# The Changing Geography of the Service Sector

# The Changing Geography of the Service Sector

D.G. Price and A.M. Blair

Belhaven Press

A division of Pinter Publishers
London and New York

© D.G. Price and A. Blair, 1989.

First published in Great Britain in 1989 by
Belhaven Press (a division of Pinter Publishers),
25 Floral Street, London WC2E 9DS

**British Library Cataloguing in Publication Data**

A CIP catalogue record for this book is available from the
British Library

ISBN 1 85293 014 4 hbk
     1 85293 065 9 pbk

**Library of Congress Cataloging-in-Publication Data**

Price, D.G. (David G.)
    The changing geography of the service sector / D.G. Price and A.M. Blair
        p.  cm.
    Bibliography: p.
    Includes index.
    ISBN 1-85293-014-4. — ISBN 1-85293-065-9 (pbk.)
    1. Service industries—Location. I. Blair, A.M. (Alastair M.)
    II. Title.
    HD9980.5.P75 1989
    338.6′042—dc19                                        88-39372
                                                              CIP

Typeset by BookEns, Saffron Walden, Essex
Printed by Biddles Ltd, Guildford and King's Lynn

# Contents

# List of Figures

# List of Tables

# Glossary

*Accessibility*. The extent to which a person or group has the opportunity to utilise a place or attribute of a place. In geographical terms accessibility is always relative.

*Agglomeration economies*. Close spatial proximity of economic activities which gives rise to mutually beneficial interactions through shared use of infrastructure and specialised services.

*Area zoning*. Division of a city or other local government area into zones designated for specific exclusive uses, for example residential, industrial or recreational.

*Automated office*. An office which uses electronic devices such as word processors, computers, fax, teletext and so on, and which is typically linked in a network with other branches, customers, or suppliers. Much routine business is handled automatically by computers.

*Big Bang*. The term used to describe the deregulation of the London Stock Exchange in 1986. It also describes the accompanying re-equipping of the Exchange with the latest information technology. Analogous to one theory of the creation of the Universe and thus supposed to indicate the significance of the event.

*Business services*. See also *producer services*—services which are for the use of commercial firms or government rather than the consumer. They are essential to a final product or consumer service, but are not offered to the consumer direct. One example is computer consultantcy.

*Business Expansion Scheme*. A British government scheme of the 1980s to encourage small businesses by giving them financial assistance.

*Cable TV*. Television programmes brought to the TV set by coaxial cable or two-way telecommunication by fibre optic cable rather than by broadcast transmissions. The more advanced systems may be used for telebanking, teleshopping and other purposes.

*Central Business District (CBD)*. The heart of an urban area, containing the main centre of commercial activity, the main shopping and office district: 'downtown' in the USA and the 'city centre' in the UK.

*Cellular radio.* A radio-based telephone system which enables the use of cordless or mobile phones. Mobility of users is complete within the 'cells' of the network which, while of limited size themselves, are linked to other cells by radio.

✓ *Central place theory.* A theory to account for the size and spacing of settlements. A normative model which states what should occur under specified conditions characterised by a network of hexagonal trade areas and a hierarchy of settlements.

*Centralisation.* The tendency for activities to group closer together in geographic space. See also *agglomeration economies*.

*Circuit courts.* A group of judicial courts served by the same judge or judges who travel from court to court according to a regular timetable.

*Commodity market.* A specialised financial market which deals exclusively in a product or commodity, not necessarily in geographical proximity to the actual physical commodity itself. Examples are the London Metal Exchange and the Chicago Wheat Exchange.

*Comprehensive education.* A non-selective system of state secondary education catering for mixed abilities in the same school, introduced in the UK in the 1960s.

*Consumer services.* Services which deal directly with the public, such as retailing. Some services, like banking, may be both consumer and producer services.

*Counter-urbanisation.* The repopulation of rural regions by urban people, usually commuters or retired persons. Usually used to describe such changes in the countryside as a whole rather than simply in the urban fringe where the process has been common for many years.

*County town* or *shire town (UK)*, *county seat (USA)*. Towns which are the seat of local government for a county. Usually also contain local branches of national government agencies and commercial organisations. Not necessarily the largest town in a county.

*Cumulative attraction.* The inherent advantages of a place which lead to its attracting further growth. A large prosperous city is more likely to attract investment because it is successful than a poor and declining one.

✓ *Decentralisation.* The movement of industry, services and people away from a centralised location to a more diffuse spatial pattern. Often inspired if not controlled by government policy.

*Deindustrialisation.* The relative decline of manufacturing industry as a source of employment and wealth creation. Used to describe the decline of much Western manufacturing industry during the recession of the 1980s.

*Deskilling.* The process of making jobs less complicated and therefore less skilled. Often used to justify less training and lower pay. Frequently alleged to be the result of computerisation.

*Diminishing returns*. A situation where the rate of increase in output from a process or job decreases as input increases.

*Distance decay*. A spatial relationship between distance and the intensity of a phenomenon. As distance from an origin increases so intensity decreases; for example, land values decline as distance from the CBD increases. An inverse distance decay shows intensity increasing with distance from an origin; for example, resident population in a modern city is usually very low in the centre and increases with distance from the centre.

*Economies of scale*. Normally average costs of production decline with increasing output. This is also true of services in many respects, for example, it is cheaper to employ one teacher for a class of 40 than four teachers each taking classes of ten. However at a certain point diseconomies of scale can set in; for example, a teacher with 400 in a class is unlikely to be very successful in educating his pupils.

*Enclosed shopping centres (ESCs) (UK), malls (USA)*. Purpose-built shopping centres usually constructed by a development company which continues to own the site and rents space to retailers. In the USA malls are likely to be in free-standing suburban locations, while in the UK ESCs are more often in town centres.

*Equity*. The notion of fairness: impartial or evenhanded distribution of a good or service to all. A principle of welfare states.

*Externalities*. The often unintended and unwanted effects of one person or organisation's activities on others. Positive externalities bring benefits; for example, a new university may provide landscaped grounds which enhance the local environment to the pleasure of all. Negative externalities create costs; for example, a new airport brings noise pollution to many who had peace and quiet before. Externalities often have a strong spatial component, frequently showing signs of distance decay effects.

*General interaction theory*. A group of geographical models which have an underlying concept of distance decay at their heart. The theory essentially tries to account for observed distance decay relationships.

*Greater London Council (GLC)*. The elected local government for the county of Greater London (UK) from 1965 to 1986 when it was abolished by central government. It was the strategic planning authority for the London metropolis and played a large part in controlling the spatial structure of the area.

*GDP/GNP*. Gross Domestic Product and Gross National Product. GDP is the measure of the market value of everything produced within a national economy, including services, during a specified time period, usually a year. GNP is GDP plus the income earned from overseas investments, less the income earned by foreign investors.

*Horizontal integration*. A firm that expands to take over rival firms in the same stage of the production process is said to be horizontally integrated; cf. *vertical integration*.

*Information technology (IT)*. Computer technology for office use—for example, word processing, fax, teletext. Its chief characteristic is that information is the commodity that is being processed.

*Infrastructure*. The physical framework of the economic system which enables all the other activities to function effectively, and including such utilities as roads, power, water and sewerage. Often extended to include anything which a firm might require in an environment, like business services.

*Inner city*. The inner urban zone adjacent to the CBD, comprising older residential and commercial districts. In most Western cities the inner city is an area of declining population and economic decay.

*Internationalisation*. The process whereby firms, organisations or administrative arrangements transcend national boundaries to bring about a global or multinational system.

*Inverse care law*. According to Hart (1971), the most needy populations receive the worst-quality health care while the least needy receive the highest-quality health care.

*Market segmentation*. The division of the population into groups, classes or segments. Different segments are associated with differing lifestyles and therefore with different purchasing behaviour. Market segmentation aims to define and identify these groups.

*Office Development Permit (ODP)*. A measure introduced by the British government in 1964 to restrict the growth of office space in London. Abolished in 1980.

*Multiplier effect*. For every job created directly in an industry there may be a certain number of other jobs created indirectly in services supplying the industry and its workers. A multiplier of 1.5, for example, means that for every job created by industry X there are an additional 1.5 jobs created elsewhere in the economy.

*Non-profit (not-for-profit) sector*. In the USA, charities, and in the UK, philanthropic organisations whose objectives are to maximise benefits to those they serve, not to shareholders. Examples are conservation trusts, housing trusts, Third World aid organisations.

*Oligopoly*. Rule by a small group. In a commercial sense it is used to indicate domination of a market by a few large firms who have an informal agreement on such matters as price levels.

*Post-industrial society*. Present day service industry-dominated Western society, where the share of employment and wealth creation attributable to manufacturing industry has declined substantially in recent years. In comparison, industrial society was dominated by manufacturing.

*Producer services*. See *business services*

*Protestant work ethic*. The idea that work is good for the soul. The view that hard work is a divinely favoured activity was particularly associated with

English-speaking Protestants between the seventeenth and twentieth centuries.

*Quango* (UK). Quasi Autonomous Non- (or National) Governmental Organisation (either definition is acceptable). An official body with some degree of independence from the government and not usually part of a Ministry or Department. Quangos often deal with obscure phenomena and are held up to ridicule as examples of bureaucracy taken to extreme.

*Rent theory*. Land users have differing abilities to pay rent and the spatial variation in the distribution of land values results in regular patterns of land use in a city. The highest-value land will be occupied by the most profitable use of land and less profitable activities will be unable to compete and will be pushed out to lower-value areas. Rent theory explains the patterns of land use by reference to land values.

*Satisficing*. The theory that people do not necessarily set out to maximise their utility but to achieve what is 'satisfactory' to them personally.

*Sogo shosha*. A Japanese industrial conglomerate. A trading organisation that provides various financial services for participating companies.

*Spatial*. Geographical, but refers to the attributes of space rather than a particular place. Spatial analysis is the study of locational patterns and processes using quantitative methods.

*Structuralism*. The idea that everything can be explained by understanding the 'structure' of a phenomenon, for example the structure of the economy and the relationship between its elements. Often used as a synonym (or euphemism) for the Marxist approach.

*Sunbelt* (USA), *Sunrise belt* (UK). The Sunbelt is the South and South-West of the USA which has seen great expansion of industry and population, allegedly drawn by the prospect of long hours of sunshine all year round. The UK Sunrise belt, on the other hand, has nothing to do with sunshine, but refers to the corridor of new high-technology industries which have located on the main route from London to South Wales which is roughly in the direction of 'sunrise' seen from South Wales and in a metaphysical sense implies that these 'sunrise' industries are associated with industrial rebirth, renewal, hope, and so on.

*Superstores*. Large supermarkets in the UK with over 25 000 square feet (2300 square metres) of selling space. Hypermarkets are over 50 000 square feet (4650 square metres).

*Technophobe*. One who has a fear of technology; for example, one who cannot bring himself to use an automated teller machine but queues to see a human bank clerk instead.

*Transnational companies*. Sometimes multinational companies (MNCs). Large corporations with substantial business interests in many countries.

*Urban fringe*. The blurred zone around cities where urban and rural activities merge. In most Western cities the urban fringe is a major area of commuter settlements and conflict over land use.

*Vertical integration*. A firm which controls the entire production process itself, from raw materials extraction to final marketing, is said to be vertically integrated; cf. *horizontal integration*.

*Weberian theory*. The industrial location theory of A. Weber, published in 1909, not to be confused with the sociological theories of M. Weber.

*Welfare state*. A system of government welfare for the whole population encompassing health, education, social security, pensions and social welfare. Common in many Western social democracies. The Welfare State (UK) originated in the Beveridge Report of 1942 and post-war legislation by the Labour government of C. Attlee.

# Preface

Writing a book on the geography of the service sector seemed to be a good idea when it was first proposed. Few would question the significance of the sector in modern advanced economies, and most would probably agree that the service sector as a whole has been relatively neglected by geographers. While the need for a textbook appeared to be irrefutable, the reality of producing one put the exercise into a different perspective. Not the least of the problems is the rapidly growing list of geographical contributions concerning the services, with academic journals likely to contain something relevant in every issue. So strongly is the tide flowing at present that it must be recorded that the present book incorporates material that had come to hand up to February 1988. Topics such as retailing, office development, health care and tourism have become sub-fields in their own right and have generated their own geographies by virtue of the amount of published work associated with them. Conversely, some areas, such as libraries and refuse collection, have not aroused much geographical interest. Space constraints forbade any attempt to provide an encyclopaedic account of the service sector and it was inevitable that selections would have to be made from the material available. We have chosen the topics and issues that seem to us to be fundamental to an understanding of the service sector, and we hope that what we offer will guide students towards such an understanding. The problem is a difficult one; the subject matter is complex and diverse, so that as yet a comprehensive explanation and a common framework of investigation have not been attained. Different viewpoints have emerged and the same issues have been approached from many different angles. In these circumstances it is worth noting the principles on which the present work is based.

Empirical description is a major element in this book because it was felt that a factual foundation is an essential basis for exploring the characteristics of the service sector. Consideration of the spatial dimension of the service sector system can only serve to improve any explanation that is offered. Throughout the text neo-classical constructs in the context of the market approach to the study of geography have been emphasised, but it is hoped that due awareness of alternative viewpoints has been shown. In choosing the market approach the authors have been guided by their own preferences and the available literature.

After a general review of the service sector in Chapter 1, the three chapters following consider the social, economic and political context in which the sector operates. Post-industrial society has advanced beyond the stage where it is principally concerned with the satisfaction of such needs as food. Increasingly it is the satisfaction of wants that matters, and the ways in which these wants are created or identified are undoubtedly related to social, economic and political factors. Therefore, it was necessary to show how these forces influence the service sector in general as well as in its specific branches. To a large extent the social, economic and political elements discussed are aspatial in character, though they might give rise to spatial patterns. One fact that clearly emerges from any investigation is that the service sector is very much an urban activity whose development has contributed significantly to the character or urban form, and a chapter is devoted to this topic.

In order to explain how changes are occurring in the service sector it is necessary to examine the processes that are moulding it. Thus, the second element in the book's basic structure focuses on processes which are likely to determine the sector's future. Dramatic effects can be expected to result from the impact of new technology, so this is an important topic. Bureaucratisation is a universal process which will probably extend its influence in the future, and in several respects epitomises the service sector for many people. Despite the emphasis in industrial geography on modern developments within the framework of a world economic system the same concern has not informed service sector studies until recently. For this reason the chapter on internationalisation touches on a topic that interests a growing number of geographers who are aware of the existence of a global service economy. In Chapter 9 it is made clear that the supply of finance and the activities of property developers play a critical role in service sector activity. All these processes contribute to the evolution of spatial patterns that concern geographers. Location is vital to the service sector. In the language of industrial geography the producer services are market-orientated and so obviously are the consumer services: the difference is that producer services can usually best serve their market by concentrating in agglomerations while the market served by consumer services generally requires a more diffuse location pattern. Distinctive spatial patterns characterise the provision of service facilities, but if improvements are sought it is necessary to understand how the facilities are used: hence the interest in studies of accessibility and the usage of facilities described in Chapter 10.

There is no overriding geographical theory to explain the development and distribution of the service sector. Such explanations as do exist are drawn from economic or social theory, with the exception of central place theory, the sole geographical contribution. Inasmuch as service activities are arranged on a hierarchical basis central place theory can be considered relevant. Public sector administrators and planners (for example, in health and education) certainly use the hierarchical principle, but in the commercial sphere (for example, in retailing) the predictive power of central place theory is too limited to make it an effective operational tool. Nevertheless, concepts such as the range of a good and the friction of distance cannot be ignored and are frequently mentioned or implied in the text. Alternative explanations based on the behavioural approach, the welfare approach, and the work of Marxist or structuralist writers have offered valuable new perspectives, some of which are included in the text.

Notwithstanding the heterogeneity of the activities which constitute the service sector and the difficulty of doing full justice to their variety, it would be wrong to suppose that it is premature to enquire into the changing geography of this sector. There is an excellent precedent in manufacturing geography, perhaps the most popular branch of economic geography in terms of coverage in the literature. Manufacturing also embraces a heterogeneous range of activities, and to the authors' knowledge not even the great compendia of commercial geography have treated manufacturing in its entirety. Manufacturing geographers have been content with a selective approach such as that adopted here, presumably because they accept that understanding of patterns and processes is preferable to a detailed account of every variation in the character and distribution of manufacturing industry. Within the space limitations of a normal text any method relying on selectivity is likely to encourage controversy. The problem already exists in the field of manufacturing geography, but the literature has been enriched by the variety of perspectives available. It is hoped that the work offered here will stimulate further debate about service sector geography.

Acknowledgements are not a ritual obligation because no academic work can be written in isolation and authors need to express their genuine and heartfelt thanks. The debt to a large number of other writers is plain from the bibliography and the references in the text. For the most part they are personally unknown to us, but we value their contribution greatly. Rosie Currell, whose advice and interest have been a constant source of inspiration, drew the maps and diagrams. The PCL library staff, not least Martin Faulkner, have been unfailingly helpful. We must thank Iain Stevenson and Sally Kilmister of Belhaven Press for their professional guidance. To some extent our thinking reflects views put forward by an anonymous adviser who deserves thanks but no blame for the final result. DGP wishes to thank Professor Emrys Jones for directing his attention to this branch of geography and for his continued interest over the years, but above all his thanks go to Patricia and Helen for their patience and unstinting willingness to provide a suitable working environment.

*David Price*
*Alasdair Blair*
*June 1988.*

# Chapter 1

# The Service Sector

'In the last three decades we have witnessed a quiet revolution in the composition of economic activity in most major developed economies. The provision of services has replaced the manufacturing of goods as the predominant production activity of advanced economies' (Inman, 1985). Given these circumstances it is obviously worth exploring the significance of the service sector, but widespread agreement with Inman's statement cannot hide the confusion about the precise character of the sector which is generated by its size and diversity. The heterogeneity of service activities has hindered systematic analysis, and there are also problems of definition and classification related to the available statistics. After discussing these problems attention in this chapter is turned to the sector's spatial and temporal characteristics in order to establish the context for succeeding chapters. Spatial patterns are considered at the global, national, regional and local scales, and, finally, changes within the sector and its place in the industrial structure over time are discussed.

## The significance of the service sector

The growth of the extractive (agriculture and mining) and the manufacturing industries has been more extensively studied than that of the service industries. The latter are sometimes erroneously regarded as a comparatively recent development, but this is to overlook the long history of administration and trade without which economic progress would have faltered, as the role of financial services in the national economy has demonstrated. Service industry in the form that we know today gained prominence during the Industrial Revolution and has matured during the current transition to a post-industrial society. Manufacturing is not necessarily a precondition for the development of service activities and many would argue that it was the financial institutions which made industrialisation possible. Certainly the notion of a sequential shift in employment structure from extractive to service industries and the presumed link between the emergence of service industries and economic development must not be accepted uncritically. Nevertheless, in most advanced industrialised countries over 50 per cent of employment is currently in the service sector, while in the USA and UK the proportion is higher than this.

Within the service sector there have been significant inter-sectoral changes. At the beginning of the century domestic service was overwhelmingly more important than it is now, and finance, real estate and commerce (especially retailing) were starting to expand. Throughout the century public administration and defence have become increasingly significant, and in the post-war period professional services such as medicine and education flourished. Currently recreational and tourist activities are expanding. The impact of this growth on employment has been evident, and the economic effect of the changes has also been significant. Much of the wealth generated by service activities derives from 'invisible' trade. Financial institutions earn much money in internal and external trade, complemented by tourism and consultancy which provide a considerable source of income on which the UK, for example, is especially reliant. Indisputably the service sector makes a great contribution to the economy, and its significance fully justifies the increasing amount of attention paid to it.

## Problems of definition and classification

P.W   Daniels (1985) suggested that 'a service may be defined as the exchange of a commodity, which may either be marketable or provided by public agencies, and which often does not have a tangible form'. He acknowledged Greenfield's comment that services frequently seem to 'pass out of existence at the same instant as they come into it'. Some economists (for example Summers, 1985) argue that the distinction between commodities and services is simple: the former can be stored while the latter cannot. Even so classification problems remain. For example, what part of a restaurant meal should be called a commodity, and is a textbook a commodity or a service? Just as difficult as distinguishing services by the nature of their end products is classifying them according to the occupational category of those who produce them. The alleged clear-cut distinction between manufacturing and service activity is illusory because tangible manufactured goods cannot be produced without involving a considerable service element. Marketing the final product is a vital process which may or may not be in the hands of the manufacturer, and in fact many workers employed by manufacturing companies are engaged in service activities although the official statistics may record them as manufacturing workers.

Service occupations are defined in the International Standard Classification of Occupations (ISCO) and most national censuses collect occupation data that can be cross-tabulated by industry. A major distinction is between 'white-collar' and 'blue-collar' jobs, though this is not very satisfactory for industries such as micro-electronics and pharmaceuticals. Unfortunately this distinction, which identifies sales staff, is less useful for enumerating administrative, technical and clerical staff who typically comprise over 30 per cent of employees in manufacturing. Despite being an inadequate basis for an analysis of service activities occupational characteristics cannot be ignored and must be acknowledged in any descriptive account of the sector.

A popular classification which has the advantage of availability of statistics is by industry sector based on a standard industrial classification scheme. Under such schemes each major sector is subdivided into a number of industry orders which can then be regarded as service industries or not. Because industry orders are usually defined according to the kind of raw material used this type of classification is not particularly appropriate for services, and there is the further problem that the British Standard Industrial Classification scheme differs from other international schemes, which makes international comparisons difficult. In practice standard industrial classification schemes are often used, and as a refinement they may be subdivided as follows (Daniels, 1982):

Tertiary: transportation and utilities (often including construction).
Quaternary: finance, insurance, trade, real estate.
Quinary: education, government, health, research.

Dawson (1982b) considered that the distinction between quaternary and quinary activities should be dropped because it has not received much support from workers in the field.

Recently much emphasis has been placed on the distinction between consumer and producer services within the service sector. Daniels (1985) placed banking, insurance and finance, professional and scientific services, and some of the miscellaneous services group in the producer services category. He also suggested that consumer and producer services could be subdivided according to their perishable, semi-durable and durable attributes as follows:

*Consumer services*
　　Perishable: yield utility over a short time (e.g. visit to a hairdresser, laundrette, football match).
　　Semi-durable: gives longer utility (e.g. dental treatment, legal advice, central heating repair).
　　Durable: gives longer-term utility (e.g. advice on education, provision of a mortgage).
*Producer services*
　　Perishable: cleaning, waste disposal, delivery service.
　　Semi-durable: advertising copy for a promotion.
　　Durable: management and building consultancy, computer consultancy.

Such a classification would be valuable for understanding the locational aspects of service activities, but the available statistics do not encourage its use. Producer services have benefited from the application of technology in ways that have not yet been matched by consumer services. Consequently, the loss of employment in traditional manufacturing is not being compensated by the creation of an equivalent number of jobs in producer services. Locationally the impact of this is great because as the traditional manufacturing areas have declined so investment has moved to areas where scarce skilled white-collar workers are available or can be attracted. Alternatively, areas of low wages and high unemployment where a semi-skilled, often female, workforce can be recruited for largely routine and semi-skilled production activities in branch plants are sought. Both trends favour locations outside the old manufacturing areas.

The dichotomy between private and public sector activities is another basis for classification. Public sector employment has expanded in the post-war years in a way which has generated much controversy. There have been disputes about the value of the public sector's contribution, and it has also been recognised that there is no single accepted definition of public service (Seeley, 1981). Some regard the public sector as privileged. For example, Eckstein and Heien (1985), using data from the USA, argued that producer services are very responsive to economic trends whereas activities tied to government decisions are not. They demonstrated the significant role of the government in the generation of American service sector jobs, and they concluded that the service sector has altered the responsiveness of the economy to market forces because it is nearly immune to the business cycle. Heated political debate may arise from this finding but geographers will be interested in the implication that locationally private services will be subject to market forces while public services may respond to other criteria.

Other dichotomies such as formal–informal, modern–traditional, footloose–tied, and office–non office, have been used in connection with the service sector. All may have their attractions, but they also have their limitations, serving to emphasise the difficulty of arriving at an acceptable working definition of the service sector. Gershuny and Miles (1983) offered a further distinction between a 'functional' and a 'commodity' classification which describes the range of service activities very well (see Table 1.1). They made an additional categorisation of the commodity classification into 'marketed' and 'non-marketed' types which is very useful, for it is clear that many functions are provided by both market and non-market suppliers (cf. private and public sectors).

The correspondence between non-marketed services and the public sector is not complete as is clear from the works of writers drawing attention to the non-profit (or not-for-profit) sector. Reiner and Wolpert (1981) suggested that changes in the amount of philanthropic flows into the non-profit service economy may provide an early indicator of metropolitan growth or decline, and they cited the case of Philadelphia. For them the non-profit sector is the voluntary or 'third' sector which is itself an important source of income and employment besides adding to the effective resources available to households. Among the donors are foundations, corporations and individuals, and their gifts are directed towards health, education, welfare, the arts and religion. Wolpert and Reiner (1984) observed that the non-profit sector was an early provider of investment for the provision and delivery of services, and so non-profit organisatons are well represented in older cities in the North-East of the USA. A 'donor transition model' was proposed which assumed that rapid economic growth yields as a by-product private fortunes and an inclination towards compensating benevolence to the growth area. In this way a frontier region can be transformed by the development of the level of facilities enjoyed by an established area. The process is inherently benevolent, paternalistic and elitist, and residents of the beneficiary area may not agree with the agenda for service provision preferred by the donors. The model is transitional in that it envisages an eventual change to democratisation in the choice of provision,

**Table 1.1** Household and government final expenditure in the service sector, classified by function and type of commodity

| *Functional classification* | *Commodity classification* | |
|---|---|---|
| | *Marketed services* | *Non-marketed services* |
| Shelter, clothing | Personal care and effects | Housing and community amenities |
| Domestic function | Household operation and domestic services | Social security and welfare services |
| Entertainment | Entertainment, recreation, cultural, hotels, cafés and package tours | Recreational, cultural and religious services |
| Transport and communications | Purchased transport and communication services | Roads, waterways, and their administrative subsidies |
| Education | Purchased education | Public education |
| Medical | Purchased medical services, medical insurance service charges | Public health service |
| Other government functions | – | General public services and economic services excluding transport and communications; defence. |

*Source*: Based on Gershuny and Miles (1983)

but the point has been made that much service provision, initially at least, is of this kind. Wolch and Geiger (1986) considered the influence of recession and the stress on privatisation associated with public sector retrenchment. They claimed that the rapid expansion of the non-profit sector is now a major form of corporate organisation. Undoubtedly its importance should not be overlooked in considering the changing geography of the service sector.

Useful though the notion of producer and consumer services is, some critics believe that it hinders conceptualisation and that the real distinction between goods and services lies in the form of labour involved and its product. Gillespie and Green (1987), for example, said that if a service involves a process normally irreproducible by other workers it entails a unique transaction between producer and consumer. Defined in this way only about 10 per cent of the economy of the UK is so composed, but they stated that service occupations account for about 50 per cent of all jobs. In their view the term 'service' connotes a type of product resulting from a 'completed' labour process. This can be accommodated within the notion that the dynamic of capitalism has engendered an increasingly complex and extended division of labour in which the locus of competitive advantage (and of capital accumulation in general) has shifted from simple productive efficiency among direct labourers to the realm of indirect labour. Producer services such as financial, legal, insurance, technical, distribution and maintenance activities can thus be regarded as indirect elements of the production process rather than as 'services'. In short, the Marxian type of analysis places the majority of services within a trend which is part of the increasing technical division of labour within production. Services such as health, education and recreation which are not considered to be producer services can be linked to the above analysis by regarding them as means of reproducing the labour force, a view asserting the paramountcy of production by subordinating the role of consumer services.

Kellerman (1985a) also envisaged division of labour, but he set his evolutionary model firmly in the context of what he called the two basic modes of economic activity, production and consumption. According to him mass production methods depended for their success on complementary services such as transport and utilities, thus creating an intermediate demand for services. Further expansion required distribution services and activities such as finance, insurance and real estate, which in their turn stimulated other economic activities. Greater division of labour on the production side led to a demand for business services, for example legal and accounting. Because there is a low elasticity for basic services rising prosperity promoted the consumption of more advanced personal services such as recreation. Greater interest in the quality of life has increased demand for health, education and entertainment, and at the same time there has been increased sophistication in business services with the development of advertising, telecommunications and information technology. Availability of information is critical to all this activity, and so, too, is the role of government which is involved as a supplier and regulator of consumption (for example, health and education) as well as a strong influence on production. Kellerman did not doubt that the processes he described were related to the nature of capitalism which, he felt, explained why North America has played a leading part in their development.

The spatial component of the growth of the service sector has received less attention than the trends displayed by the sector itself. Perhaps not enough stress has been placed on the fact that 'a major economic transformation is in progress with settlement implications as important as those assigned to the agrarian-to-industrial transformation of the past century' (Fisher and Mitchelson in Keinath, 1985). Given the problems of definition and classification discussed in this section it is not surprising that few geographical studies of the service sector have been forthcoming. Daniels (1985) spoke of 'a litany of neglect' in this respect apart from the fields of transport and retailing, but there is a burgeoning amount of literature devoted to the geography of health care, tourism and recreation, to say nothing about Daniels's own work on office growth and location. There is still no agreed overall model of the service sector and its geography, though the increasing amount of academic investigation is offering a growing understanding and insight into an unquestionably important part of the modern economy.

# Some important characteristics of service occupations

Consideration of some features of service occupations will amplify points raised in the previous section.

*Weekly earnings and industry type*

People in similar jobs (for instance, office work) may be employed in very different types of industry. Thus, a wages clerk employed by a mining company is recorded in the energy subsector, while a supermarket wages clerk is placed firmly in the service sector. Comparisons of pay for similar work in different industries may reveal whether service workers are better paid or if there are differentials between the sexes. Table 1.2 shows weekly earnings by industry groups for manual and non-manual workers according to sex in Great Britain. Women are consistently paid less than men, and non-manual workers receive more than their manual colleagues. The gap between manual and non-manual wages is actually greater in the services than in manufacturing. Female workers in distribution, hotels and catering are the lowest paid, while non-manual workers in banking, insurance and finance are the highest paid. Obviously bank managers earn more than shop assistants, and professors more than college porters, but it is worth remembering the enormous range of occupations and remunerations within the service sector. Above all, service jobs are not necessarily well paid or interesting; many are poorly paid and boring.

**Table 1.2**  Average weekly earnings by industry group, Great Britain, 1984 (£)

|  | Manual | | Non-manual | |
|---|---|---|---|---|
|  | *Male* | *Female* | *Male* | *Female* |
| Agriculture | 116.2 | – | – | – |
| Manufacturing | 158.9 | 96.0 | 213.5 | 117.2 |
| Construction | 149.4 | – | 199.2 | 101.4 |
| Distribution, hotels and catering | 125.8 | 81.7 | 174.5 | 95.4 |
| Transport and communications | 167.0 | 125.5 | 220.6 | 128.9 |
| Banking, finance, insurance, business services, etc. | 151.1 | 107.1 | 228.3 | 125.0 |
| Other services | 129.8 | 89.8 | 205.2 | 134.9 |

*Source: Regional Trends, 1985*

**Table 1.3**  Distribution of the working population according to industry, employment status and sex, UK, 1981

| Industry | Total employed thousands | Employees (male & female) as a % of all persons working in the industry | Employees Male % | Female % | Self-employed Male % | Female % |
|---|---|---|---|---|---|---|
| Agriculture | 595 | 58.3 | 43.8 | 14.6 | 36.6 | 4.7 |
| Energy and water | 663 | 99.8 | 86.8 | 10.3 | 0.1 | – |
| Metals, chemicals, etc. | 830 | 99.0 | 79.5 | 19.5 | 0.7 | 0.3 |
| Engineering | 2 699 | 98.0 | 74.0 | 24.0 | 1.8 | 0.2 |
| Other manufacturing | 2 267 | 95.7 | 55.9 | 39.7 | 3.3 | 0.8 |
| Construction | 1 429 | 71.0 | 62.7 | 8.3 | 28.1 | 0.7 |
| Distribution, catering | 4 925 | 85.4 | 39.4 | 46.0 | 9.6 | 4.9 |
| Transport | 1 426 | 93.4 | 74.8 | 18.5 | 6.2 | 0.4 |
| Banking, finance | 2 057 | 89.3 | 46.0 | 43.2 | 8.3 | 2.3 |
| Other services | 6 250 | 94.5 | 34.6 | 60.0 | 3.0 | 2.4 |
| All manufacturing | 5 796 | 97.3 | 69.5 | 27.7 | 2.1 | 0.5 |
| All services | 16 357 | 90.7 | 41.3 | 49.8 | 8.9 | 3.1 |
| All industries | 23 409 | 90.6 | 51.1 | 39.4 | 7.1 | 2.2 |

*Source: Social Trends, 1985, Tables 4.7 and 4.8*

*Employees and the self-employed*

Less than 10 per cent of the labour force is self-employed (Table 1.3), but more people in the service sector are likely to be self-employed than in manufacturing. The highest proportion of self-employed is in agriculture. The construction industry is the only service occupation with over 10 per cent self-employed: this industry includes multitudes of small builders, decorators and plumbers as well as building workers who are officially self-employed but who actually 'subcontract' to bigger firms for tax advantages.

*Contrasts in male and female employment*

Table 1.3 also illustrates the differences in male and female employment patterns. Men predominate in agriculture, energy, heavy industry, engineering and vehicles, construction and transport but women are more numerous in distribution, hotels and catering, and in other services. Banking and finance has a rough equality with only slightly more men than women. Agriculture and manufacturing are male-dominated activities, while females have a slight majority in services.

*Changes in occupations*

The services which existed in the 1880s differed greatly from those of the 1980s. Large numbers of domestic servants (upstairs and downstairs maids, butlers, cooks, gardeners, grooms, and so on), blacksmiths, flower sellers, pedlars, bootblacks and crossing sweepers were familiar characters in Victorian towns. Many of these occupations have dwindled or vanished completely. Others which are common now did not exist then, such as social workers, TV repairmen, computer programmers, air traffic controllers and video arcade managers. Some common to both eras (such as doctors, lawyers, policemen, bankers, shop assistants, printers and postmen) perform very differently nowadays. Although changes over a long period of time are obvious, change is actually continuous. During the period 1971–81 some jobs were clearly declining while others expanded (Figure 1.1). Many were production jobs that were becoming automated, but some service jobs in selling, transport and storage were also declining. Professional and managerial jobs, by contrast, expanded greatly.

Change will not cease. For example, the spread of computers will profoundly affect the services and industry. A forecast for the near-future (1980–90) in the USA foresaw a drastic decline in the number of postal clerks, compositors, typists (stenographers), schoolteachers and lecturers (Figure 1.2). Major growth areas were computer-related—systems analysts, programmers, and above all computer service technicians (110 per cent growth). Another major category of growth was in law and security—lawyers, security guards, police and prison officers. Of all the growth occupations only toolmakers and welders are clearly non-service. Aerospace and electrical engineers could be engaged in designing, selling or servicing rather than fabricating equipment. The picture is one of growth dominated by service industries, but with the type of service occupation changing significantly.

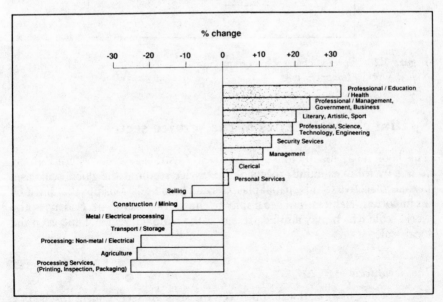

**Figure 1.1** Changes in employment by occupation group, England and Wales, 1971–81
*Source: Social Trends*, 1985, Chart 4.7

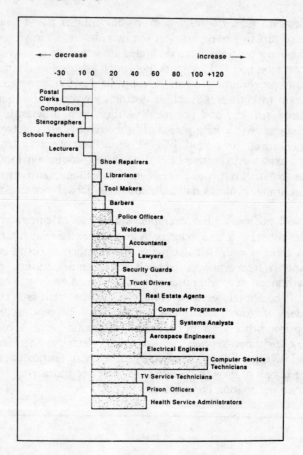

**Figure 1.2**   Expected changes in certain jobs, USA, 1980–90
*Source:* World Almanack, 1985

# Spatial characteristics of the service sector

This book refers mainly to North America, Australasia and Western Europe, so it is useful to examine aspects of the service sector at the global scale as a partial corrective to this spatial bias. Certain broad relationships that must be an important element in a geography of the service sector are evident at the world scale which may also be present at the national, regional and even the local scale.

## The global scale

The existence of a relationship between the stage of development reached by an economy and the importance of the service sector is suggested by the statistics. Table 1.4 presents some indicators relating to service industries in different types of economy using a World Bank (1983) classification based on

**Table 1.4** Changes in the service sector, world scale, 1960–81

| | Type of economy* | | | | | |
|---|---|---|---|---|---|---|
| | Low-income economies | Lower middle-income economies | Upper middle-income economies | High-income oil exporting economies | Industrial market economies | East European non-market economies |
| Average GDP/cap US$ 1981 | 270 | 880 | 2490 | 13 000 | 11 120 | n-a |
| *Annual growth rate of GDP attributable to Services (%)* | | | | | | |
| 1960–70 | 4.2 | 5.3 | 7.1 | – | 4.6 | – |
| 1970–81 | 4.6 | 6.0 | 6.5 | 12.2 | 3.6 | – |
| *Annual growth rate of total GDP for all sectors (%)* | | | | | | |
| 1960–70 | 4.6 | 5.0 | 6.4 | – | 5.1 | – |
| 1970–81 | 4.5 | 5.6 | 5.6 | 5.3 | 3.0 | – |
| *% GDP from services* | | | | | | |
| 1960 | 27 | 39 | 49 | – | 54 | – |
| 1981 | 29 | 43 | 51 | 23 | 61 | – |
| *% employment from services* | | | | | | |
| 1960 | 14 | 18 | 31 | 25 | 44 | 28 |
| 1981 | 15 | 28 | 42 | 35 | 56 | 39 |
| *% urban population* | | | | | | |
| 1960 | 17 | 24 | 45 | 30 | 68 | 48 |
| 1981 | 21 | 33 | 63 | 68 | 78 | 62 |

*Source*: World Bank (1983)
   *As defined by the World Bank 1983, 'Definitions', p.ix

income and economic-political system criteria. Particularly useful is the separate categorisation of different types of less developed country instead of lumping them together in an amorphous 'Third World' group. A number of important points about the service sector emerge from Table 1.4.

First, employment in services rises with the degree of sophistication of an economy. The poorest countries have the lowest proportion employed in services because they are more concerned with the basic production of food, raw materials and manufactured goods which require little by way of elaborate producer services. The poorer countries also have a less well-developed public sector. Social services, health and education are not so well represented in Chad or Bangladesh as in Sweden or the UK. Rising income levels are accompanied by an increase in service employment. The Eastern European non-market economies have less service employment than their development status would suggest, perhaps because of their recent emergence as compared to those of Western states and because of their traditional denigration of services for ideological reasons. In all but the low-income countries service employment increased rapidly by 10 per cent or more in the period 1960–81, and in the industrial market economies it became the dominant form of employment.

Second, GDP from services has increased to over 60 per cent in the industrial market economies. Even in the less developed nations services have begun to increase their share, particularly in the 'upper middle income' groups which include the newly industrialising nations like South Korea, Singapore and Hong Kong.

Third, rates of growth for employment and GDP have been greater for services than industry in the most developed and least developed countries. Only in the middle-income countries has industrial growth exceeded that of services. In most countries growth rates slowed down in the period 1970–81 as compared with 1960–70.

Fourth, urbanisation and services are clearly related. Most services are urban based so it is unsurprising that countries with the highest levels of service employment are also the most urbanised. Moreover the world has become a more urbanised place in the last 25 years, thus offering more opportunity for services.

Tables 1.5 and 1.6 illustrate some of these trends with reference to two selected countries representing each type of economy. Countries like India and Niger or Kenya and Thailand were overwhelmingly reliant on agriculture for employment but services accounted for a relatively large proportion of GDP (Table 1.5) because the comparatively few service employees are more productive and generate higher values than the poverty-stricken rural peasantry. Upper middle-income countries like Brazil or Iraq have experienced a large transfer of employment from agriculture to industry and services and they have also undergone spectacular urbanisation. Although some service occupations in these countries are 'modern' and well paid, many are 'traditional' and poorly paid jobs such as shoeshine boys, street hawkers and domestic servants. High-income oil exporters typified by Libya and Kuwait have seen large increases in industrial and service jobs created with the aid of their newly acquired wealth. A massive decline in agriculture and a corresponding surge in service occupations is particularly evident in Libya, and in both states urbanisation has been rapid. Sweden is a good example of a mature industrial market economy whose manufacturing has declined relatively in the last two decades. Nearly three-quarters of Sweden's GDP came from services and about two-thirds of employment is in that sector. Japan, on the other hand, has increased manufacturing employment, but even so services provided 62 per cent of GDP in 1983. Eastern European countries, where agriculture and industry retain pre-eminence in employment and in wealth creation, present a dramatic contrast. In Poland, for example, more are employed in agriculture than in services. It can be concluded from these examples that although it is difficult to equate GDP per capita with actual

**Table 1.5**
Service economy indicators, selected countries 1980, 1981

| | Service employees (%) | Urban population (%) | GDP, 1980 ($ per capita) | Agriculture | Origins of Industry | GDP (%) 1981 Services |
|---|---|---|---|---|---|---|
| India | 18 | 22.2 | 252 | 32 | 19 | 49 |
| Niger | 6 | 12.5 | 242 | 50 | 14 | 36 |
| Kenya | 12 | 14.2 | 425 | 28 | 28 | 59 |
| Thailand | 15 | 14.4 | 759 | 24 | 23 | 53 |
| Iraq | 32 | 71.6 | 1 936 | 7 | 63 | 30 |
| Brazil | 46 | 67.0 | 2 370 | 11 | 34 | 65 |
| Libya | 53 | 52.4 | 7 289 | 2 | 58 | 40 |
| Kuwait | 64 | 88.4 | 16 605 | 0 | 67 | 33 |
| Japan | 49 | 78.3 | 9 705 | 4 | 34 | 62 |
| Sweden | 61 | 87.2 | 13 513 | 3 | 24 | 73 |
| Hungary | 36 | 54.4 | 2 039 | 14 | 49 | 37 |
| Poland | 30 | 56.6 | 2 398 | 30 | 42 | 28 |

*Sources*: World Bank (1983); UN, 1983

**Table 1.6**
Service economy indicators: communications 1980, 1981

| | Passenger vehicles (per 1000 population) | Telephones (per 1000) | TV sets (per 1000) | Education spending (%) |
|---|---|---|---|---|
| India | 1.6 | 4.0 | 1.7 | 3.0 |
| Niger | 2.5 | 2.0 | 0.9 | 4.3 |
| Kenya | 6.0 | 21.0 | 4.0 | 6.1 |
| Thailand | 7.0 | 11.0 | 17.0 | 3.2 |
| Iraq | 14.0 | 26.0 | 50.0 | 3.2 |
| Brazil | 70.0 | 63.0 | 122.0 | 3.6 |
| Libya | 112.0 | – | 55.0 | 3.5 |
| Kuwait | 298.0 | 159.0 | 400.0 | 2.9 |
| Japan | 209.0 | 460.0 | 539.0 | 5.8 |
| Sweden | 347.0 | 796.0 | 381.0 | 8.2 |
| Hungary | 95.0 | 118.0 | 258.0 | 4.5 |
| Poland | 79.0 | 95.0 | 224.0 | 4.7 |

*Sources*: World Bank (1983); UN, 1983

living standards it is apparent that high GDP correlates very well with an urbanised service-orientated economy.

Because good communications permit a higher degree of interaction between individuals and organisations they provide a measure of the sophisti-

**Table 1.7**  Central government expenditure per capita (1975 dollars)

| Type of economy | Defence 1972 | 1980 | Education 1972 | 1980 | Health 1972 | 1980 |
|---|---|---|---|---|---|---|
| Low-income | 5 | 7 | 3 | 6 | 1 | 1 |
| Lower middle-income | 15 | 18 | 15 | 16 | 4 | 5 |
| Upper middle-income | 36 | 42 | 25 | 42 | 15 | 17 |
| Industrial market | 281 | 254 | 77 | 111 | 141 | 240 |

*Source*: World Bank (1983), Table 26

cation of a service economy. The service sector is heavily reliant on the exchange of information, and in many cases information is the commodity being traded. Three measures of communication differences between the various types of economy presented in Table 1.6 give an indication of personal mobility; remote communication; and information, education and entertainment receiving ability. The contrast between industrial market economies with their high volume for all indicators and the rest is very striking. Eastern European countries had relatively high rates of TV ownership but only moderate rates for telephones and cars. Oil-rich Kuwait exceeded even Japan in vehicles and Sweden in TV sets. Low degrees of interaction seem to characterise the poorer countries and there are wide gaps between the developed and Third World countries. Such gaps will probably assume greater significance when two-way cable TV systems become more common, making the importance of good communication even more apparent.

Central government expenditure (Table 1.7) displays similar trends in that the developed economies spend much more per capita on defence, education and health services than the lower-income countries. The almost non-existent health figures from low-income countries contrast starkly with the industrial countries where spending between 1972 and 1980 increased by $100 per capita. The developed countries spend a greater proportion (of a bigger total) on these services. For instance, Sweden spends 9 per cent on education and Japan 5.5 per cent, while India and Iraq spend 3.2 per cent (Table 1.6). Probably these figures understate the true level of expenditure on education in some developed countries where local government and private funding may supplement the central government input.

The greater sophistication of the service economies of developed countries is clear, yet conventionally development is measured by performance in agriculture and industry, and services rarely figure prominently in the targets set by plans for newly emergent nations. Help for the service sector is not a common feature of overseas aid programmes. Whether the levels of income, urbanisation and social welfare associated with countries whose service sectors are best developed are a cause or a consequence of development is debatable and outside the scope of this book. The point being made is that the service economy is the hallmark of the highly developed nations of the world, those countries with which this book is mainly concerned.

**Table 1.8** GDP and other indicators, Western market economies, 1981

|  | GDP per capita ($) | Origins of GDP (%) Agriculture | Industry | Services | Urban population (%) |
|---|---|---|---|---|---|
| Belgium | 11 920 | 2 | 37 | 62 | 73 |
| Canada | 11 400 | 4 | 32 | 64 | 76 |
| Denmark | 13 120 | 4 | 32 | 64 | 85 |
| West Germany | 13 450 | 2 | 46 | 49 | 85 |
| France | 12 190 | 4 | 35 | 61 | 78 |
| Italy | 6 960 | 6 | 42 | 53 | 70 |
| Netherlands | 11 790 | 4 | 33 | 63 | 76 |
| Spain | 5 640 | 7 | 36 | 57 | 75 |
| Sweden | 14 870 | 3 | 31 | 66 | 88 |
| UK | 9 110 | 2 | 33 | 65 | 91 |
| USA | 12 820 | 3 | 34 | 63 | 77 |
| Japan | 10 080 | 4 | 43 | 53 | 79 |

*Source*: World Bank (1983)
Note: due to rounding up, percentages do not always add up to 100

*National and regional scales*

All Western market economies experienced increased employment in and a greater share of GDP from services in the last two decades. Table 1.8 provides details of specific countries in 1981. The most service-orientated countries are the USA, Canada, the UK and the Scandinavian countries. Japan, Italy, Ireland, Spain, and the Netherlands have less than half their employment in services, but all derived more than half their GDP from the service sector. West Germany is a notable exception in that services account for less than half of its GDP. The relationship between the type of economy and urbanisation is also evident. Most have at least 75 per cent of their population in urban areas, and the most service-orientated tend to have over 85 per cent in urban areas; for example, Sweden, Denmark and the UK. In spatial terms there was a southward spread of higher degrees of service employment in Europe between 1960 and 1980 (Figure 1.3). The importance of urban regions is also clear (Figures 1.4 and 1.5) for the highest levels of service employment and GDP from services are in the EEC's major metropolitan regions (South-East England, the Paris Basin, Rome, Randstad-Holland, Brussels, Luxembourg, Hamburg and Copenhagen) or the major tourist areas such as South-West England and Mediterranean France.

Within the UK there is a very small primary sector of less than 6 per cent if energy and water are included and just 2.5 per cent if agriculture, forestry and fishing only are considered. Manufacturing now accounts for less than a quarter and the majority of employees are in the service sector (Table 1.9). Figure 1.6 provides a more detailed breakdown showing the various subsectors of manufacturing and service for the whole country, South-East England and Greater

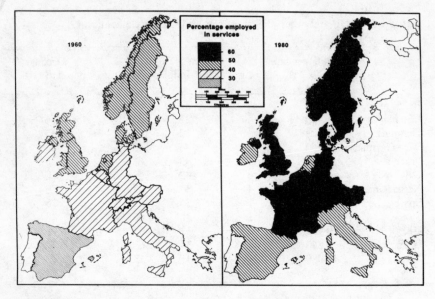

**Figure 1.3**　Employment in services, Europe, 1960 and 1980
*Source: Eurostat*, various dates

London. The importance of services in the latter two areas is very clear Table 1.10 confirms the increased importance of the services' contribution to GDP between the years 1974 and 1983, in which the role of financial services is especially noteworthy.

*The local scale*

Selected aspects of the service economy of the UK are considered next in order to illustrate small local spatial variations which are important characteristics of service provision.

　　Catering, hotels and distribution is a large subsector accounting for 13 per cent of national GDP and 21 per cent of the total labour force. At the regional level the proportion of employment in this sector is reasonably uniform, reflecting the universal demand for retailing facilities, but the areas with the highest levels of employment are all coastal counties and there is a marked concentration in South-West England (Figure 1.7). Within South-West England there are substantial deviations at the district level (Figure 1.8). Rural areas which are not major tourist destinations (e.g. Mid-Devon, Sedgemoor) have below average levels, contrasting with the coastal towns and famous tourist districts. For instance, Torbay, Sidmouth, Ilfracombe, Bude, Looe, Truro and Penwith record employment figures between 29 and 39 per cent in this sector, while Kingsbridge, Salcombe, Newquay and Holsworthy have more than 39 per cent. The West Country accounts for nearly a quarter of all holidays taken in Great Britain and this explains the above average employment levels. In London the boroughs of Westminster and Kensington, noted for their

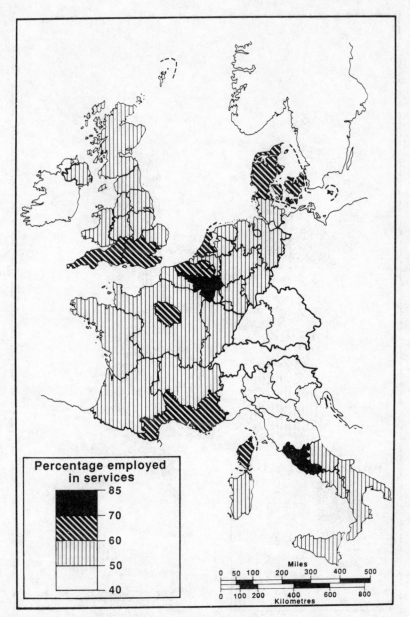

**Figure 1.4** Percentage employment in services, EEC regions, 1981
*Source: Eurostat, 1982*

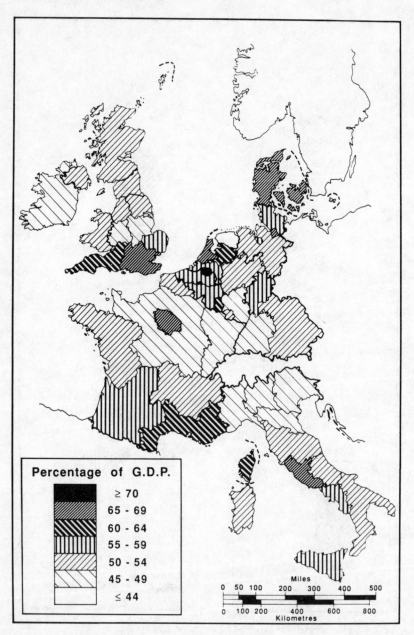

**Figure 1.5**   Percentage of GDP attributable to service sector, Western Europe, 1981
*Source: Eurostat*, 1983

**Table 1.9**  Percentage employment in the main sectors of the British economy, 1983

| | |
|---|---|
| Agriculture, forestry and fishing | 2.5 |
| Energy and water | 2.8 |
| Manufacturing | 24.75 |
| Services | 69.8 |

*Source*: *Social Trends*, 1985

**Table 1.10**  GDP by industry group, 1974 and 1983

| | 1974 | | 1983 | |
|---|---|---|---|---|
| | (£ millions) | (%) | (£ millions) | (%) |
| Agriculture | 1 558 | 2.3 | 4 177 | 1.9 |
| Energy and water | 2 689 | 4.0 | 11 208 | 5.3 |
| Manufacturing | 19 409 | 29.0 | 53 862 | 24.7 |
| Construction | 4 599 | 6.8 | 12 783 | 5.8 |
| Distribution | 8 507 | 12.7 | 29 630 | 13.7 |
| Transport | 5 002 | 7.4 | 16 054 | 7.3 |
| Financial services | 7 297 | 10.9 | 27 630 | 12.6 |
| Property ownership | 4 060 | 6.0 | 13 992 | 6.4 |
| Public administration | 4 403 | 6.5 | 14 784 | 6.7 |
| Education/health | 5 504 | 8.2 | 19 629 | 9.0 |
| Other services | 3 729 | 5.5 | 13 890 | 6.3 |
| Total | 66 648 | | 217 911 | |
| Adjustments* | 3 110 | | 10 500 | |
| Total less adjustments | 63 648 | | 207 411 | |

*Adjustments allow for depreciation of capital assets during the year

*Source*: adapted from *Regional Trends*, 1985, Table 9.4

high-quality shops, restaurants, pubs and clubs catering for tourists and others, have above average levels of employment in this sector.

Other services include many of the expanding professional occupations such as welfare, education, health, scientific and technical, the civil service and local government. This category accounted for 27 per cent of employment nationally and 22 per cent of GDP (£45 303 million) in 1983. Figure 1.7 shows that this subsector exhibits greater spatial disparity than distribution. There is a concentration of activity in the southern third of the country and particularly high levels in London, Surrey, East Sussex and Oxfordshire (all over 40 per cent). South Glamorgan, where Cardiff fulfils many government functions for Wales in the way that London does for the nation as a whole, is the only other area with a comparable figure. Oxfordshire and Surrey are well

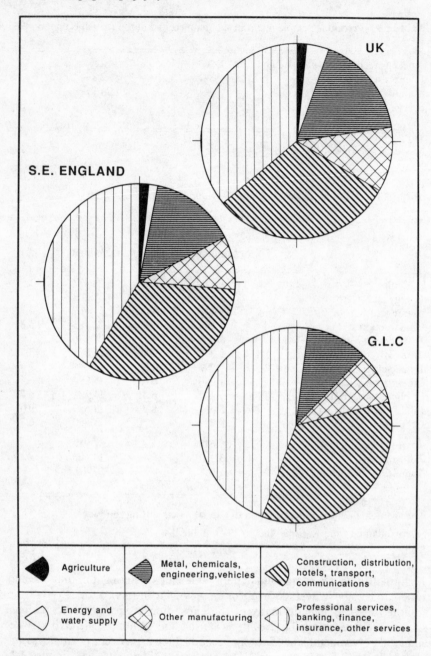

**Figure 1.6**  Employment service structure, UK, GLC and South-East England, 1981
*Source: Regional Trends*, 1985

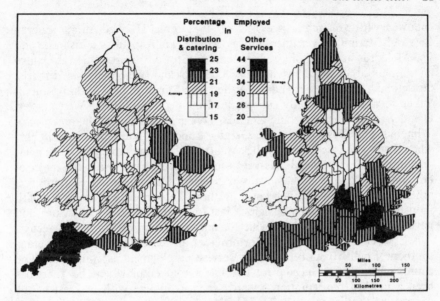

**Figure 1.7** Percentage employment in distribution and catering and other services, 1981
*Source: Regional Trends*, 1985

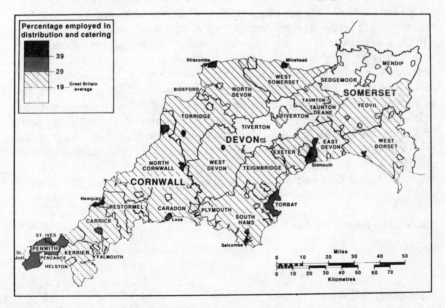

**Figure 1.8** Distribution and catering in the West Country, 1981
*Source: Key Statistics for Local Authorities in Great Britain*, London, HMSO

endowed with research organisations (for example, Harwell Atomic Energy Research Station), government offices (Ministry of Agriculture, Fisheries and Food Records at Guildford), educational institutions (universities at Oxford and Guildford), defence installations (Aldershot and Farnborough) and tourist attractions (Oxford, the Thames Valley, the Surrey hills). Within London 'other services' are heavily concentrated in the central area—Westminster, Camden, and Kensington and Chelsea. This is largely due to the presence of Whitehall and Westminster, the Greater London Council (until April 1986 when it was abolished), and the headquarters of innumerable public agencies, and semi-public trusts and pressure groups anxious to be close to the centre of decision-making. In the Midlands, and especially Derbyshire and Staffordshire, other services occupy a much lower position. These areas are concerned with industry, do not attract prestigious institutional or research activities and have lower income levels, all of which do not favour a prosperous service sector.

The service sector in Wiltshire provides an example of a fairly average southern English county as far as service employment is concerned. The county has not experienced a great decline in total employment, but there has been a marked reorientation towards services in line with the rest of the country as the figures in Table 1.11 illustrate. There are considerable variations between and within the districts that comprise Wiltshire (Figure 1.9). Salisbury district not only has the highest levels of service employment but also contains some extremely high values for urban areas. The exceptional values for Larkhill (100 per cent), Bulford (93.8 per cent) and Lyneham (93 per cent) are explained by the presence of army or air force camps. Thamesdown district is the county's major industrial area containing Swindon as its chief town. This centre has been transformed from a dependence on the railway engineering industry to become the home of many new high-technology industries that are part of the 'sunrise' belt spanning the M4 motorway. Services, though important, has a level of service employment just below the county average. West Wiltshire, with a number of small towns such as Trowbridge and Melksham which traditionally specialised in food processing industries but which are now diversifying into light engineering, is another area of below average service employment. Towns such as Warminster and Bradford-on-Avon stand out as having much higher levels of

**Table 1.11**   Employment in Wiltshire, 1975 and 1985

|                                | 1975  | 1985  |
| ------------------------------ | ----- | ----- |
| Agriculture (%)                | 3.5   | 2.7   |
| Industry (%)                   | 43.7  | 35.2  |
| Services (%)                   | 53.0  | 62.1  |
| Total employment (thousands)   | 192.3 | 197.7 |
| Service/industry ratio         | 1.4   | 2.4   |

*Source*: *Regional Trends*; Census.

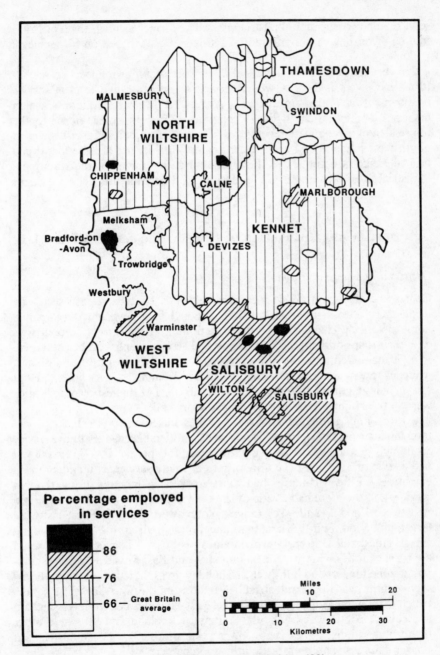

**Figure 1.9** Percentage in service employment, Wiltshire, 1981
*Source:* As Figure 1.8

service employment than the rural areas. The former woollen town of Brad-ford-on-Avon now has a substantial tourist industry based on its medieval buildings.

This brief discussion of aspects of the service sector at the local scale confirms that, even in the UK where there is a generally high level of service employment, activities are unevenly distributed. In practice there is a high degree of specialisation in local economies that does not conform to the impression of diversification conveyed by national statistics. Tourist towns in South-West England and defence centres in Wiltshire are as dependent on a limited range of activities as the old one-industry towns of the traditional industrial areas which are now in decline, and perhaps this does not augur well for the future.

# Temporal characteristics of the service sector of the UK

## Geographical change over time

Coates and Rawstron (1971) measured the impact of the service sector by using a service-to-manufacturing ratio. Although local government reorganisation, boundary changes and altered definitions make direct comparisons with their maps difficult, broad patterns and general trends can be compared. In 1961 manufacturing jobs still exceeded those in services in the Midlands, while in much of the South-East, including London, service jobs did not exceed manufacturing by a ratio of more than 1.5. The highest recorded ratios were in the Highlands, North Wales and Cornwall.

Figure 1.10 uses the methodology of Coates and Rawstron to show service-to-manufacturing ratios for 1975 and 1981. Considerable changes in the service economy's spatial expression occurred during this period. In 1975 no county had a ratio of 3 or more (i.e. three times as many service as manufacturing employees). Fifteen counties had more workers in manufacturing than in services and therefore had a ratio of less than 1. The majority (35) had a ratio of between 1 and 2, while six had a ratio of between 2 and 3. These last were Greater London, South Glamorgan and Lothian, all authorities containing capital cities, and Dorset, Gwynedd and East Sussex. Dorset and Gwynedd are rural counties with little or no industry, and East Sussex is partly a commuter zone for London: all three are holiday areas. The main area with low service ratios was in the industrial heartland from the West Yorkshire conurbation to the West Midlands, plus a broad East Midlands belt from Nottingham to Bedford. South Wales, County Durham, Cleveland and Fife were other highly industrialised areas with low service ratios. The less industrialised Border counties were more agricultural in character.

By 1981 the position had changed radically. No county had more employees in manufacturing than in services, and more than half the counties had more than twice as many employed in services as in manufacturing. The North and the Midlands were relatively less advanced in this respect. The highest levels of service employment were in London and areas to the west and south of

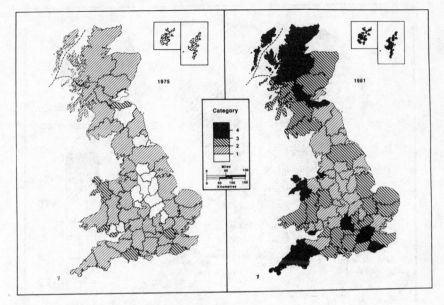

**Figure 1.10** Service-to-manufacturing ratio Great Britain, 1975 and 1981
*Source: Regional Statistics*, 1976; *Regional Trends* 1985

London (Oxfordshire, Surrey, Buckinghamshire, Berkshire and East Sussex). In Devon, Cornwall, Gwynedd, South Glamorgan and the Highlands and Islands the ratio was over 4, a remarkable change in six years.

To some extent the changed pattern results from the deindustrialisation of Britain and the massive decline in manufacturing during the recession of the late 1970s and the 1980s. Figure 1.11 indicates that many areas lost between 10 and 20 per cent of their total employment in the years 1975–81 and these losses were concentrated in manufacturing. Thus the increased service ratios in the Midlands and the North were due to a decline in manufacturing jobs rather than to an increase in services. In fact, 25 counties did experience employment growth, and five recorded increases of more than 10 per cent (the Highlands and Islands had a phenomenal 40 per cent increase due almost entirely to oil boom in the Orkneys and Shetland). Counties which benefited from employment growth also recorded additional service jobs. In counties like Oxfordshire, Buckinghamshire, Surrey, Cambridgeshire and the Highlands and Islands there was an absolute increase in service jobs to be set alongside the relative increase recorded in areas of declining total employment. Rural tourist areas and capital cities with their commuting zones (London, Edinburgh and Cardiff) witnessed an important increase in services. Interestingly, in the much heralded 'sunrise' belt from Cambridge to Bristol there has been a considerable rise in the service-to-manufacturing ratio, probably because the new microchip and biotechnology industries generate more service activities than direct manufacturing jobs.

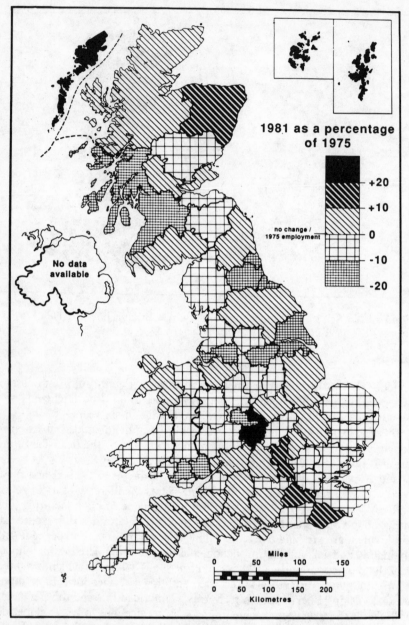

**Figure 1.11** Change in the number of employed persons. UK, 1975–81
*Source: Regional Statistics*, 1976; *Regional Trends*, 1985

**Table 1.12** Percentage of GDP attributable to the service sector, by region, UK, 1974 and 1983

|  | 1974 | 1983 |
|---|---|---|
| North | 50.1 | 55.5 |
| Yorkshire and Humberside | 51.1 | 56.0 |
| East Midlands | 48.0 | 52.5 |
| East Anglia | 57.1 | 59.7 |
| South-East | 67.0 | 68.1 |
| South-West | 61.3 | 63.4 |
| West Midlands | 46.4 | 53.2 |
| North-West | 55.0 | 58.3 |
| Wales | 53.8 | 59.5 |
| Scotland | 59.2 | 62.8 |
| Northern Ireland | 62.9 | 67.6 |

*Source*: *Regional Trends*, 1985, Table 9.4

*Changes in industrial structure*

Selected aspects of the changing industrial structure are explored in this section in order to provide more detail about some emerging trends.

Changes in GDP since 1974 are shown in Table 1.10. Agriculture, energy and water and manufacturing have declined relatively, although all increased their actual total by value. All services except construction and transport increased their share of GDP, the largest increases being in finance and business services, education and health, and other services. Overall the national share of GDP attributable to services rose from 58 per cent to 61.4 per cent in the period 1974–83. At the same time GDP increased from £68 758 million to £319 911 million, so the services were taking a bigger share of a bigger total, even allowing for the effects of inflation.

The percentage of GDP attributable to the service sector in the regions of the UK in 1974 and 1983 is shown in Table 1.12. Two major trends are evident. First, the areas with the highest proportion of service GDP were at opposite ends of the country—in the South-East and South-West and in Scotland and Northern Ireland. Second, the most rapid growth of GDP occurred in the area that had been well below average in 1974, which is clearly linked with the rising ratio of service to manufacturing employment in the Midlands and North already discussed. The southern areas grew very little in the period, perhaps because of regional policy or because other areas were catching up on earlier developments.

The growth of new firms reached 8.4 per cent in the period 1980–3, but there were wide divergences between different types of firm (Table 1.13). Only retail firms declined in number, largely due to the expansion of large chains at the expense of small shopkeepers. Agriculture, transport, catering and motor trades all grew at less than the average rate, while production firms

**Table 1.13**    Percentage growth in the number of firms in the UK, 1980–3

| | |
|---|---|
| Agriculture | 2.8 |
| Production | 10.6 |
| Construction | 15.8 |
| Transport | 3.0 |
| Wholesale | 16.7 |
| Retail | −1.9 |
| Property, finance and professional | 15.5 |
| Catering | 2.7 |
| Motor trades | 6.9 |
| All others | 23.1 |
| Total | 8.4 |

*Source*: *Regional Trends*, 1985, Table 10.10

(manufacturing, energy and water) just exceeded it. The greatest growth was in construction, wholesale, property, finance and professional, and above all in other services which grew at nearly three times the average rate. Changes in the number of firms in each sector are not necessarily a perfect indicator of growth since the size of firms is ignored, but a higher rate of increase does suggest some degree of expansion at a time of recession.

Property, finance and professional services exhibit a somewhat unexpected geographical growth pattern (Figure 1.12). Contrary to most post-war trends, London and the South-East showed well below average rates of increase, along with Merseyside and the North West. Scotland (27.9 per cent) and East Anglia (23.7 per cent) experienced the greatest increase in new firms. Scotland benefited from a vigorous policy of investment and assistance by the Highlands and Islands Development Board (HIDB 1985) which led to the creation of new companies in this area. In addition, the last phases of the off-shore oil boom were still being felt in eastern Scotland and the Northern Isles so there was a heightened demand for various services. East Anglia may have been the destination of firms leaving established centres to seek locations in county towns which was all part of the 'counter-urbanisation' trends observed in the early 1980s.

Temporal changes in geographical patterns and in the subsectoral structure of the service industry vary in their spatial incidence. Like the spatial characteristics reviewed in the previous section, the temporal characteristics discussed here lead to the conclusion that the changing geography of the service sector is too diverse in nature to be explained by simple analysis.

## Conclusion

Despite the difficulties of defining and classifying the activities comprising the service sector there can be no doubt that in modern advanced economies

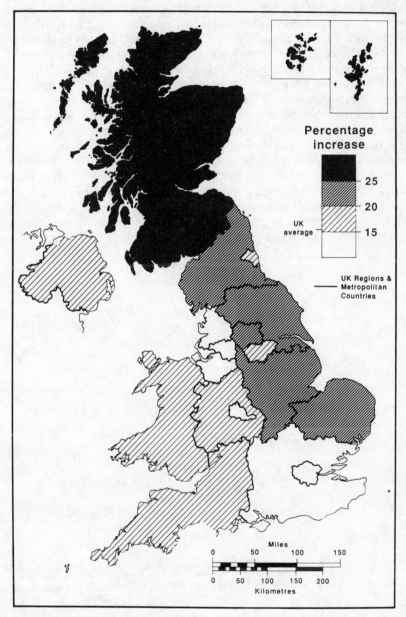

**Figure 1.12** Percentage increase in property and finance and professional services, 1980–3
*Source: Regional Trends,* 1985

services are an important element in their prosperity. Moreover, they are an element whose contribution is likely to grow in the foreseeable future. As is so often the case with economic activity, the geographical pattern produced by the distribution of services is a very uneven one, and this is true at a variety of geographical scales. Furthermore, the dynamic character of the service sector is demonstrated by change in the geographical pattern and by structural change within the sector itself. In the chapters that follow the nature of these changes and some of the reasons behind them will be explored. The so-called tertiary activities of transportation and utilities (including construction) are largely omitted from consideration except incidentally. The majority of the examples used to illustrate the concepts and themes selected for discussion are drawn from work done on office development, the producer services, retailing and wholesaling, health care, education, tourism and leisure. These activities are sufficiently representative of the services as a whole to offer the prospect of contributing insights that will help towards the understanding of the service sector's changing geography.

# Chapter 2
# The Social and Political Background

Bell (1974) drew attention to the emergence of a new type of society that he termed 'post-industrial' but it is easier to acknowledge the existence of such a society than to identify the causal factors which might provide an explanation of the change implied. Several explanations have been offered which, because of their non-spatial and even subjective character, may be regarded as of little concern to geographers. Nevertheless, there is a geographical significance because the matters discussed relate to new developments in the consumption of services, to attitudes which influence decisions, and to the recognition of trends which often display spatial variation of interest to the geographer. For example, the need for social overhead capital is universal, but the degree to which infrastructure assets belonging to the community as a whole are developed varies greatly. Similarly, the preferences that govern the actions of society are an expression of its social values that can give rise to distinctive levels of infrastructural provision. Unquestionably these concerns have a direct bearing on the character and scope of the service sector within individual countries as well as the social well-being of their populations. Social attitudes often find their expression in political actions, and in this chapter an attempt is made to discuss some of the social trends that have influenced the development of the service sector coupled with a consideration of ways in which governments have intervened to affect service provision. The purpose is to establish the context in which the development of the service sector has taken place and to act as a foil for the emphasis on economic and geographical interpretation that influences subsequent chapters.

## The Social Background: Important social trends

### Population characteristics

Throughout the Western world the post-war period witnessed an impressive growth of population with its consequent effect on the demand for services. At the simplest level governments reacted by building more schools and hospitals while retailers opened new outlets to serve the extra customers. More recently as birth rates have fallen the population growth rate has stabilised and governments are trying to implement some contraction of the system.

Population change requires readjustment in service sector provision although lead times may vary. Because there is less scope for delay in educational provision once children reach school age it is worth exploring the effects of changing population on the education service. Components of population change that are of particular interest are the changing composition of age groups, dependent on variations in the birth rate, and the growth or decline of population that accompanies population movement. Short-term prediction of the number of children requiring education is feasible if birth, death and migration rates are known. Allowing for those likely to die or migrate, it is inevitable that those currently aged up to five years will be in the six to ten age group in five years' time. Since education is compulsory it is fairly easy to predict demand for the immediate future. What is less certain are forecasts of future birth rates for long-term planning. Education planners face problems of coping with 'baby booms' where new capacity is required or when falls in the birth rate create spare capacity. The problem is that almost all long-term forecasts (more than four years ahead) are fallible. Hardly has the forecast been published than it becomes outdated. Because the lead time to build and equip schools and train teachers is long there is a danger that supply will fail to match demand. Falling birth rates are used as an argument for cutting educational expenditure. The difficulties inherent in this are shown by the experience of the UK in the 1970s and 1980s when teacher training capacity was severely reduced in anticipation of the continued fall in birth rates. However, by 1984 it was realised that birth rates were rising again and that there would soon be a need for more primary (elementary) school teachers. Apart from birth rate, the demand for education can be seriously affected by spatial redistribution of population and increasing adult participation.

Population change is rarely geographically uniform and changes resulting from alterations in the birth and death rates can have a considerable impact on the number of potential students. Declining inner cities or remote rural areas which are losing population through selective migration will have fewer students and their facilities will be threatened with closure. By contrast expanding urban and suburban areas or rural areas experiencing counter-urbanisation (Cloke, 1985) need more facilities. Typically, most migrants are young and, especially in planned new towns, often have school-age children. Throughout the developed world movement away from cities towards the suburbs and 'exurbs' and increasingly back into rural regions has been a consistent feature of the last 20 years. In the USA large interregional movements towards the Sunbelt have paralleled more local intra-metropolitan migrations. In the UK planned decentralisation through the New Towns and expanded towns programmes has been accompanied by private moves to more spacious living in the urban fringe and county towns. All these movements have necessitated changes in educational provision. As long as population continues to be spatially redistributed this is an inescapable process, however much inconvenience it causes teachers, parents and pupils who regret the closure of establishments left stranded by the flow of population away from their catchment area and to planners who have to provide new facilities in growth areas.

Similar considerations apply to other branches of service activity. Still within the public sector, the increasing separation between the inner-city location of major hospitals and the suburban residential pattern of potential patients is causing difficulties for health service planners in all parts of the Western world. It is necessary to distinguish between specialised and generalised hospital facilities because this affects the locational mobility of the institutions. There has been a movement of general hospitals to suburban sites both in the USA (Rosenberg, 1986) and in the UK as hospital building programmes have progressed, although the changes have not passed without controversy. As far as more specialised facilities such as those of London's major teaching hospitals are concerned their location reflects other require-ments than mere access to a resident population. The vast capital investment represented by a teaching hospital militates against relocation, but even where a move becomes imperative such institutions are likely to remain in inner areas. For instance, when St George's Hospital left its cramped Hyde Park Corner site in the centre of the city it moved no further than a mile or two to Wandsworth where a more spacious site for development was available. Likewise the proposed amalgamation of a number of hospitals on the banks of the Thames to form a new Westminster and Chelsea Hospital does not envisage a move to outer London. In the private sector retailers were quick to under-stand the significance of suburbanisation of population so there has been a noticeable move to suburban and out-of-town locations. This is discernible in North America and Western Europe, though the trend was constrained in the UK by planning considerations which have been recently relaxed and have led to the controversial development of 'out of town' shopping centres and malls.

## Lifestyle changes

Increased incomes among all sections of the population were a feature of the post-war period until the mid-1970s, but since then the situation has been more variable and spending power has fluctuated. Rising unemployment has also affected purchasing power. Marketing specialists accept that rising income levels affect the pattern of expenditure in that once the basic necessities of life are assured people are free to use their discretionary income as they please. This means that the market for foodstuffs is not likely to expand greatly, although this might not be true for individual items, and that the best prospects for growth are in luxury items and recreational provision. There is ample evidence to confirm the general truth of this axiom which can be shown to have had an effect on retail provision. Changes are not confined to retailing, for increased incomes tend to lead to rising expectations of the public services such as health and education. Unfortunately, the corollary of higher incomes and their effects is a reduction in facilities when personal incomes or public spending decline as the evidence of recent years demonstrates.

Demographic stabilisation does more than affect demand for school places as discussed in the previous section. It also affects the types of medical pro-vision required as well as retail and leisure facilities. Whereas during the 1960s and 1970s great emphasis was placed on serving the needs of younger people, companies are now beginning to cater for a more elderly market and they expect this trend to continue. Just as important is the breakdown of the traditional family lifestyle which provided a conceptual basis for market segmentation according to the stage reached in the family life cycle. A developmental sequence of family stages in which each stage had characteristic consumption and behaviour patterns was posited. Nowadays this view needs modification because a growing proportion of the population lives outside the traditional family lifestyle. Among the changes are delay in family formation, higher divorce rates, lower birth rates, high activity rates, earlier retirement ages and a lower proportion of older people living with their children. Such changes may be more apparent in urban than rural areas, giving rise to geographical differences. Death rates have been lowered resulting in longer periods of retirement and the emergence of a new potential market to meet the needs of older people. South coast resorts, with their concentration of elderly and retired people, have long been aware of the special problems created by this trend, but in recent years the tourist and leisure industries have turned their attention to what they recognise as a vast and expanding market.

An important trend influencing the level of disposable incomes and therefore the demand for goods and services is that of increased activity rates among the population. The larger proportion of women in employment means that an activity such as shopping that was traditionally performed by women is now being conducted jointly by working couples or else outside the shoppers' working hours. Although the time available for shopping is restricted the greater disposable income represents an advantage for the retailer which elicits a response in the form of the facilities provided. There is a greater preference for one-stop shopping which favours the larger store or centre, but conversely the large number of female part-time workers and their opportunities for using shops close to their place of work might be beneficial to town centre facilities. One outcome of the increase in the number of working women is the potential for increased consumption of convenience foods which seems to be confirmed by data relating to the purchase of frozen foods, prepared meats and fast-food products throughout the EEC. Comparable trends can be detected in respect of the consumption of services and products associated with leisure activities, and it would not be unreasonable to suppose that increased activity rates have had an effect on the demand for private education and health care.

Changing activity rates apply to employment, but also of interest to the service sector are changing participation rates in education. Conventionally the participants in education are the young who finish their compulsory school education between the ages of 15 and 19 and a proportion who go on to college or university. If education were solely confined to these groups and the proportion of young people in post-school education was fixed, it would be a simple matter to forecast future provision based on an analysis of population pyramids. Rising expectations have led to a number of changes including greater participation of females in traditional age groups; an increasing desire by mature people to complete or improve their qualifications; and mid-life career changes requiring new qualifications. The pace of change in employment making old skills obsolete and the acquisition of new ones essential has stimulated more refresher courses and retraining for adults. Involvement by hitherto non-participant groups is partly due to economic and partly to social changes. The desire by mature women in particular to acquire more qualifications after child-raising is a growing feature of post-school education. The pressures created by this new source of demand may not lead to a new pattern of provision but they might help to retain the existing facilities by justifying their continued existence.

## Increased personal mobility

An important contributory factor to the suburbanisation of population distribution is the increased personal mobility that has accompanied the growth of car ownership. The availability of a car greatly enhances an individual's flexibility of residential choice, with important results for the distribution of population. At the same time private transport can transform a person's attitude to the use of service facilities by presenting a much wider range of options than was formerly available. People with cars are willing to travel quite long distances to take advantage of medical and leisure facilities, but perhaps the impact has been most dramatic on retailing because carborne shoppers can carry greater quantities of goods than those who have no car. This has encouraged the growth of 'one-stop' shopping and the increasing preference among major store companies for out-of-town or suburban locations where ample parking space is available. It is difficult to quantify the extent to which shopping trips by car have changed at the national scale, but several smaller-scale studies indicate a conspicuous growth in car usage for shopping purposes in the suburbs and particularly at superstores or new centres. For example, it was quickly discovered at Brent Cross Shopping Centre in North London that the original provision of 3500 places was inadequate so parking was extended to 4500 places. Use of the car also affects the daily patterns of usage of stores or centres, for there is greater availability of cars for shopping at weekends or in the evening. Contrasting with these effects of increased car ownership are the negative effects of the need for medical provision to cope with accident victims and the traffic congestion that may diminish the attractiveness of a previously favoured location.

## The importance of attitudes

Consumerism, which began as a response to consumers' dissatisfactions arising in exchange relationships, has been a profound influence which has extended beyond its original focus on commercial relationships to embrace attitudes to public service provision as well. Perhaps this indicates that, basic wants having been satisfied, a more advanced stage of cultural-economic development has been initiated. Consumerism is something more than a desire to secure value for money: it includes the idea that goods and services should be rendered safe for the consumer; that the consumer has a right to be informed and protected from inadequate or misleading information; that real competition should not be limited by sellers' collusion; and that the consumer's voice should be heard. Commercial activities such as retailing and leisure provision had no alternative but to respond to the claims of consumerism, but there has been some resistance to the concept of consumer sovereignty among providers of medical and educational services. In the latter two cases, of course, attitudes may differ between the private and public providers of the service offered.

Rising expectations have been a contributory factor to consumerism. As far as education is concerned rising expectations have been expressed in an increased demand for qualifications. Hence, as education disseminates knowledge more widely ever-increasing horizons are opened to people, feeding the demand for further knowledge. Literacy and numeracy have a role to play in enhancing capabilities and raising expectations. Fostering education was a primary aim of early European socialist intellectuals like Sidney and Beatrice Webb, while trade (labour) unions encouraged the development of adult and further education among the working class. The popularity of evening classes, correspondence courses and various self-improvement residential courses amply demonstrates that education does not stop when a school or university career ends. A more demanding employment situation requiring more highly educated people is a powerful stimulus for acquiring qualifications. Although utility is an educational objective, it is also true that many students seek personal fulfilment in meeting the challenge of mastering a course of study.

Compared with the extent of publicly provided education of the sort described above which is documented, it is difficult to estimate the extent to which people educate themselves at home through reading, watching TV, listening to the radio, or engaging in educational hobbies. Part of the problem is that much home-based education is inextricably mixed with entertainment; home computers maybe used for calculating multiple regressions or zapping space invaders. By early 1985 it was estimated that 2½ million homes in Great Britain possessed a home micro-computer, proportionately more than any other Western country, although it would be foolish to assume that this equipment was wholly, or even mainly, purchased and used strictly for educational purposes. On the other hand, the British Open University, founded in 1967, is primarily educational in function. Structured reading and writing courses making use of TV and radio programmes as support material have contributed to the success of 'distance learning'. This is not a new idea (correspondence courses have a long history) but one that modern technology has made effective with all its implications for the availability of higher education to more people. Future developments of cable TV connected to home computers holds the promise of true interactive home learning. The success of the Open University suggests that the public's thirst for knowledge is far from being assuaged.

It is not easy to be precise about attitudes. For example, good health contributes so much to individual welfare that it is a prerequisite for enjoying almost every other aspect of life, though the meaning of 'good' or 'bad' health is far from clear. The WHO definition of a 'state of complete physical and mental and social well-being' provides a good starting point even though there is no absolute standard for measuring the attainment of good health in these terms because individual perceptions and aspirations vary so much that a common measure is elusive. Nevertheless, some attempts have been made to measure the 'health of a population'. The ideas expressed here conform to the notion that developments in health care provision are generally desirable because they promote human welfare. Such a liberal interpretation may well be challenged by Marxists who might regard development of this nature as a means of improving the strength and efficiency of the work-force in order to maintain the capitalist system. They would argue that this gives rise to particular geographical patterns which cannot be ignored.

Eyles and Woods (1983) discussed how attitudes to health care have altered over time. In Victorian times health was viewed very much as a matter of lack of disease, the causes of which were linked with overcrowding, insanitary conditions and poverty. Considerable philanthropic effort was devoted to remedying the situation, and although there was a large degree of success many citizens still did not enjoy good health. Today's problems are more likely to be concerned with mental health than with the diseases that exercised our Victorian forebears. Apparently success in eliminating one problem allows scope for another to emerge. Modern urban life generates stress and pressures that often lead to mental strain, and while it is disputed whether environmental conditions or social attributes are the principal cause there is agreement that the problems do become geographically concentrated (see Giggs, 1973, on schizophrenia). Geography seems to be important in other ways, too. Shannon *et al.* (1975) have argued that the manner in which medical facilities are distributed *vis-à-vis* the distribution of population has a demonstrated effect upon illness and therapeutic behaviour.

According to Eyles and Woods the welfare state has helped to redefine 'health' to embrace the social health of individuals and families and not merely the lack of physical or mental disorder. With this redefinition they claim that there has been a transition from civil to social rights. They believe that the granting of social rights by the state has not meant the application of uniform principles of allocation. Some agencies opt for a minimum level of provision (a safety net) while others favour assistance according to universalist principles; that is, to each according to his/her needs. For Eyles and Woods there is an important distinction between 'medical' and 'health care'. There is evidence of dissatisfaction with western medical standards in the upsurge of interest in alternative medicine. The growing market for health foods is one manifestation of concern with physical well-being. Providers of health services are resigned to the fact that no quantifiable and finite measure of the health problem can be devised, so that as attitudes change new difficulties will be identified and will have to be confronted.

*Changes in taste*

Lifestyle changes, increased mobility and changing attitudes mean that consumer tastes may also alter. Frequently these are too ephemeral to have much geographical significance, but some changes in taste may be important. Davies (1984) pointed out that unisex hairdressing salons, which would have had limited appeal 20 years ago and may still be unacceptable to some, have expanded in recent years. Undoubtedly this has had an impact on the retail structure of shopping districts, as has the growing involvement in do-it-yourself activities. More permissive attitudes have allowed the development of such 'twilight' activities as sex shops, though there has been powerful opposition to them in some places. For years the opening of certain shops on Sunday has been restricted in England and Wales, partly in response to religious opinion. Because the latter is felt to be less imperative nowadays pressure from interested parties advocating Sunday opening led to a marked change in government attitudes but not yet to a change in the relevant legislation. From the geographical viewpoint changes in taste may be of no more than minor importance, but they do affect the character of provision in retailing and leisure facilities so they should not be entirely ignored.

### Increased leisure time

Post-war increases in the amount of leisure time available to ordinary people due largely to the shrinking working day, the five-day week, and longer paid holidays must not delude us into supposing that mass recreation and entertainment is a modern Western phenomenon. Roman devotion to the arena, hippodrome and baths (more akin to a contemporary sports centre than a public swimming pool) is well known. The lavish provision for entertainment resulted in some of the best-known buildings of Ancient Rome including the Coliseum and the Circus Maximus which were large even by today's standards. Smaller versions were built all over the Roman Empire.

In medieval times there were holy days, local festivals, and fairs, some of which survive in watered-down form today (for example, Mardi Gras). It was only with the onset of the Industrial Revolution with the discipline of the factory and the tyranny of the clock that leisure time was cut down for the majority of people. Recent increases in leisure time have been more in the nature of a recovery from the aberration of the Industrial Revolution than a totally new trend. The 'Protestant work ethic', extolling the virtues of hard work and the generally long hours, low wages and lack of opportunity for most people in the aftermath of the Industrial Revolution, limited the time, resources and desire for leisure. Those who possessed sufficient wealth and leisure time found ample opportunity for recreational outlet. Nineteenth- and early twentieth-century popular novels about the middle and upper classes abound with detail on leisure activity (for example, *The Irish RM* by Somerville and Ross) contrasting with drinking and gambling in the local pubs relieved by the occasional works outing found in novels of working-class life like Tressell's *Ragged Trousered Philanthropists*.

The absence of mental and physical recreation contributed to the physical deterioration of health in Western urban industrial society. In England, reports like those by Rowntree and Booth shocked the middle classes into pressing government to provide more recreational opportunities for the working class. The high rate of rejection on medical grounds of volunteers for the Boer War convinced the government that something had to be done. Municipal parks, allotments and swimming baths all began to make their appearance in late Victorian times.

Thanks to the Christian heritage of the West, Sunday had always been a day of rest, but in the late nineteenth and early twentieth century the concept of the half day on Saturday became widespread. Public holidays, too, were legislated for by government, often to give the population its first taste of paid

**Table 2.1** Average hours of work,* 1973 and 1982

|  | 1973 | 1982 |
|---|---|---|
| Belgium | 40.9 | 35.6 |
| West Germany | 42.9 | 40.8 |
| France | 44.4 | 39.5 |
| Ireland | – | 41.4 |
| Italy | 41.8 | 38.1 |
| Luxembourg | 43.7 | 38.9 |
| Netherlands | 43.0 | 40.6 |
| UK | 43.4 | 41.6 |

*Manual workers: all males
Source: *Eurostat*, 1983, Table 3.18; 1973, Table 13.6.

**Table 2.2** Time use in a typical week, 1982

| Weekly hours spent on | Full-time employees | | Part-time employees | | Housewives | Retired |
|---|---|---|---|---|---|---|
|  | M | F | M | F | F | All |
| Employment and travel to work | 45.3 | 40.7 | 20.7 | 22.4 | – | – |
| Essential activities | 23.7 | 33.5 | 30.1 | 48.0 | 57.7 | 36.1 |
| Sleep | 56.4 | 57.5 | 56.6 | 57.0 | 59.2 | 60.2 |
| Free time | 42.6 | 36.3 | 60.6 | 40.6 | 51.1 | 71.7 |
| Free time per weekday | 4.0 | 3.6 | 7.8 | 4.7 | 7.0 | 9.9 |
| Free time per weekend day | 11.4 | 9.2 | 10.8 | 8.6 | 8.0 | 11.2 |

Source: *Social Trends*, 1985

leisure. Legislation to limit excessive hours of work in factories began to give factory workers more time in the evenings for other activities. Paid holidays were still rare before 1914, but after 1918 the 'week at the seaside' became more common. Since 1973 there has been a decrease in working time, as Table 2.1 indicates. The reduction in the number of hours worked and the prevalence of the five-day week clearly gives more scope for leisure pursuits. European workers enjoy more leisure time than their Japanese and American colleagues, and in fact Japanese workers sometimes have difficulty in accepting increased leisure time, preferring to do voluntary overtime instead. Communal exercises in Japanese factories may reduce the desire for after-work recreations like jogging which are popular in the West.

For professional and managerial occupations work and leisure time may become blurred. A salesman or executive may be lavishly entertained at an expense account lunch which counts as 'work time', while being expected to pore over reports at home at the weekend which counts as 'leisure time'. Even geographers on field trips enjoying the scenery and residence away from home every bit as much as if they were on holiday are in fact working. For some occupations it is becoming increasingly difficult to distinguish between work and leisure time, but there is no doubt that the available leisure time has increased in recent years.

Shorter working weeks do not necessarily mean huge increases in usable leisure time. A shorter working day may be offset by longer commuting distances. Actual free time, or disposable time, is not to be equated with 'non-work' time. Table 2.2 shows that sleep and essential activities occupy lengthy periods, leaving a comparatively limited amount of free time. Full-time employees obviously have less disposable time than part-time workers, while women may have less free time because they are coping with domestic chores and the burden of child-rearing. Retired people have most free time, but for reasons of age and finance tend to be more limited in the use they will make of it.

*Ethnic and cultural factors*

Another social change of the post-war period which is very different in character from those already discussed is connected with the scale of immigration in Europe. The immigrant population of the EEC is put at 12 million (Salt, 1985), and in many cases the ethnic groups are sharply defined in terms of their consumption and behaviour patterns. In the UK there are distinctive Indian, Pakistani and West Indian markets catered for by specialist retailers whose presence is sometimes so strong that they dominate a shopping district. Compared with other EEC countries where immigrants include large numbers of 'guest workers', immigration to the UK has been more permanent and family-based. It is too early to assess the influence of the ethnic minorities on consumer and shopping behaviour at the national scale, but the local impact of ethnic minorities is being studied in places like Bradford. Apart from distinctive religious facilities such as mosques and temples, ethnic groups may establish their own banks, insurance companies and travel agents. In other fields they usually use existing facilities such as schools and hospitals so they have not yet produced special geographical patterns for these features.

Cultural behavioural patterns based on religious, rather than ethnic, differences have long been acknowledged in studies of consumer behaviour (see, for example, Murdie, 1965). This implies a degree of segmentation in the market which may be countered by the growing interest in the development of a megacultural entity such as a standardised Euroconsumer. International advertising and awareness of developments in other countries as travel and education add to the consumers' sum of knowledge have contributed to a growing similarity in consumer tastes and preferences. Such a process has been assisted by the efforts of transnational companies distributing their products in a number of countries. Trends in fashion are quickly internationalised and the number of products that are sold under the same name in several countries confirms this; examples are Coca Cola, photographic equipment, radio and hi-fi equipment, and pharmaceutical products. These trends should not be exaggerated because there is also evidence of the strong survival of regional tastes that point to a limited geographical market for some items. Cultural differences may be present in attitudes to education and health care, but the geographical implications of this are uncertain.

## Political Background Factors

Political considerations pervade the service sector: in some cases their impact has direct geographical consequences, as in planning decisions, but political factors can have a very profound effect on service activities without being directly geographical in their impact. In this section attention will be paid to aspects of political factors that have had varying degrees of influence on service activities.

### The issue of public versus private ownership

Because consumer information is imperfect government intervenes in the allocation of health care and education by controlling its provision and regulating the standards of its practitioners. In all advanced societies entry to the medical profession is strictly controlled in terms of educational standards and length of training, and much the same is true of educational professions. Government intervention may extend to influencing the number and distribution of medical and educational establishments, and it may be used to affect the level of provision through subsidies or taxation. Intervention of this sort is practised in countries where private provision is the norm because it is realised that consumers need some protection. More serious is the debate on the virtues of public as opposed to private ownership of health and education facilities, though in practice there is dual provision in most countries. State provision of education has a longer record than that of health care services, but since 1948 a public health service has operated in the UK and its continued existence is seen to be politically desirable.

Knippenberg and van der Wusten (1984) drew attention to the sensitive nature of the relationship between church and state ever since the latter became involved in education. The issue is not confined to the Netherlands but there are indications that pressure from religious interests may no longer have the political strength it once had. Of greater importance is the fact that educational debate over public versus private provision is now a conflict between the supporters of the welfare state and the advocates of self-help. No one doubts that the vast majority of children will be educated in state schools, but political controversy exists over the desirability of allowing some people to opt out because of their wealth. Some argue that the state should not interfere with the basic freedom of parental choice, while others oppose private education on moral grounds and argue that standards in state schools would rise if the elite's children had to attend them because the rich and powerful would pressurise governments to ensure that standards were high. Critics observe that private schools receive various state subsidies including grants, tax remissions and free training of teachers. Attempts to restrict or abolish private schools in Western democracies have always failed. In 1983 the French socialist government tried to introduce various educational reforms which would have harmed the viability of private schools: the subsequent storm of protest was so great that the government retreated. In the UK eminent socialists have sent their children to private schools and such 'ethical dualism' makes it hard for them to justify implementing abolition when they are in power.

Clearly related to the issue of public versus private provision is the question of equity. Welfare state philosophy emphasises that all children should have equal access to educational opportunity. There is widespread acceptance of this view, but some demand positive discrimination to overcome social deprivation. Since the catchment areas of individual schools are likely to include pupils from particular social and economic groups the starting position for pupils is not equal spatially. Evidence suggests that pupils from a middle-class background receive more encouragement and additional help in the form of books, equipment, visits to museums, art galleries, exhibitions and the countryside than those from poorer backgrounds. Even if school provision were equal pupils from these two groups would not start from the same educational base. Often there is a double disadvantage in that working-class children are disproportionately located in inner-city areas with older buildings and equipment than those of the newer schools of the middle-class suburbs. Parent Teacher Associations in middle-class areas are more likely to raise funds for extra-curricular facilities such as computers and field trips. The desire to equalise opportunities was a prime motive in the adoption of non-selective comprehensive education in the UK, although 20 years after the movement started there are still geographical variations in the extent of comprehensivisation.

Geographically public ownership is important because it facilitates planning at a national level which in turn leads to distinctive geographical patterns. In Britain the National Health Service is organised on regional lines and the Regional Health Authorities contribute to a particular geographical pattern and organisation of health care facilities. Public education in the UK is organised on a local authority basis, but as with health care there is a hierarchical structure of facilities that corresponds to the perceived needs in specific geographical areas. Public ownership is not confined to education and health care provision: some industries are nationalised, and there are the government's own administrative activities. In the latter case the government is favourably placed to pursue its own policies, and in a spatial context this has often expressed itself in the dispersal of activities to peripheral regions.

## Control of geographical change

National and local governments influence geographical change through the planning mechanism. Control may be exercised through constraints such as planning restrictions usually operated by a system of licences (for example, Office Development Permits) or time-consuming planning enquiries. Incentives to encourage approved projects include grants, loans or tax relief, but in the case of service industries grants introduced under the Industry Act 1972 were limited. They were not available for service activities intended to meet local needs (mainly consumer services) and to be eligible firms moving from elsewhere had to create at least ten new jobs (Daniels, 1982). Regulations relating to service industries were fairly strict so that it is not surprising that they made little impact on the sector. Devices such as these may operate as an expression of regional policy or they may be limited to controlling land use within specific urban areas. Sometimes, as in France, policy is aimed at deliberate goals and development at the regional scale in designated areas, whereas elsewhere the policy has been more loosely framed as in the office dispersal policy practised in the UK.

Public policy control aimed directly at commercial development has traditionally been minimal in the USA, though some influence has been exerted through zoning. Since the National Environment Policy Act of 1969 required that the environmental effects of federal actions be evaluated there has been increased federal and state awareness of the social costs of some of their own actions and those of commercial developers. Consequently both federal and state authorities have become more willing to intervene in the shopping centre development process either by refusing permission for new schemes or by attempting to manage and shape economic growth. Compared with other countries intervention remains minimal but Dawson and Lord (1985) discussed four examples of policy intervention. Under President Carter the Community Conservation Guidance Policy operated from 1978 until 1981 and was concerned with retail location policy and the location of new retail capital development. Had the policy continued it would have helped to contain suburban growth and would have encouraged city centre investment. The community impact analysis, which had to be completed within 45 days of a formal request from a community's chief elected official opposed to a scheme, was the heart of the policy. A total of 24 studies were conducted under the terms of the policy, but the policy's impact was minimised because the Department of Housing and Urban Development had no authority over federal agencies to require them to withold federal funds from developments. Opposition to the policy was strong, and it was quickly killed off with the change of president in 1981. The Urban Development Action Grant (UDAG) programme survived the change of administration. Introduced in 1979, the programme was a pump-priming scheme involving grants and loans in severely depressed cities. In the 1978–82 some 1453 projects were funded to some extent, about a fifth of them involving retail development. The objective was to encourage investment and to create jobs in economically distressed cities, and developers quickly realised the potential for encouraging investment in shopping centres. At the state level Vermont's Act 250 of 1970 required the developers of any project exceeding 10 acres to obtain a development permit. In the decade 1970–80 some 3566 permit applications, not all of which were concerned with retailing, were reviewed and only 2.5 per cent of these were refused. The Florida Environmental Land and Water Management Act of 1972 incorporated the development of a regional impact programme (DRI). Shopping centre developments occupying more than 40 acres of land, covering 400 000 square feet of gross floor area, or providing parking for more than 2500 cars were considered substantial enough to warrant application of DRI procedures. Between 1973 and 1983 some 36 proposed shopping centre developments were deemed worthy of DRI assessment: only two were refused and none were given unconditional permission. Some applications were withdrawn for financial or other reasons, and it is difficult to evaluate the effectiveness of DRIs but Dawson and Lord (1985) conclude that while the quantity may not have been affected the quality of centre development has been improved as a result of DRI procedures. Apart from UDAG regulatory growth management policies have been introduced by state rather than federal authorities. There is evidence to suggest that the establishment of a mutually co-operative relationship between government and developer will be more productive than antagonistic conflict-based attitudes. The shopping centre industry has been more responsive to community feelings in the USA than in other countries, so that although regulation may be necessary it would be unwise to attempt the aggressive imposition of legislative programmes in a manner that might be successful elsewhere.

One of the best-known examples of planning at the regional scale with an emphasis on a service activity is the French government's development of Languedoc-Roussillon as part of the National Plan. The desire to develop a new area of the Mediterranean coast for tourism involved massive effort. $18.8 billion was invested by 1979 and five new tourist units were created in the hope that the multiplier effect would raise income and employment levels in a depressed area as well as providing new amenities. The latter has been achieved, but the other expected benefits have not materialised to the extent that the government had hoped. On a more local scale, on the south coast of England the Brighton Marina scheme entailed shops, flats, restaurants, a casino and yachting facilities and is one of the biggest of its kind in the UK. It was the subject of planning enquiries and much bitter opposition from those who claimed that its presence would mar the beauty of a magnificent stretch of coastline. Eventually planning permission was granted and the marina was built, but it was not as successful as the original promoter expected. Five big financial institutions raised over £50 million, and after many delays, which included storm damage and a further planning enquiry the marina was opened in May 1979. By this time the economic climate did not encourage the stockholders to proceed to the next stage of development. Instead, they sought advice and eventually sold out to a leisure and property group which paid £13 million for the development. Much of this money was recouped by selling a corner of the site for £10 million so that the Dee Corporation could build a Carrefour hypermarket. As now envisaged, there will be about 700 luxury residential properties, an international hotel, a sports and leisure complex including a water theme park, a multi-screen cinema, health hydro, superstore and a range of conventional shops and eating places. The project is expected to be earning £10 million a year by the early 1990s, and if it does it will have taken over 20 years to achieve this since the scheme was first approved in 1968. Another example of the way in which planning restrictions can control development is the 13-year long saga of the Brent Cross shopping centre in North London. Originally the planning application was sympathetically received by the Greater London Council Planning Department, although it was turned down on several occasions on traffic grounds. Finally the centre opened in 1976 and has been commercially successful. Similar resistance was initially experienced by superstore developers who despite the favourable change in the political climate still meet much opposition to some of their cherished ideas such as location along motorways (freeways).

Another form of political intervention is the widespread use of dispersal policies to redistribute certain activities. Regional Development policy originally concentrated on the dispersal of industry to the regions which inevitably had some effect on the service sector, but it was not until governments turned their attention to the dispersal of office activities that the service sector became a prime consideration. The British government favoured a policy of acting on those office activities over which it had most control, namely government administration. Important branches of government were moved away from London and South-East England to new locations in the North-East and Wales. An alternative strategy was to attempt to control the market through the medium of Office Development Permits which were introduced in the UK in 1964 and lasted until 1979. Here the objective was to direct office development away from London and the South-East by requiring a permit to sanction new office growth exceeding 232 square metres (2500 square feet). It was not intended to halt all office development, but it was felt that checks were needed. In 1969 the French government introduced a similar scheme to control growth in the Paris region. Both countries employed promotion agencies to encourage relocation: in the UK the Location of Offices Bureau and in France the Bureau-Province fulfilled this function, though neither was without its critics. There has been a redistribution of office activities by dispersal, and to that extent the policy has achieved a measure of success. On the other hand, dispersal has also been achieved in the USA where market forces rather than planning mechanisms have been responsible. Critics query whether we should resort to planning when market forces can produce the same result. In the USA some of the consequences of laissez-faire dispersal, especially in respect of inner cities, suggest that there are disadvantages in leaving development to chance and the operation of market forces. More attention should be paid to the costs and benefits of dispersal, but it has to be admitted that there is a gap between our theoretical knowledge of the office sector and our attempts to formulate effective office location policies. For the present, then, much office location policy proceeds by trial and error, and since Damesick (1979) reported that the office location policies of planners and developers in London were at odds there is evidently still scope for improvement.

### Control of operations

Even in advanced Western economies, with their commitment to market forces, government takes a close interest in the operation of commercial and public sector activities. Legislation in individual countries differs, but the existence of regulations controlling working hours and conditions and unfair competition is universal. A degree of restraint may be exercised on wages and prices, and as far as retailing is concerned consumers are protected by official supervision of weights and measures and by the work of public health inspectors in ensuring the maintenance of acceptable standards of hygiene, particularly in the sale of foodstuffs. In many countries, government inspectors visit schools and colleges to check the standard of educational provision.

Change in the application of these regulations occurs gradually, if at all, so that firms can take them into account in long-term planning. Other forms of government intervention are less predictable in their effects, though these may be profound. For example, changes in taxation may affect levels of demand drastically and yet they are often implemented with little prior warning. The unexpected increase of Value Added Tax in the UK from 8 to 15 per cent in 1979 probably affected sales, and certainly the changeover from the old system of purchase tax which was levied at widely differing levels to a uniform rate of Value Added Tax affected the sales of some hitherto heavily taxed items such as records and radio equipment.

In the public sector the government has a role as a protector of entry standards for practitioners in the fields of medicine and education. To some extent this involves manpower planning, but governments usually make their presence felt through financial allocations to specified services. In medicine standards are maintained by professional bodies. In education the government may lay down minimum standards of entry to teacher training but more local organisations actually determine what these standards mean in practice. Recently the question of educational standards has become highly controversial. Industry criticises education for not providing the kind of people it wants, but others claim that the aim of education is not solely to train people for jobs. Examination results are one guide to standards, and there is clear evidence of substantial variations in this measure (see Figure 2.1). Kirby (1982) showed how even within a local authority individual schools can be regarded as 'good' or 'bad'. This can lead to a self-perpetuating system with the parents of able children insisting on their going to 'good' schools, while the indifferent parent acquiesces in a place at a poorer school. 'Bad' schools can experience a negative feedback—not only do they receive weaker candidates but the latter have low expectations of themselves and therefore do not make much effort. They expect to fail and they do. Thus, on a micro-spatial scale there can be substantial variations in the chances of a pupil's receiving a good quality education, and this is a major problem for concerned governments.

Another area of interest to governments is the cost of public services. There are differences in the priority given to educational expenditure by political parties: all presumably seek to obtain value for money, but some see this in terms of reducing expenditure while others believe that better results will be forthcoming if expenditure is greater. Opponents of the current emphasis on reducing expenditure point to its adverse effects on education and the health service in the shape of reduced research output, longer waiting lists for operations, and the closure of hospitals and educational units. Supporters claim that waste is being eliminated and a more efficient service is being created. Governments may find themselves in conflict with local authorities, as is illustrated by the British Labour government's plans for introducing comprehensive education which were delayed and successfully resisted by some

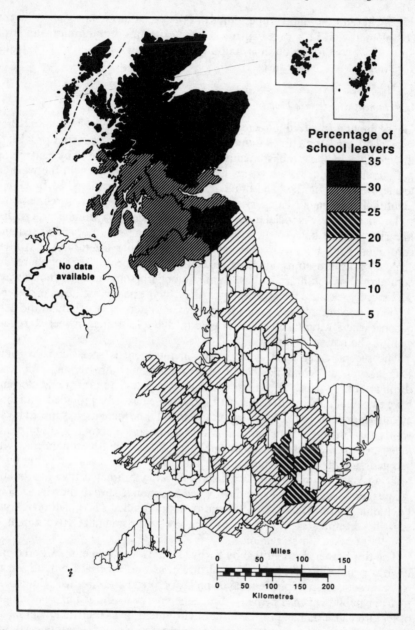

**Percentage of
school leavers**

- 35
- 30
- 25
- 20
- 15
- 10
- 5

No data
available

Miles
0    50    100    150

0   50   100   150   200
Kilometres

**Figure 2.1**   British school leavers with one or more A levels (or H grades in Scotland) 1983
*Source: Regional Trends*, 1985

Conservative local authorities during the late 1970's.

Government attempts to control the operation of services tend to apply at the national scale and are likely to result in the standardisation of quality.

They will reduce unfair competition from the use of ultra-cheap labour in the commercial world by wage control and the existence of minimum standards for working conditions, but it is doubtful whether they will eliminate all spatial variation due to these causes.

### Government and leisure provision

Government is involved in recreation by means of laws, regulations and policy statements, and sometimes may intervene directly in recreational provision, for example, by the establishment of a National Park service or by controlling a TV channel. More often government influence is felt through the work of local authorities or the local branches of national institutions. Kirby (1985) identified three major categories of government involvement in recreation.

The first of these is social investment. Governments may fund sports stadia, libraries, concert halls or theatres to provide a healthier, more educated and controlled work-force (or, more cynically, a happier electorate). Facilities such as parks, museums and libraries could not be operated free of charge by commercial or voluntary bodies. Admission charges are opposed (not always successfully) because they would deter usage by the poorer members of society. National prestige acts as a spur for government interest, especially in the field of sport where winning an Olympic gold medal, for instance, is seen to reflect well on the nation as a whole.

The second category of government involvement is social consumption. Recreation is an economic activity generating money directly and indirectly through linkage with the rest of the economy. Sports equipment and clothing have to be manufactured, transport to the venue has to be provided, and food and drink are consumed at the sports ground. Thus, recreation is linked backwards into manufacturing and forwards into service activities. Figure 2.2. illustrates the linkages created by watching sport on TV. All economic activity can generate tax for government expenditure. In fact, recreation is big business, as Martin and Mason (1980) showed. They estimated that £23 billion (27 per cent of consumer expenditure) was spent on leisure in the UK in 1979. Excluding clothing and travel, expenditure still totalled £17.25 billion (20 per cent of consumer expenditure), so it is not surprising that government is closely interested in recreation.

The third category identified by Kirby (1985) is social expense. A bored and restless population can be a political threat, as the Imperial Roman government recognised in implementing its policy of 'bread and circuses'. Entertainment at public expense helps to direct the energy of the young, who might otherwise cause damage to the local environment or to their fellow citizens. Provision of sports centres, parks, swimming pools and free concerts are examples of social expense. In Liverpool in the UK an almost immediate government response to the urban riots in 1981 was to initiate a massive Garden Festival scheme to provide jobs and a new parkland area. Increasingly social expense is extending to the costs of policing recreational events. International occasions like the Olympic Games require elaborate security arrangements to deter terrorists, and even domestic sports events may call for a police presence to control hooliganism.

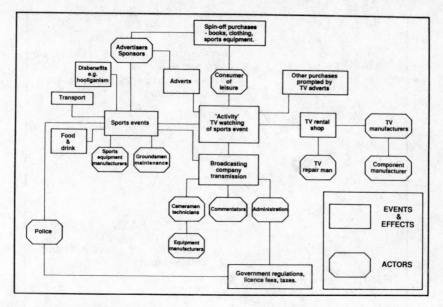

**Figure 2.2** Linkages in leisure

Provision by local authorities has increased in this century: it includes parks, gardens and sports grounds as well as buildings for concerts, plays and societies. The parks and gardens department seems innocuous enough, but leisure professionals have become more numerous. They can be motivated, not by profit, but by safeguarding their jobs or upgrading their status by controlling bigger budgets or larger staffs. This can lead to grandiose projects such as leisure centres or yachting marinas which may have little connection with the needs or wants of the local populace. According to Torkildsen (1983) the Association of Recreation Managers grew from under 100 in 1969 to over 1100 in 1981 in the UK alone. Investment in leisure facilities can contribute to the protection of the local environment and the promotion of the local economy. Modern footloose industry, especially the 'sunrise' industries, may be drawn to an area by its attractive environment as recent newspaper advertisements for computer scientists, marketing executives and graduate engineers in pleasant country towns confirm. There are many motives for local authorities to encourage recreation, including statutory obligations in the case of libraries, and are not required to make a profit. The only real constraint for them is how much the local taxpayer or ratepayer will condone. The Greater London Council (GLC, 1969) went so far as to refer to a 'theory of accessibility to public open space'. It proposed a hierarchical arrangement of parkland on central place principles whereby metropolitan parks of over 150 acres would be within 2 miles of the population served and small parks of under 5 acres would be within a quarter of a mile of users (see Figure 2.3). It was envisaged that different modes of transport would be used to reach these parks.

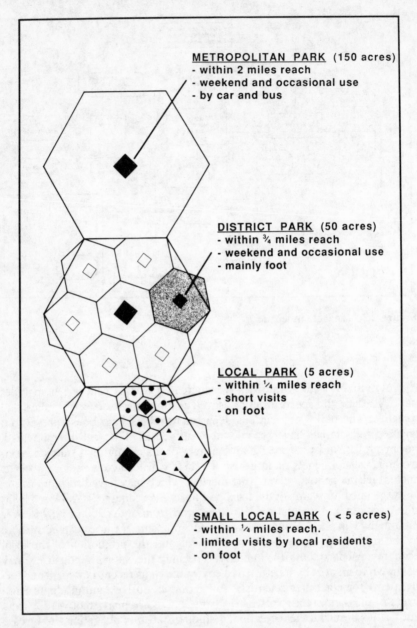

METROPOLITAN PARK (150 acres)
- within 2 miles reach
- weekend and occasional use
- by car and bus

DISTRICT PARK (50 acres)
- within ¾ miles reach
- weekend and occasional use
- mainly foot

LOCAL PARK (5 acres)
- within ¼ miles reach
- short visits
- on foot

SMALL LOCAL PARK ( < 5 acres)
- within ¼ miles reach.
- limited visits by local residents
- on foot

**Figure 2.3**   Theory of accessibility to public open space
*Source*: GLC (1969)

*Other political factors*

Governments may be aware that possession of a renowned education or medical service can enhance a country's international standing. Furthermore, where a service activity such as financial services makes a notable contribution to the country's economy the government soon becomes concerned if financial scandals threaten an institution's good name and reputation. Tourism is an activity that can help to foster a favourable image of a nation, so some governments consciously act to promote this aim. Franco's Spain and the Colonels' Greece encouraged tourism in a deliberate attempt to appease possible criticism of their right-wing governments. In this way it was hoped to win friends for their countries and possibly tacit approval for their policies. Similarly, Eastern European countries like Bulgaria have made strenuous efforts to develop tourism and to present their countries in a favourable light. Political instability in a country or the existence of active political organisations may discourage tourism, as recent experience in Ireland, Spain and Central America has shown.

There is a long history of government intervention in recreation because some recreational pursuits have been seen as harmful to the interests of the state by diverting energies or promoting disorder. Medieval European governments unsuccessfully banned football since it led to riots and diverted men from archery practice. Modern governments have laws on alochol, gambling and safety at sports grounds. They have tried to stop some activities altogether (for example, Prohibition), set age limits, established area zoning to prevent certain activities (such as bathing and hang gliding) or to restrict them to specified controlled areas (for example, red light districts or zones of tolerance). Films, TV and theatre have been subjected to censorship for both moral and political reasons. Certain types of recreation have been encouraged by the designation of National Parks, Long Distance Footpaths or Trails.

Legislation on hours of work and public holidays have provided the basic framework of leisure time. Virtually all nations have their own special national days (independence days, Victory days). There has been a tendency towards an increase in public holidays, though these are still fewer than the ancient and medieval holy days. The chief difference between ancient and modern holidays is that the latter are paid ones. Variations in laws between neighbouring states have promoted various kinds of entertainment—for example, strict gambling laws in neighbouring states helped the casinos in Las Vegas, Monte Carlo and Sun City. Local government is itself a major provider of recreation in modern states to such an extent that the vested interest of professional local authority leisure services in expansion to create and retain jobs, boost budgets, and enhance career prospects has resulted in inappropriate and large-scale prestige developments.

Adrian's (1984) comment that institutional issues have been ignored in favour of system logistics within an optimisation location-allocated framework is pertinent to a review of social and political factors. An examination of the organisational structure of the institution responsible for provision is often essential if the reasons underlying the spatial distribution of a service and the attempt to match demand and supply are to be understood. Adrian demonstrated in respect of the Sydney fire service that the role of political parties at the legislative level, the majority interest of the Board of Fire Commissioners of New South Wales in fire service financing and funding, and the direct interest of the Board in decisions affecting supply were all relevant considerations that constrained the level and distribution of provision. Without a doubt the same is true of a wide range of other services in Australia and elsewhere, and Jackson (1985) showed that this is the case as far as community health care in Victoria is concerned.

## Conclusion

However imprecise social and political factors may appear in comparison with the analytical rigour of the economists' investigations of the service sector their importance cannot be ignored because their impact on development is undeniable. Most of this chapter has been concerned with the present and the past, but there are good grounds for supposing that great weight should be attached to the way in which social and political considerations will help to shape the future of service provision. For example, Gershuny and Miles (1983), in arguing that the pattern of demand for all products produced by an economy, especially the balance between goods and services, is determined by the manner of provision for 'final functions', go on to say that innovation in the mode of provision of these functions is a major source of socio-economic change in contemporary economies. In their view, little conventional economic innovation takes place within service industries, but in fact much innovation has occurred in self-service informal modes of provision of service functions. Thus, change occurs in the organisation of the final service function rather than in the service activity which might previously have provided the function—for example, domestic washing machines replacing laundry services. Such a change is termed 'modal shift', and according to Gershuny and Miles there is a current modal shift away from the formal provision of final service functions towards an informal, extra-economic pattern demanding consumer goods and intermediate services rather than final services from the money economy. In effect, changes in the mode of service provision, which do not occur uniformly, amount to marked changes in our way of life.

Information technology is another area of great importance that will be examined again in Chapter 6. Undoubtedly access to information is of critical significance to modern life and will become increasingly so in the future. Even in the USA there has been much regulation of telecommunications services, but as that country moves away from the goal of providing a universal service towards a market-orientated information economy geographical differentials in access to information are likely to increase (Langdale, 1983). Government also has an indirect effect on innovation through environmental, safety and other regulations as well as through tax and monetary policies (Malecki, 1982). As Abler and Falk (1981) pointed out, social, political and economic systems and subsystems now consist largely of information flows, so that modern societies are flow societies in which the most advanced nations have unprecedented power to move goods, energy, people and information across unprecedented distances at unprecedented speeds. The mass media are one-way information delivery systems which confer great influence on the people who control them, but the intercommunications media which have virtually no gatekeepers have impressive organising and co-ordinating power because of their inherently interactive nature. So rapid is technological advance that nations should devise an intercommunications policy. Certainly, intercommunications technology could be used to promote spatial dispersal of activities, probably giving planners and government more control over the location of facilities. On the other hand, locational equity problems are being threatened by the rising costs of maintaining equity, which means that equity goals are being reconsidered. Yet, as Hepworth (1987) noted, markets are still the principal mechanisms for resource allocation in mixed economies and their transformation by network innovation will ultimately have a profound effect on urban and regional development. Clearly, governments cannot ignore the implications of the development of information technology and its capacity for affecting the spatial distribution of economic activity by altering the interregional geography of investment incentives and wage-determination forces.

# Chapter 3
# Economic Background Factors

Many concepts used in studying the economic geography of the service sector are derived from the discipline of economics. It is necessary, therefore, to pay some attention to economic models and reasoning inasmuch as they have made a contribution to geographical understanding before proceeding to specifically geographical analysis of the phenomena associated with the service sector. In this chapter, after a brief discussion of the role of the service sector in the economy, alternative approaches to economic analysis will be considered. For the most part the approach adopted in this book is conducted in the context of market economy concepts and the final sections of this chapter reflect this in their treatment of the problems of measuring the contribution of the service sector to the economy and the assessment of expenditure on service sector provision.

## Service activities and the economy

In advanced economies the provision of services has replaced the manufacturing of goods as the predominant economic activity to provide the motive force for post-industrial growth. Dawson (1982b) noted that in 1950 British service industries employed approximately 7.2 million people, representing 35 per cent of the work-force and contributing 41 per cent of GDP. Thirty years later the broadly comparable figures were 11.5 million, 51 per cent and 45 per cent. Depending on which source is used, an idea of the importance of services to employment can be gained. Table 3.1 provides information about service sector employment and its contribution to total civilian employment in OECD member states. At this level of analysis it is fairly easy to establish the importance of the service sector, but attempts at greater sophistication soon encounter difficulties, as will become evident when the problems of measurement are discussed.

## Some fundamental concepts and alternative approaches

Although the bulk of the literature reviewed in this book lies firmly in the market economy tradition there are other dimensions to be taken into

**Table 3.1**  Contribution of service sector employment to GDP in OECD countries

| Over 60% | 50–60% | 40–50% | Under 40% |
|---|---|---|---|
| Australia | Austria | Greece | Turkey |
| Belgium | Finland | Portugal | |
| Canada | France | Spain | |
| Denmark | West Germany | | |
| Luxembourg | Iceland | | |
| Netherlands | Ireland | | |
| Norway | Italy | | |
| Sweden | Japan | | |
| UK | New Zealand | | |
| USA | Switzerland | | |

Source: OECD Observer, 139, March 1986.

account, and readers should be aware of them. The range of ideas, all with merit, perhaps helps to explain why it is so difficult to formulate a comprehensive model to cover service activities as a whole.

*The neoclassical approach*

Neoclassical concepts resting on assumptions of economic rationality and profit maximisation have been widely applied and have stimulated much research. Losch (1954) demonstrated how a normal demand curve could be transformed into a cone that embraced the notion of distance decay and hence imparted a spatial dimension to a standard economic model. He also showed how this demand cone was incorporated into central place theory, so emphasising the theory's economic foundations. Central place theory made an important contribution to post-war geography but other economic location models have been more concerned with manufacturing than service industries, though Weberian analysis has been applied to warehouse location.

The extent to which market forces prevail has encouraged debate, and even retailing, which is sometimes claimed to represent a close approximation to a perfect market, has come under close scrutiny. Doubts have been expressed about the notion of consumer sovereignty given that supply-side considerations may determine the choice available. Similarly, the concept of *caveat emptor* (let the buyer beware) with its connotation of perfect knowledge on the consumer's part, is somewhat unrealistic. Consumers are not perfectly informed about many items which are in daily use, and studies suggest that they often do not possess complete information about the geographical location of facilities which might meet their needs. The situation is even less satisfactory in respect of medical and educational facilities where the consumer's knowledge may be too limited to allow an informed choice to be made. Consequently governments recognise that they have a responsibility to ensure that medical and educational standards reach acceptable norms. This is relatively easy to achieve where the state itself is the provider of services, but where this is not the case some system of licensing of facilities is usually in force.

Holmstrom (1985) argued that services differ from goods in ways that are economically relevant. In his view services are not storable; service quality is difficult to measure or observe; and the appropriateness of a service may be difficult to verify. Because service technology is so flexible the determinants of supply and demand will be different from those in the goods sector. It is possible, therefore, that institutions facilitating the economic exchange and production of services will exhibit idiosyncratic features. Matters of interest to economists include how well the market performs in matching the supply and demand of services as well as the effects of market structure. It is recognised that the role of reputation in service activities is important. Holmstrom commented that since services are non-storable, markets in different locations are essentially separated, and this raises the question of how demand at different locations relates to the degree of specialisation in provision. Clearly, as was suggested in the previous paragraph, there are market imperfections because complete information does not exist and so an equilibrium supply pattern is hard to attain.

Despite these limitations, the neoclassical approach has been extensively used as a basis for geographical studies of a theoretical and explanatory nature, as will be seen in the next chapter. Also, it has been adopted as the underlying assumption in the most frequently used operational models that have been employed to explore questions of accessibility and build predictive models of consumer behaviour. Gravity models exemplify the application of neoclassical concepts to the examination of the role of distance as it affects the use of facilities. Even hierarchical constructs rest on neoclassical analysis, and the same can be said for the regionalisation methods devised to assist in the location and allocation of facilities. The behaviouralist approach was a reaction against positivism and the use of neoclassical formulations. Johnston (1979), however, concluded that the behaviouralist approach failed to effect a revolution away from the spatial science paradigm with which neoclassical models are associated. For him, therefore, the behaviouralist approach was in effect an attachment to spatial science rather than an alternative to it, but there are other approaches, to which we now turn.

*The welfare approach*

D.M. Smith (1977) adapted the neoclassical approach to consider welfare. He believed that the efficiency criteria adopted in passing judgement on the spatial arrangement of human activity had to be supplemented by considerations of equity and social justice. Moreover, he felt that the sophisticated neoclassical models and methods had produced a mechanistic geography somewhat removed from reality. In espousing a welfare approach he realised that it entailed judgements about alternative structures or states of society, but he stressed that for geography the focus for concern should be to judge alternative *spatial* arrangements. Although he acknowledged that value judgements would not be divorced from recommendations for action to alter the existing arrangements, he argued that the welfare approach should provide positive knowledge and guidance in the normative realms of evaluation and policy formulation. Two value judgements underlie Smith's approach. The first is that the development of 'useful' knowledge is a superior ethic to the development of knowledge for its own sake. The second is that the focal point of human geography should be the quality of life. Both these values are open to several interpretations, but essentially Smith is concerned with efficiency in the use of resources and equity, or fairness, in the distribution of the benefits and penalties of life. Smith was critical of what he termed the capitalist-competitive materialist society, but he preferred to build on the existing intellectual tradition instead of offering a radical critique. However, he did deal with the problem of evaluating spatial distributions and the application of the welfare approach to the planning of change. He did not shrink from making suggestions about desirable forms of human spatial and societal reorganisation.

Smith's welfare approach is readily applied to analyses of the location and distribution of consumer service activities such as retailing, health care and education; it is less obviously relevant to such producer services as offices, though it is not without significance in this area. Some service activities which are not given prominence in this book, such as transport services, police, refuse and sewage disposal, can certainly be treated under the welfare approach because proximity to them has easily recognisable benefits or drawbacks.

Several economists have considered equity issues and their work, which was reviewed by Cullis and West (1979), in respect of health and education provision will be briefly discussed here. It has been pointed out that simple marginal analysis as applied to business enterprises is not necessarily suitable for studying health care. The benefits of health care are not confined to monetary gains, for they include mental benefits and the fact that improved health represents a capital asset which can contribute to increased production as well as providing time for non-market production or leisure activity. Health can be regarded as a pecuniary investment which implies some externalities, such as not passing on a contagious disease, though there are great difficulties in quantifying this. A further problem is that of 'option demand', or providing a service in case it is needed despite the fact that lack of demand at any given time might mean that it is unprofitable to provide the service on a market basis. Without doubt the supply of health care is fraught with problems that defy a simple solution.

From an individual's viewpoint it is difficult to predict when health care will be needed, so it is not easy to plan expenditure to allow for any unexpected medical expenses. While this problem can be overcome by state provision of health services or by insurance schemes, economists have noted that the existence of such schemes tends to encourage people to demand the most expensive treatment and to visit their doctors more often than is required. As a result utilisation costs are raised above the efficient level.

Imperfect consumer information is a particular characteristic of health in that there is an imbalance between the knowledge of the supplier (doctor) and the consumer (patient). Moreover, unsatisfactory treatment cannot be changed and may lead to irreparable harm. There is no real basis for consumers to shop around. Such information imbalance confers considerable monopoly power on the suppliers of medical services, and because prices can be raised or a lower quality of service offered without substantial loss of customers the normal incentives for efficiency may not be present. The existence of externalities might mean that the individual decides that the costs do not provide a sufficiently high return to justify the expenditure at the personal level although the benefits to society as a whole may be great. Thus, the operation of the market does not always lead to an efficient solution. Various equity considerations arise, for even if all have an equal chance of health care it is likely that the better informed will consume more than the others, and that raises the problem of equality of access as against equality of treatment according to need.

As even this brief summary of the economics of health illustrates, there are many difficult issues complicating the economic background to health care provision. Whereas retailing and wholesaling facilities can be provided according to commercial criteria, health care provision entails other considerations that influence its economic and geographical characteristics. Similar conclusions apply to education whose objectives can also be judged in terms of efficiency or equity. The efficiency objective would be to try to specify the amount of education that will maximise net social benefit. Costs are easy to specify but benefits are more intangible. For example, production benefits accrue if the future work-force is trained, though this is easier to determine for engineering and medicine. On the other hand, most education contains some job training element (for example, literacy and numeracy) and less easily measurable social benefits such as socialisation and the transmission of knowledge. Equity has come to the fore in the demand for 'equality of oportunity' in education, which implies that, rather than being just another consumer service, education is a process that has a fundamental effect on its recipients. Education is a major determinant of a person's lifetime income and quality of life, but this does not mean that everyone should have the same education because all do not have the same needs or aspirations. Universal 'equality of access' is the usual aim even though some argue that this is impossible to achieve given limited resources.

Some assert that the form and beneficiaries of education (with some reservations) are best determined by a free market which will give the consumer freedom of choice and which will provide the required education as a result of competition. Education is seen as an investment with a high rate of return and therefore the beneficiaries should pay for it. As with health care, the consumer does not possess perfect information so that consumer sovereignty is likely to be inhibited. Also, as with health care, education is subject to externalities, in which case a private market cannot be expected inevitably to produce an efficient allocation of resources. Among the externalities generated by education are employment benefits in the shape of greater efficiency and productivity as well as adaptability to change. Against this is the possibility that the educated may question society thus leading politicians to regard them as a social cost. There are also benefits to society in general; these may not be quantifiable, as with the case of literacy, but they may contribute to effective government. Questions of access to educational facilities have been posed: access may depend on ability to pay which raises equity questions, or it may depend on distance because of the geographical location of facilities. If facilities of varying standard exist spatial monopoly becomes a factor; bad schools may be protected from competition by distance while good schools may be out of reach of some people.

The welfare approach developed because society's resources are not in unlimited supply. This means that not all wants are likely to be satisfied and thus scarcity necessitates choice. For some the logical solution is to choose the outcome which gives the greatest excess of benefits over costs because this can be deemed an efficient allocation. This ignores the fact that benefits will probably vary according to the quantities of a good or service already consumed so that the *marginal benefit* will decline with increased consumption. Likewise scale economies derived from increased production may reduce unit costs, but eventually *diminishing returns* will set in. Alternatively equity considerations may become uppermost. Essentially there are two approaches to equity: one involves equal treatment for all, and the other entails a minimum standards level below which no one ever falls but above which there is variability. There is room for debate on this distinction, and in practice there is a greater consensus among economists about what constitutes efficiency than equity. Bramley (1986), for example, has demonstrated how difficult it is to define equal standards in local public service provision, thus highlighting the difference between theory and practice in this matter.

The welfare approach and equity considerations suggest that the market system of economic organisation cannot be expected to fulfil all of society's objectives in a wholly satisfactory way. Nevertheless, the market system is apposite for retailing and marketing, office development and many leisure facilities, and it is also relevant to health care and education even though these areas seem to be more amenable to the welfare approach. Welfare considerations can, of course, also be applied to marketing, office development, and leisure activities. Given the nature of the service sector, it is difficult to see how discussion of welfare matters can be avoided in any investigation of the distribution and utilisation of service activities and the facilities associated with them.

### The Marxist approach

The Marxian formulation is a general theory of society rather than an approach to economics (D.M. Smith, 1981). Neoclassical economics explains the relative prices of goods by assuming that land and capital as well as labour contribute and are entitled to a return which is decided by the operation of market forces. Through the Ricardian theory of value this can be linked to Marxian economics, although the latter uses the concept of value to expose the class relations responsible for the inequality manifest under capitalism. Its emphasis is on identifying those relationships of prime importance in determining a social system's overall direction of movement and change through history. The economic base or mode of production is seen as the key to understanding the interrelationships between the institutions, patterns of behaviour, beliefs and so on that make up society. The mode of production consists of the productive forces (labour, resources and equipment) and the relations of production whereby people participate in the productive process: these relations

ss cleavage. 'Surplus value' is thus a measure of the extent to which
its labour, and value and class relations are regarded as inextricable
the social practice of production under capitalism. Exploitative
_.ations, therefore, are hidden beneath the technicalities of market pricing,
resource allocation and productive functions.

Harvey (1981) believed that this viewpoint facilitates a penetrating examination of geographical phenomena. Above all, the geography of any part of the
earth must depend on the kind of society established there because different
societies characterised by different modes of production produce different
geographies. Typically, Marxist geographers have focused on the market system in the determination of land uses in respect of industrial, commercial and
residential location, and on regional and international development. Space is
not a factor in its own right, but it is legitimate to discuss the ways in which
societies produce spatial organisation and build geographical landscapes
reflecting their own requirements. Therefore, space can be analysed as an
expression of social structure. Marxist geographers have concentrated on
cultural and historical geography, urban and regional geography, economic,
political and social geography. They have mounted an attack on positivism
and have sought to develop a new synthesis in keeping with the holistic nature
of historical materialism. Few Marxist geographers have considered service
activities in detail except inasmuch as studies of land-use change accompanying office development and aspects of health care, educational and leisure provision have been informed by Marxian insights.

Massey (1984) has, however, produced a Marxist analysis in which the
economic geography of the service sector was examined. She challenged the
view that service activities were subject to different laws from manufacturing
industry on the grounds that the organisation of their labour processes was
subject to the same pressures and changes as manufacturing industry. Her
interest was in the spatial organisation of production and the geography of
occupational structure. Such questions as why different groups in society and
different parts of the social structure have particular geographical distributions interested her, and she argued that the vast majority of social forms of
capital comprise an important area of enquiry.

Massey distinguished between services geared to the reproduction of the
labour force (consumer services) and those serving other branches of industry
(producer services). She acknowledged that the distinction was not always
clear-cut. In the case of consumer services she examined the geographical differences between self-employed and family enterprises, businesses that offer
scope for capital accumulation, and state-provided services. The first two are
in conflict, especially in distribution where fully capitalised firms such as
supermarket chains are in successful competition with the independents.
Geographically there tends to be a preponderance of self-employed enterprises in South-East England, though the exact measure of concentration
varies according to the activity. By contrast, state-provided services are more
evenly distributed. Another important distinction is between high- and low-
status activities, and she showed that the latter are more likely to be
decentralised than the former—an important point in the case of office location.
Producer services are related to modern developments in the technical division

of labour, but because they depend on the market their distribution is inherently uneven. The outcome of the trends analysed, many of which are economic in character, and their effect upon social class is the development of a new use of space which produces new geographical patterns.

Massey's real point is that changes in the spatial organisation of capitalist relations of production are a response to economic and political (national and international) changes in class relations. In other words, a Western economy can only be understood by recognising its fundamentally capitalist nature. She envisaged a process of spatial change reflecting economic restructuring and social recomposition. For her, the importance of a country's geography to its social and economic reproduction has been underestimated for too long. Her analysis demonstrated that a Marxist approach can yield interesting perspectives on the geography of the service sector which differ in character from those comprising the greater part of this book.

## Explanations of the growth of service activity

Attempts to explain the growth of service activity draw on all three approaches discussed in the previous section, though the welfare approach is not prominent and the bulk of the literature is in the neoclassical tradition. There is a persistent, but misplaced, belief that whereas manufacturing is productive in the sense that tangible goods are produced the same cannot be said of services which are somehow inferior or even parasitic. At best services are dependent on manufacturing and there is a widely held view that services were led by and grew naturally following an expansion of manufacturing. As Marshall and Bachtler (1987) pointed out, the emphasis was on export-led growth and there was a danger that the fact that growth relies on effective demand, to which services may contribute, would be ignored. In practice many of the activities that are stimulated are producer services internal to the firm, so that growth may occur without necessarily developing the service sector in a particular region.

Explanations of the growth of service activity envisaging the progressive division of labour have been proposed (see pp. 5–6) by Kellerman (1985a) and by Gillespie and Green (1987). Another conventional explanation for the growth of service activity belongs to what Gershuny and Miles (1983) called an 'Engels Law' type. This is particularly appropriate for consumer services because it is claimed that income elasticity of demand for services is such that richer people tend to consume more services than the poor. Since incomes have generally risen in advanced economies the overall demand for services is increasing, but due to a 'productivity gap' the output per worker in the service industries rises more slowly than elsewhere in the economy. Hence it is easy to deduce that when the economy as a whole is growing the service sector increases in size relative to the rest of the economy. Producer services will also be affected as the result of division of labour across industrial branches in an expanding economy. Inherent in this explanation is the conclusion that (if wages and profit margins do not change relative to the rest of the economy) the service sector's prices must rise relative to the rest of the economy.

Gershuny and Miles further argue that there is a 'price elasticity of demand for services' whereby the rising relative price of the products of final service industries may lead consumers to seek to provide for service functions in innovative ways. Many of these involve do-it-yourself operations which do not themselves create new jobs but which may contribute indirectly to employment in retailing or repair and maintenance.

The core/periphery model is often used to explain relationships at a variety of spatial scales. The model posits an unequal distribution of power in economy and society, a view shared by Marxist and other writers. It is held that the core dominates the periphery in most economic, political and social respects creating a dependency which is structured through the relations of exchange between core and periphery. Because power, wealth and innovation are concentrated in the core many advantages accrue to this area to the extent that core region institutions are able to determine the progress towards development made in peripheral regions. There is abundant evidence that service activities are concentrated in such core regions as South-East England, the Paris region, Washington DC and the Australian state capitals. All these areas have been long established as cores in their respective countries, but, as Keinath (1985) observed, the old manufacturing core of the USA is declining relative to the South's 'Sun Belt' and in his view this means that it is the periphery that is growing. The assumption that there is a differential growth in services which exaggerates the dichotomy between central and peripheral regions or cities has been examined by Ley and Hutton (1987) with respect to the Canadian city of Vancouver. They described an advanced linkage between the primate city of British Columbia and its hinterland as exemplified by the powerful and complex connections between Vancouver's corporate services and the staple-dominated economy of the rest of the province. The complex corporate activities include regional and head offices of major corporations and a constellation of related producer services. A measure of the core's dominance is that while 75 per cent of British Columbia's exports by value are primary products some 70 per cent of the labour force is classified as service and is concentrated in Vancouver.

With such a variety of explanations for the growth of service activity, all of which have stimulated investigations of the sector, it is not surprising that none is regarded as comprehensive. Of the models discussed here the core/periphery model is perhaps the one with the greatest spatial applications. None of the models takes account of the possible effect of information technology which will undoubtedly have a great impact on the future geography of the service sector, but Hepworth (1987) has shown that a body of information theory is emerging which geographers must acknowledge. Information economics is concerned with how the quality and cost of information affect and are affected by the performance of a modern mixed economy. Most research under this heading has focused on revision of orthodox or neoclassical theory. Among these revisions are suggestions that the conventional model of how goods and services are produced should be changed in order to take explicit account of innovations in information technology. Traditionally the modelling of a stylised process of production fails to take note of how changes in output may arise from changes in the composition of either the capital stock or the labour force. There is a case for revising the aggregate production function by differentiating the information or non-information components of capital and labour. Information components are those used to produce, process and distribute information, and it is evident that technological advances have significantly increased the productivity of capital used for processing and distributing information. With the increase in the proportion of the labour force involved in information, and given the functional characteristics of merging computer and telecommunications technologies the growth dynamics of regional economies will be profoundly affected by innovations in powerful new (electronic) forms of information capital. Such spatio-economic impacts of technical change can neither be predicted nor explained by traditional two-factor models of regional development.

The global reach of computer networks draws attention to the need for international perspectives in studying information technology and its spatial implications. Of great importance is the fact that the extreme mobility of information as working material or electronic financial assets means that large corporate network users can transcend or selectively enter local and network markets for capital and labour. Furthermore, information space may be 'instantly' and continually transformed as government and firms configure and alter their network systems in response to underlying processes of technical, political and economic change. New technology may actually bring nearer the 'spaceless' model of neoclassical economic theory, but this does not mean we are moving towards a 'placeless' world in which equitable access to economic opportunities is assumed by the perfectly competitive working of a free-market system. Possibly network innovations only serve to highlight the different value systems underlying definitions of information and the hidden relations of corporate and governmental power which dictate and are reflected in its relative accessibility. Seen in this light information economics is a radical critique of orthodox neoclassical theory, and it certainly draws attention to the question of how information assumptions enter into and shape spatial and temporal analyses of economic phenomena. There is no doubt that future explanations of the growth of the service sector will have to include a full consideration of the role of information in this process.

## Measuring the contribution of the service sector to the economy

It is difficult to be precise about the service sector's contribution to the national economy. For example, while it is possible to determine the level of invisible exports it is not easy to establish the effect of the entire financial activities of the City of London on the UK's internal economy. Similarly, the income produced by retailing as a proportion of GDP can be assessed, but it is hard to judge the proportion of retail sales that earn foreign currency through purchases made in Spain by overseas visitors. Nevertheless commercial activities like finance and retailing can be measured in quantifiable terms, but producing a balance sheet for health, education and leisure is a much greater problem because there is no universally acceptable method of calculating the benefits, especially in the case of leisure. The cost of sunbathing on a beach, gardening or walking in the country is not great and not readily attributable within the national accounting system, though for the individuals concerned the benefits obtained may be considerable.

The debate about the contribution of education to the economy illustrates the problem of measurement and the whole issue of the value of the service sector. Kirn (1987) quoting another author, Denison, claimed that advances in knowledge have been the largest and most basic reason for the growth of productivity in the USA from 1929 to 1983, accounting for 55 per cent of the growth in actual national income per employed person during the period. Education per worker accounted for an additional 27 per cent of that growth. Figures such as these show the importance of the increasing emphasis on human capital and knowledge. Supporters of the educational contribution argue that Western society is increasingly more complex in its demands on job skills. More and more emphasis on quantitative skills arising from the growing use of computers in manufacturing industry and the service sector has led to changing demands on the education system to provide more people capable of coping with the new technology. However, so rapid are the developments in computer technology that the 'state of the art', as computer scientists like to call it, tends to change before the previous generation of hardware and software has been mastered. Despite the popular belief that future jobs will be increasingly dominated by 'high-tech' employment there is evidence that many jobs will in fact be 'low-tech' or 'no-tech'. The deskilling of some jobs has already taken place; the use of automated checkouts at supermarkets with laser scanning of product bar codes and computer calculations of the bill reduces the job of the checkout assistant to one of less skills not more. A forecast of job composition in the year 2000 (*Guardian*, 7 February 1985) predicts that, far from eliminating menial and labouring jobs, the new technology will actually increase them. Jobs will be lost in the service sector where word processors will replace the typing pool. Professional jobs will also increase, but not necessarily in the 'high-tech' industries themselves; for example, there will be extra scope in law and accounting. There is, therefore, no guarantee that training people for a high-technology future will mean that they will have jobs as computer engineers or systems analysts. Nevertheless, in France, the UK and the USA governments have pursued policies of increasing computer provision in schools and colleges in the hope of producing a technologically trained generation of workers for the twenty-first century. Even when budgets in other areas of education have been cut the computer allocation has invariably been increased.

Coates and Rawstron (1971) demonstrated a relationship between the proportion of workers with high educational qualifications and the level of economic opportunity that produces a distinctive geographical pattern with reference to Great Britain. South-East England claimed the lion's share of well-qualified workers when they wrote. Changes have occurred in the interim, and by 1981 many traditional growth areas in the British economy like the West Midlands with its car industry had gone into decline. A new dynamic region, the so-called 'Sunrise Belt', emerged west of London along the M4 motorway. Replacing the old London–Liverpool axis is the Cambridge–

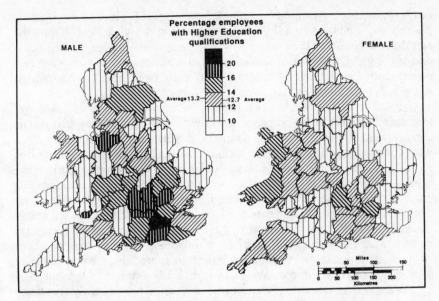

**Figure 3.1** Percentage of employees with higher educational qualifications
*Source: Regional Trends*, 1984, pp. 38–9

Swindon axis with a combination of university science parks (Cambridge, Oxford and Reading), government research establishments (Harwell, Aldermaston and Bracknell), and private firms (Sinclair Research and Acorn Computers, both at Cambridge and both now taken over by Amstrad and Olivetti respectively). Such a concentration creates a demand for highly qualified personnel so that the greatest proportion of trained workers are found in the counties of Berkshire, Buckinghamshire, Oxfordshire, Hertfordshire, Surrey, West Sussex and Cambridge (see Figure 3.1). There are lesser nodes in Cheshire and South Glamorgan. The Eastern and South-Western regions record much lower than average proportions of qualified people in residence. Wales exhibits an anomalous pattern for women, with remote Dyfed and Gwynedd possessing higher proportions of highly qualified women than men. This confirms the importance of the service sector in Wales (60 per cent of total employment, according to Williams 1985) and the fact that women are well represented in education and health which are major components of service employment. Coates and Rawstron remarked on the additional factor that the rural Welsh have traditionally valued education for their girls more highly than their English counterparts. The highest proportion of people with good educational qualifications in South-Central England is doubtless related to the better provision of educational facilities and to the economic opportunities which attract graduates from other parts of the country.

The reality of the relationship between educational provision and the level of economic activity and the proportion of highly qualified workers cannot be doubted. On the other hand, it would be too simplistic to claim that there is necessarily a causal relationship between these indicators on the evidence presented here, although there is a strong presumption that this is the case. In much the same way it would be difficult to prove that health care provision is positively related to the quality and productivity of the work-force despite the fact that the hope that these benefits will accrue from better health facilities is one of the justifications for the institution of a health service. Concentration on preventive medicine and child health can also be regarded as partially (if not wholly) justifiable in economic terms.

Tourism is a service activity that has been extensively studied as a means of assessing its contribution to economic growth and for this reason it merits careful examination. Developing countries in particular, seeing tourism as a way of financing their industrialisation and modernising their economies, regard tourism as a method of raising foreign exchange without incurring the expense of investing in sophisticated technology. Compared with exporting primary commodities over whose price the exporting country has little control, tourism allows the host nation a great deal of discretion over the prices charged for tourist goods and services. Prices can be manipulated to encourage visitors, while the high income-elasticity of tourism means that slight increases in the income of potential visitors can lead to an appreciable growth in tourist arrivals and receipts. Tourism also helps to diversify a country's economy and it can raise a large amount of foreign currency without necessarily encouraging a proportionate increase in imports. The difficulties of stimulating tourism should not be underestimated and the fact that alternative destinations can offer much the same attractions means that economies reliant on tourism can be very vulnerable. Also, the advantages of tourism may be balanced by disadvantages such as increased inflation and higher land values, the seasonality of employment, the low ratio of returns on investment, and the creation of other external costs. All these considerations apply to the advanced economies with a tourist sector just as much as to the developing countries.

The balance of payments is a much publicised economic factor associated with tourism, though it is only recently that the idea has been subjected to critical examination by economists. Airey (1978) divided the effects of tourism on the balance of payments into three categories. Primary effects occur when travellers cross an international boundary. Expenditure on accommodation, entertainment, shopping and transport can be recorded and reported separately, thus making the assessment of primary impacts possible. Secondary effects are less easy to measure. They consist of direct effects such as expenditure on overseas marketing, visible imports and payments to transport operators for their crews' expenses, and of indirect effects such as earnings gained by tourist services which are passed on to other suppliers of goods and services and which may induce imports. Induced secondary effects are payments to producers of tourist goods and services in the form of wages, salaries and rents, some of which may be remitted abroad. Flows of currency not initiated by direct tourist expenditure are termed tertiary effects; for example, clothes and travel goods purchased by home residents for travel abroad, not to mention investment opportunities created by tourist activities. Unfortunately secondary and tertiary effects are difficult to evaluate because they are not treated separately in the available statistics.

Many countries have a balance of payments deficit on tourism and seek to redress the shortfall. The amount of money spent on tourism is clearly important, but where it goes and the effects of its circulation are another matter of significance. One measure of tourism's value is its contribution to GNP, though the output of the tourist sector is likely to constitute only a small proportion of GNP (about 1 per cent in the UK). Governments can also regard tourism as a source of taxable revenue, either direct in the form of airport taxes or indirect in the form of sales taxes. On the other hand, governments cannot ignore the fact that tourism involves expenditure on their part if adequate facilities are to be provided to attract visitors; witness the Irish government's financial assistance for Knock airport. However, much of the expense of infrastructure costs for serving tourists actually falls on local communities who meet the bill from local taxes. Hence governments do not have to meet the full financial costs themselves.

Tourism's impact has been assessed in terms of the multiplier effect which has been widely applied to evaluate the influence of new enterprises on a local economy or the negative effect of a closure. In early studies of industrial development service employment was viewed as a benefit (multiplier effect) derived from the opening of a new factory. Studies of tourism reveal that the size of the tourist multiplier varies between countries depending on such factors as the volume of imported goods and services consumed by tourists, the inclination of residents to use imported goods and services, and the inhabitants' propensity to save. The higher a country's (or a region's) propensity to import the higher the leakage of money, which affects the income multiplier. There is also a sales or transactions multiplier, an output multiplier, and an employment multiplier, each of which measures a different phenomenon but all of which contribute to tourism's effects.

Although the multiplier effect is relatively easy to describe, in practice there is much complexity and confusion in applying it and the potential for error is considerable. Data problems mean the regional and local multipliers are more difficult to calculate than national ones. An estimated tourist multiplier for the UK is 1.68-1.78 compared with 0.28 for Edinburgh, 0.37 for Gwynedd, 0.26 for Lothian, and 0.30 for Skye (Mathieson and Wall, 1982). Income multipliers are useful for assessing the short-run impact of tourist expenditure and for identifying weak linkages in the economy if the data are adequate. They are less useful for long-term effects because they rest on the assumption that the structure of the economy remains unchanged.

Tourism creates employment in direct and indirect ways. The amount of direct change attributable to tourism can be measured—for example, employment in hotels, tour operation—but attempts to use employment multipliers are fraught with difficulties. Some types of tourist-generated employment, such as hotels are very labour-intensive, but as a rule there is more work for unskilled than for managerial staff. Tourism may attract workers from other sectors, such as agriculture, where they may be more beneficial to the economy as a whole. Another problem is the seasonal nature of tourist employment, which can create difficulties by necessitating an influx of migrant workers or by discouraging some enterprises from establishing themselves in an area.

On balance the benefits from tourism outweigh the drawbacks. Even so, destination areas investing their scarce resources in the development of tourism should consider the opportunity costs involved and whether an alternative activity would be more beneficial. Neglect of opportunity costs (which are notoriously difficult to measure) and the negative externalities of tourism have been partially responsible for the overemphasis placed on the value of tourism in economic development. Attention has already been drawn to the potential vulnerability of areas dependent on tourism for changes in price, fashion, or political stability can soon lead to changes in preference for tourist destination; for example, the slump in North American visitors to Europe in 1986 because of fears about terrorism and the effect of the Chernobyl nuclear reactor disaster.

Tourism has been used to illustrate the multiplier concept because of the extensive literature on this topic. Similar analyses could be undertaken to show the impact of offices on a local economy (for example, stationers, sandwich shops and other catering facilities may be very dependent on nearby offices), or the impact of educational establishments or a hospital. Lack of data has impeded such studies, but attempts have been made to show the importance of the presence of a university on its locality. There is, for example, evidence that the economic impact of overseas students on the Scottish economy is very substantial, and that this impact reaches far beyond the students' host institutions (Love and McNicoll, 1988). The universities of Oxford and Cambridge both have an enormous influence on the economies of their surrounding areas in terms of direct employment, local spending, the location of 'high-tech' industries, and the attraction of tourists and visitors. This is also true of university towns like Cambridge, Massachusetts; Montpellier, France; and Waterloo, Ontario. These cities have an important industrial base which offers alternative opportunities, whereas in small non-industrial towns like Aberystwyth; Pullman, Washington; or Armidale, New South Wales, the presence of a university is even more dominant.

Whatever the difficulties entailed in measuring the multiplier effect, there is widespread agreement that the importance of service industries depends on a country's level of economic development, although the precise relationships are often elusive (see pp. 10–12). Daniels (1982) used the number of telephones per 100 inhabitants to identify the most developed areas and his maps showed that Western Europe, North America, Japan and Australia have the highest levels of internal connectivity and can be regarded as the world's most advanced areas. Another of Daniels's observations was that many services are supplied to industrial or commercial firms rather than to individual consumers so that demand for service is often derived from the level of industrial or commercial activity. The notion of a relationship between the level of economic development and service provision has been incorporated into general models. It is suggested that there is a sequential shift from employment predominantly in primary activities to secondary (manufacturing) and eventually to service industries. Some countries are in the post-industrial stage where service industries are well established. The implication is that an economy dependent on service activities is more advanced than one still chiefly relying on manufacturing. Similarly, levels of service activity can be granted a higher status according to whether they are regarded as tertiary, quaternary or quinary. Some economies may have passed through all stages of the linear progression posited in this type of model, but this is not an immutable sequence that all countries must follow. Nor is it necessarily the case that a country whose service sector is more important than its manufacturing sector has attained a higher standard of development than a country where the reverse is true (compare Belgium and Japan).

Another conceptual problem associated with the service sector is the way in which some observers treat it as almost exclusively an internal trade sector of the local economy (except for tourism and universities), a notion that can be traced back to the Fisher–Clark hypothesis which viewed services as a tertiary stage in the developmental process. While it is still argued that service activities have less locational choice because they are almost always dependent on the prior existence of a market for their products, Stanback *et al.* (1981) claimed that many parts of the service sector are basic in nature and therefore contribute directly to the economic base of a region by bringing in money from outside. Keil and Mack (1986) sought to identify those service sector industries which are actual or potential exporters. They encountered the familiar problems in attempting this, but they developed a modification of the location quotient technique which enabled them to undertake an analysis of the service sector in Indianapolis. Of 53 service categories examined, nine were identified as having strong export potential: college and university; national security; railway; administration of economic programmes; public finance; non-commercial education and scientific research; museums, art galleries and zoos; insurance and the administration of environmental quality. If nothing else, this list highlights the variety and the potential of service activities, but what is important about their work is that they successfully challenged the idea that service activities are not wealth-creating and productive. Beyers and Alvin (1985) came to a similar conclusion a year earlier in their demonstration of the importance of export service in post-industrial society as evidenced by their study of the Puget Sound service economy.

Service activities, especially those in the public sector, have been criticised for their productivity levels, and it is often implied that there is scope for savings in what is seen as a labour-intensive area of the economy. Undoubtedly the productivity of labour in services is a key to growth as the economy becomes more service-intensive, but there are problems in measuring inputs into services. Hulten (1985), commenting on work by Kendrick (1985), demonstrated that output in the service sector grew more rapidly than output in the goods-producing sectors in the USA in the period 1948–81. However, the growth rate of total factor productivity was much lower in the former than the latter because growth in the goods-producing sector was achieved by improvements in technical and economic efficiency whereas in the service sector growth followed an increase in capital and labour inputs. Kendrick was concerned with the methodological problems of measuring productivity, but his analysis showed that the gap in productivity growth between the service sector and the goods producing sector was narrowing. Within the service sector retail and wholesale trade experienced productivity improvements comparable with the goods sector, whereas finance and real estate experienced poor (often negative) productivity trends. There is hope that with the recent increase in its capital-to-labour ratio the financial sector may achieve significant labour productivity gains in the future. The technical nature of

Kendrick's work must be seen against the background of another debate. In the USA the question of the efficiency of a national industrial policy in reversing the erosion of the manufacturing sector is perhaps the converse of concern over the growth of the service sector. It is feared that the decline in the manufacturing sector will lead to a decline in the growth of labour productivity for the economy as a whole. Real wage incomes thus grow less rapidly. Further, because of their intangible nature services tend to be domestically produced and consumed so that world trade in goods overshadows world trade in services. Consequently, a decline in the manufacturing sector may weaken a country's balance of payments position. There is also a fear that a service economy cannot be transformed easily into a military economy in time of war. Some advocate the use of industrial policies to reverse the trend to a service economy, but there is real concern about the economic impact of such a step and the importance of measuring service sector productivity to the resolution of this debate is clear (Inman, 1985).

Services play a vital role in international trade. Thus, if income from investments (as payments for services of capital) is included, services constituted approximately 25 per cent of world transactions in 1980, and even without investment income their share was 17 per cent. In both categories the USA is by far the dominant exporter (Inman, 1985). These figures are impressive, especially when it is realised that world trade in services has grown over the last decade. Statistics of international transactions usually distinguish between factor and non-factor services. The former are direct services rendered by the factors of production such as interest payments and wages to foreign workers, regardless of output. Non-factor services are those which require the addition of intermediate inputs of labour and/or capital for their production; for example, passenger fees for transport. In the domestic economy virtually all services are non-factor services (Kravis, 1985).

Whether international service transactions will continue to grow at their present relative rate is debatable, but it seems likely that service trade expansion will require increased direct involvement in foreign countries (a matter further discussed in Chapter 8) which will not be without its difficulties. Exported services have a special relation to cultural and political objectives as well as to security requirements. As the largest exporter of services the USA is aware of this, and it also has to confront the problem that the import of services can be controlled by licences, fees and special taxes. The American authorities are sensitive to barriers to services and, given their comparative advantage in this area, they acknowledge the need for an international agreement on trade. Currently there are restrictions regulating the operations of telecommunications, banking, aviation and shipping but not insurance. One obstacle to regulation is the increasing tendency to combine a number of different services under one corporate management. The importance of international trade in services to the economies of the developed world is clear. Some of the consequences of this are relevant to the changing geography of the service sector, for the future of international fnancial centres seems to be assured and there are good prospects of an increased spread of transnational service operations.

**Table 3.2** Central government expenditure on various sectors ($ per capita)

|  | Defence | Education | Health |
|---|---|---|---|
| Spain | 41 | 64 | 7 |
| Italy | 66 | 164 | 246 |
| New Zealand | 83 | 237 | 248 |
| UK | 246 | 45 | 217 |
| Austria | 71 | 229 | 302 |
| Finland | 107 | 280 | 199 |
| Australia | 170 | 152 | 182 |
| Canada | 136 | 68 | 118 |
| Netherlands | 208 | 495 | 447 |
| Belgium | 206 | 551 | 63 |
| France | 208 | 258 | 431 |
| USA | 392 | 49 | 193 |
| West Germany | 225 | 22 | 463 |
| Sweden | 288 | 460 | 87 |
| Switzerland | 189 | 62 | 215 |

*Source*: World Bank (1983)

Note: Because of variations in the way public expenditure is dealt with in different countries, the above figures need to be interpreted with care. Thus while defence expenditure in all states is invariably a matter for central government, education is sometimes largely handled by local authorities. The figure of $45 for the UK, for example, presents a false impression since an additional $330 is met by local authority expenditure.* In the case of the USA and West Germany the figures represent federal expenditure and ignore the contribution of the individual states.
*Based on 1983 average exchange rates of 1 US$ = £0.6896

# Expenditure on service sector provision

Private investment expenditure on office development, retailing and wholesaling, and leisure provision is considerable, but statistics are not readily available. Some idea of the scale of investment comes from the following figures. In 1976 total private construction in the USA accounted for the expenditure of $51 984 million, of which $17 152 million (33 per cent) was for non-residential buildings. Expenditure on office buildings totalled $2917 million, or 5.6 per cent total construction and 17 per cent of non-residentail construction, according to Armstrong (1979). Investment in retailing is considerable, as is indicated by the estimated £60 million cost of the Eldon Square Shopping Centre in Newcastle-upon-Tyne (Bunce, 1983) and the £250 million invested in Tyneside's Metro Centre (*The Times*, 12 January 1987). An estimated £250 million is required to develop the Runnymede out-of-town retail and leisure

**Table 3.3**   Per capita health spending, 1982 ($)

| | |
|---|---|
| 200–400 | Portugal, Greece |
| 400–600 | Ireland, Spain, New Zealand, UK |
| 600–800 | Austria, Italy, Japan, Finland, Belgium, Denmárk, Luxembourg |
| 800–1000 | Netherlands, Australia, West Germany, Iceland, Norway |
| 1000–1200 | France, Canada, Switzerland |
| 1200–1400 | USA, Sweden |

*Source*: *OECD Observer*, November 1985.

complex near London's Heathrow airport (*The Times*, 22 January 1987). Both these latter developments combine leisure facilities with retailing and may be indicative of a future trend. Evidently vast sums are needed for modern developments.

More information is available about public expenditure. For example, OECD (1987) figures suggest that there has been a radical shift in the structure of spending on education. Most striking has been the sharp fall in capital spending, though in all member countries except New Zealand and the UK current spending (over half of which is on teachers' salaries) has increased at a faster rate than overall spending on education. Salaries have actually tended to rise less rapidly than current outlays as a whole, partly because of the drop in the number of teachers. Also important is the shift in the relative importance of different levels of education with nursery and elementary school stages benefiting from increased spending compared with a decline in expenditure on higher education. Secondary education claims about half the share of GNP devoted to education, and the average cost per pupil has risen in almost all countries except the Netherlands and New Zealand. In most OECD countries education is largely financed from public funds, but the private sector also plays a role and may be subsidised to some extent. Total public subsidies to private education as a percentage of total educational expenditure range from less than 1 per cent in Sweden to almost 65 per cent in the Netherlands. Table 3.2 shows the percentage of real GDP accounted for by public expenditure to have declined slightly or remained steady except in Australia and Luxembourg (Sweden and Switzerland also showed small increases). A decline does not necessarily mean that education has been singled out for hard treatment, for in the UK case the decline of percentage GDP expended on education from 5.8 in 1975 to 4.6 in 1983 reflects the decline in public expenditure for in both years education's share of real total public outlays was 42 per cent.

More money is spent on health care, the second largest social programme after pensions in OECD countries, making health one of the largest single overall expenditure categories in these nations. Between 1960 and 1983 health expenditure for public programmes increased from 18 per cent of social spending to almost 25 per cent and from 4.2 per cent to 7.6 per cent of GDP. Over this period total real health care expenditures increased 60 per cent faster than real GDP, and 40 per cent faster over the years 1975–83. Analysis indicates that rising health care prices were the major factor behind the growth in expenditure, with more intensive use of services coming second. Average per capita health spending was $790 in 1982, ranging from $252 in Greece to $1388 in the USA. There was a statistically significant relationship in which each $100 difference in GDP is associated with a $10 difference in per capita health spending. Table 3.3 illustrates the range of health spending among OECD countries. Throughout the 23 OECD member countries the bulk of health expenditure comes form private sources, and this proportion has risen from 62 per cent in 1960 to 79 per cent in 1982. Although these figures give some idea of the sums spent on health care, they also indicate that health care systems are structurally diverse and based on different underlying principles, thus emphasising the difficulty of making generalisations.

One aspect of public expenditure on services which has not received much attention in the literature was raised by Holmes (1985). He observed that in affluent Western societies policies of economic welfare and social justice have increasingly acquired a geographical dimension as governments seek to ensure comparable living standards and access to services regardless of location. This requires special assistance programmes for marginal regions, which are usually sparsely settled, economically backward and retain certain characteristics of a pioneer zone—Holmes was writing of Australia's pastoral zone. Earlier goals of national development, which often focused on these zones, are becoming submerged within new-found goals of social equity. Increased public intervention also implies increased dependence and increased sensitivity to changes in public policies. This heightened dependence is a major difference between marginal regions and the more densely settled, economically viable, readily serviced cores.

Norway, Finland and Sweden are also countries whose desire to preserve the national settlement system demands substantial transfers to marginal regions. Australia has engaged in a marked expansion in special assistance programmes to people in sparsely settled areas. Initially focusing on basic education and health services and on income tax relief, these have been progressively expanded and diversified into most aspects of transport, communications, fuel, electricity, drought relief and rural financial assistance. All of this requires substantial funds, but assistance programmes have not been carefully thought out and implemented. Australia is not unique in facing the problem of a dispersed settlement pattern that poses very severe servicing problems requiring costly solutions. Private sector investment and employment have declined while at the same time there have been increased expectations in the public sector whose heavy costs are not recovered from remote consumers. The survival of the population in the pastoral zone depends on public assistance, and the debate now centres on quality-of-life issues: are isolated people entitled to equivalent services at identical prices to those available to city consumers? In effect, locational disadvantage is being equated with social disadvantage. Despite the successes achieved in Australia the government will continue to face problems and it is clear that the issue of public expenditure on service infrastructure has a profound influence on settlement patterns and their viability which is by no means confined to the example dealt with by Holmes. For example, just one of the questions raised is the extent to which governments should endeavour to rationalise service provision by encouraging a restructuring of land use and settlement in remote areas.

## Conclusion

In keeping with the approach adopted in this book the contribution of service activities has been largely explored in market economy terms using employment and financial data in particular. Given the framework adopted in the remainder of this work, it is useful to be reminded that there are alternative bases for moving towards an explanation of the changing geography of the service sector. Questions of equity and the moral dimension are the basis for the welfare approach, but latterly Marxist writers have focused on the way in which social and spatial changes are interrelated. They view service activities in the context of the social relations of production and they aim to explain and interpret the spatial organisation of the social relations of capitalist production. Whatever the validity of these critiques of orthodox thinking it cannot be denied that a sound knowledge of economic concepts and background factors is essential to an understanding of the service sector. Here, various models that attempt to explain the growth of the service sector have been discussed and attention has been paid to the measurement of the sector's contribution to the economy. Debate about the value of the service activities was illustrated with special reference to education and tourism, respectively a predominantly public and private mode of provision. Relationships between service activity and development were examined, and it was shown that services have basic as well as non-basic attributes. Because of its importance to the economy's future prospects the problem of productivity levels in the service sector was addressed. Also explored was the importance of the sector's contribution to international trade. Finally, the vexed question of expenditure on services, especially public expenditure, was raised and some spatial implications were discussed. In seeking to understand the geography of the service sector social and political factors are incontestably important, but the bulk of the geographical literature on this topic derives, at least in part, from economic principles and hence justifies the significance attached to economic considerations in this chapter.

# Chapter 4
# The Location of Service Activities

Geographers are naturally interested in the factors that influence location patterns. Traditional location theory, with its emphasis on transport and labour costs as well as the importance of agglomeration, should not be regarded as inappropriate in respect of service activities. Watts (1987), with the example of producer services in mind, warns against this simplistic view. Weberian theory has also been specifically applied to warehouse location problems, but because of its focus on the size of market area Loschian theory seems to be more readily applicable to manufacturing and services. Market areas also figure prominently in Christaller's central place theory, widely regarded as the geographical theory *par excellence* and certainly one which attempts to provide a rationale for the location of service activities. This theory has stimulated many hypotheses and an impressive quantity of work that has expanded empirical knowledge of the service sector, yet many question its usefulness as an analytical tool for planning or predicting developments in the provision of service facilities. In addition to central place studies, general interaction theory and urban land-use models have been employed to further understanding. Attempts have been made to develop public facility location theory, while others have emphasised supply and demand considerations. As an alternative to this work which assumes economic rationality, alternative behavioural explanations have been offered. It is the purpose of this chapter to review the body of work referred to in this paragraph.

## General locational characteristics of service activities

Because the locational requirements of service activities vary a classification must be devised. Wood (1986) emphasised the distinction between consumer-orientated and producer-orientated service activities. The former are likely to exhibit a widespread distribution in order to serve the interests of the consumers wherever they may be, whereas the latter are more likely to be concentrated in important business centres. Corporate and competitive behaviour in the producer services sector means that it is responsive to technical innovations and pressures on labour productivity, and this is likely to affect locational change. Consumer services, on the other hand, will respond to variations in prosperity levels so that they will tend to reinforce spatial contrasts in disposable income.

Alexander (1979) classified office activities according to the market areas they served and showed that while many activities fall into the same functional category it is the size of their market area that influences their locational requirements. Thus, banks and insurance offices seek different locations according to whether they are serving a local or a national/international market. Companies that are large enough to need an organisational hierarchy may have headquarters offices operating at the national/international level and branch offices serving regional or even local markets. In such companies there are likely to be strong links influencing their offices at all levels of the hierarchy and possibly also affecting their locational strategy.

Alexander's classification incorporates the concept of a spatial hierarchy as a rational basis for distinguishing between patterns of apparently similar activities (for example, shops, insurance offices, hospitals). A hierarchical structure helps to explain why there is unevenness in the distribution of facilities leading to the clustering of activities in particular places. The reality of a hierarchy is very clear in respect of some service activities such as health care and education because the hierarchical concept is accepted by those responsible for planning the service and locating its facilities. In the commercial world the situation is more fluid and company planning is not necessarily dominated by hierarchical constraints. There has been a long-standing division of opinion between those who view the provision of commercial service facilities as conforming to a recognisable hierarchical structure characterised by distinctive levels and those who can only detect a continuum in which there are no readily distinguishable breaks between one level and the next. Few, however, would deny that some places are more important than others, and the merit of Alexander's market area approach is that it offers a geographical dimension to the distinction between places and activities of different degrees of importance.

Implicit in the market area approach is the concept of *access*. It is assumed that the location chosen by an activity ensures that the client or customer has access to the service. It is also implied that if the cost of gaining access to a service, in time or money, is too great the client or customer will look elsewhere. In the modern world access is not confined to personal travel by the users of a service who may be able to satisfy their wants simply by communicating with the provider of the service by letter, telephone or telex. The question of access is regarded as very important in the case of publicly provided services because equity considerations are raised, but it may also be crucial to the commercial success of retail or leisure facilities. Accordingly, the literature is comparatively rich in studies of access to health, education, retail and leisure facilities.

## Location theory and service activities

Concepts relating to hierarchical structure, accessibility and the size of market areas have been embodied in a variety of theoretical formulations. Whatever the limitations of these theories, they do attempt an explanation of the underlying factors influencing the location of service industries, and to that extent they help to clarify thinking.

*Central place theory*

Since service activities have undoubtedly grown in response to demand efforts have been made to model the distribution of settlements whose prime purpose is to provide goods and services to the surrounding area. Such settlements are called 'central places', and it was the aim of Walther Christaller (1933) to devise a 'central place theory' that would discover the laws governing the number, size and distribution of central places. If the theory proved to be valid there would be an explanation for existing distributions and a basis for predicting future patterns. Most of the investigations conducted to test the theory were concerned with retail provision, though the theory is applicable to services such as health care and educational provision which are also influenced by the distribution of population.

Christaller's ideas aroused little interest until after the Second World War. Losch (1954) proposed an alternative version of the theory which many consider to be closer to reality but which has been so difficult to operationalise that it has received less attention than Christaller's ideas (but see Beavon, 1977). Christaller's theory is not examined in full here because readily accessible accounts exist elsewhere (see, for example, King, 1984). Instead, some key concepts which do provide insights aiding our understanding of service activity location will be discussed. A major criticism made by Vance (1970) was that central place theory presented a closed system, whereas the main metropolitan centres around which central place systems develop owed their origin to external forces. Vance was especially concerned with the role of trade and wholesaling in influencing the settlement pattern and hence the location of activities. Other critics (such as Dawson, 1979; and Davies, 1976) claim that the theory has so many limitations that it has little practical value for marketing studies for which it might seem particularly appropriate. Both concede that the theory's popularity among planners may have given it an indirect influence on the development of shopping provision. Brown (1987b), another critic, felt that despite its undoubted shortcomings central place theory is unlikely to be superseded until a theoretical framework is established with change as its *raison d'être*. Central place ideas are more relevant to health care and educational provision. Public service facilities are usually planned in a longer-term context than is usual in retailing and are less subject to commercial constraints. Urban geographers who are perhaps less concerned with its possible commercial applications believe that central place theory provides insights into the nature of urban systems in general. For example, Herbert and Thomas (1982) argue that the research generated by central place theory has provided much of conceptual and methodological value. Daniels (1982) commented that it is 'the principles used to derive the model and their particular contribution to understanding the location of service industries which are of interest'.

Christaller believed that the size of a market area served from a given place would be determined by the distance people were prepared to travel to purchase a specific item, and he defined that distance as *the range of a good*. It was noted that people's willingness to travel depended on the type of good in that some items would attract customers from greater distances than others. Implicit in Christaller's work, although he did not use the term, is the notion of a *threshold* (the minimum number of customers needed to support an activity) because a market area whose range was not sufficient to embrace a threshold population would be doomed to failure. Items which had a longer range were termed *higher-order goods* and because they required larger market areas there would be fewer centres providing them. These high-order centres would also offer low-order goods so that they could provide cusotmers with a better range of choice than was available in lower-order centres. In this way the central place system became hierarchically structured, and it was proposed in the theory that there would be a constant ratio of higher- to lower-order centres that would be reflected in the spacing of centres and in the size of market areas. A host of empirical tests have verified many of Christaller's principles, but because his initial simplifying assumptions are nowhere met in reality the precise patterns he predicted have not been matched in the real world. Nevertheless, the key concepts referred to in this paragraph remain as useful aids in explaining the geographical pattern of service provision.

Despite the theory's limitations the hierarchical construct is acknowledged as having provided extremely useful terms of reference and organisational concepts within which to examine systematic regularities in settlements and shopping centres (Davies, 1976). Many of the studies have been descriptive but the pioneering work of Berry (1967) and his associates adhered more strictly to a theoretical approach. Planning studies intended to act as guidelines for the development of centres, such as the Dutch polderlands and neighbourhoods in British New Towns, have commonly adopted notional standards about the future size, capacities and spacing arrangements of settlements or shopping centres. British planners adopted the hierarchical concept as the main organisational principle in their plans for retail provision, and they have also applied it to the provision of educational, medical and other welfare services. The concepts can be applied at the *intra-urban* as well as the *inter-urban* levels. Christaller was aware that his theory stressed the economic pull of urban centres and he noted:

> There is also a branch of the economy that avoids central places and the agglomeration of industry. This is tourism. Tourism is drawn to the periphery of settlement districts as it searches for a position in the highest mountains, in the most lonely woods, along the remotest beaches (Christaller, 1933, Baskin's translation 1964, p. 95).

This suggestion that there is a sort of symbiotic relationship between central places and tourist centres despite the apparent antithesis between their requirements contains a measure of truth, but in other respects central place concepts are applicable to the provision of leisure and tourist facilities.

*General interaction theory*

Although it is not directly derived from central place theory, what has been termed 'general interaction theory' (Davies, 1976) does draw on some of the former's concepts. Essentially, general interaction theory is a theory of movement concerned with the controls affecting the interaction between people and places. It is not a formally constituted theory with a set of underlying assumptions comparable to central place theory, and in fact it makes use of a gravity concept analogous to Newton's law in physics. Interaction theory has been widely applied to various forms of population movement and therefore it is applicable to problems pertaining to the use of retailing, health, educational or leisure facilities.

The initial work was done in the marketing field by W. Reilly, who introduced his law of retail gravitation in 1929. Because extended accounts exist elsewhere (see, for example, Davies, 1976) the concept will not be examined in detail here. However, as originally formulated, the law aimed to calculate the amount of attraction exerted by one town compared with another on the area that lay between them, but this was soon modified to calculate the 'break-point' which effectively marked the boundary of the market area between the two places. Customers on one side of the break-point were more likely to shop at the nearest centre, and by making the same calculation to find the break-point between a specific town and its immediate rivals that town's market area could be delimited. When the towns are of similar size this model works well, but if the centres are of different sizes and therefore likely to offer different types of good a single line is not suitable for representing the probable variations in shopping patterns. Thus, it is best to use the break-point model in conjunction with a hierarchical classification of centres so that places of the same order are being compared.

The break-point model also fails to take account of overlapping trade areas. Huff (1963) addressed this problem in the intra-urban setting by assessing the probabilities of customers choosing to visit one of a number of competing centres. Probability values can be plotted and contour lines drawn to indicate the customers' relative preferences for any centre. Such a modification identifies the break-point and provides much additional information. A further development employed the market potential concept, which has usually been applied on a national scale to determine the relative proximity of provincial cities to the main markets in a country. Strict definitions applied to the market potential model permitted its use in forecasting the growth capacities of shopping centres. For example, the Lakshmanan and Hansen (1965) model attempted to predict the actual sales volume of various major shopping centres in Baltimore given alternative planning policies about their future arrangement. The model is a complex one but it has been widely used for planning purposes.

General interaction theory is valuable as the basis of an operational approach to planning and market research. It allows for far more variability in consumer movements than central place theory and may therefore be more applicable to situations in which consumers enjoy considerable freedom of movement. Since the theory applies to the aggregate level of population movement it may not account for all possibilities, and in some cases the latter may be a significant proportion of the whole. Interaction models are not without their problems, however valuable experts may find them. Recently, for example, the British Department of the Environment ruled that submissions to planning enquiries using results based on the Lakshmanan and Hansen model are not admissible because they confuse non-expert participants (Breheny *et al.*, 1981).

*Public facility location theory*

The approach whereby location is analysed in terms of economic rationality and the assumption that market considerations are paramount can be applied to the public sector, but it is usually recognised that in the case of public facilities equity principles have to be taken into account. Central place theory, with its emphasis on hierarchical principles, has provided a framework for public facility planners, who as far as possible try to devise a system of public provision meeting equity considerations by matching the twin constraints of perceived needs and cost factors.

Critics believe that this is inadequate, arguing that there are circumstances in which location in space has a bearing on what benefits an individual or group receives, and they highlight the importance of externalities and accessibility in this context. D.M. Smith (1977) mentioned the concept of *place utility* as a convenient means of organising discussion of consumption in space. Individuals may have different personal utility functions which may not correspond to a group utility function. It has also been found that once a residential location choice has been made a large number of other consumption decisions are pre-empted by virtue of the social, economic and environmental considerations associated with place of residence. What is true of residential choice by individuals applies equally to the selection of a location for a public facility which can alter the environmental and perhaps the social and economic attributes of a place. Smith thought that as each location decision is made some people and some places gain while others lose. He was concerned to show that there is a general welfare approach to location/allocation problems and that a spatial perspective has a distinctive contribution to make to planning a redistributive activity.

Inequality of access to public services is inevitable by virtue of the discrete locations of the facilities that provide them. This raises the question of access to sources of human need or want satisfaction which in turn directs attention to the importance of location and distance. Geography is clearly relevant, but the geographical viewpoint does not hold the key to all that matters, even in the specifically spatial differentiation of human life chances. The broader structure of society in all its dimensions continually constrains what can be achieved by spatial reorganisation alone. Even so, geographers have made important contributions to investigating the question of accessibility using a variety of techniques including sophisticated gravity modelling. Analyses of spatial hierarchical organisations and the planning of improved hierarchical structures have been undertaken, and considerable attention has been devoted to regionalisation in devising optimum service areas for specified features such as hospitals and schools. Studies of public service provision in which equity considerations are prominent differ from studies of other forms of service provision in their emphasis rather than their method, but there are significant differences in the location patterns that result when equity instead of profit is the guiding principle in decision-making.

# Urban land-use models

*General land-use models*

The familiar models of Burgess, Hoyt, and Harris and Ullman commonly discussed in urban geography texts are of little practical consequence to the geography of services. They do, however, distinguish between the central business district (CBD) and outlying parts of an urban area, a distinction that has been at the heart of a number of hierarchical schemes proposed for the intraurban level. The CBD is the chief location for retail and high-level office activity capitalising on its accessibility and it is also highly prized by high-level educational and medical facilities, not to mention tourist attractions such as museums, art galleries and theatres.

Hierarchical schemes for outlying districts date from the 1930s (for example, Proudfoot, 1937), but in recent years Berry's (1967) formulation has been widely adopted. He distinguished between nucleated centres clustering around street intersections of varying degrees of importance, ribbon developments stretching along major roads, and specialised functional areas characterised by groups of related types of establishment held together by close linkages and economies arising from comparison shopping and advertising. Berry's scheme was more applicable to North America than to Europe where zoning restrictions had curtailed ribbon development. He also conceded that his typology failed to capture the real diversity of intra-urban facilities. Dawson (1983) modified Berry's classification to take account of innovations in tenant policy, design, location and development practices with particular reference to modern planned shopping centres. All these models are descriptive in character and, as Davies (1976) noted, there have been few attempts to construct theories or concepts about the particular locational attributes of business activities in the central area, let alone the subsidiary centres. His own comprehensive model of the central area retailing structure utilised the components of Berry's typology, and later Potter (1982) propounded a three-stage evolutionary model of the urban retailing system which was a graphical and developmental extension of Berry's typology. Neither model is general enough to include all service activities, nor are they good bases for prediction.

*Rent theory*

Hierarchical urban land use models have been criticised for lacking explanatory power, and some advocate an analysis based on the nature of competition among different types of land use for specific sites. Rent theory has been used mainly, but not exclusively, in respect of retailing activities. It is assumed that activities with the greatest need for access to the market would pay the highest rents to secure this benefit. Consequently activities would be arranged in concentric zones at distances from the centre determined by their rent-paying abilities. Garner (1966) applied this model to the internal differentiation of regional, community and neighbourhood centres suggesting that in each type of nucleus the highest-order functions would be closest to the centre and the lowest in the outer concentric zone.

Although rent theory offers an attractive explanation for the general pattern of uses within a centre, the concept of rent used is an abstract one which may not correspond to the contract rent actually asked for a site. Length of lease and actual ownership of a site may further complicate matters so that the observed pattern may deviate considerably from that predicted by rent theory. Bateman (1985) confirmed that, in the case of the property market: 'It would be simplistic indeed to offer an explanation for office development in classic bid-rent theory terms, since utility maximisation by an occupier may be a secondary consideration for development to profit maximisation for the financial institution.' Daniels (1985) also criticised rent theory models and noted that in reality there are many obstacles to the operation of the free market postulated by the model. He further observed that some service firms might prefer to be remote from their competitors in order to 'corner' a specified market in preference to the agglomeration economies afforded by a central location. Under modern conditions when decentralisaiton of facilities is common the CBD may no longer be the most accessible point for consumers to reach, and this limits the usefulness of the model. On the other hand, rent theory principles may still influence the distribution of facilities within a centre, even one that is newly planned. Attention is still being paid to understanding the development of nuclei within urban areas, as Erickson (1986) recently showed. Whereas rent theory relies heavily on economic rationality to explain the patterns observed, Erickson stressed that the processes involved are not well understood and that what is required is a general equilibrium approach including the role of suburban municipalities in influencing the supply of sites through zoning and other public actions.

## Scale economies and location

Scale, with its influence on production costs and level of profitability, affects location. Scale economies may derive from aspatial factors such as variations in levels of demand within the economy, but here we are concerned with external economies that are commonly achieved by means of agglomeration. The economies to be derived are not only related directly to the physical size of the agglomeration but also indirectly and fundamentally to other advantages of convenience resulting from competition between firms in a spatial setting (Toyne, 1974). Neither economies of scale nor agglomeration factors can be ignored when dealing with the location of service activities.

### Economies of scale

Competitive forces may mean that survival depends on taking advantage of scale economies. Unless the market for goods and services also expands, the increasing size of individual operating units means that fewer of them will be required. This results in *concentration* of the number of outlets which may be expressed geographically by increased *centralisation*. Concentration can also make itself felt in terms of the ownership of firms, for individual firms may increase their size by takeover or merger, thus reducing the total number of independent companies.

The trend towards larger retail stores, warehouses, hospitals, schools and hotels is often accompanied by centralisation of facilities. Sometimes the geographical pattern may remain quite widespread, but closer inspection often reveals that the bulk of provision is actually concentrated in relatively few locations; for example, hotels are well dispersed but the majority of beds are found in a few particularly well-favoured centres. Organisational concentration among manufacturing firms means that fewer headquarters offices are required, though the average size of individual units may be greater. Certainly the larger number of new office blocks conveys the impression that this is happening, but it is not easy to demonstrate that such a trend is occurring because of the variety in size of the market area offices serve and the fact that many firms only need small offices.

Many retail companies have embarked on a policy of increasing their average store size. Under a rationalisation programme during the 1970s the British supermarket chain Tesco reduced the number of its London stores from 223 to 98 but at the same time increased sales volume and floor space (Dawson, 1982a). Press announcements suggest that this process will continue as companies, Tesco included, state their preference for out-of-town locations suitable for very large stores. The Tesco example illustrates geographical concentration of facilities into fewer locations, although the resultant distribution was evidently intended to serve the same geographical areas. Within retailing scale economies can also be attained by organisational change, and British figures show that multiple firms are claiming a larger share of the market at the expense of independents and co-operatives (see Table 4.1). Increasingly multiples are large enough to serve the whole British market, and in some cases firms have become transnational in their scope. Boots, Marks and Spencer, Burton, Laura Ashley, Lasky and Habitat are examples of British companies with considerable overseas operations.

Change in hospital size in the UK illustrates the influence of scale economies on health care provision (see Table 4.2). Small hospitals of under 25 beds remain the most numerous size group despite a fall in their percentage share from 81 per cent in 1959 to 77 per cent in 1985. Hospitals with fewer than 50 beds declined at a faster rate, but small hospitals have not suffered the same degree of closure as small shops. In fact, in August 1974 a paper was issued on community hospitals confirming the need for units to be situated close to the residences of patients in need but no longer requiring the specialist services of district general hopsitals. Many existing local and 'cottage' hospitals were suitable for this purpose which benefits certain classes of patient and which can employ trained local staff who prefer to work on a part-time basis. The advantages of community hospitals were noted by Haynes and Bentham (1979) in their study of some of the problems caused by the closure of small East Anglian hospitals on completion of a large new hospital at Kings Lynn, a rather peripheral urban focus for the region.

Medium-sized hospitals (250–999 beds) recorded the greatest numerical growth. Proportionately, their share rose from 15 per cent in 1959 to 21 per

**Table 4.1**   Retail sales by organisation type, UK 1961–84 (per cent)

a) 1961–1980

|  | *1961* | *1966* | *1971* | *1976* | *1978* | *1980* |
|---|---|---|---|---|---|---|
| Multiples | 28.2 | 33.0 | 36.4 | 40.1 | 42.2 | 42.8 |
| Independents | 53.9 | 49.9 | 48.1 | 43.0 | 41.0 | 40.7 |
| Co-op Societies | 9.5 | 7.7 | 5.8 | 6.2 | 6.0 | 5.8 |
| Dept. stores (inc. Co-op) | 5.9 | 5.7 | 5.8 | 6.0 | 5.8 | 5.7 |
| Mail order | 2.5 | 3.7 | 3.9 | 4.7 | 5.0 | 5.0 |

*Source:* P. J. McGoldrick in Davies and Rogers 1984, p. 35.

b) 1980–1984

|  | *1980* | *1984* |
|---|---|---|
| Multiples | 47.2 | 52.4 |
| Independents | 46.3 | 42.3 |
| Co-ops | 6.5 | 5.3 |

*Source:* Retailing Inquiry 1986

cent in 1980, while the share of allocated beds rose from 37 per cent to 58 per cent. In this period the optimum size for a district hospital was thought to be 820 beds, but because of the expense in 1975 the government health department offered an alternative concept in hospital design called the 'nucleus hospital'. This is a standardised scheme for a 300-bed unit with the usual supporting services costing £6 million at 1975 prices and so designed that further modules could be added when the need arose (Levitt, 1977). The very largest hospitals with over 2000 beds totalled 28 in 1959 but by 1976 this size category had been totally eliminated. All were psychiatric hopsitals and a change in medical thinking probably accounts for this outcome which appears to be at variance with the notion of scale economies. Overall the rationalisation of hospital provision produced a fall of 457 (19 per cent) in the number of hospitals, and a 20 per cent decline in the number of allocated beds from 455 138 to 363 395.

Primary health care facilities were also affected by scale economies, as evidenced by the growth of group practices with three or more medical practitioners. Legally all medical practitioners are considered to be equal, so a group practice cannot properly be regarded as operating at a higher level in a hierarchy of medical services (Phillips, 1981). Group practices do, however, allow for the sharing of expenses and a better level of provision of support workers. For example, there must be at least one full-time member of staff on

**Table 4.2** Distribution of British public hospitals by size and number of allocated beds

*(a) Hospitals*

| | 1959 | 1969 | 1976 | 1979 | 1980 | 1985 | change 1959-85 (%) |
|---|---|---|---|---|---|---|---|
| All hospitals | 2 441 | 2 293 | 2 126 | 2 023 | 1 984 | 1 862 | −23.7 |
| <50 beds | 977 | 825 | 762 | 742 | 727 | 723 | −26.0 |
| 50–249 | 1 011 | 991 | 895 | 819 | 802 | 709 | −29.9 |
| 250–449 | 243 | 254 | 246 | 243 | 239 | 236 | −2.0 |
| 500–999 | 119 | 149 | 171 | 178 | 180 | 176 | +47.9 |
| 1000–1999 | 63 | 65 | 52 | 41 | 36 | 18 | −71.4 |
| >2000 | 28 | 9 | – | – | – | – | −100.0 |

*(b) Allocated beds (thousands)*

| | 1959 | 1969 | 1976 | 1979 | 1980 | 1985 | change 1959-85 (%) |
|---|---|---|---|---|---|---|---|
| All hospitals | 455.1 | 436.8 | 391.8 | 370.6 | 363.4 | 325.5 | −28.5 |
| <50 beds | 24.9 | 21.5 | 20.4 | 19.6 | 18.9 | 17.9 | −28.1 |
| 50–249 | 116.6 | 111.7 | 101.5 | 92.5 | 90.2 | 80.3 | −31.1 |
| 250–499 | 84.1 | 88.9 | 88.5 | 88.1 | 87.4 | 86.7 | +3.1 |
| 500–999 | 82.2 | 102.3 | 114.3 | 120.7 | 123.4 | 119.9 | +45.7 |
| 1000–1999 | 81.8 | 92.6 | 67.1 | 49.7 | 43.4 | 20.6 | −75.0 |
| >2000 | 65.3 | 19.8 | – | – | – | – | −100.0 |

*(c) Share of provisions (%)*

| | Hospitals | | | | Allocated beds | | |
|---|---|---|---|---|---|---|---|
| | 1959 | 1980 | 1985 | | 1959 | 1980 | 1985 |
| Hospital size | | | | | | | |
| Small (<250 beds) | 81.4 | 77.1 | 76.9 | | 31.1 | 30.0 | 30.2 |
| Medium (250–999) | 14.8 | 21.1 | 22.1 | | 36.6 | 58.0 | 63.5 |
| Large (>1000) | 3.7 | 1.8 | 1.0 | | 32.3 | 11.9 | 6.3 |

*Source: Health and Personal Social Statistics for England, 1982 and 1987*

secretarial, nursery-receptionist, or medico-social work in a group practice. Since it is both government and British Medical Association policy to encourage group practice and an allowance is paid the trend towards group practice is assured. The figures in Table 4.3 suggest that the preferred size is a practice of three doctors. There are fewer single-handed practices than there used to be, which in fact means that provision in central locations where these practices

**Table 4.3** General medical practitioners in England: organisation by practices

| Type of practitioner | 1961 | 1971 | 1981 | 1985 |
|---|---|---|---|---|
| All practitioners (total) | 20 865 | 20 597 | 24 359 | 26 190 |
| Unrestricted practitioners (total) | 18 905 | 19 374 | 22 304 | 24 035 |
| Single handed practices | 5 337 | 3 954 | 2 990 | 2 915 |
| In partnership of 2 doctors | 6 384 | 4 552 | 4 004 | 3 880 |
| In partnership of 3 doctors | 4 008 | 4 911 | 5 132 | 4 986 |
| in partnership of 4 doctors | 1 984 | 3 232 | 4 255 | 4 352 |
| In partnership of 5 doctors | 715 | 1 490 | 2 940 | 3 610 |
| In partnership of 6 or more doctors | 450 | 1 235 | 2 983 | 4 292 |

*Source:* Health and Personal Social Service Statistics for England, 1982 and 1987. HMSO

Note: an unrestricted principal (practitioner) provides the full range of general medical services and whose list is not limited to any particular group of persons. In a few cases (about 20) such practitioners may be relieved of the liability to have patients assigned to them or be exempted from liability for emergency calls out-of-hours from patients other than their own.

The difference between the totals for all practitioners and unrestricted practitioners is accounted for by restricted principals, assistants and trainees.

were most numerous has been reduced, which might have serious repercussions for public accessibility.

Similar tendencies can be observed in the field of education, which has become more complex and specialised. The range of specialist teachers and equipment (computers and laboratories) has grown and because many items are not divisible they must be concentrated in fewer and larger schools. Except in remote rural areas where the alternatives to small schools would mean increased hardship and cost in transporting pupils over long distances, it is felt that small schools with small classes deprive children of the intellectual and social stimulus of interaction with their peers. This is especially true if age-groups are mixed where there are too few pupils or teachers to justify separate year classes. Under such circumstances younger pupils may be intimidated or older ones held back as teachers strive to satisfy the needs of all age groups. By contrast the village school can be viewed as a cherished component of a rural utopia in which small classes facilitate close contact and personal supervision of a child's progress. This is preferred to the alleged impersonal and alienating atmosphere of the giant urban comprehensive or high schools where teachers have little hope of even remembering the names of all their pupils, let alone treating them as individuals. Both images are probably sustained more by the mass media than empirical research, though the available evidence points to the impoverishment of resources in small schools. What cannot be denied is that there has been an overall trend towards larger schools at the secondary level and the closure of many of the smallest village schools.

Since there is still scope for further economies of scale, especially in response to technological advances, locational change can be expected to continue. The process will not be unabated because eventually diseconomies of scale will become manifest as in the case of additional travelling imposed on patients as hospital size increases. The consumer orientation of much of the service sector's activity will ensure that the scale of facilities will not grow to the extent that users are prevented or dissuaded from making use of them.

*Agglomeration*

Hotelling's ice-cream vendors exemplified the economic rationale for clustering of economic activities, and other studies have emphasised the role of *linkage*. Daniels (1982) noted that agglomeration strongly influences the location of producer services relying on links with other activities rather than meeting the demands of final consumers. Producer services function largely by exchanging information, and he suggested that the volume, variety and importance of those linkages to individual producer services will determine the significance attached to ease of contact with appropriate sources. Ease of contact relates to the time taken to attend meetings and accordingly 'information-rich' activities of a managerial or professional character will tend to group together. Thus the location pattern that evolves is one in which the largest clusters in the most contact-rich environments attract a disproportionate share of any additonal producer services attracted into the system. Pred (1977) believed that where specialised information was essential to a firm this would depend on spatially biased considerations such as face-to-face meetings, letters or telephone if proximity of the participants means that it can be obtained more cheaply than when they are far apart. Hence certain financial institutions and exchanges need to be close together, an extra advantage of which is that by their proximity they can tap a very large labour catchment area.

The agglomeration principle is not confined to producer services, as evidenced by the concentration of offices in the financial district of London. On a smaller scale agglomeration economies also benefit consumer services, as any shopping district illustrates. It is widely acknowledged that a cluster of shops collectively attracts more customers than the same number of similar-sized shops occupying isolated free standing sites. Even within a shopping district cumulative attraction is a consideration proved by the strong tendency for shops like jewellers and footwear specialists to locate close together. Because much the same conclusions apply to wholesaling, health care, education and leisure facilities the importance of agglomeration in the service sector cannot be ignored.

# Alternative approaches to the location of service activities

Apart from specific weaknesses in individual theories there has been a general criticism of the reliance on economic rationality in location theory. Various writers demonstrated that the goal of profit-maximisation is an elusive one because of the uncertainty of knowing whether maximum profits have actually been attained or where that could be done (Tiebout, 1957). Firms probably give more emphasis to sales maximisation because it is easier to assess where most sales can be achieved. Sales maximisation models are well suited to the analysis of consumer services, with their preference for market orientation. Agglomerations are conducive to sales maximisation, but the interest in achieving greater sales potential led to the development of concepts involving strategic location designed to diminish a competitor's access to a market. This focused attention on decision-making within the firm. Simon (1959) introduced the idea of satisficing behaviour according to which decision-makers did not seek optimal solutions. Instead possible actions are evaluated according to whether or not their expected outcomes are satisfactory or unsatisfactory, for example, whether a satisfactory income can be obtained from a given activity in a particular location. This may be a very appropriate way of judging the success of small businesses (and perhaps large ones) under independent ownership or management such as are commonly encountered in the service sector.

Increasing awareness of a subjective element in location decision-making led some to question the normative basis of economic models as they explored the greater flexibility offered by behaviouralist models. Such models allow for the decision-maker's perception of the business environment as an influence on choice, and they take account of the modifications that may occur as a result of the search and learning processes undergone by those who make decisions. The internal environment of the firm, inasmuch as it affects decision-making, is considered to be an important factor. Furthermore, it is recognised that decision-making may not be an individual matter but that it may have to conform to the needs of an organisation and to the rules and procedures laid down by that organisation. Frequently the decision-maker is provided with a number of alternatives from which the most suitable, rather than the optimum, must be chosen. Proponents of this approach hoped that the investigation of behavioural processes would provide increased conceptual knowledge, increased understanding, higher levels of explanation and improved predictive power.

Among the components of the behavioural approach identified by Golledge et al. (1972) are decision-making and choice behaviour, search and learning, information spread, and perception. Studies of the service sector have been undertaken within this framework, as evidenced by the interest in search and learning and perception as they affect consumer behaviour. Insights have been gained into how consumers view stores and how they decide what and where to purchase. Work has also been done in the same vein on the utilisation of health facilities. Edwards (1983) provided an example of the application of a decision process model to the problem of locational choice for office firms. Another aspect of decision-making concerns the effects of organisational change and the locational implications of the restructuring of relations between head offices and branches. This work, mostly applied to industrial firms, is equally relevant to service activities. Information spread is usually associated with diffusion models, and there is a strong tradition of enquiry based on the diffusion of information or innovation between the nodes in a system of cities, or between regions, that ultimately derives from

Hagerstrand's (1967) pioneering work. Availability of information reinforces the attractiveness of agglomerations, but while this might suggest that the central place hierarchy would exert a strong influence on the location and concentration of business services this is a subject that arouses controversy. Stanback (1979) advanced the thesis that in the contemporary urban system information diffusion can be achieved, even when information-orientated services are concentrated in a limited number of urban areas, without concentration at the top of the hierarchy. He supported this view with evidence from a number of metropolitan centres in the USA which had significant business service functions in 1960 and which experienced the most rapid growth of employment in the USA in the same services during the next decade. The conclusion was that services did not have to be in New York to flourish, but Wheeler (1986) challenged the Stanback hypothesis following his study of corporate spatial links with financial institutions in the American metropolitan hierarchy. Evidently the issue has not yet been resolved. Also within the framework of studies of information diffusion are analyses of the geographical dispersion of a company's activities as the company expands and as its knowledge of its operating environment increases. Watts (1975), for example, used the diffusion model in his study of the spread of the retail outlets of the pharmacy chain Boots, in Britain and Bird and Witherwick (1986) examined the growth of Marks and Spencer, a major British food and clothing retailer, in a similar way.

Behaviouralists are also interested in business organisation, for this, too, has locational consequences. Taylor and Thrift (1983) were proponents of a broad geography of business organisation, and their framework included a theoretical account revolving round the notion of segmentation and its historical development. Perhaps the most distinctive changes in capitalist economies have occurred through fission, primarily in response to new conditions of competition and crisis which favours concentration and centralisation of capital. The process of segmentation results from the emergence of new dominant segments which are both the causes and consequences of crises of accumulation, and over time the typical capitalist economy becomes more complex and interrelated.

The present pattern of segmentation (allowing for problems of definition) rests on a dichotomy between large and small firms. Small firms usually operate at one site, whereas large firms have a number of sites. The smaller-firm segment is distributed across all sections of the economy and is probably biased towards non-manufacturing. A high rate of replacement characterises the small-firm segment which is further categorised by 'laggard' firms. These latter may be classed as 'craftsman' or 'satisfied', intermediate, and leaders. Intermediates can be classed as 'satellites' or 'loyal opposition'. Satellites include subcontractors and franchisees, among whom there may be a high rate of replacement. By contrast the loyal opposition is very stable because it has identified a niche in the market and because it is not worth the effort for large firms to try to dislodge this type of enterprise. Leader small firms also have a high replacement rate, partly because they tend to be innovative.

In the large-business segment there are multi-divisional and global corporations which are often becoming more diversified. Within a multi-divisional company product-cycle analogues seem appropriate. There are leader activities which are the firm's innovators carrying a high risk but also the prospect of high profits. Laggards will be that part of the company producing products for which demand is tailing off, while the intermediates, which yield steady profits, are the heart of the operation. Support companies provide general services ranging from management services to computing time. The three types described here can be seen as the international organisational subforms of particular stages in the classical three-part manufacturing cycle, but they also fit a parallel three-part market cycle appropriate for banking and finance, retailing and distribution, and services. Every multi-divisional corporation is to varying degrees caught on an 'innovation treadmill', though very large firms have the advantage that they can adapt to changes in the economic environment. Global corporations, on the other hand, are emergent and have a high rate of replacement. Such corporations relate to the internationalisation of capital and the new international division of labour, and for them no spatial frontier exists. Within this category, too, there are leaders, intermediates, laggard and support companies. This interest in business organisation is relevant to the understanding of such a dynamic area as the service sector, but Taylor and Thrift showed that different aspects of location theory apply to different segments of business organisation, thus pointing to a link between location theory and business organisation theory.

Undoubtedly location theory emphasises demand considerations, but the level of demand or the factors that influence it are not explicitly examined except in so far as they are affected by distance. The prevailing notion of consumer sovereignty leads to neglect of the importance of supply considerations. Little has been said about the powerful forces that mould demand, and it may be claimed that work on the service industry has scarcely ventured beyond a strict neoclassical formulation and a preoccupation with patterns rather than processes. Terms like 'managerialism', 'Weberian', 'structuralism' and 'reproduction of the labour force' have been introduced into the literature chiefly in respect of residential location. Kirby (1985) called for a movement away from 'management-oriented, site-based empirical studies' towards conceptual and theoretical research on leisure provision. He referred to researchers in political science and economics who are seeking an evaluation of the environment which recognises the role of economic systems, social values and the state.

Kirby's view refutes the idea that people control and determine their own existence and looks to a higher level of explanation for this state of affairs than that provided by geography alone. He appeals to the tradition of emphasis on social relations, political struggles and the role of the state for the greatest returns in analyses of fundamentally complex and important phenomena. Other workers have adopted a similar stance in relation to public service provision beyond the field of leisure. The idea that the market can be moulded to influence the consumer is not necessarily restricted to wide-ranging explanations of the nature of society and the state. For example, a more narrowly focused view is expressed by Bateman (1985) in his study of the role of property developers in office location. In his opinion early development may have occurred in response to a need, but today's speculative office development is not directly linked to the needs and wants of the final users: instead, it is a vehicle for large-scale investment of finance. Property development is highly dependent on compliance with the requirements of major financial investors, and since office activities are quite mobile they may well have to move to what is available. Hence the supply side might be more significant than the demand side in determining where development occurs.

The role of developers has also been examined in respect of modern retailing facilities (Dawson 1983; and Dawson and Lord 1985). The scale of investment in planned shopping centres is high and the rents required to achieve an acceptable return often preclude the participation of small independent retailers by favouring the multiple. Consequently, concern has been expressed that the pattern of retail provision is becoming increasingly managed and is changing in character as the balance of multiples in shopping centres far outweighs that in traditional high streets (Bunce, 1983). Consumers seem to favour the change, if the commercial success of shopping centres is any guide, but whether the new trends meet the needs of all consumers is open to question. Poor and immobile members of society would doubtless agree that the existence of very real wants will not necessarily guarantee that the suppliers of those wants will respond by providing them for they might not deem the perceived demand to be large enough to justify their interest. Commercially this may be defensible because businesses do not purport to be philanthropic in their outlook, but it does emphasise that consumers can only look to the service that is provided which may be very different from what they would prefer. There is, therefore, a case for paying as much attention to supply factors as is given to demand considerations if the geography of service provision is to be explained.

## Conclusion

Central place theory has been extensively used to provide insights into the distribution of retailing, health and educational facilities, and by implication it is relevant to the concentration of business services in certain centres. Of particular importance are the concepts of hierarchical provision and consumer access. Urban land-use models and rent theory also contribute to the understanding of service sector location, as do the impact of economies of scale and agglomeration economies. Neither can behavioural and welfare considerations be ignored, and it is clear that the factors influencing or controlling the supply of facilities are important. Geographers are undeniably interested in the locational attributes of service activities, and it is not surprising that location theory has been called to their aid. Storper (1985), however, has pointed to the problems of using a logical *abstraction* to gain insight into a *concrete* phenomenon such as locational behaviour. Daniels (1985) also commented on the futility of searching for a single theory once the factors affecting the location of services are enumerated. Whatever explanation is applicable to individual activities it remains true that services are not uniformly distributed in geographical space, which is sufficient reason for geographers to investigate their characteristics.

# Chapter 5
# The Impact on Urban Form

Despite the tendency to relegate the study of urban form to a minor role in geographical studies, the physical impact of the economic, social and political factors already discussed is too important to be overlooked entirely. Smailes's (1953) interest in the 'townscape' directed attention to the street plan of a town, the architectural style of its buildings, and the pattern of land use. Geographers have not devoted much attention to architectural style but the approach advocated by Smailes has increased understanding of urban growth. Description was the essential characteristic, and although it did lead to the formulation of some generalisations their analytical power was considered to be weak. Among the generalisations attempted was the investigation of the relationship between form and function as in the urban land-use models of Burgess (1923), Hoyt (1939) and Harris and Ullman (1945). Such inductive models purport to show important relationships but are in fact no more than constructs based on observations from a large number of American cities. Carter (1972) reviewed these models critically and exposed their limitations. However, he acknowledged that studies of urban retail location, by trying to relate form to function, built on and extended the concepts implicit in the early land-use models.

Proudfoot's (1937) fivefold typology of retail structure cities in the USA was matched by a comparable scheme advanced by the British planner Burns in 1959. Gradually in the 1960s the twin strands of urban land-use models and central place theory were united in an increasing number of studies. Prominent among them was Berry's (1967) typology, elements of which can be traced in Potter's (1982) account of the urban retailing structure of Stockport and in Dawson's (1983) classification of shopping centres. He defined the latter as planned units distinctive from a shopping district or area, and identified six main types which were further divided into 15 subtypes. Efforts have been made to achieve greater understanding of the CBD, and the core-frame model proposed by Horwood and Boyce (1959) focused on the CBD's internal structure. Davies (1976) observed that there had been few attempts to construct theories or concepts about the particular locational attributes of business activities inside the central area, but in 1972 he proposed a comprehensive model of central area retailing structures combining Berry's nucelated, ribbon and specialist functions. His ideas were later used by Brown (1987c) in a study of Belfast.

The dynamism of retailing, its high degree of visibility in urban areas, and its impact on individuals may account for the prominence given to studies of the retail sector. Nevertheless, other work, such as Whitehand's (1967) on the nature of urban fringe belts, is of interest. In Whitehand's view the CBD changes its location only slowly relative to the built-up area as a whole, and in general its form and function reflect current conditions. By contrast the fringe belt is subject to centrifugal forces, but urban extension is rarely continuous. Instead, it is cyclical with periods of rapid outward growth alternating with quiescent periods. The basic constraint is lack of economic dynamism, which leaves its mark as a fixation line in the land-use pattern. When renewed growth occurs there are marked contrasts in the pattern of landholding on either side of the fixation line. During the period of stability the town may require land for schools, hospitals, parks and many other uses, so that the urban fringe will be characterised by development, sometimes extensive, of public utilities. When there is an economic upswing residential building may be resumed and the former fringe belt with its institutional uses will become fossilised in the urban landscape. In addition to the great public sector institutions, industrial and commercial activities have shown a preference for urban fringe locations as the examples of planned shopping centres, superstores or hypermarkets, and office parks illustrate. Whitehand believed that because of the forces at work urban plans throughout the country would display many common features, and he felt that the characteristics of Edwardian fringe belts were typical of the Western world as a whole.

An interest in urban morphology is not enough. Carter (1972) addressed the problem by referring to work published by the planner Foley in 1964. Foley presented a matrix with two columns representing spatial and aspatial aspects, and three rows distinguishing between normative or cultural, functional organisational, and physical aspects. The reconciliation of spatial and aspatial aspects of activities investigated by geographers is a continuing difficulty, but the geographer's interest in urban morphology is justified. The components of the urban structure are observable and produce patterns that are a legitimate object of geographical enquiry. However dangerous it might be to infer processes from observed patterns it seems perverse to ignore the patterns that may result from processes that have been identified and studied. As the nature of the service sector functions changes in response to modern conditions so we can expect the physical structure of urban areas to be modified. There may be practical advantages to be gained from such inquiries, but in any case they are likely to add to our understanding of the activities themselves and the areas in which they are located. Accordingly this chapter deals with the spatial and physical aspects of service sector activities that result in land-use patterns. These include linkages, spatially conceived, and the spatial pattern of establishments by functional type. In addition to paying attention to the geographical expression of specified functional activities, aspects of temporal change which are the outcome of dynamic influences will also be considered.

## Functional areas as elements of urban form

Commerical or business activities encourage people to live in cities, and over 20 years ago Murphy (1966) noted that these occupations were the main employers in American cities. He further remarked that in cities varying commercial patterns become apparent and serve to differentiate the interior of the city as well as generating interaction between the inhabitants of urban areas. In his view commercial patterns could throw light on the structure and operations of the city, and this idea will be examined in more detail in this section.

### Retailing and wholesaling

Developments in retailing and wholesaling are currently modifying the form of cities, and it is these rather than the nature of such world-renowned shopping streets as Oxford Street, Fifth Avenue and the Rue de Rivoli that are of concern here. Powerful interests, principally manifested through the mechanism of planning procedures, have protected the status of the CBD in the UK. Following wartime destruction, certain town centres were rebuilt to carefully designed plans as in Coventry and Plymouth, while New Towns such as Crawley, Basildon and, most recently, Milton Keynes also possessed planned centres. The authorities were naturally anxious to protect their investment in such centres so they were resistant to the emergence of out-of-town regional shopping centres of the successful North American type. There were also social and environmental objections to suburban and out-of-town development, but despite a change in attitude towards the latter there are still strong interests keen to secure the future of the CBD. Even in the USA attempts are being made to revive downtown areas. Apart from the post-war reconstruction schemes and the New Town precincts in the UK, attempts have been made to refurbish older town centres, particularly in the declining heavy industrial areas.

Since 1950 the planned shopping centre has become a dominant component of the American retailing landscape, and Rogers (1984) regarded the development and expansion of the American shopping centre industry as the most significant structural change in recent years. From 1964 to 1980 planned shopping centres in the USA increased from 7600 to 22 050 and probably accounted for 42 per cent of all retail sales in 1980. Sizes vary and more than half the centres are under 9300 square meters (100 000 square feet) in extent, but there are 268 centres with over 93 000 square metres (1 million square feet) of floorspace (Lord, 1985). Smaller centres with less than 200 000 square feet (18 600 square metres) of gross leasable area account for 86 per cent of the total shopping space and 52 per cent of their sales. Several development companies were involved: Dawson (1983) cited the Taubman Company which in 30 years developed 6 million square metres of centre space, most of which it sold off. Initially growth was concentrated in the industrial North-East and California, but after 1960 westward and southward spread occurred, tempered by a hierarchical diffusion pattern in which the innovation first appeared in the largest or second largest cities within states. Even though recent expansion has been in the southern states and Sunbelt cities development expertise has remained mainly north-eastern in origin. Since the schemes depend on private enterprise they have sought the most profitable locations in surburban middle- and higher-income districts and there has been no pressure from local authorities comparable to that in the UK to favour central areas. Very few centres exist in inner suburban or ghetto areas. Many of the early centres are now 16–25 years old and in need of renovation. Some major development companies are acknowledging this 'life-cycle' factor and now devote one-third to half of their resources to centre renovation or expansion. James (1985) described the effect of the new trend on downtown Denver by reference to the proposal to renovate the 30-year-old Cherry Creek Centre or else to revitalise the downtown area itself.

Shopping centre expansion has been accompanied by CBD decline to the extent that often the CBD accounts for less than 10 per cent of a city's or Standard Metropolitan Statistical Area's retail sales. For example, in 1977 the Memphis CBD accounted for only 3.5 per cent of the city's total retail sales, but there were three retail centres within the city whose sales each exceeded this level (Lord, 1985). Although shopping centres are frequently important focal points in the community, their similarity in appearance probably results from the dominance of the industry by a small number of developers and national chain stores. Trends such as the slowdown in the demand for retail goods as population growth declines, the lack of increase in real incomes, and the rapidly increasing costs of non-retail items may affect future location decisions and development policies. Furthermore, development costs are rising and there is concern about the environmental impact of large malls.

The new markets that have been identified consist of middle markets, the CBD, and infill areas. Middle markets are either small metropolitan markets or areas of non-metropolitan status with 15 000–50 000 population. Centres catering for this type of market cover 18 500–70 000 square metres. Unlike the metropolitan suburban centres which achieved success by spatially segmenting the metropolitan market, the middle markets thrive on the spatial aggregation (either multi-county or multi-city) of previously separate markets. The performance of these centres suggests that there may be a trend towards smaller units in the future. With public sector support CBDs are now looking more attractive to developers, and there is also scope for development of infill locations which lie between the CBD and the first ring of suburban malls.

Powerful centrifugal forces have encouraged decentralisation and suburbanisation. From the 1950s onwards the phenomenon was reported in North America (Kellerman, 1985b), and it has been recognised in other parts of the world as well. Increased personal mobility of consumers, central area decline, the availability of sites in the suburbs and administrative considerations such as planning controls and urban tax structures were among the reasons proffered to explain this trend. Planning constraints have restrained decentralisation in the UK compared with North America, though forces favouring dispersal are becoming stronger in the UK. In the UK property development companies switched their attention from the office and housing fields to town centre shopping facilities during the period 1965–80 (Davies,

1984). They sought to satisfy the demand from multiple retailers for new sites in favourable trading circumstances and they elected to achieve this through the agency of enclosed shopping centres (ESCs). Some of the early 'Arndale' centres were little more than appendages to the established shopping streets, but by the mid-1970s much larger schemes such as Nottingham's Victoria and Broadmarsh centres were introduced followed by the very large Eldon Square scheme in Newcastle. Property developers co-operated with local authorities in many of these schemes, though the latter's role may diminish in future because of the economic and political climate. Bennison and Davies (1980) recorded an increase in the size of centres in the years 1965–80 and increasing specialisation of function (especially by the reduction in the number of other business activities). Greater commercial success has accompanied this trend in their opinion. Among the characteristics of ESCs are the greater likelihood of underground or rooftop service facilities and second- or third-floor shopping levels. They have better than average car parking allocations and more frequently incorporate a bus station. Future changes may be expected because of the reduced availability of sites, but classification is not easy owing to the variety among existing schemes. Bunce (1983) showed how ESCs have diffused southwards, and although he was concerned about some of the problems they pose he recognised their popularity with customers.

Currently the balance seems to be tipping in favour of out-of-town centres. Hillier Parker reported that in mid-1986 some 47 million square feet (4.4 million square metres) of new development was proposed in Britain, representing a more than 200 per cent increase on the 15 million square feet (1.4 million square metres) planned when the present retail boom started. The most significant finding was that planned or proposed out-of-town schemes will soon outstrip town-centre developments. There were plans for 30 million square feet (2.8 million square metres) of out-of-town shopping, with 80 per cent of the proposals being made between March and June 1986. Up to March 1986 out-of-town schemes totalled 16.2 million square feet (1.5 million square metres)—compared with 5.2 million square feet (480 000 square metres) in 1985—as against 15.6 million square feet (1.4 million square metres) in town centres. Particularly interesting is the fact that some 10 million square feet (930 000 square metres) of the proposed space under consideration is located close to the M25 motorway which encircles London. Traditional town centre developers scarcely figure in the out-of-town proposals, whose average size was 437,959 square feet (40 688 square metres) compared with 133,551 square feet (12 407 square metres) for town centre developments. Even though the planning system is no longer the obstacle that it once was, it is difficult to say whether these proposals will come to fruition. Equally critical for developers is the prospect that several rival schemes could obtain planning permission in a given area which would raise financial difficulties. In these circumstances market forces would come into play whereas hitherto once planning permission had been obtained it was unlikely that a rival centre could be built nearby (*The Times* July 1986).

Market segmentation evidenced by specialist theme centres, mutli-use centres, or factory outlet (off-price) centres have been popular in North America, and already a multi-use centre has appeared in the UK at Gateshead's Metroland.

Such centres are growth points in an industry whose rate of expansion has declined as population and income growth have slowed down while interest rates have risen. Regional shopping centres have not developed so rapidly of late, partly because the market position of department stores, the usual anchor tenants, has weakened. Also the space needed for regional shopping centres entails high building costs which affect the rents paid by tenants. Neighbourhood shopping centres are easier to fit into existing built-up areas, and so may become more popular in the immediate future.

Delobez (1985) discussed the development of shopping centres in the Paris region. According to her there were 99 centres in the Ile de France with at least 3,000 square metres (32 000 square feet) of gross leasable area and ten businesses in January 1983 accounting for a quarter of the total number of centres in France. Development began in the 1950s when the tradition of individual shops was breaking down and a number of small centres emerged. In 1959 a large development was built, but the majority of centres constructed prior to 1971 simply reproduced the traditional model of daily convenience goods centres built in a residential block, so that, apart from size, these centres were little different from their predecessors. From 1972 to 1974 there was a period of peak activity in which centres serving 250 000–700 000 people were developed, though in an area containing 12 million people such centres were subregional rather than regional in scale. Growth slowed down after 1975, partly because of tax restrictions, the approach of saturation, a decline in the growth rate of retail demand, and the effect of economic recession in the wake of the 1973 oil crisis. Without a doubt the sales area in the Ile de France has increased, mainly by new building but with some extension to existing capacity, though there have been problems. Traders in centres have complained about collective charges such as maintenance costs and publicity campaigns, which cost from 10 000 to 20 000 francs per square metre in 1983, rather than rents. In practice very few small independent traders have gone into shopping centres in the Paris region and they are almost absent from regional shopping centres. Big commercial firms and franchisers are more favourably placed, and the shopping centres have proved to be a useful tool for commercial concentration. Even so, some of the prestigious department stores had doubts about their involvement in regional shopping centres and there were a few closures, but despite their difficulties in integrating themselves into shopping centres these shops have not been unsuccessful in the Ile de France centres. Spatially the pattern of centres is not uniform in that a transitional zone between the inner and outer suburbs has benefited most from the establishment of centres.

Reliance on shopping centre development for meeting a city's retail needs is likely to prove inflexible and inadequate as the case of Canberra, Australia, illustrates (Dawson, 1985). Canberra is very dependent on the whims of politicians and public policy and shopping centre development has been plagued by plans that over- or underestimated growth in what is a totally planned new capital city. Retail units are provided in shopping centres planned on a hierarchical arrangement and virtually no other retailing is allowed. Each type of shopping centre was intended to meet a particular range of consumer needs in terms of accessibility, variety of goods, and convenience. Private enterprise funds, constructs and operates centres, and it can exercise its own judgement in respect of the detailed timing, store and tenant mix, precise size of centres, their marketing and redevelopment or rehabilitation needs. Actually there are long lead times in acquiring land for development, but perhaps a more serious problem is that the rigid hierarchical schemes make naive assumptions about consumer behaviour. Such assumptions may once have been justified but they are no longer so. Canberra's experience clearly demonstrates that shopping centres alone will not meet consumers' needs, and that, however significant their impact on urban form, they cannot be the sole components of future retail structure.

Besides planned shopping centres large individual stores affect urban form. A few of these stores locate in central areas, but the majority are situated in suburban, edge-of-town or out-of-town locations. Conventionally superstores are large shops selling food as well as other commodities which provide an opportunity for genuine one-stop shopping. Notwithstanding this, definitions of superstores vary (Price, 1985), but the increasing importance of this type of grocery trading is incontestable. In Britain superstores developed first in the North but now the South-East is catching up and London is a battleground for development as major operators struggle to secure a share of a lucrative market. While it had authority the Greater London Council preferred central area development and was prepared to accept about 90 stores compared with the 120 outlets sought by the companies themselves. An interesting development is the joint venture between the supermarket company Tesco and Marks and Spencer, whose first combined out-of-town development was opened at Broxbourne in Hertfordshire in February 1988. Perhaps this signifies a move towards North American practice where similar schemes are common, but hitherto in Britain superstores have not been closely associated with stores of comparable size as a rule. Although Marks and Spencer is not a specialist grocery retailer, food sales are an important element in its retail strategy. Significantly the company is trying to adapt to the new trading circumstances by retaining its traditional shopping street base while also taking advantage of edge-of-town opportunities. The company will have completed by the end of 1988 a £1.5 million store refurbishment programme and it intends to open nearly 500 000 square feet (46 000 square metres) of new shopping space in high street locations each year. Currently, however, it has a dozen edge-of-town developments which will add 1.5 million square feet (139 000 square metres) of selling space and the same number are at the planning stage. Europe's experience has been similar to Britain's in respect of superstores. France played a prominent role in the emergence of hypermarkets (a term reserved for superstores with over 5000 square metres (54 000 square feet) of selling space). West Germany has more superstores than any other Western European country, though the individual units are usually smaller than their French counterparts.

Retail warehouses selling non-food items have been more important than superstores in stimulating retail suburbanisation in the UK (Jones, 1984). During the period 1979–81 some 196 retail warehouses were opened by 12 of the major operators—three times the number of superstores opened. While it may be true that the customers come from the more mobile and affluent suburban sections of society, Jones argued that development strategies geared to raising profit levels are the important element in helping to explain innovations in retailing style. These innovations in their turn created a demand for out-of-town sites. Geographically retail warehouses are concentrated in the major conurbations, but less than half were located within or adjacent to a shopping centre.

Another type of single-store development which originated in the USA in the 1920s but which did not develop rapidly until the early 1960s is the convenience store (Jones, 1988). In North America the total number of convenience stores rose from 2500 in 1960 to 58 000 in the mid-1980s. A large number of chains, each with its own unique store layout and design, are involved. Southlands Corporation, trading as 7-Eleven and Quick Mart, is the largest operator with 8000 stores in 41 American states and five Canadian provinces. Other major chains include Circle K (2700 stores), Convenience Food Marts (1200 stores), and National Convenience Stores (1100 stores). Franchising forms a significant element in the organisation of some major chains, and recently joint stores and petrol stations have become increasingly common in the USA. The convenience store has been adopted in the UK, where stores occupying between 50 and 300 square metres (540–3200 square feet) of retail floorspace have been developed in residential areas. Location is important, for store operators try to be close to the central or focal point of a residential area for the convenience of pedestrian shoppers while at the same time offering adjacent car parking to attract passing motorists. Convenience is expressed in a number of ways such as opening hours of at least 16 hours per day, seven-day opening, and a self-service layout with a product range geared to meeting the emergency and impulse needs of the local population. It has been found that convenience stores are useful for 'topping up' a consumer's requirments to supplement one-stop shopping at large superstores. Also, as discretionary income has increased so a greater premium is placed on convenience rather than cheapness in shopping.

Three types of convenience store operation can be identified in the UK. A small group of specialist companies, among whom Sperrings, Misselbrook and Weston, and 7-Eleven are prominent, have embarked on convenience store programmes. Initial development has been concentrated in Greater London and southern England. By 1986 Sperrings, which started in Southampton, had 60 stores in southern England and many of these were franchised. Misselbrook and Weston also started in Southampton and by 1986 had 50 stores, almost all of which are within neighbourhood shopping districts serving residential areas of 3500–8000 people. This company favours sites close to hairdressers, sub-post offices, chemists, public houses (inns), youth clubs, schools and health centres, and with access to car parking. Most 7-Eleven stores are in busy suburban shopping areas within Greater London. Circle K and Lalani Foods are two smaller specialist convenience store groups operating in London. A second type of convenience store involves the conversion of existing shops to a new trading format, a trend in which voluntary groups are playing a major role. Spar, for example, launched an 'Eight till Late' conversion programme in 1981, and by 1986 some 1000 of Spar's 2700 outlets had been converted to this format, which according to Spar can double a store's customers and increase turnover by 60 per cent. Mace introduced their Convenience Express scheme in 1985. Cullens, an independent supermarket operator, has embarked on a conversion programme and has ambitious plans for expansion. Major petroleum companies seeking to exploit the market presented by the 20 million cars driving onto petrol station forecourts each week have developed the third type of convenience store. Included under this heading are Texaco's Star Food Shops, Murco's Shopstop, BP's Foodplan, Ultramar's Ultraspar, and Total's Petropolis. If they are to be successful forecourt convenience stores may need to attract pedestrian customers as well as motorists.

Convenience store operators stress that they are not in direct competition with large supermarket and superstore groups, but if they adopt aggressive marketing strategies they may further reduce the economic viability of small supermarkets and independent shopkeepers. This may lead to closures, but there are likely to be 4000–6000 convenience stores trading in the UK in the mid-1990s and they may provide a valuable improvement in the level of retail provision for some sections of the population. So far convenience stores have been concentrated in southern England where disposable incomes are highest, rather than elsewhere in the country where the concept may not prove so successful. Nevertheless, the voluntary groups and the petroleum companies already have national networks available should they wish to expand their operations. Although the British stores differ in trading style and product range from the original North American counterparts they both represent a new element in the changing structure of retail geography which may contribute to the revitalisation of traditional shopping areas.

Wholesaling has also moved outwards. Traditional land-use models place wholesaling in a fringe zone adjacent to the CBD. As Tunbridge (1986) put it, warehouses benefit from the good access but poor environment of the 'zone of discard' in the CBD. Some clustering of wholesaling premises occurred in this zone, especially if a well-defined market in the core was being served. Events overtook the conditions assumed in the traditional models because many inner-city depots were multi-storey and not very well adapted to modern handling techniques and equipment. The increasing cost of operating a central facility was a problem, so inner-city sites are giving way to purpose-built single-storey buildings on suburban sites often located on industrial estates. Space and rent considerations, not to mention costly delays occasioned by traffic congestion in the inner areas, put a premium on non-central sites with easy access to motorways. Disused sites such as those in London's docklands may be particularly attractive, but perhaps the most dramatic expression of decentralisation has been the migration of city wholesale markets for fresh foods. Covent Garden (fruit and vegetables), Billingsgate (fish), and Smithfield (meat) markets in London have moved, and in Paris Les Halles moved out to Rungis. Similar developments have occurred in other European cities, prompted by the decline in wholesale market trade caused by the bypassing of central markets as large integrated wholesalers take complete control over fruit and vegetable wholesaling to their own depots and retailers. The process of decentralisation is well illustrated by the wholesaling parks developed as transhipment centres. Dawson (1982a) reported that there were

30 of these in Europe in the late 1970s, including that at Toulouse which comprised 33 enterprises. He also noted the emergence of specialist cold storage facilities such as Frigoscandia Food Town at Kings Lynn. These new developments provide access to larger markets compared with the smaller geographical areas served from the traditional small warehouses, especially those in ports like London or Liverpool. Nor must it be forgotten that retailers have increasingly come to exert control over distribution and in so doing are helping to change the geography of physical distribution systems (Sparks, 1986). Stimulated by changes in retailing, major store groups are looking closely at their distribution systems. Tesco is developing new-style warehouses called composites which carry most of the goods needed by a large store chain in a single depot. Each composite will be about 250 000 square feet (23 000 square metres) in size and will be fully computerised for stock control purposes; they will be capable of handling 30 million cases a year. Composite systems are based on cost-effectiveness and should reduce distribution costs by 15 per cent. A particular advantage over single systems lies in the better utilisation of vehicle fleets. Superstores run by Tesco will receive several deliveries every working day, leading to 'just-in-time' deliveries which will substantially reduce the storage space required at stores. Compared with traditional systems which might require as much as 60 per cent of a store's space for storage, composites are expected to reduce this need to 25 per cent and the aim is to go lower than this. Tesco has joined with four distribution specialists to introduce the new system, but it is not alone in doing so, for Marks and Spencer and J. Sainsbury and other grocery chains are developing this type of facility. Wholesaling, like retailing, is a dynamic service activity which has a visible presence in urban areas. As this discussion has shown, important changes are occurring in retailing and wholesaling provision that are having a significant effect on urban form.

*Office activities*

Business, insurance and financial activities require much office space and they are prominent in outlying areas as well as in the CBD. A simple distinction between *general* and *headquarters* offices is useful because the former are diverse in nature, may be small, and may serve comparatively localised markets. Since a central location is not necessarily essential for them they are often among the first to decentralise. As with retailing, there has been much suburbanisation of office activities, and the number of specialised office parks (analogous to industrial estates) in the suburbs is growing. Headquarters offices are usually larger and aim to serve national or international markets. They may benefit from a central location which makes them accessible to a large pool of skilled labour, but they will seek such a situation because they have linkages with other firms, have a pressing need for good communications with others which are encouraged by proximity, and have a requirement for a prestigious location. The outcome of these influences is the development of office quarters which are distinctive components of the urban landscape in major cities. Since Chapter 7 provides more details of the nature and geographical extent of office activities, the impact of offices on urban form is only briefly discussed here.

Goddard (1967) identified the City district as the major financial centre and Westminster as the main centre for government offices in London. Others have noted the presence of general offices in Westminster. The City has long been recognised as a distinctive area within London, and in the post-war period the increasing number of high-rise buildings has given it a marked and controversial physical form. City activities thrive on the receipt, exchange and manipulation of information, and in the past there was good reason to value proximity as an aid to face-to-face communication. Modern communication systems have not obviated this need, for businessmen still believe that they gain much from personal contacts which are often no more than the exchange of gossip over lunch. Claims for the importance of linkages are not figments of the City's imagination. Daniels (1982) quoted a Manchester study showing that banks, insurance offices, accountants and lawyers had strong working links, and even outside this core group there were lesser linkages. All of this encourages clustering in a central location. Another type of need is ease of access to government officials which may be necessary for the smooth working of a firm. For this reason the head offices of national and international companies seek a location close to the government offices in the Whitehall area of Westminster. Because there are powerful competing interests such as retailing the West End office quarter is less conspicuous than that of the City though in fact it possesses more office space. Apart from the intermingling of other activities offices may not be so obvious in the West End because they occupy older premises which for reasons of architectural merit are preserved, as for example in Portland Place and Cavendish Square. It is also true that a West End address is prestigious and this in itself is a factor which attracts firms. In the City and the West End the concentration of offices has a multiplier effect in that shops catering for office supplies are numerous; pubs, restaurants, cafés and sandwich shops abound, and various business services such as printers and telex bureaux are present.

Downtown Manhattan, at the southern end of Manhattan Island, is a financial centre challenging the City of London since the federal government relaxed its regulations in 1978 to create what amounts to a financial 'free-trade zone'. Midtown Manhattan (like London's West End) has more office space— 13.9 million square metres (149.6 million square feet) compared with 8.4 million square metres (90.4 million square feet) (Bateman, 1985)—and since 1950 has emerged as a centre for corporate headquarters and foreign banks which increased in number from 50 in 1972 to 250 in 1980. For a while midtown Manhattan outstripped the older centre, but rent differentials are narrowing which suggests that the downtown area is recovering. North America pioneered the skyscraper and contributed to what has become the hallmark of thriving office centres throughout the world. New York typifies this development.

The examples of London and New York illustrate that there may be differentiation in office quarters within cities giving rise to distinctive urban areas. The pattern is repeated, albeit on a smaller scale, in other major cities even down to quite low levels in the urban hierarchy. Instead of having specialised office areas in different parts of the city, smaller centres may possess identifiable sectors with particular activities within a single office quarter.

Large provincial cities are increasingly coming to acquire high-rise office buildings which make the office quarter instantly recognisable, and even a modest country market town is likely to exhibit some clustering of office activities to form a mini or incipient office district.

*Medical and educational facilities*

Medical and educational institutions are organisations which make an important contribution to urban form. Whitehand's model would seem to be appropriate for studying the location of these institutions, though many teaching hospitals and universities lie within the central areas of cities rather than on the fringe or even the former fringe.

Specialised medical facilities at the upper end of the medical services hierarchy tend to be associated with larger hospitals. It is frequently pointed out that famous teaching hospitals are situated in inner-city areas from which the local population has migrated; for example, Sydney (D. M. Smith, 1979) and Chicago (Morrill and Earickson, 1968b). Recent attempts to redistribute resources within the British National Health Service (NHS) by relating financial allocations to local resident population led to fierce protests from London teaching hospitals which feel that this criterion harms them unduly even though allowances are made for their teaching functions. The size of the investment in a major hospital makes relocation impracticable in the short term, and there is the argument that patients benefit from a central location because they can share public transport facilities and the highway network. Large teaching hospitals, notable features in the urban landscape in their own right, have a multiplier effect manifested by the presence of ancillary facilities such as medical bookshops and shops selling surgical instruments, medical supplies or florists. Ambulance depots may also be close at hand.

In very large cities specialised medical areas may develop, as was recognised by Berry (1967) in his classification of the commercial structure of the North American city. London's Harley Street, which has an international reputation, is a classic example. Here are to be found surgeries (or medical offices) of specialist consultants, and such is the prestige of a Harley Street address that some medical premises round the corner in another street nevertheless carry a Harley Street address. Ancillary medical facilities are located in surrounding streets. Apart from its plethora of brass plates, Harley Street differs little from surrounding streets in its appearance. This is also true of other medical facilities. For example, family planning clinics are not great consumers of space and are scarcely distinguishable from neighbouring commercial premises. However, these clinics often seek a central location; a study of the distribution of clinics in London showed that whereas basic services were very widely distributed the more specialist family planning services were highly centralised (Price and Cummings, 1977). Clinic users confirmed that they preferred to use central London clinics, either to preserve their anonymity or else because of the convenience of visiting a facility close to their workplace.

Primary health care is dispensed from surgeries which may be part of a doctor's house or a former residence that has been converted. Little is done to enhance the appearance of medical offices for, unlike shops, they are not intended to attract the passing customer. They are rarely sufficiently concentrated to make a significant impact on urban form. Knox (1978; 1979a and b) found that in Aberdeen, Dundee, Glasgow and Edinburgh there were few surgeries located in the CBDs, few in post-war peripheral estates and a relative concentration in poorer inner-city areas. Thus, there is a parallel with the mismatch between the location of teaching hospitals and the resident population and it was felt that the relatively poor people in peripheral housing estates were disadvantaged. As long ago as 1920 the case for concentrating primary care personnel under one roof was advanced, and the concept of health centres was included in the Act of Parliament, passed in 1946, which set up the NHS. Such centres were intended to house doctors, dentists, pharmacists, nurses, opticians, family planning clinics, baby clinics and other community services. The British Medical Association recommended that a viable health centre should accommodate ten medical practitioners serving an average of 25 000 people. Facilities of this sort would be large enough to become conspicuous features in the urban landscape, but by 1958 only ten centres had been opened. Even in 1969 only 131 were operating, with a further 79 under construction (Phillips, 1981).

Educational establishments are also major space consumers. Higher (post-school) education has heavy space demands for laboratories, libraries, lecture theatres and halls of residence. Major cities such as London, Paris and New York possess several higher education institutions which collectively occupy a large area within the city. Imposing buildings like King's College in London may be compared with the larger hospitals in their impact on urban form, but the original building in the Strand is only part of King's. University expansion was accompanied by the acquisition of nearby properties to house offices and academic departments. In this instance the use of the buildings has changed but not their appearance. Around London University's Senate House, itself a landmark, there is a veritable university quarter consisting of Birkbeck College, University College, the London University Students' Union and other premises in Torrington Square, Woburn Square, Gordon Square and Bedford Way. The Latin Quarter around the Sorbonne is another university-related area which, like London, has its full complement of service trades like bookshops and coffee bars. A similar quarter can be identified in Ann Arbor, Michigan, or Toronto, Ontario. British provincial universities like Manchester, Liverpool, Leeds, Sheffield and Bristol have all expanded from fairly restricted sites by purchasing surrounding property. Sometimes the need to build new facilities for engineering, medicine and science requires the demolition of older property, and in Bristol the dominant position of these new developments on a hill overlooking the city centre has had a notable impact on the city skyline. Elsewhere in Bristol the new Arts Faculty building is housed in a clever conversion of premises undertaken to preserve the character of the area though its use has changed greatly. Extreme examples of the effect of university institutions on urban form are provided by Oxford, Cambridge, Heidelberg and Princeton which were virtually created by the universities that still dominate them. More recently the British post-war campus universities like Sussex or East Anglia have become renowned for their spacious settings in

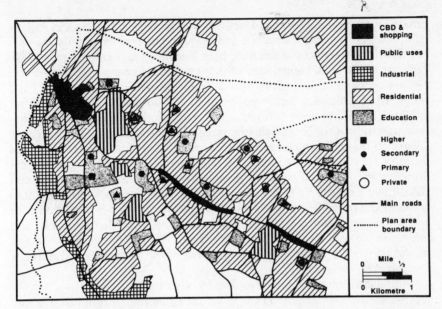

**Figure 5.1** Education provision and urban land use in the central part of the London Borough of Hillingdon, 1986
*Sources*: London Borough of Hillingdon and field work, 1986

urban fringe locations. In this respect they follow the examples of many North American and Australian universities. Some North American institutions like Berkeley, California, and Cambridge, Massachusetts, are self-contained communities, or towns within towns, on the edge of cities.

Schools and colleges also contribute to the spatial land-use structure of towns. A few occupy central locations, but the majority are situated elsewhere. Part of the London Borough of Hillingdon (Figure 5.1) shows quite clearly how educational uses are not only widespread but also make extensive use of land with their buildings and playing fields. Located for convenient access to residential areas and avoidance of industrial and commercial activities, educational land uses are an important component of city structures. Large playing fields help to soften the landscape by providing green space, and in certain areas the playing fields are available to meet local recreational demand outside school hours. In the same way school halls may provide a meeting place for local societies thus contributing to the enrichment of community life. Some authorities deliberately design school premises to be multi-purpose for this reason.

*Leisure and recreation facilities*

What Burkart and Medlik (1981) referred to as infrastructural and superstructural facilities serve the leisure and recreational needs of visiting tourists and local residents. The infrastructure consists of all forms of construction at or below ground level including lines of access and communications (roads and railways) and facilities providing essential services such as light, heat, power, water, drainage and sewage. The resident population benefits from these services which have been calculated as accounting for 15–20 per cent of the total capital cost of development (Lawson and Baud-Bovy, 1977). Superstructural facilities include traffic terminals, hotels, theatres and shops, all of which are highly visible in the urban landscape. Ideally infrastructure should precede superstructure, but resorts tend to develop spontaneously without the benefit of a preconceived plan so that many tourist centres fail to offer the optimum provision by modern standards. Usually superstructural facilities are planned individually by their operators, which results in great diversity and a lack of coherent planning in many instances. Lawson and Baud-Bovy attribute 50–60 per cent of capital costs in tourist development to accommodation and catering facilities. A further 10–15 per cent should be added for other tourist facilities. Superstructure costs, then, are the most important element in tourist development and this is reflected in the contribution they make to the visible components of the geographical features of tourism.

Natural attractions not complemented by other tourist facilities rarely satisfy tourists in their own right. There is a built environment of tourism whose history extends back to Roman times when spas were significant. Today winter and coastal resorts are more popular and produce distinctive urban forms. Resorts include some spas for health and entertainment (Baden-Baden, Bath, Vichy), climatic resorts for convalescence (Menton), Alpine resorts (Chamonix, Zermatt) and seaside resorts (Bordighera, Brighton and Deauville). Robinson (1976) offered an alternative categorisation of places developed exclusively as resorts (Blackpool, Monte Carlo, Languedoc-Rousillon, Niagara Falls) and places developed incidentally as resorts (Stratford-on-Avon, Miami, Williamsburg).

Tourist development usually begins round a core, often the seafront, and expands outwards. The core contains the major shops, catering and entertainment facilities, and hotels. As the resort grows a concentric pattern of architectural and social stratification takes shape. Imposing private residences and hotels occupy the prime locations, while boarding houses and bed-and-breakfast accommodation are found in less central positions. Frequently the core is aligned along a route linking the railway station with the 'front' producing a characteristic T-shape in the layout of the core and frontal amenities of a seaside resort. Later expansion may result in linear development along the coast to create an unbroken line of accommodation and other resort facilities which may ultimately form a coastal conurbation (for example, Brighton). Radial expansion along routeways may also occur, and while there may be few facilities capable of attracting tourists on their own there may be golf courses, tennis courts, or attractively laid out parks, as in Brighton's London Road, which contribute to the town's appeal by enhancing its image.

The world's major cities attract large numbers of tourists; for example, over 60 per cent of overseas tourists visiting the UK in 1982 spent some time in London. Hotels are needed to accommodate these visitors and many former residential neighbourhoods in the inner areas have been invaded by new hotels. Covent Garden and St Katherine's Dock are examples of former com-

**Table 5.1** Percentage of hotel bed-spaces in England located in London, 1983

| Size of establishment (no. of bedrooms) | Distribution of bed-spaces (%) |
|---|---|
| 1– 3 | 0.02 |
| 4– 10 | 0.25 |
| 11– 15 | 0.48 |
| 16– 28 | 0.95 |
| 29– 50 | 1.64 |
| 51–100 | 2.39 |
| 101–200 | 3.39 |
| 200+ | 11.19 |

*Source:* British Tourist Authority, *Digest of Tourist Statistics, 1984–5.*

mercial areas where hotels have replaced older functions. Some modern hotels may be aesthetically displeasing to many observers but well-designed hotels can make a positive contribution to the rehabilitation of decaying inner-city areas. London's share of the total number of bed-spaces in England is 20.34 per cent, and, as the figures in Table 5.1 show, over half of this share was in the largest size category of hotel.

Conference centres are a comparatively recent form of tourist development. Burtenshaw (1985) cites the Cologne Exhibition Centre in West Germany, a 212 000 square metre (2.28 million square feet) complex which holds 26 fairs and 800 conferences a year. It employs 370 staff and has an estimated employment multiplier of 40 000. Some 17 per cent of local businesses can claim 20 per cent extra turnover directly attributable to trade fairs. In London conferences generate sums of £150 million per annum with delegates spending £68–£98 per day. Of this, 43 per cent filters down to hotels, 31 per cent to shops and 12 per cent to restaurants. British Rail Eastern Region alone announced earnings of £300 000 generated by conference travel. An indication of the value of conferences and the need to provide centres for them is the importance Brighton, Blackpool and Bournemouth attach to attracting the annual Party Political Conferences. Similarly, party conventions in the USA generate huge revenues for cities with appropriate facilities, like Atlanta, Georgia.

Hotels and conference centres cater for visitors rather than residents. Recreation facilities, on the other hand, are probably equally well, if not better, used by the local population. Many regard the central city's recreational facilities as the city itself. London may thus be associated with the West End theatre district, the Royal Parks and the Leicester Square cinemas (movie theatres), while New York may be synonymous with Broadway. Although capital or primate cities are usually the places with the most impressive array of recreational facilities, smaller cities have their complement of theatres, restaurants and cinemas.

Most of the large prestigious luxury cinemas which are the first to obtain

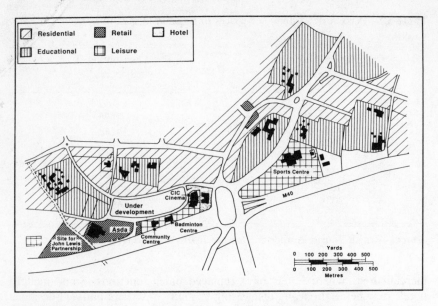

**Figure 5.2** An out-of-town service sector complex, High Wycombe, 1987

new releases are situated in city centres. Leicester Square in London is well known for its cinemas, and because film releases generally follow a hierarchical principle in the UK the first showings occur here or elsewhere in the West End. A few weeks later the London suburbs and major provincial centres like Birmingham and Manchester can show the films, and eventually they reach smaller towns and provincial suburbs. Cinemas remain an important form of entertainment and the buildings designed for film shows still make a distinctive contribution to the urban fabric. Cinema attendances have, however, declined and many have been converted to other uses. Closures have been especially concentrated in the suburbs and smaller towns, and frequently the cinema itself has disappeared as its site has been used for redevelopment. In common with other activities described in this chapter cinemas have decentralised, as was apparent when suburban cinemas first opened, but currently the prospect of building out-of-town multi-screen cinemas seems to be interesting promoters. One such venture situated close to a motorway interchange near the small town of High Wycombe opened in July 1987 and is proving very successful. There is a parallel here with out-of-town shopping centres, and the developments at High Wycombe (see Figure 5.2) may well herald a future trend in cinema location. Cinema attendances are beginning to rise again and in anticipation of the new demand multi-screen cinemas (multiplexes) are also being built in central areas.

Live theatres, which are older institutions than cinemas, have long been associated with cities. In the London of Shakespeare's day, theatres were located in the contemporary urban fringe beyond the city boundaries in the entertainment district of Southwark. Today theatres locate in the centre, with London's Shaftesbury Avenue or New York's Broadway being flourishing centres. As Figure 5.3 illustrates, London has a very high density of theatres

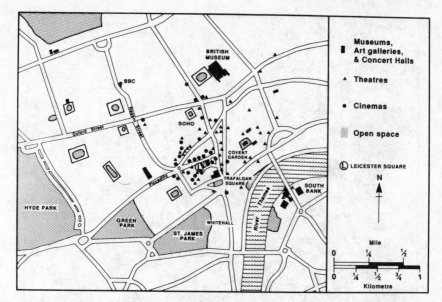

**Figure 5.3** Principal places of entertainment in Central London

in the West End. Where theatres concentrate together as they do along Shaftesbury Avenue, they comprise a pervasive element in the urban scene, especially when they are illuminated at night.

Parks and gardens, which may result from deliberate planning or historical accident, greatly influence the urban morphology of several great cities. Newer cities in North America and Australia laid out in the nineteenth and twentieth centuries contained parkland as an integral part, witness Australia's 'parkland towns' (Williams, 1966), of which Adelaide, with its grid square plan and ring of parkland round the city centre, is a typical example. New York's Central Park was designed by Frederick Law Olmstead and Calvert de Vaux during the years 1857–76. In an area of over 800 acres (3.2 square kilometres) something of the woodland typical of that encountered by the first Dutch Settlers has been retained, and the whole area of open parkland can be regarded as the finest feature of the island of Manhattan. The park, which is now designated a National Historic Landmark, is over one-and-a-half miles long and is nearly a mile wide, and forms a remarkable lung in the middle of such a congested area. It is also an effective 'break' between different types of urban land use. Recognition of the need for recreational space for urban crowds could not be met by throwing open land formerly reserved for the reigning families as in the case of the Luxembourg Gardens in Paris or Kensington Gardens in London, but apart from Central Park New York City made early provision for public space by purchasing large private estates to establish Prospect Park in Brooklyn (1859) and Bronx Park (1884).

Older European cities differ in being the product of centuries of accretion and successive generations of planning overlaid on one another. Royal palaces and ancient defensive works provide Copenhagen with the bulk of its open space and parkland in the city centre (see Figure 5.4). The Renaissance defen-

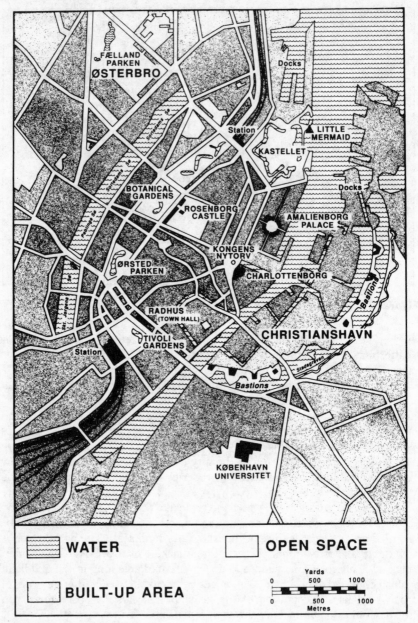

**Figure 5.4** Central Copenhagen
*Source:* Copenhagen City map, 1980

sive work of the Kastellet and the bastions of the Christianshaven are still obviously warlike in origin, but the Botanical Gardens are less clearly sited on the ramparts. The canals ringing the city centre are further relics of the old water barrier on the landward side. Together with the Rosenborg castle grounds and the Tivoli gardens, 9 per cent of Copenhagen's land area is taken up by parkland and open space. London has a similar proportion, but much of it is concentrated in the Royal Parks of the West End, which makes the capital appear greener than it really is. Many cities possess far more open space: the Hague, 22 per cent; Berlin, 13 per cent; Vienna, 25 per cent; Oslo, 45 per cent; and Stockholm, 56 per cent (Darin-Drabkin, 1977).

Technically parks and gardens may not be regarded as part of the service sector, particularly as many park employees are not classified as service workers. However, their function is recreational and they do attract ancillary activities such as restaurants, cafés, open air theatres, and provision for playing games. So important are these open spaces that new parks were created as cities expanded; for example, Victoria Park in the East London district of Stepney and Battery Park at the southernmost tip of Manhattan. In time these sub-urban parks were bypassed, though they remained in the urban structure. Fashions changed, and from the 1880s in Britain emphasis was placed on smaller parks, gardens and recreation grounds. By 1900 specially designed children's playgrounds were being introduced. Individual town corporations and private philanthropists participated in these developments, but interest varied so levels of provision differed between cities. A further development in the late nineteenth and early twentieth centuries was the emergence of gran-diose 'amusement' parks and pleasure gardens ranging from the elegance of Copenhagen's Tivoli Gardens to the brash commercial funfairs of the Coney Island, Battersea or Barry Island variety. These amusement parks were often permanent forms of travelling funfair, but the modern version culminates in the highly sophisticated technical wizardry of something like Disneyland and other 'theme parks'.

# Conclusion

The service sector plays a vital role in the life and development of urban areas, and despite the comparative neglect of recent times there is ample justi-fication for the 'resurgence of interest in urban morphology' (Freeman, 1987). Shopping streets, office areas, hospital and educational precincts, and leisure and recreational facilities have their own distinctive characteristics which help to mould the appearance of an urban area and the way it works. These activities illustrate the effect powerful centrifugal forces can have in modifiying the form of the built-up area, but they also provide examples of the rival centripetal forces that act to preserve the dominance of central areas. The resolution of the conflicts engendered by these opposing tendencies helps to account for the dynamism that affects and reshapes urban morphology.

Many examples cited in this chapter have been drawn from capital cities. Places of this size are so large that it is difficult to visualise the total impact of the various functions that have been discussed. At a smaller scale it is possible to understand just how much service activities contribute to the features of cities. Figure 5.5 depicts the location and distribution of recent and planned large developments in the service industries in Miami and Dade County. It should be remembered that the total contributions of service activities to Miami's urban fabric is actually greater than is shown here because older

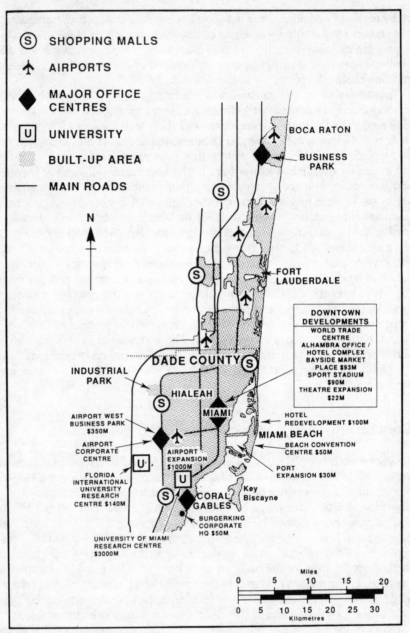

**S** SHOPPING MALLS

✈ AIRPORTS

◆ MAJOR OFFICE CENTRES

[U] UNIVERSITY

▒ BUILT-UP AREA

— MAIN ROADS

N

BOCA RATON

BUSINESS PARK

FORT LAUDERDALE

**DOWNTOWN DEVELOPMENTS**
WORLD TRADE CENTRE
ALHAMBRA OFFICE / HOTEL COMPLEX
BAYSIDE MARKET PLACE $93M
SPORT STADIUM $90M
THEATRE EXPANSION $22M

INDUSTRIAL PARK

DADE COUNTY

HIALEAH

MIAMI

HOTEL REDEVELOPMENT $100M

MIAMI BEACH

AIRPORT WEST BUSINESS PARK $350M

BEACH CONVENTION CENTRE $50M

AIRPORT CORPORATE CENTRE

AIRPORT EXPANSION $1000M

PORT EXPANSION $30M

FLORIDA INTERNATIONAL UNIVERSITY RESEARCH CENTRE $140M

Key Biscayne

CORAL GABLES

BURGERKING CORPORATE HQ $50M

UNIVERSITY OF MIAMI RESEARCH CENTRE $3000M

Miles
0    5    10    15    20

0    5    10    15    20    25    30
Kilometres

**Figure 5.5** Recent and planned large development in the service industry in Miami and Dade county, Florida, 1987
*Source: Fortune,* June 1987

developments are not included on the map. Retailing is represented by a number of new shopping malls; office activities by business parks, the Coral Gables office centre and the corporate headquarters of Burger King; education by research centres; and, not unexpectedly, there is a range of tourist developments, including airports. Specific new health care projects are not large enough to be shown here, but Miami regards itself as a health-care mecca with an impressive amount of hospital provision. Although the majority of the schemes depicted are suburban or edge-of-town in location there is also evidence of vitality in the downtown area. An indication of the thriving nature of Miami's service sector is provided by the amount of investment entailed in these developments. The example of Miami encapsulates the dynamism and extent of service sector activities within a city and makes an appropriate conclusion to this discussion of the importance of services in urban morphology. Like most cities with a flourishing service economy Miami is constantly changing and growing.

*Chapter 6*

# Technological Influences and their Locational Significance

Unquestionably technological innovations that characterised the Industrial Revolution profoundly affected the geography of manufacturing industry. Service activities are now in the forefront of technological development and locational consequences derive from this. Much technological development is *internal* to the sector in that new equipment and ideas become part of the operation of service industries, but there are many *external* technological developments influencing the demand for and utilisation of services. Transport innovation, so crucial to the Industrial Revolution, is also an external factor of great significance to the service sector. Formerly the emphasis was on the physical transfer of goods, and this remains important in the distribution field. Improvements in personal mobility have widened residential choice for employees and their firms, helped tourism to flourish, and modified patterns of consumer usage in respect of retail, medical and leisure facilities. Vital to the service sector are changes in telecommunications and information technology which facilitate the flow of ideas and help to transform urban and regional systems by doing so. Here recent developments in transport are briefly discussed before the characteristics of the new technology are examined. The impact of the new technology on employment is considered, and the effects on producer and consumer services are explored.

## Recent transport developments

*Private cars*

Cars have greatly influenced the development of a range of services (for example, out-of-town shopping centres) and have been a major force in encouraging decentralisation and suburbanisation. Table 6.1 shows the growth of private car ownership in advanced countries. The USA and Sweden, with very high levels of ownership, exhibited little growth between 1975 and 1983. High car ownership does not mean that *all* the population will drive; some will be too young, others too old, and along with the disabled and those who do not want or need to drive they comprise a substantial minority. Hence there are limits to the growth of this innovation, but formerly less affluent nations like Greece and Spain are now in a phase of rapid expansion. The fig-

**Table 6.1** Growth of private car ownership (per 1000 population) in advanced nations, 1975 and 1983

|  | 1975 | 1983 | Increase (%) |
|---|---|---|---|
| Belgium | 267 | 331 | 24 |
| Denmark | 256 | 272 | 6 |
| West Germany | 289 | 400 | 38 |
| Greece | 49 | 109 | 122 |
| France | 290 | 372 | 28 |
| Ireland | 165 | 206 | 25 |
| Italy | 270 | 345 | 28 |
| Luxembourg | 357 | 385 | 8 |
| Netherlands | 254 | 332 | 31 |
| Portugal | 84 | n.a. | n.a. |
| Spain | 119 | 228 | 92 |
| Sweden | 336 | 361 | 7 |
| UK | 249 | 318 | 28 |
| USA | 495 | 535 | 8 |
| Japan | 143 | 224 | 57 |

*Source*: *Eurostat Review*, 1986, Table 3.2.1.
n.a. = not available

ures suggest that trends associated with the availability of motor cars will show no signs of abating.

## Railways

Goods traffic has suffered greater relative decline than passenger traffic in most countries (see Table 6.2). Rail passenger traffic increased in France, the Netherlands and Denmark, and even in the UK there has been a slight rise to compensate for the fall in goods traffic. Evidently the railways have not gone into terminal decline. Considerable advances in the use of computers for signalling and general passenger services have made an impact. In France and Japan new high-speed trains have outclassed the domestic airlines for speed, comfort and price. Railways suffer from governments' unwillingness to invest in them compared with their readiness to subsidise road transport by paying for new roads. On the other hand, developments such as the Channel Tunnel should stimulate rail freight and passenger traffic between the UK and France.

## Aviation

Air travel is a classic example of high technology having vast repercussions on a range of other activities. Foreign tourism has been a notable beneficiary. American tourists, for example, have few options but to fly if they wish to

**Table 6.2**   Changes in goods and passenger traffic on railways in Europe 1975–83/84

|  | Index of Goods Traffic 1984 1975 = 100 | Index of Passengers carried 1983 1975 = 100 |
|---|---|---|
| Belgium | 120 | 82 |
| Denmark | 94 | 156 |
| West Germany | 109 | 105 |
| Greece | 78 | 92 |
| France | 88 | 111 |
| Ireland | 100 | 93 |
| Italy | 111 | 98 |
| Luxembourg | 115 | 100 |
| Netherlands | 60 | 115 |
| UK | 95 | 104 |

*Source: Eurostat Review*, 1986, Tables 7.2.5 and 7.2.6.

travel outside North America, and in the 1960s and 1970s the growth of the package tour industry was based on the ability to fill aircraft seats at reduced costs by flying large parties abroad to cheap destinations in the sun. Civil aviation trends during the 1970s are illustrated in Table 6.3. In contrast to the experience elsewhere the number of American airlines declined greatly as did the figures for the number of passenger-kilometres flown, chiefly because oil price rises and hence fare increases have hit the airlines badly. Aircraft numbers generally declined owing to increases in the capacity of aircraft such as the Boeing 747 (the 'Jumbo Jet'). Tourism, on which aviation depends so heavily, is a notoriously fickle trade, as the widespread desertion of Europe by Americans reacting to exaggerated fears of terrorism testifies.

## The characteristics of the new technology

While high levels of communication distinguish the service economy and great advances have been made in telecommunications, the vast and growing amount of conventional mail carried in the advanced nations should not be overlooked. Except for Spain and Portugal mail deliveries increased substantially between 1975 and 1984 (see Table 6.4). Large quantities of direct mail contributed to this, and the practice of sharing or selling mailing lists has increased the likelihood of an individual's receiving mailshots from organisations like charities, Reader's Digest and other mail order companies. Increasingly magazines and journals regularly mail their subscribers—11 million *National Geographic* magazines are despatched each month. Although people write fewer personal letters, they continue to receive much mail ranging from credit card prospectuses to tax demands, bills, offers of timeshare apartments and bookclub lists. An efficient postal system which takes advantage of transport

**Table 6.3** Changes in civil aviation in advanced nations 1972–81

| | No. of Airlines | | Aircraft | | Passenger-kilometres (millions) | |
|---|---|---|---|---|---|---|
| | 1972 | 1981 | 1972 | 1981 | 1972 | 1981 |
| Belgium | 1 | 1 | 27 | 26 | 6 325 | 5 197 |
| Denmark | * | * | * | * | * | 2 970 |
| West Germany | 1 | 1 | 78 | 96 | 18 956 | 21 635 |
| Greece | 1 | 1 | 43 | 44 | 5 207 | 5 184 |
| France | 2 | 2 | 126 | 121 | 27 700 | 31 876 |
| Ireland | 1 | 1 | 16 | 19 | 2 695 | 2 270 |
| Italy | 1 | 1 | 79 | 61 | 17 052 | 12 044 |
| Luxembourg | 0 | 1 | 0 | 9 | 0 | 27 |
| Netherlands | 1 | 1 | 52 | 52 | 15 123 | 15 168 |
| Portugal | 1 | 1 | 19 | 31 | 5 683 | 4 008 |
| Spain | 1 | 1 | 76 | 88 | 13 607 | 15 280 |
| Sweden | 1 | 1 | 74 | 86 | 13 156 | 10 318 |
| UK | 3 | 2 | 209 | 187 | 39 017 | 44 145 |
| USA | 14 | 5 | 1 843 | 1 160 | 418 716 | 231 770 |
| Japan | 1 | 1 | 80 | 83 | 23 458 | 31 916 |

*Source: Eurostat,* 1974; 1976
* Denmark counted in with Sweden (SAS)

and other innovations is indispensable for modern business. Telex, by contrast, is a purely business form of communication and the rise in telex subscribers reflects the higher levels of information exchange in the commercial world. Growth has been greatest in the less advanced Western countries but Japan recorded a decline, possibly because of advances in other forms of communication. As Dicken (1986) observed, the transformation of global communications was very much a post-war event. International telex traffic grew rapidly after 1950, and since 1965 the use of satellites has vastly expanded possibilities. Compared with the 240 telephone conversations or two television channels carried simultaneously by the Intelsat I satellite in 1965 it is predicted that by the year 2000 the Intelsat system will carry 700 000 international voice circuits.

Advances in electronics have accompanied changes in telecommunications. Better capacity and reliability resulted when microchips replaced transistors, while improvements in computers, and notably in the software packages available, have facilitated the processing of vast quantities of data and enhanced the information available to managers. Simultaneously optical fibre development has widened the scope of telecommunications systems. Prior to 1950 improvements in electronics, telecommunications and computers tended to occur separately, but more recently they have converged and together they comprise information technology (Daniels, 1985). Devices linking computers

**Table 6.4** Indices of communication in the advanced world, 1975 and 1983

|  | Letters posted | | Telex subscribers | |
|  | 1983 (millions) | Increase since 1975 (%) | 1983 (thousands) | Increase since 1975 (%) |
| --- | --- | --- | --- | --- |
| Belgium | 2 910 | 23 | 228.0 | 59 |
| Denmark | 1 468 | 52 | 11.3 | 65 |
| Germany FR | 14 898 | 42 | 148.4 | 48 |
| Greece | n.a. | n.a. | 14.8 | 134 |
| France | 14 687 | 24 | 95.4 | 124 |
| Ireland | n.a. | n.a. | 6.5 | 126 |
| Italy | 6 802 | 4 | 50.1 | 177 |
| Luxembourg | 228 | 38 | 2.0 | n.a. |
| Netherlands | 4 697 | 24 | 35.7 | 58 |
| UK | 12 510 | 19 | 92.6 | 61 |
| Spain | 4 350 | −8 | 29.2 | 162 |
| Portugal | 477 | −12 | 11.7 | 414 |
| Sweden | 2 989 | 53 | 15.8 | 56 |
| USA | n.a. | n.a. | 178.6 | 40 |
| Japan | 16 231 | n.a. | 60.0 | −24 |

*Source: Eurostat Review*, 1986, Tables 7.1.1 and 7.1.3
n.a. = not available

together transformed their scope. Henceforth machines in branch offices could interrogate those in head office thus creating the potential for radical change, and much effort has been devoted to making machines at different locations work together (Hepworth, 1987). The new technology can be applied to office activities in the form of mechanisation, computer aids, office information systems, and decision support systems (Daniels, 1985). Currently micro-processors represent the leading edge of change because the automation of certain processes such as the creation, manipulation, storage, duplication and transfer of different types of information in an electronic format depends on them. The possibility of a fully automated office incorporating work stations, local area networks, central facilities, private branch exchanges and external facilities now exists.

By altering the ways in which individual office workers interact, innovations in telecommunications might have a considerable spatial impact. Telex speeded communication between parties, and the teletext system of West Germany, Sweden and the UK has the advantage of permitting the transmission of documents. A striking example of the locational implications of the fax machine is provided by the editor of the newly launched magazine, *Landscape*, who works from home in Jersey far from his staff in

London. In his own words: 'I might simply be in the next room rather than 200 miles across the Channel. Proofs appear instantaneously from the publisher in Cornwall; articles arrive from London in two or three minutes' (*Sunday Telegraph*, 22 November 1987).

Another example of the way in which facsimile transmission may effect major changes in distribution and service activities is provided by the national press in the UK which is sending pages to provincial printing centres by facsimile transmission. International editions are being sent from the UK to continental Europe and North America by satellite. The outcome of this is that the traditional use of railfreight to despatch newspapers from London to stations throughout the country where wholesalers collect them for delivery to newsagents has undergone change. In the face of road competition and the emergence of devolved printing centres British Rail decided to discontinue its delivery train network for national newspapers from July 1988.

Cellular radio, represented by Cellnet and Racal-Vodafone in the UK, promises even greater locational flexibility for some activities, offering mobile communications enabling salesmen to place orders while on the move and allowing key staff to be contacted wherever they are. Because the radio signals employed are not strong enough to travel very far and coverage is dependent on low-power radio stations the system's geographical extent is limited. The places from which calls can be made are restricted, but calls can be made or received from any part of the world. At present the system is strongly biased towards London and South-East England, with some extensions which mirror the motorway network.

Data are most effectively transmitted in digital rather than analogue form because switching (connecting one subscriber to another) can be done electronically. Fibre optic cables greatly reduced transmission costs, but installation is only justified if the volume of use is high and so the benefits are likely to accrue to the biggest users. Hence, networks are likely to reinforce the existing business hierarchy in the immediate future. Gillespie and Goddard (1986) noted that fully electronic exchanges are needed to achieve all the benefits of switching. Unfortunately some areas of the UK already possess semi-automatic exchanges which will have to be amortised before being replaced by completely electronic facilities, and this means there will be lags in provision. Value Added Network Services (VANS) provided by private companies are a new feature of the competitive telecommunications environment—for example, Mercury and Cellnet—but outside the UK's core area British Telecom is a monopoly provider. Although the information economy is big business for producers, within the EEC there is a marked disparity in the uptake of services depending on whether the firms in a region are local or national/international in outlook.

However limitless potential developments arising from the rapid rate of innovation may seem to be they all represent elements in the telecommunications–transport trade-off. Much depends on how distance-sensitive the new developments are, and this may reflect the pricing system adopted for them. Formerly proximity reduced movement costs and encouraged the growth of office quarters, but high operating costs in agglomerations may make other locations more attractive, especially if telecommunications enable business to be transacted satisfactorily. It is assumed that the additional telecommunications cost consequent upon a move will be more than offset by the savings from relinquishing expensive central office space (Erickson, 1986). A differential pricing system could encourage or retard such a trend. For example, standard postal rates apply irrespective of distance according to the nature of the items carried, and are thus neutral as far as locational opportunities are concerned. If prices varied according to the true costs of supplying the service to an individual consumer this might diminish the attractiveness of a freestanding or suburban location. Neither the telephone nor video-conferencing have yet replaced the importance attached to face-to-face contacts, and in practice the telephone seems to be a vehicle for arranging meetings instead of a substitute for them (Daniels, 1985). Ley (1985) confirmed this by studying two firms located respectively in downtown and suburban Vancouver. Surprisingly the managers of the suburban firm who expressed concern at loss of contacts actually work for one of the leading firms in communication technology. Nevertheless, geographers should be interested in the prospect of telecommunications technology making urban agglomeration economies and central place principles obsolete. It is too early to be certain of the locational impact of the opportunities afforded, but without a doubt the service sector has been in the forefront in taking advantage of the advances that have been made.

## New technology and service employment

In the leading advanced economies, where service sector occupations are the chief source of employment, deindustrialisation has occurred and the problem of what to do with the surplus labour is an acute one. Can the service sector absorb the affected workers and how will its ability to do so be affected by technological change? The answer to the latter question requires identification of the information economy occupations which Porat (1977) defined according to the types of job people do. He used the notion of an 'information worker' whose job is primarily concerned with the generation, manipulation, transformation, or processing of information. Seen in these terms employment in the information sector has grown rapidly in Western countries (Gassman, 1981). Even so the outlook is uncertain. No longer is the white-collar worker protected from the effects of automation and the deskilling of white-collar work has become a reality. Extra staff recruited by banks and insurance companies have masked the problem, for the additional work generated by the new methods has been carried out by a declining rate of staff expansion. There will be place- and sector-specific employment effects of information technology depending on a number of factors such as diffusion rates, trends in the demand for services, the size and distribution of the firms adopting the new technology, the effects of merger and reorganisation, the ease with which new technology can be used within different types of services, and the willingness of workers to co-operate with the changes in work practices, job specifications or job status (Daniels, 1985).

Instead of creating new jobs it is feared that information technology will destroy them. Rajan and Cooke (1986), in their study of insurance, building societies and banking, refuse to be dogmatic on this point. They found that extensive applications of information technology in financial institutions have not caused job displacement, and in fact there has been a 40 per cent increase in jobs and a rise in the volume of business done by banks. Thus, increased demand derived in part from the opportunities provided by the new technology may offset the number of old-fashioned clerks displaced by the new equipment. For example, the introduction of credit cards created 15 000 new jobs, and they estimated that improved cost-effectiveness in banks led to a 30 per cent increase in business volume which may have produced 20 000 new jobs. Considerable manpower resources are also required at the design and implementation stage, although thereafter manpower economies may be achieved. Other factors include employee resistance to change which may retard the introduction of new methods so delaying the job losses, and the attitude of customers who prefer personal service, as evidenced by the resistance to self-service in banks. The scope for radical restructuring dependent on the introduction of new technology is greater in large units than in smaller ones in which the automation of one task will have little effect on staff levels because the total staff is so small that it will be needed entirely to deal with other non-automated services. Furthermore, the paternalistic culture of most financial institutions favours incremental rather than wholesale change. It is not inevitable that the introduction of information technology will destroy jobs, but there is little in Rajan and Cooke's analysis to suggest that the new technology will create enough new jobs to compensate for the loss attributable to deindustrialisation.

Some attempts have been made to assess the impact of technological change on the spatial patterns of employment in the UK in major corporations. Peck and Townsend (1987) state that the large manufacturing plants have been disproportionately affected by corporate restructuring. Moreover, large corporations tend to introduce changes simultaneously at a large number of locations so the effect is widespread. Within a firm important technological changes can involve a reallocation of financial resources accompanied by the rationalisation of other activities. Spatial restructuring is a complex process operating at various levels within a firm which may lead to changes in employment totals, employment skill mix, and in female and part-time employment. That somewhat similar considerations apply to service sector firms seems likely. Enderwick (1987) examined the strategy and structure of service sector transnationals and found that, compared with the 1960s and early 1970s, higher value added per head is sought from contemporary overseas investment. Internationally traded services are attractive because they are generally labour-intensive (for example, computer software, consultancy) and offer high value added. Because services have a low import content their domestic income and employment multipliers are increased. Service investments benefit from the growing importance of service output and employment in advanced economies which results in possible compatability between incoming factors (management, capital, service technologies) and locational factors such as skilled labour. Although international service transactions are of increasing significance international market penetration in services is low, and the implication is that such service investments offer great potential in financial and employment terms. Enderwick, however, thought that services are unlikely to make up for the loss of manufacturing jobs in the peripheral regions.

Green and Howells (1987) confirmed this and drew attention to the service sector's heterogeneity in the wide range and quality of jobs it offers. Important differences arise due to distinctions between producer and consumer services, between public and private sectors, and between information and non-information occupations in the service sector. Such distinctions are crucial because employment prospects and their regional impact vary with them. For example, education, medicine, and local and national government administration generated much employment in the early 1970s only to become vulnerable to cuts in the 1980s. Conversely, private producer and consumer services have expanded, and managerial and high-level non-manual jobs have increased. The demand for predominantly female part-time labour has remained high and should be taken into account when assessing the amount of employment generated by new developments in the service sector. Spatial disparities in the service sector are crucial because of its total size, but the high-order services offering the best employment prospects are overwhelmingly concentrated in southern Britain, particularly in the London metropolitan region. This area is well provided with 'novel, innovative and technically oriented services' which seem to assure its future, but elsewhere the prospects are less bright so it cannot be assumed that services will compensate for manufacturing job losses.

Debate continues on the employment consequences of technological innovation in the services sector. Awareness of growth prospects is balanced by justifiable fears that the automation implied in innovation will not stimulate the creation of enough jobs to offset losses elsewhere in the economy. There seems little hope that the peripheral regions which have suffered so badly from deindustrialisation will benefit greatly from the changes taking place. Wood (1986) recorded a 4 per cent growth in service sector employment between 1975 and 1981 compared with a 19 per cent decline in manufacturing, and in commenting on different growth and decline trends among services he emphasised that service activities are increasingly interwoven into the production process itself. Areas with declining manufacturing are therefore disadvantaged. Hepworth (1986) substantiated this conclusion in arguing that the relatively highly paid producer services providing information outputs are attractive and beneficial for an economy. Non-information activities (such as hair styling, laundering, car repairing and purveying food and drink) tend to be low-paid and perhaps less useful in regenerating an economy. Whatever the overall effect of the new technology on total employment, it is clear that its impact will be spatially uneven.

# New technology and producer services

A visible consequence of new technology in relation to producer services is the boom in demand for 'high-tech' office units. Anticipating the effects of deregulation of the London Stock Exchange in October 1986, developers forecast a need for 'high-tech' office units of 10 000 square feet (930 square metres) at a rent of £30 per square foot (£2.79 per square metre) per annum. Office blocks built in the 1960s became obsolete because modern telecommunications, computer ducts and air conditioning have specific space requirements such as a height of 12–14 feet (3.7–4.3 metres) between floors in the shell of the building and large open plan dealing/trading floors. In order to retain London's status as a world financial centre massive increases in office space have been proposed which will have a profound effect on the City's layout and appearance. Typical of the purpose-built computerised trading floors that have replaced the Stock Exchange site on which trading has taken place since 1801 is the Ebbgate House headquarters of the Barclays de Zoete Wedd merchant bank group. Here 60 trading stations serviced by £18 million worth of computers have been installed in premises that cost £5 million to rent. So-called 'fast-track' building methods have been developed, involving steel-framed buildings with many prefabricated elements. New attitudes to the exploitation of air rights have emerged with an increase in plans that link buildings on opposite sides of a road, or by supporting buildings on piles to span a feature such as a railway station. Compared with the revolution caused by the mechanisation of office functions at the turn of the century by the typewriter and the telephone the pace of modern innovation is very swift indeed.

Gillespie and Goddard (1986) referred to telecommunications as the 'electronic highways' of the future which will influence the geography of economic opportunity in the emerging 'information economy' in much the same way as the railways affected the structural change of the industrial economy. Advances in telecommunications technology cannot be divorced from changes in the nature of the economic base embodied in the term 'post-industrial society'. Whereas the manufacturing economy relied on the key strategic resource of 'finance capital' the post-industrial society looks to 'knowledge' as a prime resource. Instead of transforming finance capital to achieve economic benefit as manufacturing did, in a post-industrial society it is knowledge that has to be transformed. That knowledge must be in a form that can be exchanged, processed, transferred, manipulated and applied in a multitude of ways and among a multitude of uses. Currently society's economic base is being altered by the application of information but, as Gillespie and Goddard warn, there are winners and losers in the new situation. Because knowledge and information are becoming marketable commodities access to them is being restricted, and in particular the largest corporations are exploiting the new technology to extend their control over global markets. In the absence of policy intervention, geographical divisions will probably be exacerbated by developments in the information economy. Already London and South-East England claim an above average share of information workers so that there is regional dependency within the UK whereby much of a region's economy (for example, the northern region) is controlled from external headquarters. To date British developments have reinforced the existing business hierarchy, and Wheeler (1986) found that in the USA the high-order financial institutions were not decentralising. Fears have been expressed that instead of a convergence between cores and peripheries that would reduce inequalities between regions the reverse is more likely to happen.

Although service industries have the choice of a much wider range of locations than formerly, inertia factors seem to have retarded the degree of change. Also, the vision of the home as a workplace for a large proportion of the workforce remains a distant goal. Nevertheless, attempts have been made to model the process of change in the light of technological innovation. Rothwell (1982), who was concerned with industrial change, envisaged initial growth of small firms followed by an intermediate phase of rationalisation and consolidation. Finally, when maturity and market saturation are attained, large firms are usual. At this stage price competition is fierce, and because productivity (influenced by technology) outstrips demand jobs are lost. To effect this a suitable innovation structure must be created consisting of a set of favourable supply factors (technical, financial, manpower), demand factors (innovation-orientated procurement), and an appropriate overall environment (local houses and communications). Similar considerations doubtless apply to the service sector in which small firms, for whom local markets are vital, are so prominent. More specific to the service sector is the four-stage model proposed by Nilles *et al.* (Daniels, 1985) in which the first stage is one of centralisation. This corresponds to the current dominant mode for most information-using industries, and is followed by decentralisation, usually involving the outward extension of a firm's communication boundaries as distinctive subunits move. Fragmentation of this sort may affect branch banks or accounting sections who use mail and telecommunications to maintain contact with head office. Dispersion may occur later when a central or local computer and workstations for employees can provide the information needed for work. Eventually a stage of diffusion will be reached with individuals working at home and only a small core of senior personnel being concentrated at a single location.

This idealised model has not been extensively tested by empirical research, though many find it intuitively appealing as a guide to further development. A recent study of the Canadian situation (Hepworth, 1986; 1987) explored the geography of technological change in the information economy and its implications in detail. Computer networks can be regarded as information technology and as spatial systems, and in the Canadian example it was shown that firms have penetrated new regional markets which, at the international level, are 'unprotected' by tariff barriers. This means that the telecommunications-transport trade-off is of greater significance than previously assumed, and it applies to movements of people as well as material inputs into production. Adopting a phrase popular with geographers, Hepworth said that today's distributional issues centre on who gets what information where, and he illustrated this by reference to computer-related, printing and publishing, and research and development occupations.

Traditionally the spatial impact of technological change has been investigated with the aid of theories of regional development resting on the role of information in space and contact systems, the hierarchical structure of diffusion processes, and the locus of corporate control in urban and regional systems.

There is evidence that multi-locational manufacturing firms extend head office control over dispersed operations through their complex networks. With the enlargement of information space to the global scale there is scope for producer services to sell variegated information to firms and governments in the international 'network marketplace'. Opportunities for transforming the space economy certainly exist, but the telecommunications–transportation trade-off which should act as the foundation for this process remains an elusive concept. Canadian evidence suggests that computer networks are highly centralised structures despite the technical feasibility of distributing data-processing hardware. Computer power also raises labour productivity, though the geographical concentration of head offices means that regional variations in productivity bear little relation to the spatial distribution of capital investment. Computer networks may be horizontal (industry-wide) or vertical (function-deep), a feature whose full significance has not yet been realised because thinking is still biased towards information as innovation diffusion and towards control over organisations or regions. There has also been a tendency to treat information workers as a residual category of 'non-productive' employees. The implication of these ideas is that dramatic changes in the geography and organisation of producer services will occur once the full significance of the current technical revolution has been grasped.

Computers were introduced to Canada in 1952 and now 75 per cent of them are used in service industries. Major investments in computer networks were concentrated in the late 1970s, and in 1983 nearly two-thirds of computer capacity was located in Ontario, a far cry from the spatial convergence resulting from decentralisation and dispersion that was supposed to happen. About 90 per cent of the computers are in head offices in Ottawa and Toronto, the national centres of federal government and corporate institutions. Much computer power is applied to routine transactions and administrative applications (such as payroll processing), but networks are essentially instruments of organisational control so strategic network applications (such as decision-support analysis) are of growing importance,.

Possibly we are on the threshold of great changes as further developments implement Local Area Networks (LANs) and their interconnection to create a fully integrated, two-level system for controlling the entire process by which goods and services are distributed. Production and distribution services in all sectors are likely to be radically altered to produce a new geography of economic opportunity. Consequently, the 'distance-shrinking' and 'space-adjusting' characteristics of the new information technology have increased rather than diminished geography's potential contribution to the public debate on the distribution issues raised by the 'information revolution'. Closed production function models of economic growth are no longer appropriate for application to the spatial organisation of information capital, not least because information-based economies are 'open'. A new form of interregional trade in information services has been created, both in an intra-corporate and a market context. For the time being, however, companies are ignoring the opportunities for decentralisation afforded by technical innovations and are using hierarchical systems to maintain and support centralised organisational structures.

The Canadian evidence can be complemented by studies of computer services in the UK. Computer services, an application of information technology, conventionally include computer data-processing services, consultancy, recruitment and training, and software provision. This simple classification is now difficult to apply because of the emergence of turnkey systems, maintenance, telecommunication and automation and because the subsectors are becoming less distinct. The market for computer services is large: in 1984 it was estimated to be $40 billion in the USA and $12.9 billion in Western Europe (of which $2.1 billion was accounted for by the UK). Employment in computer services in the UK expanded from 31 000 in 1971 to over 81 000 in 1981, and there was a marked spatial bias towards South-East England. After considering these general points Howells (1987) focused on the software industry. Since the UK accounts for 5 per cent of the world's software market and itself supplies only 2–3 per cent of that market balance of payments problems arise. Despite the rapid growth of small firms the top ten British companies controlled 22.1 per cent of the market in 1984, and it seems that a bifurcation process (a small number of giant organisations and a mass of small firms), which is characteristic of the service economy of the UK as a whole, is taking place. Large firms are also important because much British software development has arisen from the in-house computing departments of transnational companies, so growth has not been endogenous. Recently many large firms have transferred their computer service operations, which are independent of the general strategies and constraints of the parent firm, to separate profit centres. As hardware sales slow down hardware manufacturers are increasingly attracted to the software market. This, and the trend to 'firmware' (software embedded into the manufacturer's hardware through read-only memories), would favour those areas where hardware manufacturers are concentrated. Relative shifts between large and small firms, along with the decline of user dominance in the software industry, may produce important spatial consequences. There is scope for fragmentation and dispersal of the computer service industry similar to that encouraged by the adoption of distance working in the insurance industry. Vincent *et al.* (1987) examined the role of the technical consultant with reference to the British government's MAPCON (Microelectronics Applications Project Consultancy Scheme) initiative. Judged by the distribution of the Department of Trade and Industry authorised consultants there is an 'information-rich' South-East, but great tracts of the country lie in an 'information desert'. Most consultants are located along the London–Birmingham–Manchester axis and there is some clustering along the M4 motorway. Compared with the traditional manufacturing regions South-East England has a more generalist environment in terms of industrial expertise, though consultancy skills seem to be becoming more closely matched to regional economic activity. Both studies reviewed here confirm that in total more activities occur in South-East England than elsewhere, and though that region may have slower growth rates of firms than other parts it also experiences lower death rates.

Another perspective on the process of decentralisation connected with information technology is offered by Erickson (1986) who studied multinucleation in the metropolitan economies of Boston, Milwaukee and

Minneapolis-St Paul. He was interested in the telecommunications–transportation trade-off for he believed that the decision to locate is a function of the potential profitability of the investment. Revenue from some types of establishment will not be affected by a suburban fringe situation and a cost-minimisation model would be suitable for analysing their locations. A profit-maximisation model would be more appropriate for activities whose market is spatially restricted. This distinction, which indicates an important constraint on the wholesale readjustment of locations in the wake of innovation, should be remembered when considering the implications of new technology.

New opportunities do not mean that the conventional office is doomed to extinction. Installation expenses and the attitudes of office employees and their unions may delay the introduction of equipment in particular offices. Responses to a 1980 survey (Daniels, 1983b) of 304 business service offices in eight provincial centres to discover whether information technology was well known and used showed that attitudes of banking, insurance and finance offices, and professional and scientific services differed little, except that banks had a higher rate of usage than most. Banks and insurance offices needed data-transmission facilities whereas consulting engineers required computers with graphics capabilities. Daniels concluded that possession of telex and internal computing facilities increases the chances that other equipment will be used, and he also noted that some items are more readily accepted than others; for example, computers in preference to word processors.

As yet there has not been a wholesale transformation of the location of producer service activities in response to the new opportunities, possibly because the existing investment in offices is a powerful factor in locational inertia. A slower rate of innovation may permit greater locational adjustment because of the financial implications of giving firms time for the necessary investment changes needed. Faster innovations may simply put pressure on existing space. Nevertheless, office parks are already being developed in North America and Europe, and this trend may increase because the new technology is giving the decision-maker greater locational choice.

# New technology and consumer services

The anticipated reduction of intra-firm costs makes information technology attractive to producer service companies, and the same arguments apply if there is a high volume of business between two or more companies. Consumer service companies benefit from using the new technical equipment for intra-firm operations such as accounting and stock control procedures. Customers, however, may be less impressed. Teleshopping is a feasible system with scope for altering the relationship between retailer and customer. Viewdata systems can display goods in the consumer's home and allow purchases to be made from there. The system can apply to stocks and shares, holidays and theatre performances as well as retailing. Cable TV may facilitate the development of channels specialising in retail advertising, though American experience has not been very encouraging. 'Informercials' have been more successful. The problem is that individual customers may perceive no advantage to themselves and may be reluctant to change their  habits or instal home equipment to enable a new system to work.

In 1983 there were over 30 000 cable broadcasting systems in Britain covering 2.3 million subscribers. The number of subscribers has fallen by about 25 per cent since 1976, largely due to the closure of older systems installed in areas of poor transmission which became redundant when new local transmitters were opened (Table 6.5). However, local authorities and housing associations on new estates have also introduced new systems. Two-way cable TV communications can be used for teleshopping or telebanking; some British building societies do offer a telebanking service though the practice is not widespread. Compared with other countries—Belgium, 64 per cent of households; Netherlands 55 per cent; France, 37 per cent; the USA, 22 per cent; and Ireland, 23 per cent—Britain, with 14 per cent, had a very low proportion of TV households cabled in 1981 (Gershuny and Miles, 1983), but the figures are deceptive since most of the installations are basic coaxial cables lacking two-way communication capability. Britain's fibre optic cable systems are more advanced than those of European rivals,  though the prospects for a communications revolution are hampered by the vast disruption and expense entailed in providing mass connections to a national cable network. Consequently the government is being cautious despite the attraction of a cable network connecting every house and workplace as a means of revolutionising communication. Not the least deterrent to such a massive undertaking is the risk that further technological advance may render it obsolete.

Cable TV derives from a medium primarily offering a form of one-way entertainment, education and information. It is one aspect of technology in the home which has shown a general increase. Countries with the highest ownership levels of TV sets (Table 6.6) have a slower rate of increase than less favoured nations, probably because saturation levels are being reached. Similar considerations doubtless apply to telephones, though their faster rate of expansion presumably reflects their greater use in business activities (Table 6.7). Table 6.8 details changes in home technology. Unlike automation in the office, labour-saving innovations in the home do not replace people in the same way. Very few householders had servants to replace, and some new goods such as videos and freezers had no non-technological analogues. What these new devices have substituted for is services outside the home. A freezer

**Table 6.5**  Subscribers to cable TV systems
(as a percentage of TV licence holders) in the UK

|      |      |
| ---- | ---- |
| 1961 | 4.8  |
| 1971 | 13.2 |
| 1976 | 14.2 |
| 1980 | 13.8 |
| 1983 | 12.3 |

*Source: Social Trends*, 1985, Table 9.13

Technological influences and their locational significance 129

**Table 6.6**  Television set ownership

|  | Sets per 1000 population | | Increase in sets, |
|---|---|---|---|
|  | 1975 | 1983 | 1975–83 (%) |
| Denmark | 308 | 369 | 20 |
| West Germany | 305 | 335 | 10 |
| Greece | 106 | 257 | 142 |
| Ireland | 178 | 206 | 16 |
| Netherlands | 259 | 310 | 20 |
| UK | 315 | 328 | 4 |

*Source: Eurostat Review,* 1986

**Table 6.7**  Telephone installations (per 1000 inhabitants)

|  | 1975 | 1983 | Increase (%) |
|---|---|---|---|
| Belgium | 286 | 417 | 46 |
| Denmark | 450 | 719 | 60 |
| West Germany | 317 | 572 | 80 |
| Greece | 221 | 336 | 52 |
| France | 262 | 544 | 108 |
| Ireland | 138 | 235 | 70 |
| Italy | 259 | 405 | 56 |
| Luxembourg | 412 | 587 | 42 |
| Netherlands | 244 | 380 | 56 |
| Portugal | 113 | 169 | 50 |
| Spain | 220 | 352 | 60 |
| Sweden | 661 | 890 | 35 |
| UK | 376 | 520 | 38 |
| USA | 686 | 768* | 12 |
| Japan | 354 | 520 | 47 |

*Source: Eurostat Review,* 1986, Table 3.2.3
* 1982

permits bulk purchase so that the frequent visits to a corner shop are no longer necessary, a factor which has contributed to the decline in numbers of small shops. Similarly, the ability to watch TV and rent or purchase home video feature films has affected cinema attendances adversely.

Retail banking provides a widespread and visible manifestation of technical innovation affecting the consumer in the automated teller machine (ATM). A personal magnetically encoded plastic card usable in any ATM will call up an account, check a balance, withdraw cash and in some cases deposit cash, summon a statement or make a complaint. ATMs have greatly increased the convenience and flexibility of bank accounts by facilitating speedy, almost effortless, cash withdrawal nationwide. Department stores, shopping arcades

**Table 6.8** Percentage of households in possession of certain durable goods, England, 1970–84

|                   | 1970 | 1979 | 1984 |
|-------------------|------|------|------|
| Central heating   | 32.5 | 56.9 | 66.8 |
| Washing machine   | 64.7 | 74.2 | 79.1 |
| Refrigerator      | 70.1 | 92.5 | 94.4 |
| Freezer           | –    | 43.9 | 60.5 |
| Telephone         | 37.5 | 69.6 | 78.1 |
| Television        | 91.5 | 91.0 | 97.7 |
| Colour TV         | –    | 68.0 | 81.9 |
| Video             | –    | –    | 21.2 |

*Source: Regional Statistics, 1976, Regional Trends, 1986*

and student unions are places other than banks where ATMs can also be found. In 1971 Citicorp became the first bank in the USA to open ATMs, and by 1987 more than 80 per cent of their customers used them for over half of their transactions. If customers were to be attracted, Citicorp found that technology had to be user-friendly and thoroughly reliable, which meant investing in research and development. The latest idea, the Citi Station, has three to ten lanes and is 'a gas station for money'. Customers drive up to the ATM and conduct a transaction without leaving the car: the ATM even adjusts itself automatically to the height of the car (Norton, 1987). Citicorp realises that, however seductive the new technology is for them and for most of their customers, there will always be 'technophobes' who refuse to deal with a machine. Each Citi Station, therefore, will have one human teller. The Lloyds Bank Cashpoint card (Table 6.9) is a good example of a British ATM network. It grew from 308 outlets in 1974 to 1700 in 1986, in which year there were an additional 2000 outlets available through reciprocal arrangements with Barclays and the Royal Bank of Scotland. Following the normal pattern of diffusion most early Cashpoint machines were in the bigger branches, with London having a disproportionate share. This dominance was reduced by 1981 by diffusion down the urban hierarchy, although the more remote rural branches have yet to be reached.

Enthusiasm for technology should not disguise the serious problems associated with some new developments. Even a comparatively minor technical innovation like 'cashless shopping' can run into difficulties, as the case of the British Connect debit card system, intended to replace cheque and cash payments to retailers, illustrates. The system involves wiping a customer's card through a machine at the point of sale which allows the retailer to debit the relevant account automatically. There was opposition from retailers to the bank's proposed charge for the service. Instead of a fixed sum per transaction as applied to ordinary credit cards retailers were to be charged a percentage of the value of each transaction. Retailers accused the bank of abusing its dominant position in the credit card market by trying to force its new card on them, and

**Table 6.9** Lloyds Bank Cashpoint card outlets, 1974-86

|  | *1974* | *1981* | *1986* |
|---|---|---|---|
| London | 70 | 106 | n.a. |
| Provincial | 238 | 664 | n.a. |
| Total Lloyds | 308 | 770 | 1700 |
| Other compatible outlets | 0 | 0 | 2000+ |
| Total Cashpoint outlets | 308 | 770 | 3700 |

*Source*: Lloyds Bank, 1974; 1981; 1986

they alleged that the proposed new charge would have to be passed on to customers in the form of higher prices. These problems are not insurmountable, but they help to explain why delays may occur in the adoption of technological innovations.

Experience with a pilot Electronic Funds Transfer at Point of Sale (EFTPOS) scheme introduced in Northampton in England in 1985 by the Anglia Building Society and ICL revealed other difficulties. Under this scheme more than 70 000 consumers were able to buy goods and services at 100 retail outlets without using cash, credit card or personal cheque. A card authorises a direct transfer of funds from an Anglia account to the retailer, but customers seem to dislike the immediate debiting of their accounts as against the period of grace allowed by a normal credit card. Perhaps more worrying for the ultimate acceptance of the concept is that the system gives the bank a *de facto* record of their spending habits which customers may prefer to keep a mystery. Retailers and the bank have more to gain, but retailers are unhappy about having to lease or buy computer terminals and changing their working practices to accommodate them. Since the English system uses a single magnetic strip encoding on the back of the bank card the whole idea may be overtaken by technological progress in the shape of a competitive French system employing silicon chip technology. The French 'smart card' uses a wafer thin silicon chip inside the card which can store far more information than can be contained on a single magnetic strip.

Although automated goods handling may enhance the prospects of home-based buying in the grocery field, the effect is likely to be socially divisive because the rich rather than the poor will possess computers. Home-based buying would require fewer workers at check-out points so that retail employment opportunities may diminish despite the transfer of a few to packing and delivery. Developments in telecommunications will probably strengthen the trading power of multiples, and because it will reduce the need for personal contact there may be more centralisation of provision in the largest branch outlets. Large towns will be more affected by the changes than small ones. As a by-product of the development there will be smaller stocks in stores but more frequent deliveries. A major social change arising from the new circumstances is the availability of seven-day access to many services now available only on weekdays, though in the case of shopping the transformation of habits depends on legislative not technological change. Davies (1984) described the efforts of one local authority to use technology for the benefit of the disadvantaged. The British supermarket Tesco co-operated in an experiment at Gateshead in northern England offering computer shopping to the disadvantaged, who could use computers installed in public branch libraries for this purpose. Another computer in the Social Services Department was available for the bedridden who could phone their requirements to the Department which would take the necessary action.

Although videotex is technically feasible, one firm (Kays) already having a complete home shopping system set up and ready to run with more than 35 000 lines, it is unlikely to be successful until a large enough user base exists. That is, there must be enough customers in possession of the technology to use such a system. The market cannot expand until the range of goods and services on offer make it irresistible to more people, and American experience suggests that there is much consumer resistance from customers who would prefer to browse through a catalogue instead of looking at wares on a screen. One experiment in the West Midlands of Britain operated by Viewtel aimed to promote supermarket shopping in conjunction with Carrefour, but despite an annual turnover of £250 000 per year the service was terminated after two years as not economically viable. Various teleshopping projects are being evaluated in several countries, though doubts remain about the system's probable appeal.

Technological advances offer great potential benefits in medicine. Increasingly complex and expensive machinery is being used to raise standards of medical treatment, but unfortunately some sophisticated techniques are becoming so expensive that they may not be generally available to the public. There are ethical problems stemming from the fact that high technology activities like heart transplants might claim a disproportionate share of resources compared with the benefits they confer and may have to be paid for by a reduction in other services. Shortage of money has limited the number of renal dialysis machines available to British patients so that treatment cannot be supplied to all who need it. Conversely, improved technology offers the prospect of cures where previously none existed, and so the expectations of what can be realistically attained by health care are increased. Technological advances seem to have frustrated the visions of the founders of the British National Health Service who believed that when the deficiencies in health that they perceived had been overcome expenditure on health care would decline. Instead, health care expenditure continues to rise and technological developments will probably ensure the continuance of this trend as long as the public perceive the prospect of improved health as the outcome. Whether the medical profession would accede to home treatment services and teleconsulting is doubtful, for the problems are greater than those already encountered with teleshopping. Geographically, technical advances in medicine will have little impact on the current patterns of provision because they will be applied in the existing hospital facilities.

Computers and video technology offer great scope in education. For example, schools and colleges in a given area could jointly benefit from a specialist lecture reaching them over a television network. Such loosening of spatial constraints would be of great potential benefit in rural areas where children could stay in their small local schools under the supervision of one teacher but with access to a wider world through electronic contacts. Not the least benefit from this would be a reduction in the transport cost of bussing the children to urban centres. In reality the likelihood is that television networks for schools are now more likely to exist in urban centres than in widespread rural areas. Distance learning, like the British Open University, has demonstrated some of the possibilities new forms of learning can provide but in all probability the new technology will take its place alongside other educational equipment such as tape recorders, TV and radio broadcasts, and slide or film projectors as one of the many methods used by the teacher.

Leisure activities have benefited from technological advances, notably in respect of home entertainment. Technology has also contributed to tourism by encouraging a greater awareness of places, and it has enabled people to develop counter-attractions (for example, artificial ski-runs) to potentially over-used natural facilities. Modern air conditioning and central heating are among some of the technological developments that have improved the comfort of hotels, so helping to boost tourism. As already mentioned, tourism has benefited from transport innovations, and so have wholesaling and retailing. Studies by Watts (1975) and McKinnon (1981) showed how the location of wholesale depot systems has changed in response to transport developments, notably technical improvements in road vehicles, and changes in the nature of markets. Even this brief statement demonstrates that no type of consumer service is immune to the effect of technological innovation, which frequently has important geographical consequences as well.

## Conclusion

The service sector is at the forefront of the response to the exciting prospects created by technological advances and their impact on the information economy. In some quarters there is an almost euphoric sense of limitless possibilities arising from this situation. This is to ignore the huge scale of investment required to make information technology effective and the risks of being led into blind alleys as developing systems are overtaken by still more powerful technological achievements. Geographical change will occur, but at a more subtle pace than the term 'revolution' suggests. At the global scale London and New York will remain leading financial centres taking full advantage of the available technology, but Tokyo, Hong Kong and Singapore are rivals which may become the foci of a burgeoning Pacific economy comparable to the North Atlantic economy that has prospered for so long. National urban systems may experience some change as individual places rise or fall within the hierarchy, though there is reason to believe that the existing hierarchical structure will itself exert a strong influence on technological diffusion. Perhaps some new information centres comparable to the railway towns of the Industrial Revolution will emerge, but there are good grounds for supposing that there will be much inertia in the urban system. Within towns and cities morphological and functional changes will occur in the Central Business District (CBD) and the process of decentralisation and suburbanisation will benefit from technical advance. There are doubts about the service sector's ability to compensate fully for the employment losses caused by deindustrialisation. It also seems likely that for both producer and consumer services the strength of large companies will be enhanced, and that the rationalisation of organisational structure this may well imply will have geographical consequences. Some consumer resistance to technological innovations has been encountered and may retard development, but overall the pace of change is such that its geographical impact will be considerable.

*leave out.*

# Chapter 7

# Bureaucratisation

Bureaucracy, for some the hallmark of office activity, is essential for the efficient dispatch of business. The term may evoke ideas of unnecessary official procedures and red tape, but it originally meant a system of administration designed to dispose of a large body of work in a routine manner. As Pinch (1985) pointed out, M. Weber explored the nature of bureaucracy, and, even though his ideas have been criticised, his thesis that 'bureaucratic administration means fundamentally the exercise of control on the basis of knowledge' is a very useful guideline for reaching an understanding of the relationship between services and office space in city and region. Manufacturing industry could not function without its own internal office system providing services within firms. Shops, schools, hospitals, health centres, hotels and amusement centres all need offices to ensure the smooth running of their operations. Whether in the private or the public sector, office activity is ubiquitous. An office collects, processes and exchanges information and these are functions which have expanded enormously in the twentieth century and have come to epitomise service sector developments.

Alexander (1979) tried to classify office jobs (Table 7.1), but his classification is not acceptable to all. Obviously office jobs are not synonymous with non-manual jobs, for teachers and retail sales assistants are white-collar workers who do not operate in offices. Because occupational statistics are not always available in the disaggregated form given in Table 7.1, it is sometimes necessary to refer to *office-type jobs*. Many of the activities listed in the classification are not performed in office buildings. A further problem is that offices 'attached' to manufacturing premises account for an unknown number of workers who may be classified as manufacturing workers. There is a significant number in this category in the UK, and estimates made elsewhere range from one-third in all cities in the USA to 55 per cent in Sydney, Australia (Alexander, 1979). Alexander also considered the growth of office-type employment in selected countries over a ten-year period, and he found that within the office sector clerical jobs accounted for the largest number of people and were the fastest-growing activity. However, technological developments have already slowed the growth rate and may transform the employment prospects of these workers.

Bureaucratisation is most evident at the urban scale where office quarters are such a conspicuous feature or urban morphology. This aspect of office

**Table 7.1**   Classification of office jobs

| Occupation group | Examples |
| --- | --- |
| *White-collar jobs regarded as office jobs* | |
| Professional and technical | Architects, engineers, surveyors, law professionals, draughtsmen and technicians, professional and technical not elsewhere classified |
| Administrative, executive | Government administrative, executive officials, private sector employers, directors, managers, workers on own account |
| Clerical | Bookkeepers and cashiers, stenographers and typists, office machine operators, receptionists, other clerical workers |
| Sales | Insurance, real estate salesmen, auctioneers, valuers, commerical travellers, manufacturers' agents |
| Communications | Telephone, telegraph and related operators, postmasters, postmen and messengers |
| *White-collar jobs not regarded as office jobs* | |
| Professional | Scientists, medical practitioners, dentists, nurses, other professional medical, teachers, clergy |
| Sales | Proprietors and shopkeepers, retail and wholesale trade salesmen, shop assistants |

*Source*: Alexander (1979, 3).

space in the city was discussed in Chapter 5 and the impact of technological developments which are especially relevant to office activities was considered in Chapter 6. Here attention is focused on geographical patterns at varying scales. The treatment is largely empirical in order to indicate the character and extent of bureaucratisation. The greater weight attached to national and local government patterns reflect, the availability of suitable data for geographical analysis and the importance of these activities, but the private sector is not ignored.

# The geographical pattern of public sector office activities

By the 1980s industrial countries had an average of 9 per cent employment in central government and 12 per cent in local government, compared with 23 per cent and 4 per cent respectively in developing countries (World Bank, 1983). The post-war growth in numbers of government employees slowed down to 2½–5 per cent per annum in industrial countries by 1980. The UK and Canada were among the first to show a decline as a result of government policies. In the UK public administration and defence (excluding members of the armed services) accounted for 1,549,000 employees, or 6.7 per cent of civilian workers in 1982. There were a further 323,000 employed in the armed services (Central Office of Information, 1984). In 1972 the gross domestic product of public administration was £3743 million (6.7 per cent) and this rose to £16 724 million (7.2 per cent) in 1982. Evidently public administration is a large and important sector of the economy, and because of its all-pervading role in setting standards, enforcing regulations and guiding policies, it directly and indirectly affects every other sector. Since all parts of the country require administration, administrators must be widely distributed although in practice the geographical distribution may be uneven. Unlike the private sector, public sector office activity is not under an obligation to make a profit, so that the spatial patterns of public administration tend to reflect the distribution of needs or the objectives of government policy as in the case of deliberate office dispersal. We now turn to the examination of office activities connected with public administration, defence, police and the law at various spatial scales.

*International organisations*

International organisations and their staffs have increased in number in the post-war period. The biggest international body is the United Nations Organisation (UN) founded in October 1945 in the aftermath of a catastrophic war when it was widely felt that greater international co-operation would help to prevent further conflict by binding the nations together. Specialist agencies within the UN included UNESCO, FAO, WHO, and there were also 'organs' such as Unicef and UNCTAD. The headquarters of these agencies display an interesting pattern. Apart from the General Assembly and Security Council in New York, nine of the agencies are in North America, one in Asia, two in Africa, and twenty in Europe, with nine in Geneva alone. Geneva has also attracted other non-UN international bodies such as the European Free Trade Association and the World Council of Churches. A prime reason for this choice of location is that Geneva was the home of the UN's predecessor, the League of Nations, and had many facilities when the war ended. Each of the 32 UN agencies (see Table 7.2) requires staff and buildings. Since a primary function of most of these bodies is to collect, collate, publish and disseminate information to member governments, commerce and the general public, there are large numbers of researchers, statisticians, journalists, and, not least, translators as well as the secretariat.

Another extensive international bureaucracy is that of the European Economic Community (EEC). With its 12 member states the EEC has extensive problems producing translations, for, unlike the UN which limits translations to English, French, Russian, Chinese, Spanish and Arabic, the EEC must translate into the languages of all member countries. The headquarters of the Commissions in Brussels and the distinctive office block of the

**Table 7.2**    International organisations and their headquarters

## 1.  United Nations

(a)  *United Nations organs*

International Court of Justice, The Hague
UN Centre for Human Settlements (HABITAT), Nairobi
United Nations Children's Fund (UNICEF), New York
United Nations Conference on Trade & Development (UNCTAD), Geneva
United Nations Development Programme (UNDP), Nairobi
United Nations Disaster Relief Office (UNDRO), Geneva
United Nations Environmental Programme (UNEP), Nairobi
United Nations Fund for Population Activities (UNFPA), New York
United Nations High Commission for Refugees (UNCHR), Geneva
United Nations Industrial Development Organisation (UNIDO), Vienna
United Nations Institute for Training & Research (UNITAR), New York
United Nations Relief and Works Agency for Palestinian Refugees (UNRWA), Vienna
United Nations University, Tokyo
World Food Council (WFC), Rome
World Food Programme (WFP), Rome

(b)  *Specialised Agencies*

International Labour Organisation (ILO), Geneva
Food and Agriculture Organisation (FAO), Rome
United Nations Educational Scientific & Cultural Organisation (UNESCO), Paris
World Health Organisation (WHO), Geneva
International Bank for Reconstruction and Development (IBRD), Washington, DC
International Development Association (IDA), Washington, DC
International Finance Corporation (IFC), Washington, DC
International Monetary Fund (IMF), Washington, DC
International Civil Aviation Organisation (ICAO), Montreal
Universal Postal Union (UPU), Berne
International Telecommunications Union (ITU), Geneva
World Meteorological Organisation (WMO), Geneva
International Maritime Organisation (IMO), London
World Intellectual Property Organisation (WIPO), Geneva
International Fund for Agricultural Development (IFAD), Rome
International Atomic Energy Agency (IAEA), Vienna
General Agreement on Tariffs and Trade (GATT), Geneva

## 2.  EEC

Commission, Brussels
Council of Ministers, Brussels
European Parliament, Brussels, Strasbourg and Luxembourg
European Court of Justice, Luxembourg
European Investment Bank (EIB), Luxembourg

## 3.  Other international organisations

Council of Europe, Strasbourg

European Free Trade Association (EFTA), Geneva
North Atlantic Treaty Organisation (NATO), Brussels
Organisation for Economic Cooperation and Development (OECD), Paris
Association of South-East Asian Nations (ASEAN), Jakarta
Caribbean Community and Common Market (CARICOM), Georgetown, Guyana
Council for Mutual Economic Assistance (COMECON), Moscow
League of Arab States, Tunis
Organisation of African Unity (OAU), Addis Ababa
Organisation of American States (OAS), Washington, DC
Organisation of Petroleum Exporting Countries (OPEC), Vienna
World Council of Churches, Geneva

*Source: Whitaker's Almanack*, 1987, pp. 962–75

Berlaymont Building is becoming as recognisable in news reports as the White House or Houses of Parliament. The Council of Ministers is also housed in Brussels, but the European Court of Justice and the European Investment Bank are located in Luxembourg. The European Parliament is curiously located in three places—Strasbourg, Luxembourg and Brussels. Since this must involve considerable cost, inconvenience and extra travel for members, civil servants and documents, the arrangement is clearly meant to demonstrate a political point about European unity. No single nation is to be regarded as the headquarters of the Community. Each member country has its own EEC branch information office, usually in the capital. The EEC is notoriously bureaucratic, for its objectives involve 'harmonising' many different systems of economic activity, which inevitably generates much paper work.

Several other international organisations also have large office complexes, and most of them have chosen to locate in the same cities as the UN or the EEC. Examples include the Organisation for Economic Co-operation and Development (OECD) in Paris, EFTA in Geneva, and the Council of Europe in Strasbourg. The North Atlantic Treaty Organisation (NATO) has its main headquarters in Brussels, though its tactical command centres are more widely scattered—NATO naval headquarters, for example, are buried deep beneath suburban Northwood in north-west London. Rome and Vienna are two other centres favoured by international organisations (see Figure 7.1): the Organisation of Petroleum Exporting Countries (OPEC), for example, has its headquarters in non-oil-producing Vienna. Such concentrations of international organisations help to give a cosmopolitan flavour to cities. Brussels, in particular, has a multilingual, multi-cultural atmosphere created by such things as TV channels in most community languages expressly provided for expatriate civil servants of the Commission and Parliament.

*National government organisations*

National governments generally concentrate their civil service headquarters in enclaves close to the legislative building. In London Whitehall is close to the Palace of Westminster, and in Washington a plethora of Federal Agencies and Departments of State are near to Capitol Hill. Individual office blocks,

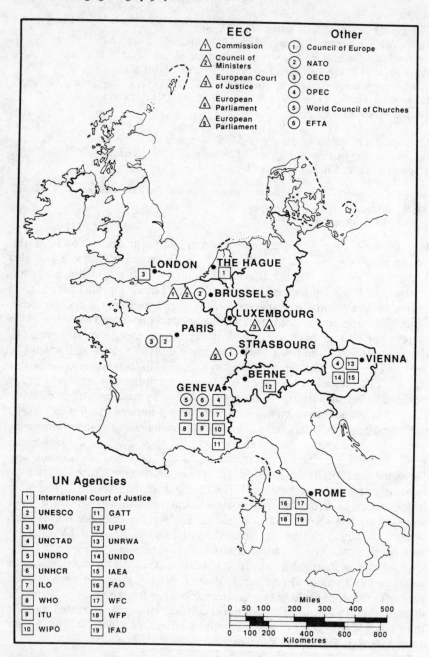

**Figure 7.1** International organisation HQs in Europe
*Source: Whitaker's Almanack*, 1987

**Table 7.3** Expenditure on Civil Service as a percentage of total national budget, selected countries, 1979–80

| Rank | | |
|---|---|---|
| 1 | Mali | 55.8 |
| 4 | Greece | 45.7 |
| 7 | Senegal | 42.7 |
| 9 | Zaire | 41.5 |
| 24 | Morocco | 32.8 |
| 38 | Uruguay | 29.2 |
| 46 | Ghana | 26.4 |
| 60 | New Zealand | 19.9 |
| 64 | Belgium | 15.4 |
| 66 | France | 15.05 |
| 68 | Denmark | 14.2 |
| 71 | UK | 13.8 |
| 72 | Indonesia | 13.7 |
| 73 | South Korea | 13.7 |
| 75 | Ireland | 12.5 |
| 77 | Italy | 12.1 |
| 80 | USA | 11.4 |
| 82 | Finland | 10.6 |
| 84 | Canada | 9.9 |
| 85 | Netherlands | 9.8 |
| 87 | West Germany | 9.4 |
| 90 | Sweden | 6.5 |
| 91 | Switzerland | 6.3 |

*Source*: G. Kurian, *The New Book of World Rankings*, New York, Facts on File
    Publications, 1984

like the Ministry of Defence along Whitehall and the Pentagon in Washington, are large enough to overshadow their surroundings, and the whole complex of government offices forms a distinctive unit in the urban landscape.

The more developed nations spend proportionately less on their civil services than the less developed countries (see Table 7.3). The apparently huge spending on the civil service in some developing countries is deceptive because they spend much more on administration than on welfare, whereas in the developed countries the reverse is true. Developing countries often have an especially well-developed bureaucratic framework in the capital city, but are often less well organised in functions like health and education elsewhere in their countries. The spatial organisation of administration depends on the nature of the state: in federal nations like the USA individual states administer functions such as education which in unitary states (such as France) are the prerogative of the national government though even in these countries some responsibilities may be devolved to local authorities. However far responsibilities are devolved some sort of spatial administrative framework is necessary. Bennett (1980) examined the different methods of distributing functions over space and saw it as a problem of assigning departmental functions at appropriate spatial scales. He identified four guiding principles. The *service principle* entails a separate administrative department for each group of people or problem; for example, Bureau of Indian Affairs, department for the unemployed. The *purpose principle* requires separate administrative departments for each expenditure function; for example, defence, health, agriculture. This is the normal structure in the UK. The *process principle* is based on different departments for each type of staff expenditure; for example, engineers, accountants, architects. This method is more common in industrial companies than in government. Finally, the *area principle* or 'layer cake' federalism is marked by administrative departments for each territorial unit and total devolution to lower geographical levels; for example, the Northern Ireland Office deals with many functions in the province which are under separate ministries in the rest of the country.

Most governments mix the four principles to produce extremely complex structures, which were often adopted in a piecemeal fashion and endure through inertia. Reforms of administration are rarely so sweeping as to obliterate previous structures. The result may be a labyrinth of varying procedures and systems even within one country. What Bennett (1980) called the 'marble cake' or cafeteria system is the product of functional fragmentation. Here different functions serve a variety of geographical areas with the disadvantage that co-ordination is difficult and costly. There is a danger of wasteful overlap when rival agencies compete for the same 'client'; for example, in the UK the Nature Conservancy gives grants to farmers to conserve habitats while the Ministry of Agriculture awards grants to destroy them in the interests of increased food production. At the opposite extreme is the centralised 'package' approach with a single multi-purpose organisation at each level to administer all functions. Though this has theoretical advantages it is often large and unwieldy in practice and is usually employed to deal with relatively small and simple areas such as the Falkland Islands.

National government is subdivided into a number of executive branches. Normally these are centrally controlled ministries or departments headed by a Minister or Secretary of State; for example, the Ministry of Defence in the UK, and the State Department in the USA. There are also government agencies which assist in carrying out specialised functions. Sometimes these have a 'parent' ministry, as in the case of the British Forestry Commission which is answerable to the Ministry of Agriculture; in the USA, the US Geological Survey is part of the Department of the Interior. If they are not directly attached they are known as 'quangos', a term usually meaning 'quasi-autonomous non-governmental organisations'. Sometimes 'national government' is substituted for 'non-governmental', for, as the Central Office of Information (1984) points out, there is no readily accepted definition, though everybody knows what quangos are. Examples of quangos include the Commission of Northern Lighthouses, University Grants Committee, Commission for Racial Equality, National Radiological Protection Board, National Economic Development Office, and the Home Grown Cereal Authority in Britain and The Veterans' Administration and the Environmental Protection Agency in the USA. There are three types of quango: executive bodies; advisory bodies; and tribunals. Explosive growth of quangos during the 1960s and

**Table 7.4** Civil servants in post by region, UK, 1984 (full-time equivalents in thousands)

| Department | Total | N | Y&H | EM | EA | SE | SW | WM | NW | W | Sc | Elsewhere |
|---|---|---|---|---|---|---|---|---|---|---|---|---|
| | | | | | | Regions | | | | | | |
| Agriculture | 11.8 | 0.5 | 0.7 | 0.6 | 1.2 | 5.5 | 1.3 | 0.8 | 0.4 | 0.5 | 0.3 | - |
| Customs and Excise | 25.1 | 0.7 | 1.2 | 0.7 | 0.9 | 13.6 | 1.2 | 1.0 | 2.4 | 0.6 | 2.1 | 0.7 |
| Defence | 202.9 | 5.3 | 8.4 | 6.2 | 2.5 | 75.0 | 46.9 | 10.0 | 11.0 | 8.6 | 20.7 | 8.3 |
| DES | 2.4 | 0.6 | 0.1 | - | - | 1.5 | 0.1 | 0.1 | 0.1 | - | - | - |
| Employment | 57.1 | 3.8 | 6.5 | 3.1 | 1.3 | 15.9 | 3.6 | 5.4 | 8.6 | 3.1 | 5.9 | - |
| Environment | 49.4 | 1.1 | 2.1 | 1.5 | 1.1 | 24.0 | 5.1 | 2.1 | 2.1 | 6.2 | 2.9 | 1.0 |
| DHSS | 90.3 | 15.4 | 6.2 | 5.1 | 1.7 | 25.4 | 4.3 | 6.2 | 14.0 | 4.0 | 7.9 | - |
| Home Office | 35.3 | 1.9 | 2.7 | 2.8 | 1.5 | 16.0 | 3.1 | 2.8 | 3.6 | 0.8 | - | - |
| HMSO | 3.8 | - | - | - | 1.1 | 1.5 | 0.2 | - | 0.7 | - | 0.2 | 0.1 |
| Treasury | 3.7 | - | - | - | 0.2 | 2.7 | 0.3 | - | 0.1 | 0.1 | 0.2 | - |
| Inland Revenue | 70.5 | 3.4 | 6.3 | 3.0 | 1.8 | 22.5 | 4.4 | 5.1 | 10.5 | 5.3 | 7.0 | 1.2 |
| National Savings | 8.0 | 2.2 | - | - | - | 0.2 | - | - | 2.5 | - | 3.2 | - |
| Scottish Office | 10.2 | - | - | - | - | - | - | - | - | - | 10.2 | - |
| DTI | 12.8 | 0.3 | 0.2 | 0.1 | 0.1 | 8.5 | 0.3 | 0.2 | 0.4 | 1.8 | 0.9 | - |
| Others | 49.2 | 1.0 | 1.0 | 1.3 | 0.8 | 25.4 | 4.1 | 1.0 | 3.2 | 4.9 | 3.6 | 2.8 |
| Totals | 632.0 | 36.1 | 35.6 | 24.5 | 14.2 | 237.7 | 74.8 | 34.8 | 59.6 | 35.9 | 65.2 | 14 |
| (%) | 100.0 | 5.7 | 5.6 | 3.8 | 2.2 | 37.5 | 11.8 | 5.5 | 9.4 | 5.6 | 10.3 | 2 |
| Change since 1979 (%) | -13.7 | -14.8 | -6.6 | -15.2 | -11.8 | -18.6 | -10.7 | -5.6 | -12.1 | -11.8 | -7.9 | -9.1 |

*Source: Regional Trends*, 1985, Table 7.3, p. 93.

Abbreviations used in Table 7.4
N-North; Y&H-Yorkshire and Humberside; EM-East Midlands; EA-East Anglia;
SE-South-East; SW-South-West; WM-West Midlands; NW-North-West; W-Wales;
Sc-Scotland; Elsewhere-other locations not specified
Customs-Customs and Excise
DES-Department of Education and Science
DHSS-Department of Health and Social Security
DTI-Department of Trade and Industry
HMSO-Her Majesty's Stationery Office

1970s produced many hundreds of organisations, all with staffs and buildings. Several hundred of the more obscure and bizarrely titled were abolished after 1979 as the Conservative administration tried to cut expenditure. In the USA the federal government has 'executive' agencies such as the Council on Environmental Quality, the Office of Science and Technology Policy, and the Central Intelligence Agency which are not part of regular government departments. Other agencies like the National Park Service (Department of the Interior) or the FBI (Department of Justice) are directly responsible to the parent department.

The regional distribution of administration is often highly biased towards the centres of government to the extent that central government becomes synonymous with its principal location—Whitehall and Washington for instance. Table 7.4 shows the distribution of civil servants in the regions of the UK by departmental function, and the overwhelming concentration in South-East England is very evident. Since 1979 the reduction in the number of civil servants has been proportionately higher in South-East England because it has been policy to cut administration more than the actual services, which has hit Whitehall. Most departments have a heavy locational bias towards South-East England: 72 per cent of the Treasury staff, 66 per cent of the Department of Trade and Industry, and 62 per cent of the Department of Education and Science are found in South-East England. Departments with little or no representation in London are National Savings, which was deliberately relocated in the 1950s and 1960s (Premium Bonds to Lytham St Anne's, Lancashire, and National Savings Accounts to Glasgow), and not surprisingly the Scottish and Welsh Offices. Of the other departments, Defence has a lower proportion but very high absolute numbers of civil servants in South-East England. There are also high numbers of defence personnel and civil servants in South-West England. Defence accounts for a high proportion of civil service employment (31.9 per cent of all civil servants work for the Ministry of Defence) because industrial civil servants are included—those who make weapons, ammunition, aircraft, tanks and ships. Important defence bases at Plymouth, Portsmouth and Aldershot as well as units such as the Admiralty at Bath generate much associated civilian employment and help to explain the amount of defence employment in South-East and South-West England. Departments requiring a high degree of contact with the public, such as Health and Social Security, Inland Revenue, and Employment, and more evenly distributed, but they too have high concentrations of staff in South-East England. In line with government office dispersal policy the Department of Health and Social Security conducts much of its operations in Newcastle, and another example of this deliberate location policy is the transfer of the Royal Mint from a cramped site near the Tower of London to a greenfield site at Llantrisant, South Wales.

*The spatial organisation of a government department*
The British Ministry of Agriculture, Fisheries and Food (MAFF) provides a good example of the spatial oranisation of a government department. With 11 800 civil servants the MAFF was one of the smaller departments, though Scotland and Northern Ireland have their own agriculture departments drawn from their respective regional offices. Some 46 per cent of MAFF civil servants are located in South-East England, where the expected concentration in Whitehall is complemented by the existence of many laboratories and research stations in the region (see Figure 7.2). Because MAFF is responsible for plant and animal health it maintains a large number of veterinary and plant pathology specialists. It also has an international func-

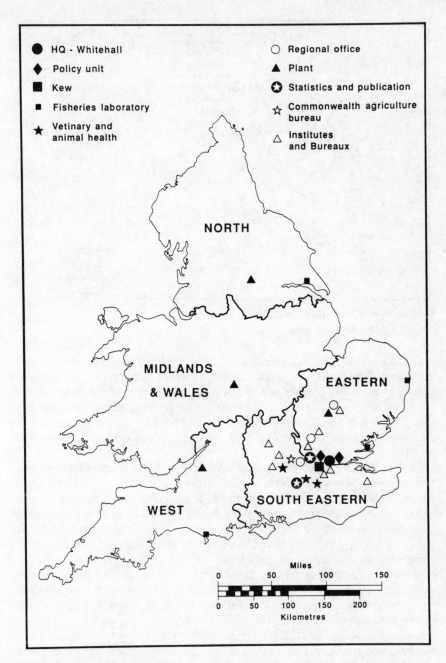

**Figure 7.2**  MAFF organisation
*Source: Whitaker's Almanack, 1984*

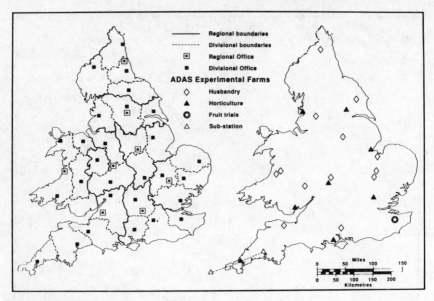

**Figure 7.3**   ADAS offices
*Source*: ADAS, *Annual Report*, 1976.

tion in its role of running several Commonwealth agricultural bureaux and institutes; for example, Rothampstead research station at Harpenden. MAFF's regional organisation does not correspond with the standard regions so comparisons are difficult. Each large region has its own regional headquarters. One function of MAFF is to conduct the annual June census of farms, and this employs large numbers of civil servants to process and analyse the results.

MAFF also has its own specialist agency, the (Agricultural Development and Advisory Service (ADAS), which is responsible for practical day-to-day liaison with farmers. ADAS officers form the agricultural extension service of MAFF. They advise farmers on everything from grant applications for new buildings to monitoring sheep dipping, and for this reason they have to be well distributed geographically. Hence ADAS has a regional and divisional structure covering groups of counties; for example, the Cambridge regional office serves the whole of the eastern region and is subdivided into divisions each with its own office, as shown in Figure 7.3. Another branch of ADAS is concerned with research and development on experimental farms and research stations.

Since 1945 advice has been freely available to farmers on demand, but the recession-induced cutbacks in government have led to the closure of some experimental stations and a suggestion of privatising the whole service. Body (1984) showed how MAFF and its clients are clearly related when he noted how the concentration of power in Whitehall had encouraged no less than 67 agricultural interest groups and lobbying organisations in addition to the old established National Farmers' Union to locate in the West End of London. Not only does government form concentrations of offices in a city, but it also brings its associates in its train. Doubtless the same is true for other departments.

*The growth and impact of bureaucracy: the example of defence*
As warfare becomes more complex and sophisticated so more civilians are employed in manufacturing and maintaining weapons, clothing and transport. The work-force in catering, cleaning and administration also expands. A comparison of nations with over 250 000 armed servicemen reveals the truth of this observation. Raw numbers of soldiers are no guide to their quality, as, for example, in India and Turkey whose large armies contain conscripts in contrast to the smaller but highly technically equipped military force of the UK. Hence the ratio of three civilians to one armed serviceman is common in the advanced nations. Countries like Poland and Spain, whose armed forces are less sophisticatedly equipped have a two to one ratio, while in Third World countries like India and Pakistan the ratio is one to one (see Table 7.5).

In addition to the civil servants in places like Whitehall and the Pentagon there is employment for civilians on military bases. Often these bases are located in rural areas and provide welcome jobs. Todd (1980) demonstrated that the small Canadian community of Gimli, Manitoba, with 1,000 inhabitants, had 193 direct civilian jobs and 63 indirect or induced jobs in the town itself due to the presence of a local air station. This station injected $2.8 million into the community annually. In the USA it has been estimated that major military bases (those with over 2,000 personnel) employ 831 000 civilians as well as 1.6 million servicemen. Army towns like Aldershot or naval bases like Portsmouth in the UK are also well-known as providers of civilian employment and contributors to the level of service activities.

*The spatial organisation of other services: the example of the law*
Two aspects of law enforcement illustrate the importance of spatial organisation. First, police authorities in the UK are organised on territorial lines which may cover a county or groups of counties as in the Thames valley and West Midlands. An exception is the Royal Ulster Constabulary, which has responsibility for the whole province. Each police force is a separate body under a Chief Constable, but ultimately control lies with the local authority, except for London's Metropolitan Police Force which is directly responsible to a government minister, the Home Secretary. Although various constabularies evolved to cover their own areas, the growing range of problems with a wider spatial dimension (for example, terrorism, industrial disputes, and criminals operating nationally or internationally) prompted increased cooperation among police forces. In the USA there are separate police forces at town and city, state and federal levels, plus the Federal Bureau of Investigation (FBI) and US marshals. France, with its greater centralisation, has a national police force and certain functions are given over to paramilitary forces like the Compagnies Republicaines de Securité (CRS).

Britain's 52 police forces have 132 500 regular officers and there are also 7900 in the Royal Ulster Constabulary. The density of police coverage varies spatially (Figure 7.4) with the big cities and Northern Ireland having the highest proportion of police to inhabitants; the Metropolitan Police Force

**Table 7.5**   Defence statistics for all countries with armed forces of over 250,000 1980

| | Armed forces | Soldiers per 1000 civilians | Defence spending (% GNP) | Ratio of civilian defence workers and civil servants to armed forces |
|---|---|---|---|---|
| China | 4,750,000 | 4.0* | 6.7 | 1.5:1 |
| USSR | 3,673,000 | 18.4 | 10.7 | 3.0:1 |
| USA | 2,049,100 | 10.4 | 5.2 | 3.0:1 |
| India | 1,104,000 | 2.0 | 2.9 | 1.5:1 |
| Vietnam | 1,029,000 | 12.9 | 10.6 | 1.5:1 |
| North Korea | 782,000 | 34.9 | 6.2 | 1.5:1 |
| South Korea | 601,600 | 15.6 | 5.5 | 1.5:1 |
| Turkey | 569,000 | 13.0 | 4.1 | 1.5:1 |
| France | 504,630 | 9.4 | 3.9 | 3.0:1 |
| West Germany | 495,000 | 8.0 | 3.2 | 2.5:1 |
| Taiwan | 451,000 | 27.5 | 6.5 | 1.5:1 |
| Pakistan | 450,600 | 6.3 | 5.1 | 1.0:1 |
| Egypt | 367,000 | 8.8 | 9.9 | 1.5:1 |
| Italy | 366,000 | 6.4 | 2.4 | 2.5:1 |
| UK | 343,646 | 5.7 | 4.8 | 3.0:1 |
| Spain | 342,000 | 8.7 | 1.8 | 2.0:1 |
| Poland | 319,000 | 12.3 | 2.9 | 2.0:1 |
| Indonesia | 273,000 | 1.7 | 3.6 | 1.0:1 |
| Brazil | 272,550 | 3.9 | 0.8 | 1.5:1 |
| Iraq | 252,250 | 11.2 | 8.0 | 1.0:1 |
| Yugoslavia | 252,000 | 11.8 | 4.1 | 1.5:1 |

\* estimate
*Sources:* G. Kurian (1984), *The New Book of World Rankings*, New York, Facts on File Publications, 1984; and M. Kidron and D. Smith, *The War Atlas*, London, Pan, 1983, Map 27.

alone has 26 000 officers. Rural areas are not so intensively policed because problems associated with crime and disorder or traffic congestion are less acute there. In order to release as many uniformed officers as possible for operational duties police authorities employ 35 000 civilians on administrative duties in England and Wales and 2300 in Scotland. Increasing use of computers calls for more programmers, many of whom are civilians. There are also 4700 traffic wardens in England and Wales, and 570 in Scotland (Central Office of Information, 1984). In the USA the proportion of civilians to officers varies considerably (see Table 7.6). In Chicago it is 1:6, but in Jacksonville, Florida, it is 1:1.5. Despite the impression given on British and American TV, relatively little time is spent out on the streets by police officers. Much of their time (up to half for a British constable) is spent in administrative tasks.

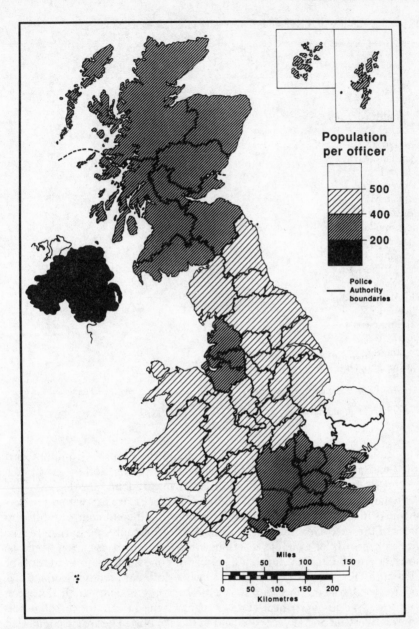

**Figure 7.4** Police manpower
*Source: Regional Trends*, 1985, Table 5.7

The second aspect of law enforcement with a spatial dimension is that of the courts. In Britain magistrates courts deal with the majority of criminal cases, but more serious cases are the province of the Crown Courts. There are some 700 magistrates courts and 90 Crown Courts in all. The most serious crimes (such as murder and terrorism) are dealt with by High Court judges.

**Table 7.6**  Police and civilian employees in large cities, USA, 1982

|  | *Police* | *Civilians* |
| --- | --- | --- |
| Atlanta, GA | 1 340 | 283 |
| Baltimore, MD | 3 056 | 525 |
| Boston, MA | 1 737 | 392 |
| Chicago, IL | 12 562 | 2 463 |
| Cleveland, OH | 1 947 | 331 |
| Dallas, TX | 1 996 | 573 |
| Denver, CO | 1 388 | 303 |
| Detroit, MI | 4 092 | 613 |
| Houston, TX | 3 345 | 1 074 |
| Jacksonville, FL | 903 | 664 |
| Los Angeles, CA | 6 861 | 2 441 |
| Memphis, TN | 1 200 | 298 |
| New Orleans, LA | 1 355 | 503 |
| New York, NY | 22 855 | 5 876 |
| Philadelphia, PA | 7 377 | 904 |
| Phoenix, AZ | 1 621 | 694 |
| San Francisco, CA | 1 971 | 508 |
| Seattle, WA | 1 007 | 371 |
| Tucson, AZ | 557 | 182 |
| Washington, DC | 3 861 | 524 |

*Source: World Almanac,* 1984

The Royal Courts of Justice in the Strand and the Central Criminal Court (the Old Bailey) form the core of London's legal quarter, and the traditional Inns of Court as well as the offices of law firms are found nearby.

England and Wales are subdivided into circuits (Figure 7.5) with three tiers of courts in each. Circuit judges sit in sessions in different courts at different times of the year. Generally cases go to the nearest court appropriate for the level concerned; for example, a serious crime committed in Devon would be heard at Exeter Crown Court but a less serious one might go to Barnstaple or Plymouth. The Scottish system is somewhat different because Scotland has its own legal system more closely resembling those of continental European countries. Sheriff courts hear cases brought by the Procurator Fiscal, a full-time civil servant and lawyer based at the sheriff court. The sparse population and low crime rate in the Highlands and Islands requires a special solution which entails groups of courts served by a panel of sheriffs who move in much the same way as English circuit judges. Thus the courts are organised on a territorial and hierarchical basis which has analogies with central place networks, even to the extent that the travelling sheriffs of northern Scotland appear to have much in common with the operators of periodic markets.

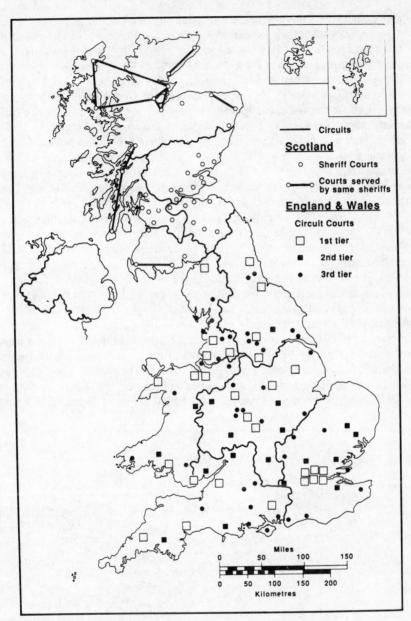

**Figure 7.5**   Circuit and sheriff courts
*Source: Whitaker's Almanack*, 1987

*Local government*

Local government authorities perform an administrative role and provide services such as education. In federal countries the component states have considerable autonomy except in matters of national defence, foreign affairs and national taxes. Although federal laws on education, consumer rights and welfare guide the individual states in adopting compatible practices, states can act in a contrary way. Within states there is a lower tier of local government corresponding with what is usually meant by local government in unitary systems. The latter have nothing comparable to state governments, and there is little scope for local authority defiance of the national government in a unitary state as the dispute between the Conservative government and the Labour-controlled metropolitan counties and Greater London Council demonstrated. Finance is the key to local government (Bennett, 1980). Authorities capable of raising taxes can fund their programmes. Local taxes are usually additional to national taxes, and in some countries revenue may be raised by scales taxes or local income taxes. In Britain local revenue is raised by a tax on property though it is proposed to replace this with a flat-rate tax on individuals or poll tax. Local property taxes have risen in recent years, but despite the resentment this has caused much local government activity is actually funded directly by the national government.

The chief spatial expressions of local government are the division of territory into units of management and the selection of a centre for administration. Population and geographical size are the two main criteria for designating an area, and many studies, theoretical and practical, have been conducted to establish deisrable or optimum sizes. Changes in the human geography of a country rapidly outdate existing boundaries, but constant reorganisation of local government is inconvenient and disruptive. Most local authorities are suboptimal from the moment they are announced because the processes of change are continuous. Thus, as suburbs spread across the city boundaries the movement of population affects the city's tax base leading to declining revenues without a comparable reduction in cost. Some believe that

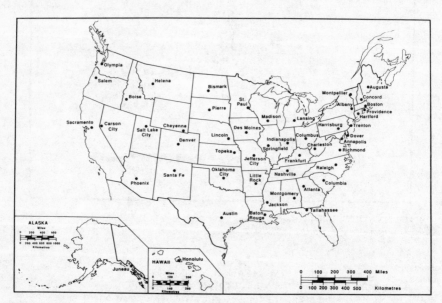

**Figure 7.6** State capitals, USA
*Source: Times Concise Atlas of the World*

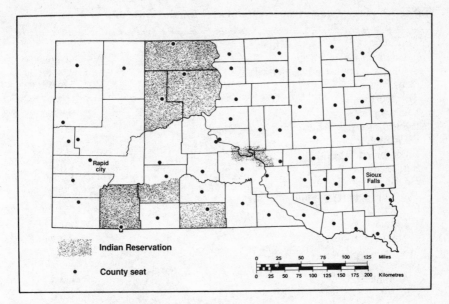

**Figure 7.7** Counties and county seats, South Dakota

this problem would have been reduced had the city region concept been adopted in the 1974 reorganisation of local government in Great Britain.

In the USA states vary greatly in population and size, and many have revenues exceeding those of several independent nations. State capitals (Figure 7.6) are the administrative centres, but they are rarely the state's major city. With the exceptions of Atlanta, Boston, Salt Lake City and Phoenix, American state capitals are relatively small and unknown outside the country or state itself. How many non-Americans could name the states of which Bismark, Pierre, Olympia and Montpellier are capitals? The late settlement of the Mid-west and Great Plains allowed a straightforward geometrical division of states into counties, as is illustrated by the case of South Dakota (Figure 7.7). Rivers make obvious boundaries, but otherwise the areas are regular and in most cases the county seat is close to the county's geometrical centre.

Local authorities employ over 2½ million people in Great Britain (Table 7.7), most dealing with actual services but many in administrative and clerical jobs; for example, there are 424 000 administrators in education compared with 600 000 teachers and lecturers. Separate figures are not given for other services, though many of the 'miscellaneous' services are central adminis-trative jobs. Geographically council staffs have to be housed in the adminis-trative centre, and the 'County' or 'Shire' halls are usually well-known land-marks in county towns. Like American state capitals, English county towns are not necessarily the largest town in the local authority area. Table 7.8 shows that in South-West England county towns range in population size from 14 000 for Dorchester to 524 000 for Bristol. County towns usually have a higher proportion of employment in 'other services' than the rest of their county. Apart from containing the local government headquarters, the county

**Table 7.7**   Local authority manpower, Great Britain, 1984 (thousands)

| | |
|---|---:|
| Education | |
|    Lecturers and teachers | 608.6 |
|    Others (administration, clerical) | 424.8 |
| Construction | 132.9 |
| Transport | 27.7 |
| Social services | 251.4 |
| Public libraries and museums | 37.0 |
| Recreation | 87.0 |
| Environmental health | 23.4 |
| Refuse collection | 51.0 |
| Housing | 62.2 |
| Town and country planning | 23.0 |
| Fire service | |
|    Regular | 40.5 |
|    Administration, etc. | 5.7 |
| Miscellaneous services | 288.5 |
| Police | |
|    All ranks | 134.5 |
|    Cadets | 1.0 |
|    Civilians | 41.1 |
|    Traffic wardens | 5.5 |
| Agency staff | 0.6 |
| Magistrates courts/district courts | 9.3 |
| Probation officers | 5.9 |
| Others | 5.7 |
| | |
| Total | 2,267.4 |

*Source: Social Trends*, 1985, Table 4.11, p. 65.

**Table 7.8**   County Towns in South-West England: population and 'other' services employment

| County | Town | Population | Percentage of 'other' services in town | Percentage of 'other' services in county |
|---|---|---|---|---|
| Avon | Bristol | 524 371 | 47.3 | 35.0 |
| Cornwall | Truro | 18 557 | 44.7 | 34.7 |
| Devon | Exeter | 91 938 | 43.2 | 37.8 |
| Gloucestershire | Gloucester | 108 150 | 32.4 | 32.3 |
| Somerset | Taunton | 48 863 | 41.7 | 30.9 |
| Wiltshire | Trowbridge | 27 476 | 29.3 | 36.8 |
| Dorset | Dorchester | 14 225 | 51.8 | 37.2 |

*Source: Regional Trends*, 1985.

town is likely to accommodate the local head offices of national concerns such as the gas and electricity boards, representatives of central government, various quangos, and a host of voluntary 'county' organisations affected by proximity to the official bodies.

## Private sector office activities

The more readily available data relating to the public sector must not be allowed to obscure the importance of private sector office activity. Many office staff appear in the statistics as manufacturing workers, but one service industry category in the British Standard Industrial Classification has thrived in recent years. Insurance, banking, finance and business services comprise the traditional 'City' occupations that are the heart of the private sector's office activities, and they contribute much to the character of the world's renowned office quarters. Some indication of the scope of the British financial sector is provided by Table 7.9, from which it will be seen that in addition to the banks there are several specialised finance activities which together make up a complex whole. As with the public sector, it is possible to consider patterns of office activities at different geographical scales.

*International operations*
At the international level private sector office activities may be operating in a global market or they may be part of a transnational firm aiming to serve a

**Table 7.9**   The British financial sector

| Banking system | Specialised Finance |
| --- | --- |
| Bank of England | Finance Houses |
| Clearing Banks | Leasing companies |
| (Barclays, Lloyds, Midland, | |
| National Westminster, | |
| Bank of Scotland, Clydesdale and | |
| Royal Bank of Scotland) | Factoring companies |
| National Girobank | Finance Corporations |
| Trustees Savings Bank (TSB) | Pension funds |
| Overseas banks | Investment trusts |
| Merchant banks | Unit trusts |
| Discount market | Building societies |
| National Savings Bank | Insurance market |
| | Stock Exchange |
| | Foreign exchange market |
| | London gold market |
| | Commodity market |
| | Futures market |

*Source*: COI (1984)

particular geographical market. The former includes the insurance, banking and finance activities taking place in important world financial centres like London, New York, Paris, Tokyo and Hong Kong. These money markets exercise a great influence on investment flows throughout the world and they are major contributors to national economies in the form of 'invisible exports'. Banks and insurance companies, for example, may have branch offices in overseas financial centres, but much of the business transacted can be effectively conducted with the aid of modern telecommunications and computing equipment. Activities of this sort are considered in more detail in the next chapter.

Many large business enterprises are transnational in scope; for example, IBM has a presence in 80 countries and ICI in nearly 50, and in both cases over a quarter of their employees work outside the home country. As Dicken and Lloyd (1981) pointed out, transnationals are not confined to American-owned firms, nor are they confined to industrial companies. In effect there has been an internationalisation of production and capital which has had repercussions on the location of office activities. Also, as business enterprises have become larger they have had to modify their internal organisational structures. Arrangements may differ in detail, but in general large firms are hierarchical in structure. It is possible to distinguish between top-level decisions and control, day-to-day administration, and basic work processes. Each of these levels has different locational requirements. A transnational company can easily transmit its top-level decisions from the headquarters site to the subsidiary headquarters offices in overseas countries. Both these levels require 'information-rich' environments, which usually means being close to the main business and government centres in the case of the top-level decision-making unit. The second-level units need not be located in a capital city, although overseas subsidiary offices do tend to locate in or close to the capital city of the country in which they operate; for example, the clustering of American-owned company offices around London, Paris and Brussels. The third-level activities tend to be located according to the requirements of the production process concerned, and in this case the office work is 'attached'.

*National and regional patterns*

Daniels (1982) noted the very high degree of spatial concentration in the location of producer services in Europe and North America. The search for supporting services, clients, prestige, and access to information and the media gave rise to 'corporate complexes' which are aggregations of headquarters offices, business services, advertising agencies and so on.

*Fortune International* (1987) shows the trend in the USA (Table 7.10 and Figure 7.8). New York is the major centre with 72 of the 500 firms, followed by Los Angeles, Dallas and Chicago. Relatively few places dominate the list, and 40 per cent of the top 500 firms are to be found in the 11 leading cities. It is noteworthy that the financial sector is well represented in these cities. Sixty-five per cent of the New York firms are in insurance, banking, finance and savings; 57 per cent in Los Angeles, and 100 per cent of the firms in Hartford, the next most important city. There are numerous smaller corpor-

**Table 7.10** Leading centres of service industries in the USA, 1987

| City | Number of firms with HQ in city | No. in finance sector |
| --- | --- | --- |
| New York, NY | 72 | 47 |
| Los Angeles, CA | 26 | 15 |
| Dallas, TX | 17 | 5 |
| Chicago, IL | 16 | 6 |
| San Francisco, CA | 13 | 5 |
| Houston, TX | 12 | 5 |
| Minneapolis/St Paul, MN | 10 | 7 |
| Philadelphia, PA | 10 | 7 |
| Hartford, CT | 10 | 10 |
| Boston, MA | 9 | 7 |
| Miami, FL | 7 | 5 |
| Phoenix, AZ | 7 | 3 |
| St Louis, MO | 7 | 4 |
| Atlanta, GA | 7 | 2 |
| Columbus, OH | 6 | 3 |
| Seattle, WA | 6 | 3 |
| Washington, DC | 6 | 5 |
| Detroit, MI | 6 | 4 |
| Richmond, VA | 6 | 2 |
| Cincinnatti, OH | 6 | 3 |
| Wilmington, DE | 5 | 2 |
| Baltimore, MD | 5 | 4 |
| Charlotte, NC | 5 | 2 |
| Newark, NJ | 5 | 4 |
| San Diego, CA | 5 | 3 |
| Pittsburgh, PA | 4 | 2 |
| Nashville, TN | 4 | 2 |
| Louisville, KY | 4 | 2 |
| Milwaukee, WI | 4 | 3 |
| Cleveland, OH | 4 | 3 |
| Jacksonville, FL | 4 | 2 |
| Fort Wayne, IN | 4 | 2 |

*Source: Fortune International* (1987)

ate complexes from Nashville to Seattle and Phoenix to Cincinnati. Four main regional concentrations can be distinguished in Figure 7.8: New York–New England; the West Coast around Los Angeles; Texas (Dallas–Fort Worth–Houston); and a diffuse Midwest-South area stretching from Minneapolis to Miami in which there are numerous medium and small corporate centres. With the exception of Phoenix, the South-West and mountain states have a great dearth of corporate centres. The corporate centre pattern mirrors the distribution of the population and manufacturing industry. Like London, New York has retained its paramount position in financial services even though it has had to face the challenge of the rise of the Sunbelt cities.

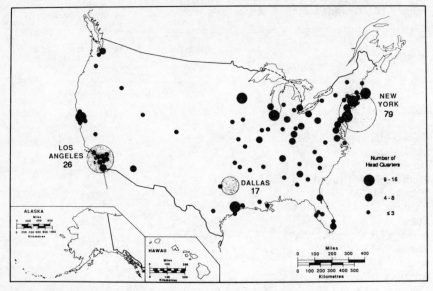

**Figure 7.8**   Service sector corporate office centres, USA, 1986
*Source: Fortune International* (1987)

*California case study*

The Los Angeles area is the second most important service sector corporate centre after New York and Figure 7.9 shows the location of the leading firms' headquarters according to type of firm. Downtown Los Angeles itself has the major share, but suburban centres such as Beverly Hills, Burbank and Glendale are also significant. Beverly Hills and Burbank are the headquarters of the entertainment industry, with important film and TV studios (for example, Walt Disney) being located there. Nevertheless, the most striking feature is the emphasis on finance. The total assets of financial corporation headquarters in the Los Angeles area are huge ($325 billion). As can be seen from Figure 7.10, downtown Los Angeles has the greatest concentration of assets. Banks, savings, investment companies, financial corporations and life assurance firms are to be found in Los Angeles. Savings companies in particular are highly concentrated in California.

*Other aspects of national and regional patterns*

In Britain and France there is considerable regional concentration of office activity, and to a lesser extent this is also true of West Germany and Italy. Bateman (1985) described the British office market as unbalanced, with over half of it being in South-East England. In fact, London accounted for 37.6 per cent of the country's total office space in 1982, but elsewhere Manchester and Liverpool were of some importance and rents (a measure of demand) were relatively high in Birmingham, Bristol, Cardiff, Leeds, Glasgow and Edinburgh. There was some evidence that Brighton and Bournemouth were

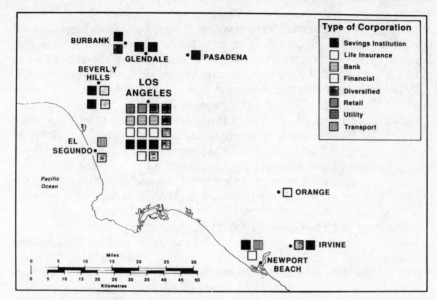

**Figure 7.9** Corporate Headquarters, Los Angeles area, 1986
*Source: Fortune International* (1987)

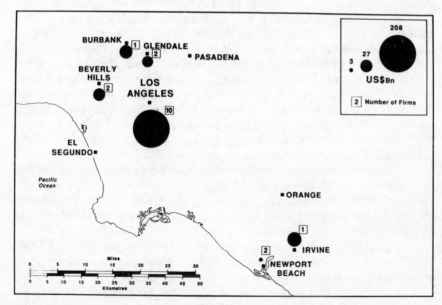

**Figure 7.10** Total assets of financial corporations with headquarters in the Los Angeles area, 1986
*Source: Fortune International* (1987)

important office centres enjoying lower rents than London. A second tier of provincial centres includes Nottingham, Sheffield and Coventry, but in Leicester overdevelopment resulted in an excess supply and low rents. Building trends suggest that this pattern will remain unchanged for some time to come. It should be remembered that the figures quoted here include public as well as private offices, but the pattern of the latter is clear.

Paris contains over 50 per cent of French office space and approximately two-thirds of Parisian workers are employed in the service sector. Some 96 per cent of French banks have their headquarters in Paris, and over 40 per cent of those employed in French banking, insurance and finance work in the Ile de France region. Compared with other European countries the French provincial office market is poorly developed, though Lyons and Marseilles have experienced some office growth. In Canada, Toronto, Calgary and Edmonton are the most important centres.

In such a brief review of private sector office distribution it has been possible to do little more than highlight the leading office growth centres, but some emphasis should be given to two important trends. Suburbanisation of offices is a global phenomenon and, in his study of Melbourne, Edgington (1982) observed that whereas planners were trying to retain the CBD's competitive edge, offices, except for banking and finance, which moved to the suburbs also reduced their spatial linkages so the attraction of the CBD's agglomeration economies diminished. Kellerman and Krakover (1986) examined decentralisation from another perspective. According to them leading and trailing sectors have been identified in the literature. A suggested order of suburbanisation was population, manufacturing, retailing, business services and wholesaling. Evidence from Philadelphia supported this suggestion, but within the city's urban field it was found that the fastest growth rates were in business services followed by wholesaling, FIRE (finance, insurance and real estate), retailing, population and manufacturing. Complex spatial changes accompany this sequence: population has the furthest outlying peak, FIRE has a secondary spatial growth peak located beyond the boundary of the urban field, retailing is double-peaked, services and wholesaling are suburban in their growth, and manufacturing is undergoing a general decline. On this evidence services, wholesaling and FIRE are trailing sectors, while population and retailing are leading sectors developing peaks of growth in the outer areas. Possibly, therefore, these two activities are indicators of future developments in other services.

In a post-industrial setting such as the Dallas-Fort Worth region Rees (1978) found that manufacturing headquarters and their associated office activities are often spatially dispersed in order to adapt to polynuclear cities. In such areas the direct impact of the headquarters may be minimal. Wheeler and Brown (1985) described a shift in the corporate influence within the USA from the North-East to the South and West, not so much as a result of relocation as because of the growth of metropolitan areas in the South and West. Even so, non-Sunbelt firms dominate the Sunbelt economy and control much of the investment there. These authors found support for a four-stage model proposed by Semple and Phipps (1982). This model states that the spatial evolution of corporate power initially begins with concentration in a single national centre (such as New York) and perhaps some minor regional concentrations. At the second stage there is dispersal to a number of dominant regional centres so that no clearly distinguished national headquarters centre remains. In the next stage there is further dispersion to satellite and other urban centres within a region, thus reducing the dominance of regional centres. Finally 'national maturity', an idealised end-point with no dominant national or regional centres, is attained. For the period 1960–80 the South experienced a growing corporate influence and the number of metropolitan areas having major corporate headquarters increased. Houston, Dallas-Fort Worth, Richmond and Greensboro-Winston-Salem were leading centres, but some future convergence can be predicted as corporate importance and population size move closer towards equilibrium.

Contrasting with offices serving national and regional markets are those that serve local needs. This type of office locates in general accordance with central place principles. Banks, insurance offices, accountants, solicitors, estate agents, auctioneers and valuers are found in towns of all sizes and in some villages. There is a parallel with retail provision, and as with retailing there is an intra-urban hierarchical pattern. At this level office activities are geographically widespread and present in all regions.

## Conclusion

Office jobs are rightly regarded as the most significant source of new service jobs in the post-war period. Many of these jobs were in manufacturing industry rather than in the service sector as defined in Chapter 1, but it is very difficult to distinguish between the geographical patterns formed by service sector and non-service sector office activities, if indeed such differences exist. In addition to their importance as a source of employment offices are perhaps the most visible evidence of a service sector presence in the urban landscape, especially since skyscrapers began to dominate the skyline.

The availability of data is such that in this chapter more attention has been paid to public sector activities, though this can be justified because the growth of public sector employment has played a prominent part in the recent expansion of service activities, not least in the UK. It was shown that the work of international and national civil servants creates distinctive concentrations of activity, and that in the case of the latter these concentrations are widely diffused throughout the national space. Despite the greater attention given to government civil servants the number of local government employees actually exceeds those in central government employment. However, this statement must be treated with caution because many local government workers perform blue-collar rather than white-collar jobs. Geographical patterns can be discerned at the international, national, regional and local levels for public and private sector activities, and there are many similarities between the two sectors in this respect.

*Chapter 8*

# Internationalisation: The Growth of Transnational Operations

Traditionally financial institutions have engaged in international activity and the penetration of overseas markets with beneficial results for the national economy in the shape of 'invisible exports'. Usually presented as a straightforward venture, international lending by private banks also conforms to government objectives and has geopolitical overtones in what some have termed 'finance capitalism' (Fryer, 1987). Prominent among the lending countries are the USA, the UK, West Germany and, increasingly, Japan. Like the UK, the USA aims to expand its service exports in an attempt to regain some of the ground lost to Japan in manufacturing. Undoubtedly there is great interest in the export of services, and this has been accompanied by a growth in service sector transnational companies. Firms of this type are not new, they have long existed but since the 1970s there has been a new phase of international production which has found its expression in the global corporation (Taylor and Thrift, 1982) and in the rise of service sector transnationals (Enderwick, 1987). In the remainder of this chapter the development of transnational service activitites and the world's leading corporations will be considered. This will be followed by a discussion of the internationalisation of producer and consumer services.

## The development of transnational activities

Recent work on the global manufacturing economy emphasises the importance of transnational (multinational) companies. One consequence of this form of organisation is that it leads to a spatial division of production. Obviously this also applies to manufacturing-related services performed by the companies themselves. Businesses may benefit from operating in a transnational context if this permits them to avoid the penalties of tariff or tax barriers. Mergers and acquisitions have contributed to the transnational trend, often resulting in conglomerates that have a service element. Retail and wholesale firms, and even health and education services, have engaged in transnational activities, but financial, hotel, and tourist operators are longer established participants in this field. So powerful have transnationals become that fears have been expressed about the power they wield in respect of the spatial distribution of international monetary reserves (Leahy and Hill, 1981).

Dicken (1986) suggested that overseas investment is either *market-orientated* or *supply (cost)-orientated*. The former enables firms to locate in order to serve an overseas market directly. Much of the internationalisation of service firms has been of this type, which Dicken regarded as a form of *horizontal expansion* across national boundaries. Harrington *et al.* (1986) explored this notion in greater detail with reference to Canadian companies located in western New York. Supply-orientated investments are the dominant motivation for firms in the natural resource industries whose sources of supply may be highly localised. Such investments may be the first stage in a sequence of *vertical integration* and they have become more important for manufacturing firms. Perhaps this kind of orientation is of greatest significance in the service sector for tourist operators who may be linked to specific locations in foreign countries.

Early explanations of international production have focused on the very large, oligopolistic, mostly American enterprises. Schoenberger (1985), in discussing the role of oligopoly and 'ownership advantages', noted that this led to a preference for market-orientation. He concluded that a manufacturing company's decision to invest in the USA is not necessarily a decision to produce there for the investment may be concerned with producer services. He believed that much foreign investment is in technology-intensive activities for which a market location is very appropriate. Since transnationals vary in size explanations based on the largest firms are unlikely to encompass the full range of diversity that is present. Dunning (1983) proposed a framework for understanding the phenomenon of international production, and he envisaged the need for three facilitating conditions: first were ownership-specific advantages not possessed by competitors; second was internalisation, whereby the ownership-specific advantages can best be exploited by the firm itself rather than by selling or leasing them; third were location-specific advantages making it more profitable to produce or operate overseas.

F. W. Woolworth's pre-war expansion from the USA to the UK exemplifies the ownership-specific advantages of a well-known name. Woolworths in the UK are no longer American-owned, but Marks and Spencer have also adopted the policy of trading on the name to enter an overseas market. Hotel companies also seek to exploit their reputation for supplying a known standard of service that will ease the burden of choice for travellers, particularly business executives, when they are abroad. A traveller knows exactly what to expect of a Holiday Inn or a Hilton. Similar advantages exist for insurance, banking and consultancy services, all of which benefit from the ability to protect the company's name and to ensure its sales outlets. Access to particular markets is an additional location-specific advantage.

Advanced economies possess the advantages noted by Dunning, which is important because the demand for services is highly income-elastic. This is especially true of tourism, whose future seems to be promising as prosperity rises and given that a large proportion of the world's population has not experienced the pleasures of international travel. If tourism expands, its internationalisation will inevitably become greater. Tourist operators are naturally more likely to be involved overseas than retailers, but several retailing firms are transnational in scope and possibly there will be more internationalisation of health and education services as income increases. Holmstrom (1985) observed that the determinants of supply and demand for services and for the goods sector differ. In his view institutions facilitating the economic exchange and production of services will exhibit idiosyncratic features. Economically relevant differences include the fact that services are not storable, the difficulty of measuring and observing service quality, the problem of verifying the appropriateness of a service, and the greater flexibility of service than production technology. Holmstrom noted that in employment terms a service economy already exists, although micro-economic theories remain strongly rooted in the industrial paradigm which may have restricted understanding of the importance of service transnationals.

Internationally tradable services offer considerable investment potential. Such services are generally labour-intensive (for example, computer software, consultancy) and offer high value added. Because of their typically low import content they have favourable domestic income and employment multipliers. Services can be classified according to the degree to which they are internationally traded (Boddewyn in Enderwick, 1987). Foreign-tradable services create a commodity distinct from the production process that can be exported; for example, computer software. Location-based services require a foreign presence, generally because consumption cannot be separated from production; for example, hotel accommodation. There are also combinations or 'mixed' services where locational substitution is possible. Price competition is important. Almost any service is tradable and individuals may incur considerable time and travel costs to consume location-bound services, which suggests that cost competitiveness will be an important determinant of the propensity of trade services. Technical innovation encourages trade in services by facilitating the international exchange of electronically encodeable data, and because the conjunction of communications, information processing and storage technology permits the locational and temporal separation of service production and consumption.

Enderwick (1987) showed that a large proportion of the overseas market for services is met by direct investment instead of exports, which is not the case with manufacturing. Thus, in 1974, of the estimated $50 billion of services sold by American companies, $43 billion (86 per cent) was attributable to off-shore sales. Service sector transnationals exhibit considerable product specialisation. Since their competitive assets are likely to be of low technological complexity compared with manufactured goods, their main sources of competitive advantage are differential access to and ability to process and apply information. Government-induced market imperfections such as differential regulation and minimum standards are of assistance here. The technical conditions associated with information markets (a tendency towards monopoly provision, economies of learning and doing, and the high 'experience' content of information) suggest that many services will favour barriers to entry built upon first-move advantages and benefit of incumbency.

Economies of scale are less important to service sector transnationals than to their manufacturing counterparts, but they may be more dependent on agglomeration economies. Reliance on specialised information sources and specific skills make locations like the CBD, where financial, business and commercial interests congregate, attractive. Conversely there is evidence that the above average-size transnational service companies are less dependent on agglomeration effects than other service firms because they can benefit from the internalisation of economies previously consumed as externalities and from their privileged access to parent services. Service sector transnationals have a marked spatial concentration. About 70 per cent of the total stock of service investment is located in the advanced economies. Apart from banking and insurance, there is little investment in the developing countries, and frequently such investment is actually made in tax havens or offshore banking centres. Within the host country geographical clustering is often complex, with multi-location affiliates, which suggests that benefits accrue from a concentrated presence reinforced by mutliple representation. Uneven spatial distribution at the international level and within individual countries is the typical pattern. Within countries big business functions (research and development, financial control, senior management) are becoming centralised in core regions and cities.

Relations between service transnationals and client industries are interesting for they help to explain the role of linkage. About 50 per cent of marketed service demand is intermediate rather than final. High-technology services have particularly close linkages with their clients (often high-technology goods industries) because joint access to a pool of skilled labour, major government departments and universities is crucial. These activities are mainly producer services whose growth has been stimulated by a number of factors. One outcome has been the extension of the inter-industry division of labour resulting in the expansion of activities such as distribution, banking, insurance and finance to serve the needs of material producers. Complex problems of administration and control, as geographical and industrial diversification have been pursued, have stimulated the growth of managerial organisation. Many firms have based their product differentiation strategies on the conjunction of material and non-material goods (for example, computer hardware and software), while the rapid development of new user industries, such as investment management, computers and data processing, means that the demand for services like advertising has grown.

# The world's leading corporations: a review

Large corporations, often transnational in their business interests and ownership, dominate economic activity in the developed world. Because big corporations maintain a diversified profile it is often difficult to label a company as 'manufacturer', 'retailer' or 'financier'. Many engage in all three activities and the importance of each may vary significantly from year to year. Takeovers and mergers leading to vast and complex organisations, encompassing everything from mining through newspapers to property development, further complicate the pattern. Corporations may search out new fields of interest simply to spread the risks in uncertain markets or to utilise spare capital. BAT Industries began life as a tobacco company but, faced with increased hostility to smoking in the 1960s and 1970s, diversified into paper and packaging and retailing to safeguard its corporate future should smoking ever be outlawed. Elders IXL (Australia) is another complex conglomerate resulting from takeovers and mergers. The company has interests in woolbroking, brewing and investments which, through its traditional linkages with the British wool trade, has been able to diversify its British operations by promoting Australian lager and by purchasing a major brewery. The Japanese sogo shosha, which are trading and finance corporations to which groups of related and sometimes unrelated companies belong, are notable examples of diversified conglomerates. Taylor and Thrift (1982) consider that if the associated banks of the sogo shosha were included in the groups' total turnover figures these conglomerates would easily rank as the world's biggest companies, but in practice the banks are enumerated separately.

In terms of turnover value the oil industry, with 17 representatives, dominated the world's 50 largest corporations in 1985 (Table 8.1). Normally regarded as a primary and secondary activity engaged in extracting and refining petroleum, the oil industry actually has substantial service functions. The sogo shosha are the next biggest group, accounting for 20 per cent of the turnover of the top 50 with many fewer representatives than the oil industry. Manufacturers, especially automobile manufacturers, are the other major grouping, but four retailers, three communications services and one utility are represented. Although three companies are too diversified to permit easy labelling they all have some service functions. Some interesting features emerge when the top 50 firms are ranked (Figure 8.1). While oil companies take first and second place, four of the top ten corporations are sogo shosha and the top ten account for over 40 per cent of total turnover. Table 8.2 shows that American firms make up 46 per cent of the total; Japan is the second leading nation, and the European countries each contribute one or two firms. Mexico, with its Petróleos Mexicanos (PEMEX) state oil company, is the only non-developed country appearing in the list. Royal Dutch Shell and Unilever, both of which are Anglo-Dutch, are interesting examples of truly transnational ownership.

### The world's largest service companies

The world's largest service corporations (Table 8.3) are involved in either distribution or communications. Excluding the sogo shosha, the biggest service company in the world is Sears Roebuck, the American general merchandising distribution company. Sears Roebuck had a 1985 turnover of £29.7 billion, which is bigger than the combined GNPs of Bulgaria and Egypt. AT&T (American Telephone and Telegraph) has a bigger turnover than the combined GNPs of Portugal and Colombia. These figures serve as an indication of the scale and significance of modern giant corporations in the service sector.

### Japanese corporations

The top seven Japanese corporations are all sogo shosha (Table 8.4), four of which are among the world's top ten. With the exception of Mitsubishi, none of them is a household name in the West. Those Japanese companies which are

**Table 8.1** Activities and turnover of the world's 50 leading corporations, 1985

| Type of activity | Number of firms | Total turnover (£ billions) | Share of turnover of top 50 (%) |
|---|---|---|---|
| Oil industry | 17 | 438.4 | 36.4 |
| Sogo shosha | 7 | 248.2 | 20.8 |
| Car manufacturers | 6 | 162.5 | 13.6 |
| Other manufacture | 9 | 164.7 | 13.8 |
| Retail Distribution | 4 | 73.2 | 6.1 |
| Communications | 3 | 50.9 | 4.3 |
| Diversified corpn. | 3 | 43.1 | 3.6 |
| Utility | 1 | 11.4 | 1.0 |

*Source: Times 1000*, 1985–6

**Table 8.2** Nationality of the world's 50 leading corporations

| Nationality | Number of firms |
|---|---|
| USA | 23 |
| Japan | 13 |
| West Germany | 4 |
| UK | 2 |
| UK/Netherlands | 2 |
| France | 2 |
| Italy | 2 |
| Netherlands | 1 |
| Mexico | 1 |

*Source: Times 1000*, 1985–6

not sogo shosha are, by contrast, very familiar manufacturers of consumer goods; for example Toyota, Hitachi and Nissan. The sogo shosha include finance houses, investment trusts and banks, usually set up in order to facilitate exports of manufactured goods. Mitsubishi, for example, has its own bank and investment trust which are transnational in operation but not owner-ship—there are branches of the Mitsubishi Bank, for example, in London and other capital cities.

Japanese companies employ contrasting policies abroad. Panasonic UK does not manufacture its electrical products in the UK, but simply imports them and employs only 246 in marketing and distribution. Sony UK, on the

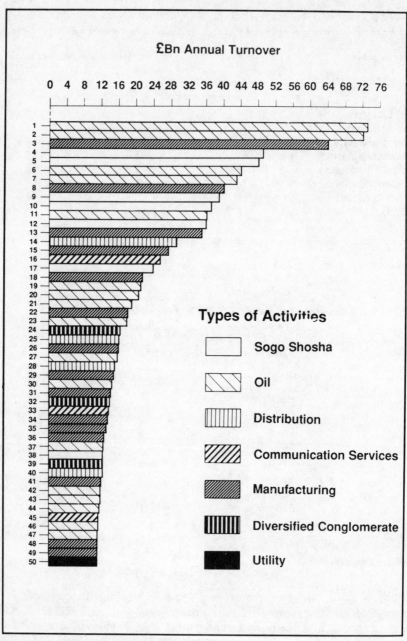

**Figure 8.1** World's 50 largest industrial groupings, 1985
*Source: Times 1000*, 1985-6

**Table 8.3** World's largest service companies, 1985

| Rank | Company | Activity | Nationality | turnover (£ billion) |
|------|---------|----------|-------------|-----------|
| 14 | Sears Roebuck | Distribution | USA | 29.7 |
| 16 | AT & T | Telecommunications | USA | 25.4 |
| 25 | K-Mart Corp. | Retailing | USA | 16.1 |
| 28 | Safeway Stores | Retailing | USA | 15.0 |
| 33 | Nippon T & T | Telecommunications | Japan | 13.8 |
| 40 | Kroger | Retailing | USA | 12.2 |
| 45 | Deutche Bundespost | Postal service | West Germany | 11.6 |

*Source: Times 1000*, 1985–6

**Table 8.4** Japan's largest corporations, 1985

| World rank | Company | | Sales (£ billions) |
|------------|---------|--|-------|
| 4 | Mitsui | (sogo shosha) | 49.8 |
| 5 | Mitsubishi | (sogo shosha) | 48.6 |
| 9 | C. Itoh | (sogo shosha) | 39.9 |
| 10 | Marubeni | (sogo shosha) | 37.0 |
| 12 | Sumitomo | (sogo shosha) | 36.2 |
| 17 | Nissho Iwai | (sogo shosha) | 23.9 |
| 22 | Toyota | | 18.1 |
| 33 | Nippon T & T | | 13.8 |
| 34 | Hitachi | | 13.4 |
| 35 | Nissan | | 13.2 |
| 38 | Toyo Menka | (sogo shosha) | 12.4 |
| 44 | Nippon Oil | | 11.8 |
| 50 | Tokyo Electric Power | | 11.4 |

*Source: Times 1000*, 1985–6

other hand, manufactures and markets its televisions, cassette recorders and radios in the UK, employing some 1800 people mostly at a factory in Bridgend, West Glamorgan. The turnover of both companies is much the same, £193 million for Panasonic and £192 million for Sony in 1985.

*Australian companies*

Service and raw materials corporations dominate Australian business (Table 8.5), but the image of Australia as a producer of primary products is only

**Table 8.5** Leading Australian Companies, 1985

| Company | Activity | Turnover (£ millions) |
|---|---|---|
| Elders IXL | Woolbroking, brewing, finance | 2866 |
| Coles & Co | Retail stores | 2786 |
| Broken Hill Pty | Iron and steel | 2760 |
| Woolworth's | Retail stores | 1890 |
| CRA | Mining | 1757 |
| Myer Emporium | Department stores | 1488 |
| Pioneer Concrete | Holding Company (manufacturing) | 1237 |
| ACI International | Holding Company (packaging) | 1096 |
| News Corporation | Newspapers | 955 |
| CSR | Holding company (sugar, building, etc) | 984 |
| Thomas Nationwide | Road haulage | 895 |
| Amatil | Holding company (diverse) | 787 |
| Dunlop Olympic | Tyres and clothing | 751 |
| ICI Australia | Chemicals | 760 |
| Ampol | Oil | 751 |
| Boral | Quarrying, gas transport | 698 |
| Burns Philp & Co | Wholesale merchants, shipping | 599 |
| Alcoa | Aluminium | 589 |
| Comalco | Aluminium | 570 |
| Australian National Industries | Drop press forging | 517 |

*Source: Times 1000*, 1985-6

partly borne out by the facts. Of eight corporations with a turnover exceeding £1 billion in 1985 four were service companies, two were diversified holding companies, and only two were in mining or heavy industry. Retail stores have a relatively higher ranking in the Australian business structure than they do in other developed countries. By comparison Sears Roebuck ranks 14th in the USA, Marks and Spencer 25th in the UK, and Carrefour 50th in Western Europe. Nevertheless, in absolute terms they are all bigger than the leading Australian retailer, Coles and Co. Sears Roebuck is actually ten times as large. Australian corporate headquarters are restricted in location to Adelaide, Melbourne and Sydney.

*British companies*

Service firms account for 46 per cent of the top 50 British firms, reflecting the high proportion of the economy devoted to services (Table 8.6). As a historical relic of London's hegemony in international trade during the nineteenth century many British firms specialise in international trade and commodity broking—for example, Dalgety, S. and W. Berisford—but large utility and

**Table 8.6** Leading service firms, UK, 1985

| UK rank | Firm | Activity | Turnover (£ billions) |
|---|---|---|---|
| 3 | BAT Industries* | Diversified | 14.4 |
| 6 | Electricity Council | Utility | 9.5 |
| 9 | British Telecom | Communications | 6.8 |
| 10 | British Gas | Utility | 6.3 |
| 13 | S. & W. Berisford | Merchanting | 5.7 |
| 14 | Grand Metropolitan | Hotels, etc | 5.05 |
| 16 | Philbro Saloamon | Commodity broking | 4.7 |
| 20 | Dalgety | Merchanting | 3.0 |
| 25 | Marks & Spencer | Retail | 3.2 |
| 26 | Allied Lyons* | Brewing, hotels | 3.1 |
| 27 | J. Sainsbury | Retail | 2.9 |
| 28 | Post Office | Postal service | 2.8 |
| 30 | British Rail | Railway service | 2.8 |
| 32 | George Weston Holdings* | Food distribution | 2.7 |
| 33 | Tesco | Retail | 2.5 |
| 34 | Lonconex | Commodity broker | 2.5 |
| 35 | British Airways | Airline | 2.5 |
| 39 | Hanson Trust* | Diversified | 2.3 |
| 45 | Inchcape | Merchanting | 2.0 |
| 46 | Reed International* | Publishing | 2.0 |
| 47 | Boots Company* | Pharmaceuticals | 2.0 |
| 48 | Great Universal Stores | Retail | 2.0 |
| 49 | Sears* | Footwear/stores | 2.0 |

*Source: Times 1000.* 1985–6
\* Mixed manufacturing/service conglomerate

communications corporations dominate the top 20. 'Chain' retailers like Marks and Spencer, Sainsbury and Tesco are also significant. Various conglomerates, like BAT, Allied Lyons, Hanson Trust and Reed International, have both manufacturing and service functions. BAT, for instance, now obtains only 50 per cent of its profits from tobacco; its financial services, led by Eagle Star and Allied Dunbar, account for 20 per cent; its retailing interests include Argos and Best Seller shops in the UK and People's Drug Stores in the USA (*Guardian*, May 1987).

*Foreign firms in the UK*

The extent of internationalisation is well illustrated by considering foreign firms in the UK. Some 28 per cent of *Times 1000* companies are foreign-owned. Manufacturing firms (167) exceed service sector companies (121), but a large number of significant service sector firms appear in the list (see Table 8.7). The largest number of foreign service sector firms are closely related to

**Table 8.7** Main activities of leading foreign firms in the UK

|  | *Number of firms* |
|---|---|
| *Manufacturing* | |
| Oil production | 11 |
| Metals | 13 |
| Chemicals | 35 |
| Pharmaceuticals | 16 |
| Vehicles | 9 |
| Electronics | 17 |
| Engineering | 25 |
| Other manufacturing | 3 |
| Civil engineering and construction | 7 |
| Food, drink and tobacco | 16 |
| Computers and business equipment | 7 |
| Packaging | 2 |
| Household consumer goods | 6 |
| *Services* | |
| Publishing | 6 |
| Shipping | 3 |
| Motor vehicle distribution | 16 |
| Oil/petroleum distribution | 9 |
| Industrial business services | 12 |
| Commodity trading/merchants | 13 |
| Wine merchants | 3 |
| Metal and ore traders/merchants | 7 |
| Food marketing and distribution | 12 |
| Food retailing | 1 |
| Insurance | 3 |
| Electronics distribution | 14 |
| Consumer services | 5 |
| Travel, hotels and leisure | 6 |
| Advertising agencies | 8 |
| Security services | 2 |
| Newsagents | 1 |

*Source: Times 1000, 1985–6*
*Note:* a small number of firms are counted twice when they are involved in both manufacturing and distribution. This applies to one firm in food and three in electronics.

manufacturers and are in effect their sales branches. Motor vehicle distribution, electronic goods distribution, food distribution and oil distribution account for 42 per cent of the foreign service firms.

Industrial business services and advertising agencies are the most numerous of the other firms (16 per cent), while commodity trading and metal trading between them account for a further 16 per cent. These firms are located in the

UK because of the City of London's pre-eminence in international trade and finance. Relatively fewer foreign firms are directly involved in consumer services, although there are representatives of travel, hotel and retail firms to be found. The size of these firms is noteworthy for none has a turnover of less than £43 million. Most of these foreign firms have gravitated to London, thereby illustrating the characteristics of spatial concentration and agglomeration that Enderwick suggested (see p. 165). Also, as Enderwick indicated, most are concerned with producer services.

Over half the foreign firms are American (Table 8.8). The majority of the rest are from other advanced nations, but even the leading European countries (France and West Germany) have only a tenth of the representation of the Americans. Japanese investment in the UK increased dramatically to a total of $4125 million in the financial year 1986–7. In all some 73 Japanese manufacturing companies are established in the UK, and there is a growing service element, including about 40 banks and other financial institutions.

At first sight there is a surprisingly large contingent of firms from small island states, though closer examination proves that these firms are not native Cayman or Netherlands Antilles firms, but British, European or American companies domiciled in tax havens. Figure 8.2 shows the location of the home countries of the leading foreign firms in the UK and Enderwick's (1987) observation that the absence of regulations in island tax havens is attractive to transnationals is borne out.

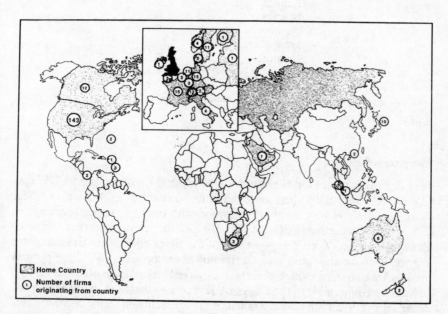

**Figure 8.2** Home countries of 279 foreign firms in the *Times 1000* list of leading firms in the UK
*Source: Times 1000*, 1985–6

**Table 8.8** Nationality of leading foreign firms in the UK (per cent)

|  | % |
|---|---|
| USA | 51.2 |
| West Germany | 5.3 |
| France | 5.3 |
| Canada | 4.3 |
| Switzerland | 4.3 |
| Netherlands | 3.9 |
| Sweden | 3.9 |
| Japan | 3.9 |
| Australia | 2.1 |
| Denmark | 1.7 |
| Italy | 1.4 |
| Norway | 1.4 |
| Luxembourg | 1.0 |
| Liechtenstein | 1.0 |
| Netherlands Antilles | 1.0 |
| South Africa | 1.0 |
| Belgium | 1.0 |
| New Zealand | 0.7 |
| Panama | 0.7 |
| Malaysia | 0.3 |
| Ireland | 0.3 |
| Singapore | 0.3 |
| Finland | 0.3 |
| Bahrain | 0.3 |
| Cayman Islands | 0.3 |
| Hong Kong | 0.3 |
| Bermuda | 0.3 |
| Jersey | 0.3 |
| Guernsey | 0.3 |

*Source: Times 1000, 1985–6*

*European service firms*

Service firms account for 24 per cent of the top 500 European (non-UK) firms (Tables 8.9 and 8.10). Just over half are domiciled in France or West Germany; Italy is very poorly represented with only one major service firm (Rinacentre Department Stores). Retailing is the most important sector of European services with nearly a third of the firms falling into this category. France leads in this field and Carrefour is its top firm. Wholesaling and utilities are also significant, but there is a marked lack of large producer service companies comparable to the USA or UK. Possibly there are many small producer service firms which have failed to justify inclusion in the list, but even so this indicates an interesting difference in the service sector structures of Europe compared with those of the USA and the UK. Transport is better represented, by such airlines as SAS, Lufthansa and Air France. The only European

**Table 8.9** Nationality of leading European service firms

|  | *Number* |
| --- | --- |
| West Germany | 30 |
| France | 33 |
| Sweden | 14 |
| Belgium | 8 |
| Netherlands | 13 |
| Italy | 1 |
| Finland | 3 |
| Switzerland | 7 |
| Austria | 2 |
| Spain | 6 |
| Denmark | 4 |

*Source: Times 1000*, 1985–6

**Table 8.10** Activities of leading European service firms

| | |
| --- | --- |
| Postal/telecom | 3 |
| Utility | 22 |
| Wholesale | 22 |
| Retail | 38 |
| Airline | 8 |
| Shipping | 4 |
| Publishing | 7 |
| Advertising | 3 |
| Tourism | 3 |
| Investments | 2 |
| Transport | 3 |
| Import/export | 4 |
| Other | 2 |

*Source: Times 1000*, 1985–6

service corporation to appear in the world top fifty is Deutsche Bundespost, the West German postal and telecommunications service.

Evidently service sector firms are well represented among the world's leading corporations, and many of them are transnational in their scope. Figure 8.3 showing the headquarters location of leading American subsidiary companies in Europe, gives some idea of the geographical impact of transnationals. London, Paris, Brussels and Antwerp are the preferred locations, as might be expected from transnational firms seeking the most important and prestigious centres.

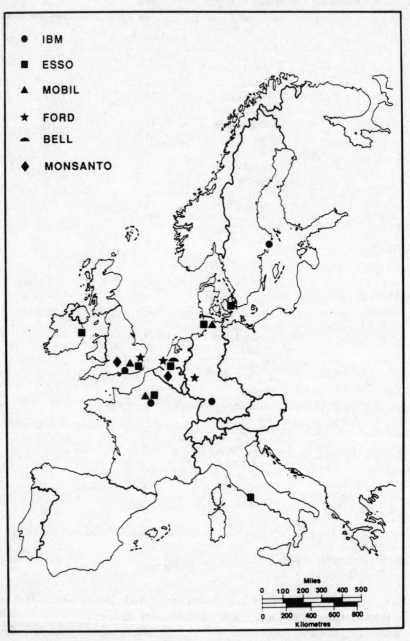

**Figure 8.3**   Headquarters of leading American subsidiary companies in Europe
*Source: Times 1000*, 1985–6

# The internationalisation of producer services

The UK and the USA have long relied on overseas trade as a vital element in their economies and this has given rise to many service activities. Definitions, however, again present a problem. For example, governments may purchase commodities such as educational or medical equipment in order to deliver services. In this case the commodities can be regarded as intermediate products used as an input in the production of services, and it is the final product that has to be classified as a service or not. Another problem is that normally the production and consumption of services is necessarily simultaneous, so that inventories of services cannot be maintained. Consequently it is difficult to measure the actual extent to which nations absorb services, but the simplest way of showing the contribution of services is to record the percentage of GDP expended on specified areas of spending. Summers (1985) attempted to do this using 1975 figures, and he showed that the percentage share of GDP devoted to services rose with national income levels. Balance of payments figures can be used as a measure of international trade in services, but they must be used with caution because there is evidence that the cost of a service within a country varies with income levels. Prices of services are higher relative to commodities in the richer countries, suggesting that the market for services in poorer countries is likely to be limited by the comparative inability of users to pay. For this reason trade in services will probably be largely confined to advanced economies with broadly comparable income levels, and within this group certain countries have developed a competitive advantage arising from their experience and knowledge of the market's needs.

The USA is seeking to capitalise on its acquired advantage in its role as the largest exporter of services. Apart from the economic incentive, there is the fact that services often have a special relation to cultural and political objectives and also to security requirements. An increasing proportion of world trade is in services (Stalson, 1985), and in balance of payments terms services accounted for over a third of the USA's exports in 1980 and nearly 25 per cent of its imports (Kravis, 1985). Another definitional problem has to be confronted here because statistics of international transactions usually include what economists call 'factor' and 'non-factor' services. The former refer to direct services rendered by factors of production such as interest payments on foreign capital or wages to foreign workers irrespective of the output. Non-factor services are those requiring the addition of intermediate inputs to labour and/or capital for their production. In the latter category transport (including freight, passenger fees and travel) account for around 70 per cent of the total; business and professional services are an important component and government transactions make up a good part of the balance. Non-factor services constitute only 9 per cent of the export total of the USA and 11 per cent of its import total. On the other hand, this understates the true position because the value of distributive services in international transactions is included in the value of a commodity or service trade, but this is not the case for domestic statistics. Nevertheless, it is clear that investment income from overseas operations by transnational companies makes an important contribution to the American balance of payments position.

Figures relating to service exports probably fail to indicate the real position since most estimates of service trade are based on extrapolation from industry surveys. Such data are inherently poor, and in some cases (such as computer and data-processing services) no information is collected. Kirkland (1987) commented that, compared with the approximately 10 000 categories of goods recorded by the US Commerce Department, only about 40 categories of services are examined. Consequently the US Congress Office of Technology Assessments (OTA) recently claimed that the true value of the USA's service exports may be twice as large as the official statistics suggest. The OTA also noted that the revenues of overseas subsidiaries of American advertising agencies, investment banks, insurers, consultants, and so on, will not be recorded in the American data if the buyers and sellers of the services concerned are in the same country. Offshore sales of this type are estimated to have totalled about $100 billion in 1983. American forecasting agencies predict that the USA's surplus on trade in services will rise noticeably at least up to 1990. In 1986 the total service surplus on the American current account was $22 billion and the surplus on service trade was $3 billion; actual service exports amounted to $48 billion, which is some indication of the volume of trade involved. The figures essentially measure shifts in the flow of international investments and are not helpful in identifying the competitive advantage of services for trading purposes. It is likely that the surplus on investment income enjoyed by the USA for most of the twentieth century will turn into a deficit, so it is important to identify tradable services. Hopes are pinned on a recovery in transportation, a rise in foreign visitors to the USA, and especially in what have been called 'brainpower-driven' services (data-processing and computer services, software production, management skills, design and financial services). The UK has similar aspirations and Japan is becoming increasingly active in this area.

Due to its central role in organising nineteenth-century world trade the UK was the first truly international centre of finance. The City of London built up a complex network of institutions to finance international trade in a wide range of commodities and this infrastructure survived the decline of the empire. The expertise and contacts available to City financiers helped the UK to retain its importance in world terms, as commodity markets illustrate. Most of the sales negotiated in London relate to consignments which never pass through British ports. Close links with finance, shipping and insurance, not the physical presence of the commodity, determine the London location of markets for cocoa, coffee, grain, rubber, soya bean meal, oil, sugar, wool, metal and potatoes. This explains why so many international commodity brokers and merchants appear in the list of major service firms in the UK (see Table 8.6).

Since financial services are not tangible in the same way as a shipload of grain or iron ore. British statistics refer to them as 'invisible'. In fact, the invisible sector contributes greatly to the British economy, so that the former 'workshop of the world' is perhaps more accurately described as the 'counting house of the world'. In 1964 the £543 million deficit on visible trade was partly offset by a £170 million surplus on invisible trade, leaving a balance of payments deficit of £373 million. By 1985 the comparable figures were a visible deficit of £2111 million, and invisible trade of £5713 million, and a balance of payments surplus of £3602 million (*UK Balance of Payments*, 1986). Evidently invisible trade has assumed ever-growing significance in the economy of the UK over the last 20 years. Table 8.11 shows the net overseas earnings of UK financial institutions in 1975 and 1985. The most striking changes have been the relative decline of commodity trading and the rise of pension funds, unit trusts and brokerage. It is important to remember that as figures of net earnings the data do not indicate the gross extent of activity overseas, but it is net figures which are most significant in a market economy. Investment overseas, especially of the pension funds, is particularly important because it reflects increasing international awareness and the growing ease with which funds can be transferred round the world.

In 1986 the City of London's net overseas earnings totalled £9375 million (42 per cent up on the £6645 million earned in 1985). Although brokers and securities dealers did well in the wake of the Big Bang the biggest increases were achieved by insurance companies and banks. Insurance earnings rose from £2910 million in 1985 to £4260 million in 1986, and underwriting earnings were up from £1060 million to £1740 million. Since this represents the receipt of premiums it must be pointed out that some of these gains may be offset by claims in future years. Profits from overseas subsidiaries of British insurance companies also did well, rising from £43 million to £723 million. Banks improved their net overseas earnings from £1310 million in 1985 to £2360 million in 1986. There was a £320 million rise in portfolio investment income earned abroad by banks and a £366 million fall in the investment due from British branches to overseas banking parents. The banks earned £1210

**Table 8.11** Net overseas earnings of British financial institutions, 1975 and 1985 (£ millions)

|                     | 1975 | 1985 |
| ------------------- | ---- | ---- |
| Insurance           | 450  | 3318 |
| Banking             | 7    | 2071 |
| Leasing             | –    | 66   |
| Commodity trading   | 299  | 618  |
| Investment trusts   | 41   | 159  |
| Unit trusts         | 9    | 100  |
| Pension funds       | 16   | 692  |
| Brokerage           | 207  | 560  |
| Total net earnings  | 1029 | 7584 |

*Source: UK Balance of Payments*, 1986, London, HMSO, Table 6.1.

million from financial services (foreign exchange dealing, new issues fees, portfolio management) though these figures have not risen in line with expectations since 1983, when £726 million was earned. Net earnings by the Stock Exchange rose from £106 million to £157 million, and investment income abroad of securities dealers increased from £318 million to £552 million (*The Times*, 31 July 1987). These are impressive figures, but they obscure an important consideration in that they do not distinguish clearly between tradable services and investment income.

### Financial services

Banks, finance houses, credit corporations, insurance companies, investment trusts, leasing houses and other purveyors of money have frequently located in foreign countries especially since the 1970s to assist their own countrymen engaged in importing and exporting. Hence, international operations usually locate in countries which are major trading partners and show a preference for clustering in the principal financial districts. Primarily international finance began as a producer service, a role it retains, but some firms have also conducted consumer business on a large scale. For example, the American firm Salomon Brothers has entered the British mortgage market, lending $500 million in one year (Kirkland, 1987). Credit card companies like American Express, Diners Club, Master Card and Visa operate world-wide. Master Card is the American firm Citicorp's credit card, but there is a reciprocal agreement with Access in the UK and Eurocard in Europe that enables customers to use their cards in foreign outlets. Other credit card companies have similar arrangements. There has been increasing mutual penetration of each other's home markets by the large international finance companies. Stimson and Adrian (1987) present an interesting case study of the role of foreign investment and investor attitudes with particular reference to property development in Australian state capitals. The UK is still the major source of direct foreign investment in urban real estate, much of which is for office development, but Asian investment is increasing. Malaysia is the main source of Asia funds, though there has been growing penetration from Japan and Hong Kong. Australia has experienced greater internationalisation of its property market, which has been a critical element in the country's integration into the world economy. Like their manufacturing counterparts, service sector transnationals are playing a leading role in the dynamic which is forging this integrated economy.

### Banks

London, New York and Tokyo are the world's three major financial centres, but, as Table 8.12 shows, Paris, Frankfurt, Osaka, San Francisco, Düsseldorf, Montreal and Hong Kong are also important. Daniels (1986b) showed that foreign banks in London and New York were very similar in their location decision-making behaviour and in the demands they placed on the local metropolitan economy. For the time being there is little dispersal outside London or New York, though high costs in New York may encourage

**Table 8.12** World's largest banks, 1982

|  | Deposits ($ billions) | HQ location |
|---|---|---|
| Bank of America | 95.037 | San Francisco, USA |
| Banque National de Paris | 90.677 | Paris, France |
| Crédit Lyonnais | 83.59 | Paris, France |
| Barclays Bank plc | 80.81 | London, UK |
| Crédit Agricole Mutuelle | 78.38 | Paris, France |
| Deutsche Bank | 75.81 | Frankfurt, West Germany |
| Citibank | 74.54 | New York, USA |
| Société Générale | 73.29 | Paris, France |
| Midland Bank plc | 71.21 | London, UK |
| Dai-Ichi Kangyo Bank Ltd | 69.3 | Tokyo, Japan |
| Fuji Bank Ltd | 65.93 | Tokyo, Japan |
| Sumitomo Bank | 65.04 | Osaka, Japan |
| Royal Bank of Canada | 63.9 | Montreal, Canada |
| Mitsubishi Bank | 63.3 | Tokyo, Japan |
| Sanwa Bank | 61.0 | Osaka, Japan |
| Chase Manhattan Bank | 59.31 | New York, USA |
| Dresdner Bank | 52.2 | Frankfurt, West Germany |
| Westdeutsche Landesbank | 52.4 | Düsseldorf, West Germany |
| Industrial Bank of Japan | 52.1 | Tokyo, Japan |
| Hong Kong & Shanghai Bank | 51.66 | Hong Kong |
| Lloyds Bank plc | 51.3 | London, UK |
| Barclays Bank International | 51.3 | London, UK |
| Bank of Tokyo Ltd | 50.9 | Tokyo, Japan |

*Source: World Almanac*, 1984

decentralisation in the future. Daniels found that most banks ranked agglomeration economies highly, especially since they are increasing their use of external intermediate services (such as legal specialists).

Some of the largest banks have extensive overseas interests in the developed and developing worlds. In the 1970s massive loans were extended to Third World countries in the hope of promoting economic development and ultimately creating new developed nations. Japan's transformation from a medieval agrarian state to a world industrial and financial giant was seen as a precedent. In the event Third World countries failed to develop fast enough to match their population growth and the markets for their products did not give returns equal to servicing the debts let alone paying them off. The risk of default by countries unable to repay (Mexico, for example, owed $40 billion) and yet clamouring for more loans provoked a serious crisis. In 1987 Citicorp wrote off its Third World debts as the least odious option, and many banks now consider it safer to concentrate on financing the developed world and such newly industrialising nations as Korea and Taiwan.

Capital has become footloose (Taylor and Thrift, 1982) as resources are more easily transferred around the world due to improved channels of communication and a general relaxation of government controls. International banks have become more widely diffused in this congenial environment. Japanese banks expanded rapidly in the 1970s and 1980s, some 69 per cent of their overseas branches being in Europe and North America. Because Japanese banks have very close links with industry and many are parts of sogo shosha, their spread to overseas locations has been part of Japanese trading expansion. Australian banks provide an interesting smaller-scale example. The pattern of overseas representation of Australian banks can be related to the pattern of trade financing and to traditional involvement even if the areas concerned are not currently important in trade (Hirst *et al.* 1982; Hirst and Taylor 1985). Australian banks, therefore, have strong ties with New Zealand, the UK, and Papua New Guinea on historical and economic grounds, but are principally involved in many small Pacific island groups as a relic of past colonial administration rather than for any pressing trading function. Links with the USA and Japan reflect realities. Unlike their British, American and Japanese counterparts, Australian banks have relatively little representation on mainland Europe because they lack historical or trading links with that area.

Although Australian banks are significant in international terms, they are not truly global in comparison with some American and British banks. In Hirst and Taylor's view Australian banks have entered the third of four stages in the model of bank internationalisation. In the first stage correspondent relationships with overseas banks are established in order to finance trade. This is followed by the establishment of representative offices and banks overseas to enable a bank to serve the offshore needs of its domestic customers. Effectively the bank is trying to protect its business with its domestic customers. The next stage sees the acquisition of foreign customers and involvement in third-country transactions. This necessitates developing an international network of points of representation as a defensive move to retain the bank's competitive advantage. Finally, when international business has become a large and increasing share of the bank's business, the third-stage activities are deepened and strenthened. Hirst and Taylor illustrate their argument by reference to recent developments in the Australia and New Zealand Banking Group (ANZ), which acquired the British-based Grindlays Bank in 1984. ANZ is the first Australian bank to secure a presence in Japan, but expansion has also meant buying into the Third World debt problem.

*British banks overseas*
Figure 8.4 shows the overseas networks of two major British banks, Barclays and Lloyds. While both banks have interests in North America and Europe their other global connections are very different. Barclays is more heavily involved in Africa than Lloyds which is more committed to South America. It seems that, although the market in the developed world is ample for both, the Third World is less able to sustain too many foreign banks. A long history of financial involvement in trade and former colonies influences the banks' areas of interest. Both banks have a large number of subsidiary investment trusts and holding companies in the Channel Islands, the Isle of Man and various Caribbean islands. Such diversity gives banks a great deal of flexibility in transferring funds, in safeguarding themselves from unfavourable trends in

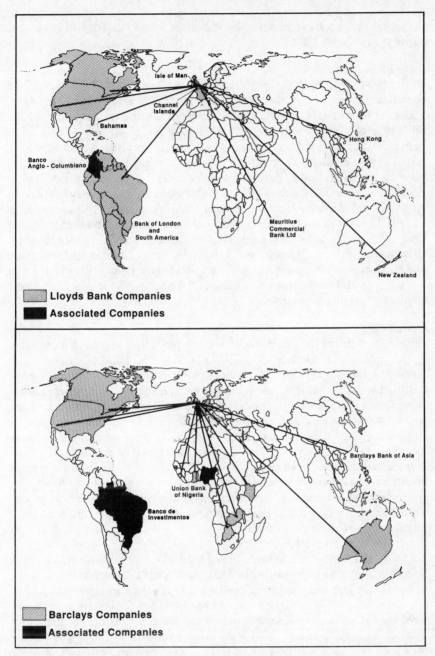

**Figure 8.4**  Overseas interests of Barclays Bank and Lloyds Bank
*Source: Whitaker's Almanack,* 1984

any one country, and it permits the manipulation of currency to become a business in its own right.

*Foreign banks in the UK*
Of the 600 foreign banking institutions in the UK about half are 'recognised banks', which means that they can engage in a full range of banking services. 'Licensed deposit-taking institutions' are banks which are not permitted the full range of services and are restricted to specific activities (Table 8.13). There are also representative offices of foreign banks which do not appear in this list whose functions are not those of bankers but of intermediaries between clients and other banks. Fully 61 per cent of banking institutions in Britain have non-UK origins. The biggest share goes to European and American banks, though there are large numbers of Middle Eastern and Japanese banks as well. London has long been a favoured location for Arab oil money, and every oil state has its London bank. Despite ideological contempt for the capitalist world, Eastern Europe also has its banks in London because trade makes it necessary for the communist world to have financial institutions in the UK. A significant category of bank is 'International' for which no single country or origin can be given.

*Insurance*
Table 8.11 confirms the pre-eminence of insurance as a source of income for British financial institutions in 1975 and 1985. In both years insurance accounted for 44 per cent of earnings, although the absolute total grew greatly. Insurance has three main components; insurance companies, Lloyds (where much insurance is underwritten), and insurance brokers. Each sector's overseas earnings are shown in Table 8.14. Companies such as Prudential, Sun Alliance and Eagle Star have four sources of overseas income—from underwriting directly with foreign clients, indirectly from overseas subsidiaries, from property rents and sales abroad, and from general investments in other countries. Income from portfolio investments has grown greatly from 42 per cent to 67 per cent of insurance companies' overseas profits. This is another indication of the broadening of the interests of financial institutions from their original functions which is analogous to the trend in consumer financial institutions.

Lloyd's of London (not to be confused with Lloyds Bank with which it has no connection) is a unique institution with world-wide significance in insurance, especially for maritime and aviation risks. Lloyd's is an incorporated society of private insurers; it is not a company but a market for insurance administered by the Council of Lloyd's. Individual underwriters act on their own account and are in competition with other members of Lloyd's and other insurance companies. In 1984 there were 21 600 members grouped into 400 syndicates (Central Office of Information, 1984). Interestingly, the share of Lloyd's overseas income derived from underwriting declined from 83 per cent in 1975 to 60 per cent in 1985. It has been replaced by increases in portfolio investments. The final sector is brokerage, which accounts for 20 per cent of foreign earnings. Brokers are simply intermediaries between insurance companies and clients.

**Table 8.13** National origins of banking institutions in the UK, 1986

| Country | Banks | Deposit-taking Institutions | Total | % |
|---|---|---|---|---|
| UK | 62 | 172 | 234 | (39.1) |
| North America | 47 | 19 | 66 | (11.0) |
| EEC | 60 | 19 | 79 | (13.2) |
| Other Western Europe | 17 | 10 | 27 | (4.5) |
| Eastern Europe | 4 | 2 | 6 | (1.0) |
| Middle East | 17 | 20 | 37 | (6.2) |
| Japan | 27 | – | 27 | (4.5) |
| Other Asia | 25 | 10 | 35 | (5.8) |
| Africa | 5 | 8 | 13 | (2.1) |
| Australasia | 8 | 4 | 12 | (2.0) |
| South America | 11 | 1 | 12 | (2.0) |
| 'International' | 22 | 29 | 51 | (8.5) |
| Total | 305 | 294 | 599 | (100) |

*Source: Whitaker's Almanack*, 1987, 1147–51.

**Table 8.14** Overseas earnings of British insurance institutions, 1975 and 1985 (£ millions)

| | 1975 | 1985 |
|---|---|---|
| *Credits* | | |
| Companies | | |
|     Underwriting | 31 | 331 |
|     Overseas subsidiaries | 46 | 105 |
|     Property income | 4 | 22 |
|     Portfolio investments | 59 | 954 |
| Lloyds | | |
|     Underwriting | 166 | 729 |
|     Portfolio investment | 34 | 479 |
| Brokers | 115 | 664 |
| *Debits* | | |
| Overseas affiliates | 5 | −34 |
| *Net earnings* | 450 | 3318 |

*Source:* as Table 8.11.

The UK has about 850 insurance companies, of whom 20 per cent are from overseas. British insurers handle some 20 per cent of general insurance placed on the international market. About half of the non-life insurance business in the UK originated from 100 overseas nations. International insurance is strongly related to industry and trade, and much is concerned with commercial property.

*Advertising agencies*

Advertising epitomises a producer service dealing in intangibles. Advertising agents sell ideas and their success is measured in the increased sales of their clients' products or increased votes for a political party. For years American advertising agencies dominated the market and even now half the major agencies in the UK are American-owned. The early development of commercial television in the USA helped the development of advertising firms, and the later diffusion of TV in the rest of the world allowed the American expertise to be exported. However, in recent years the American hegemony has been challenged by the British company Saatchi and Saatchi, whose phenomenal success (turnover is nearly £700 million greater than its nearest British rival) derived from a number of fruitful campaigns. The Conservative Party election advertising in 1979, 1983 and 1987 were all designed by Saatchi, as were British Airways promotions and the British Gas privatisation. In advertising nothing succeeds like success, and clients clamour for a proven agency to advertise their wares. So successful has Saatchi and Saatchi become that by 1987 it was the world's largest advertising conglomerate and was buying up American firms including related management consultants (Kirkland, 1987).

Britain's top 13 advertising companies had a turnover of £1951 million in 1986 (Table 8.15). American firms accounted for 31 per cent, but Saatchi and

**Table 8.15** Advertising agencies in the UK

| Company | Turnover (£ millions) | Employees | Nationality |
|---|---|---|---|
| Saatchi & Saatchi | 855.4 | 3748 | UK |
| Interpublic | 168.6 | 856 | USA |
| J. Walter Thompson UK Holdings | 166.2 | 977 | USA |
| Mills & Allen International | 137.1 | 2568 | UK |
| Geers Gross | 121.9 | 306 | UK |
| Sewgent Holdings | 92.3 | 440 | USA |
| Charles Barker Group | 74.7 | 1729 | UK |
| Foote Cone & Belding | 71.3 | 451 | USA |
| Ted Bates Holdings | 58.7 | 281 | USA |
| Boase Massini Pollitt | 58.4 | 618 | UK |
| Lowe Howard-Spink Campbell | 52.1 | 144 | UK |
| Brunning Group | 48.7 | 744 | UK |
| Benton & Bowles Holdings | 46.2 | 249 | USA |

*Source: Times 1000, 1986*

Saatchi alone accounted for 44 per cent and the remaining British agencies only achieved a quarter of the total. Daniels (1985) showed that advertising is highly spatially concentrated. In the USA, 96 of the top 200 firms are located in New York and they accounted for 90 per cent of the client revenue. Advertising agencies need access to the media as well as clients, which is another reason for their location in major cities. Associated with them are various subsidiary services such as designers and graphic art suppliers.

Dicken (1986) made a comparison between advertising agencies' growth patterns and those of transnational banks, except that in advertising the American firms were even more dominant. Of the world's 50 leading agencies 36 are based in the USA and a further ten are Japanese. The American agencies are strongly transnational in their operations and obtain an increasing proportion of their income from their overseas offices. The major concentrations are in the advanced economies, but the global spread of activity is very extensive and half the offices are in developing countries. J. Walter Thompson has offices in 30 of the 65 countries in which American firms operate, while McCann-Erickson is represented in all 65.

## The internationalisation of consumer services

Apart from transport agencies, the principal beneficiaries of trade in consumer services are hotels and shops, though medical and educational institutions also profit from serving overseas visitors. As with producer services, this element of international trade in services is being accompanied by an expansion of overseas investment in various companies.

### Tourist services

Tourism provides a visible manifestation of the potential contribution of overseas expenditure to a country's economy. In the first five months of 1987 alone visitors to the UK spent a record £1.9 billion, but this must be balanced against overseas expenditure by Britons which rose to £2 billion (the actual deficit was £85 million). Travel agents were quick to open overseas branches to promote their business, but hotel groups were equally eager to establish themselves abroad. The growth of transnationals, whose executives spend much time in international travel, has encouraged this trend. Executives demand a reliably high standard of service wherever they may be, and they frequently want conference and recreation facilities on site. Many transnational hotel chains have worked hard to promote a 'brand image' appealing to their target markets. In addition to the standard of room accommodation this might include the provision of transport between the airport and the hotel as well as a reservation service for other hotels in the chain. A United Nations survey identified 26 leading transnational hotel chains that accounted for almost 80 per cent of all foreign-operated hotels in 1978, of which eight were American, six British and five French (Dicken, 1986). Holiday Inns, an American firm, owned over 100 hotels outside North America. Inter-Continental, Hilton International and Sheraton all owned more than 60 foreign hotels, while Trust House Forte, the largest British group, had over 50 foreign hotels. Club Méditerranée, a French concern, catered for recreational rather than business users. Unlike their manufacturing counterparts, transnational hotel groups do not usually wholly finance their operations in individual countries; instead, a good deal of capital participation from the host country is common, but the most important consideration is the contractual relationship that ensures the maintenance of the brand image.

Transnational hotel groups, which may themselves be part of larger transnational conglomerates, exist in a very dynamic milieu. Pan Am started Inter-Continental in the 1940s but airlines really became a major force in hotel provision in the 1960s. In this way economies generated by newer and larger aircraft could be passed on to the customer (thus encouraging more people to fly) rather than being siphoned off by a tour operator or travel agent. Airlines sometimes co-operated with each other to protect their business, as in the case of the European Hotel Consortium in which five leading European airlines and five European banks collaborated to build medium-priced hotels in European cities faced with a shortage. Oil companies also became involved: Esso, with nearly 50 hotels and motels in Western Europe, moved into this area of trade in the 1960s, while Gulf Oil joined Pan Am to build a hotel chain in Europe. Often hotel groups move into foreign territories by acquiring or merging with an existing hotel, thereby avoiding development costs at a new and probably inferior site. As recently as September 1987, the Aliegis Corporation sold Hilton International to the British firm Ladbroke in order to concentrate on its main business, United Airlines. For £645 million Ladbroke's acquired 92 hotels, just under half of which are run on management contract, with more than 35 000 bedrooms in 44 countries. The geographical extent of Hilton hotels is shown in Figure 8.5. Ladbroke began as an off-track betting chain, but it has now diversified into hotels which are intended to provide about half its profits and in addition it has extensive interests in consumer retailing (*The Times*, 5 September 1987).

*Retailing and wholesaling*

Successful retailers can achieve scale economies by expanding into transnational activities, and the existence of the EEC has created opportunities for this process. One of the largest organisations is the wholesaler-sponsored voluntary group contractual grocery chain Spar, which has interests in 17 countries. Végé, a similar group, operates in 12 countries and has almost 13 000 affiliated shops served from about 300 warehouses run by 87 wholesalers. If a national market is regarded as saturated a company may look abroad; thus Vroom and Dreesman, a Dutch department store chain, acquired substantial interests in the USA and Kuwait. C & A is another Dutch firm with large numbers of outlets in the UK, France and Switzerland. By the late 1970s several British companies were trading in France, mostly in the non-food trades. Among the firms involved were Burton (45 stores), Laskys (15), Laura Ashley (7), Habitat (6) and Marks and Spencer (3). In 1979 there were almost 2000 stores (excluding those in transnational contractual chains) in France operated by non-French companies or with substantial foreign

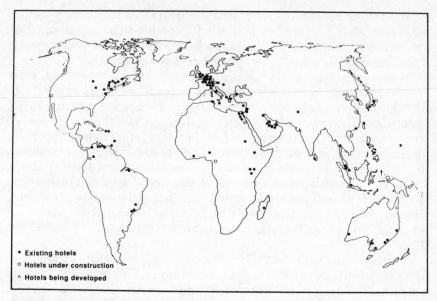

**Figure 8.5** Distribution of Hilton hotels
*Source: The Times*, 5 September 1987

ownership of share capital. Even food retailers established non-food links overseas by co-operating with other companies. For example, Sainsbury (UK) and GB-Inno-BM SA (Belgium) planned to develop do-it-yourself centres in Belgium, but this is only a small part of the Belgian firm's activity for it also has links with West Germany, the Netherlands and France (Dawson, 1982a). American convenience store companies have begun to expand into Europe, South-East Asia, South America and Australia during the last decade, so the extent of transnational involvement by firms on both sides of the Atlantic is considerable.

The existence of the European Community does not of itself give rise to pan-European marketing, pan-European distribution channels, and pan-European brands. White (1984) argued that genuinely transnational distributors represent a tiny proportion of retail activities in virtually every European country, and that few retailers with international networks are actually trying to achieve a co-ordinated transnational positioning in the market. In practice local distribution systems are determinedly heterogeneous and internationally co-ordinated manufacturer brands thrive on this heterogeneity. Nevertheless, Western Europe is more or less homogeneous in cultural terms, and there are common trends affecting retailing despite the existence of a divide between countries north and south of the Alps. Thus, the number of retail outlets per capita is declining, multiples are gaining an increasing market share, self-service is becoming more widespread, superstores and hypermarkets are becoming important in food retailing, and discount outlets are notably successful in textiles, food, furniture, carpets and electrical goods. Throughout Europe retail outlets are becoming increasingly similar, and the same applies to North America and Japan. In the Nordic countries and

Switzerland co-operatives have proved strong enough to resist the growth of multiples, while elsewhere in northern Europe the voluntary groups have enabled independent retailers to claim a larger share of trade than they have been able to do in Italy, Spain, Portugal or even France.

As far as retailing is concerned there are degrees of internationality. There are internationally interrelated voluntary groups (primarily in groceries) such as Spar, Végé, A and O, and Centra, and there are also international buying groups operating in a number of sectors. At the top end of this activity are two major department store groups, but there are other groups operating in textiles, shoes, and jewellery. Another type of operation is that conducted by multiple retailers trading under a common name and style in several countries. Franchising is an extension of this type of activity. Finally, there are diversified retail operations with subsidiaries and associated companies carrying on different trades in different countries under different names: for example Britain's BAT's retail division has grocery chains in the UK and USA.

White found no more than 115 companies trading in at least two European countries, more than half of which were involved in only two or three countries. Less than 20 per cent were in more than five countries, and a large proportion of these were voluntary or buying groups which are international more in name than operation. Grocers, clothing, shoes and mail order were the only retail categories that had as many as ten international operators, so it is not surprising that these four categories account for about 60 per cent of the total organisations and outlets involved. France is the most internationally minded country (with over 25 per cent of the international organisations) and, together with West Germany, the Netherlands and the UK, accounts for over 80 per cent of the total number of operations. On a per capita basis the Netherlands, Sweden and Switzerland do well. On average international retailers engage in four countries, though the rationale for their choice is not always obvious. Geographical contiguity is more or less general, but language does not seem to be a dominant consideration in that few organisations cover the three French-speaking countries, the three German-speaking countries (Luxembourg and Liechtenstein are ignored in this analysis) or the three Nordic countries. Finland is the only country that appears to be immune to foreign interests in its retail sector.

So far the dynamics of retailing have meant that multiples have been preoccupied with developing in their home countries, an activity that has fully engaged management. Nevertheless, certain circumstances favour overseas operations. For example, where the home market position is so strong and perhaps diversified that further growth is inhibited, firms like GB-Inno in Belgium or the Ahold Group in the Netherlands have looked abroad for new opportunities. Alternatively, a successful new concept may be transferred from one country to another as in the case of Carrefour's hypermarket concept which diffused from France. In some crowded and fragmented sectors like clothing, shoes and manufacturers' tied outlets overseas markets help to develop exports, as the Bally footwear chain and Benetton clothing shops have demonstrated. For the most part moves into overseas markets have been achieved through the medium of new stores or franchises rather than by acquisitions or mergers; the latter have been less fashionable than joint ventures, franchising and shops-within-shops. On the other hand several European companies have entered the American and Canadian markets by merger and acquisition, as the example of Marks and Spencer, discussed below, illustrates.

Transnational retail chains should be able to offer greatly enhanced buying power which offers the prospect of increased discounts. Suppliers dealing with a familiar retailer across frontiers are presented with a potentially valuable channel for entering new markets; retailers using suppliers familiar with a new market can to some extent simplify the overall buying process by centralised quality control and testing which allows for a reduction in the total number of suppliers to be dealt with. This may be the case in theory, but in reality things seem to be different. Retailers are actually faced with a diversity of markets in the countries they serve, and though they may occupy similar price or image positions in different countries their market share may be very different. In individual countries retailers need to offer a range of merchandise that will appeal to customers accustomed to local brands, local manufacturers, local forms of packaging, and local styles of labelling and point-of-sale presentation. In European supermarkets the vast majority of branded food products are locally produced (even if internationally known), and it may be difficult to change this pattern. Even international buying groups seem to avoid dealing with brands for international distribution. At the department-store level there appears to be a bespoke buying service which allows suppliers of novelties to gain rapid international distribution in prestige outlets. International buying power has proved to be effective, with own label goods promoted by chains such as C&A, Mothercare, Bally, and Marks and Spencer, all of which buy centrally to supply their international operations. For the supplier this may well represent the best way of developing an international business. At least some of the private label supplies of Carrefour and Makro are internationally purchased.

For the time being there does not seem to be a strong underlying trend towards more international distribution chains leading to more usefully accessible pan-European marketing channels. It may be that retailers have correctly identified a wish among consumers to retain their national identities in respect of their purchasing behaviour. Also, it is clear from the foregoing discussion that transnational retailing is not necessarily a straightforward enterprise. Scope for development will probably be limited to relatively simple retail concepts, often with a strong factory link, and predominantly own-label, as in the case of Laura Ashley and Benetton. Changes will probably be confined to a limited range of 'old' retail types such as clothing and shoes, though 'new' types such as computer shops may also do well. At a more complex level effects are likely to be confined to what are, in effect, 'skimming' or 'creaming' operations like Marks and Spencer, or simple discount activities. Franchising will probably be important in all developments. Genuinely transnational retailing is on a small scale in Europe and only slow growth is to be expected so it is not surprising that European firms have proceeded carefully in extending their participation beyond their own continent.

European firms have nevertheless invested in North America. Dawson

(1982a) referred to Cavenham's ownership of the 500 stores in the Grand Union chain and Tengelman's 42 per cent capital stake in A and P. Recently Sainsbury increased its 28.5 per cent holding to take full control of Shaw's Supermarkets, which runs 49 New England stores. This was thought to have cost up to $261 million (£132 million) and was justified as part of a long-term strategy to reduce dependence on British food retailing (*The Times*, 20 June 1987). North America offers a large market provided the necessary adjustments in marketing management and distribution techniques can be made. Mothercare, a specialist baby products retailer, has succeeded in this, but Marks and Spencer has experienced problems. In 1972 the firm acquired the Canadian D'Allaird (100 outlets) and the People's Stores (80 outlets) and they have also opened another 70 Marks and Spencer shops. The USA was to be entered under the D'Allaird banner but the newest acquisitions in shopping malls in New York state may operate under the English name. This cautious approach, given that New York state is well within reach of the Toronto-based management, suggests that there is a learning curve in overseas operations. Initially the Canadian shops of Marks and Spencer were up to 25 000 square feet (2300 square metres) in selling area, but this was reduced to 10 000 square feet (930 square metres) in the light of experience, and all outlets were located in shopping malls. The new shops in the USA, with about 4000 square feet (375 square metres) of selling space, are comparatively small and offer only women's outerwear. In general locally produced goods are sold in the Canadian shops and currently the American shops are being supplied from Canada. British suppliers are close enough to serve the seven stores in France, the two in Belgium and one in Dublin that are operated by Marks and Spencer. Despite this overseas involvement, Marks and Spencer still obtains 98 per cent of its business from the UK (*The Times*, 30 December 1986), a statistic which helps to put transnational activity into perspective. Wholesaling companies like Booker McConnell are transnational in scope and many American firms have been active in neighbouring Canada. Location is an important consideration in transnational retailing and wholesaling, for very few days developments occur on new sites. The preferred mode of expansion is to acquire an existing store or chain of shops because this permits better store location assessment and reduces the risks inherent in trading abroad—even a well-run company like Marks and Spencer can make mistakes that necessitate policy reappriasal and perhaps the relocation of stores.

Further evidence of Marks and Spencer's interest in North American operations is its purchase of Brooks Brothers, a select American retailing chain selling primarily classic men's clothing to establishment east coasters but with 12 per cent of sales coming from womenswear. Brooks has 47 stores in the USA and 21 outlets in Japan. Part of the deal concluded with the Canadian Campeau Corporation, which sold Brooks to Marks and Spencer for about $750 million, allows Marks and Spencer a three-year exclusive right to rent space for food retailing in the Campeau department stores of its choice. Virtually none of these stores currently retails food. Potentially this gives Marks and Spencer access to up to 800 department stores and would provide a good base for the extension of the company's North American operations. More importantly, the agreement would give Marks and Spencer time to explore the supply and distribution sides of a food retailing operation in North America. In the UK Marks and Spencer has based its success in food retailing by relying to a great extent on establishing sound relationships with manufacturers and distributors. Many of these companies already have a presence in North America and would welcome an opportunity to duplicate their working relationship on that side of the Atlantic. Buying a specialist food retailer on the east coast would help Marks and Spencer to secure its suppliers without whom the company has little chance of succeeding (*The Times*, 9 March 1988).

## Health and education

Contrasting with their importance in domestic economies, health and education activities are only minor items in international service transactions. Barriers reduce the free movement of practitioners between countries. Certification problems, although not insurmountable, act as a brake on movement by medical practitioners, while travel expenses tend to limit the international flow of patients. Similarly in education, at least at school level, rigid regulations usually impose standards that have to be met before a teacher trained in one country can take up a post in another. In many cases the language barrier is sufficient to restrain movement of personnel. Teachers moving to another country generally do so on an individual basis and are not selling their services in a way that would figure in balance of payments statistics. A relatively small number of foreign pupils may attend fee-paying schools in a particular county and thereby contribute to that country's foreign earnings, but this is not a very significant contribution to the total.

Despite their modest contribution to international trade figures neither health nor education can be ignored in a discussion of internationalisation. Barriers can be overcome by establishing hospitals, schools or colleges overseas, and this is done on a growing scale. Private medicine in the UK includes American-owned operations; for example, Hospital Corporation of America (HCA) in Southampton. In fact, HCA, the biggest operator of private hospitals in the USA, has acquired 28 hospitals abroad and has signed contracts to run nine others. American expertise in medical technology and management is also being exported, the latter in an effort to reduce or control health costs in the client country (Kirkland, 1987). Schools serving foreign communities exist wherever sufficient numbers of a national group can justify their presence. Hence there are schools in the UK for the American, French and Japanese communities, among others. Such activities hardly represent an expanding area of investment in the field of international services, but there has been an increase in foreign-owned tertiary educational institutions in Europe. Thus, some American universities have units in the UK or in Europe and others have arrangements for their students to take advantage of programmes of study in European colleges. The American College in Paris is a well-established example of this type of institution. A parallel development is the opening by Philadelphia's Temple University of a Japanese campus in Tokyo.

## Conclusion

Concern with transnational manufacturing activity has perhaps obscured the importance of internationalisation in the service sector. In any case, definitional problems concerning the available data probably understate the true significance of service activities, though their contribution to international trade statistics is impressive. It is often difficult to identify the service component in the activities of major conglomerates, which may lead to further understatement. There are good commercial reasons why successful companies should want to expand overseas, especially since the emergence of an integrated global economy, but one motive for moving abroad is to circumvent barriers to operation. Barriers may include the imposition of special taxes, fees, or licensing requirements, and, if these amount to a sufficient restraint on trade, companies will benefit from establishing overseas branches. Internationalisation has proceeded furthest in producer services, particularly in the financial sector where it comprises a significant element in the total amount of activity. Tourism apart, overseas operations have not yet reached the same level of importance for consumer services, but it seems safe to predict that internationalisation will continue to influence service sector development.

# Chapter 9

# Finance and Property Development

The changes occurring in the service sector cannot be understood without some knowledge of the contribution made by methods of financing and the nature of property development. Investment capital is a prerequisite for the production of any good or service, and for such a dynamic activity as the provision of services the means of raising finance are very important. This is especially true as the increasing role of information technology is transforming a hitherto labour-intensive field into a more capital-intensive one. Given that finance is available the arena in which the interplay of competing forces is resolved is the real property market in urban areas, and it is necessary to be aware of the characteristics of this market in order to comprehend the processes that are taking place. All service firms require a site and a building in which to operate. Sometimes existing properties are used, and occasionally this involves a change of use for the building, but frequently the new service activities take place in purpose-built office buildings, shopping centres or leisure centres. Property development greatly influences the supply of premises and hence the location of service activities. Consequently the process of property development is a vital element in the growth of the service sector, and it is one which makes a distinctive contribution to the urban fabric. Knowledge of how property is developed would certainly contribute to our understanding of the pattern of service sector facilities, but unfortunately 'The property market is paranoically secretive about its activities'. So wrote Green (1986) about the situation in London which she contrasted with the availability of a central register of property ownership to the citizens of Paris, New York, Oslo and Rome. Though the British Land Registry records properties, both freehold and leasehold, that have changed hands since 1879, few people other than conveyancing solicitors are allowed access to this source. As a result, information about the ownership of buildings in England and Wales which may influence a property development strategy is very difficult to obtain. Undoubtedly the two processes of financial provision and property development have an enormous influence on the changing geography of the service sector and for this reason they must be discussed. In this chapter a theoretical perspective on the real property market precedes discussion of the means of financing private sector services and the ways in which property development has affected the private sector. Empirical information about the latter is of value because it shows how the detailed pattern of service provision is often influenced by ownership and company policies. Finally, attention is paid to financial consideration and property development as they affect the public sector.

## The nature of the real property market

Goodall (1972) argued that the outcome of uncoordinated decisions relating to the use of land and buildings within an urban area is not chaos because there is an underlying rationale and order due to the effectiveness of market price as a means of resource allocation. There is a market in urban real property involving transactions between owners of real property and those who wish to purchase space and buildings for business or residential purposes. Such a market for urban land and buildings is an expression of rational behaviour in that space and location are economic commodities subject to supply and demand forces and private behaviour which is guided by profit- and satisfaction-maximisation requirements. Land and building uses are undoubtedly responsive to changes in costs and demand. Conflicting demands and supply are resolved by competitive bidding, and for practical purposes the usual emphasis is on the price or value determination of urban real property, although there is scope for discussing the nature of the values and the resultant distribution of activities in urban space. Normally it is the real property market (which means that there must be a building) rather than the land market that matters, but the value of redevelopment sites must not be ignored. While there is usually only one price under discussion, the urban real property market really entails trading in three goods: land, buildings and location. Because of the durability of real property, ownership and the right of use may be separable. Where owners are not users they treat property as an investment, and they must believe that they will secure an adequate return by renting. Users, on the other hand, must be convinced that it is better to rent than to buy.

The real property market comprises a series of submarkets of varying degrees of complexity and overlap; for example, there are submarkets for shops, industrial premises and residences. There will be differences in the number of buyers and sellers, the role played by intermediaries, and the incidence of legislation and other restraints. The market price reflects economic decisions by buyers and sellers with respect to the future productivity of a property assessed on the basis of its anticipated net income in various uses. Buyers have a ceiling price and sellers a floor price, but the price of any real property is related to that of other real properties. The efficiency with which the urban real property market actually establishes similar prices for properties with the same amenity, risk and prospective income characteristics is dependent on the type of property, market structure, and the effectiveness of market communication. Suburban houses are more likely to form a true market than a non-standardised   property of high unit value such as a first-class shopping facility. The urban   real   property market is more complex than the rent theory models discussed in Chapter 4 presuppose, but despite the complications and imperfections that arise in practice the principles of price determination remain valid.

Real property is not a single interest comprising either undeveloped land or land with buildings and other site improvements. More often than not real property transactions are not particularly concerned with the land and buildings themselves but with interests in or rights over land. Thus, a shopkeeper purchasing a lease is obtaining the use of premises supplied by the landlord, subject to conditions that may be laid down in the agreement. Anyone assuming ownership takes over the obligations assumed by the predecessor to the title, and this means that there may be more than one marketable interest in the same parcel of real property. Such a multiplicity of interests in real property arises because different persons place different subjective values on these interests based on their varied assessments of the future, their asset preferences, and the amount of capital they own or can borrow. Further complications may occur because landlords sometimes accept lower rent increases in return for a specified reduction in capital payment from a financially sound tenant, a tendency which favours multiple retailers at the expense of independents who may have submitted a higher rental bid to secure the use of a property. Tax factors can complicate matters further in that where rents, but not capital payments, are tax-deductible expenses the prospective user will prefer rent payments. Leaseholders may themselves sublet, adding further complexity to the market. The real property market is strongly influenced by ownership and legal factors and restraints so that virtually every real property is subject to different controls and agreements. Legal and social constraints are major factors in the compartmentalisation of transactions into submarkets, and sometimes transactions are sheltered from the market process as in deals between government authorities, divisions of a corporation, or members of a family. Because real property leases do not lapse simultaneously everywhere the economic forces discussed in rent theory influence only the broader features of the situation.

Even allowing for fast-track building methods, the yearly flow of new buildings has only a minor quantitative effect on the total stock, and new buildings tend to supplement rather than replace existing buildings. The result is that rents and prices respond comparatively slowly to demand conditions, and in any case change is difficult to perceive. Various government measures influence, or perhaps interfere with, the market allocation of real properties. Subsidised interest rates and government grants will affect the market, while the imposition of estate duty may speed the break-up of estates so releasing property to the market.

If demand cannot be accommodated within the existing stock of real property, development, which is rarely carried out by the person who will use the property, may occur. Developers will be concerned with optimum capital expenditure, the price to be paid for acquiring interests in the land, and the minimal net return required to justify a particular development. The marginal net return needed is likely to rise as capital expenditure increases to compensate for the higher risks involved, but eventually the marginal net return expected from the development will fall. This is because building costs will rise with increasing height of the property so that the capital sum required to produce a given rise in revenue will be greater. Moreover, rents or prices per unit of accommodation tend to fall as the amount of accommodation provided on a given site increases. The outcome is that the developer who proposes the highest capital expenditure may not secure a site because there is still the question of the residual left over to purchase the interest after all other development costs have been considered. The sum to purchase the interests will depend on the anticipated income from the developed property, capital expenditure other than the purchase of those interests, and the return expected on capital expenditure by the developer. In practice, therefore, there is a relationship between capital expenditure and expected income which is subject to diminishing returns.

The existence of the firm theoretical base reviewed by Goodall helps to explain how property development has affected the private sector provision of the buildings in which service activities are housed. Empirical information about property development and the impact of ownership and company policies on service provision is not readily available, but in the pages that follow many details are provided of the situation in London which may be taken as representative of the processes operating in Western cities in respect of office, retail and hotel properties. First, however, it is necessary to consider how finance is obtained to assist development.

## Finance for development in the private sector

Capital markets provide most finance for private sector development, though help may be forthcoming from government sources, not least in the form of tax concessions. The topic of raising finance for development has been comparatively neglected in the geographical literature, but there are indications of a growing interest in this area. Gertler (1986) investigated the regional dynamics of manufacturing and non-manufacturing investment in Canada. He found that manufacturing still accounts for a major proportion of total private capital accumulation and consistently leads investment in other sectors of the economy. He concluded that this meant that technological change has involved the replacement of labour by capital over time, but it is evident that future studies may find that the same process is affecting the service sector with the rise in information technology, so that proportionately more private investment will be directed towards service activities.

Evidence from the USA (Florida and Kenney, 1988) suggests that venture capital plays a critical role in technological innovation and regional development by providing funds and helping to organise embryonic technology-orientated industries. The active nature of venture capital investing has ensured that the industry is relatively 'fixed' spatially, although theoretically it could be footloose. Since venture capital investing is heavily dependent on information-sharing achieved through personalised, informal and localised networks there is a tendency for the firms involved to cluster. Such clustering occurs either in centres with a high concentration of financial resources like New York, or else where there are high concentrations of technology-intensive

**Table 9.1** Unincorporated businesses' and industrial and commercial companies' deposits with and borrowing from UK banks, in sterling at constant 1975 prices (1975 = 100)

| End-year | Unincorporated businesses[1] | | | Industrial and commercial companies | | |
| | Deposits | Borrowing | Net deposits | Deposits | Borrowing | Net borrowing |
| --- | --- | --- | --- | --- | --- | --- |
| 1975 | 100.0 | 100.0 | 100.0 | 100.0 | 100.0 | 100.0 |
| 1976 | 94.6 | 94.7 | 94.4 | 98.9 | 98.4 | 97.9 |
| 1977 | 100.9 | 107.0 | 88.4 | 104.7 | 99.0 | 93.7 |
| 1978 | 105.6 | 118.0 | 88.8 | 109.6 | 101.2 | 93.3 |
| 1979 | 106.3 | 135.1 | 67.1 | 93.7 | 101.7 | 111.2 |
| 1980 | 104.7[2] | 152.0[3] | 40.2 | 96.8[4] | 107.2[5] | 117.0 |

[1] Unincorporated businesses: personal sector excluding persons, households and individual trusts.
[2] £8854 million at current values.
[3] £7416 million at current values.
[4] £14 152 million at current values.
[5] £32 269 million at current values.
*Source:* Bannock, 1981

businesses as in California. New York and Massachusetts account for approximately 60 per cent of the total American venture capital pool with Chicago, Minneapolis and Dallas acting as lesser centres. New York and Chicago are overwhelmingly export-orientated in that they provide funds for other regions, while California is more tightly integrated and indigenously focused: Boston to some extent combines both attributes. There seems little doubt that the existence of sources of finance such as venture capital greatly accelerates the pace of technological innovation, and this is just as important for the service sector as it is for manufacturing.

A major difficulty in financing arises because so many service sector firms are small and have problems in providing funds to promote growth. According to Bannock (1981) the banks play a crucial role in financing small firms in the UK providing at least two-thirds of their funds from institutional sources. Employment in small service firms has been more buoyant than in manufacturing firms, and Table 9.1 shows that advances to unincorporated businesses (which include manufacturing as well as service businesses) rose steeply in real terms between 1977 and 1980, and much faster than those to industrial and commercial businesses. The latter hardly grew at all until 1980. The trend reveals that banks lent to small businesses on an increasing scale as the recession deepened, and evidently finance was forthcoming even for small firms.

Long-term finance for smaller firms can be obtained under three schemes. Since 1980 the Stock Exchange has operated an Unlisted Securities Market (USM) from which small firms derive the benefit of Stock Exchange listing. Jarrett and Wright (1982) noted that in 1981 just over 50 per cent of the firms benefiting from this facility were in the service sector. Under the Loan Guarantee Scheme, introduced in 1981, over 14 per cent (nearly 11 per cent by value) of the loans made in the first year of operation were to retailing firms. Financial institutions have also helped small enterprises by providing funds for managers wishing to buy out their firms, although the main beneficiaries have been in manufacturing and not the service sector.

Mason (1987) reviewed the sources of finance available to small businesses. By January 1986 some 17 000 companies had shared £554 million in loans under the scheme and over 120 000 unemployed people had been helped to set up in business by qualifying under the Enterprise Allowance Scheme during the first four years of its operation. By September 1986 the USM had enabled 500 member companies to raise over £1000 million and 71 of these companies subsequently graduated to a full listing on the London Stock Exchange. The expansion of the over-the-counter (OTC) market has provided a source of equity capital for small unlisted companies, and the Business Expansion Scheme (BES) introduced in 1983 has channelled equity finance to small, unquoted firms by offering tax breaks to private investors. In 1983–4 715 businesses raised £105 million under the scheme and in the following year 787 businesses raised £140 million. Apparently two-thirds of the companies funded under the BES in 1983–4 could not have raised the equity from any other source. While the advantages of these schemes have not been confined to service firms, the development of a venture capital industry in the UK has helped the process of service sector expansion.

Mason, though impressed with the availability of finance for small businesses in the UK, found that 'neither the improvements nor the benefits have been felt equally in all regions of the country'. The availability of finance is disproportionately concentrated in London and South-East England. Mason identified five categories within the British venture capital industry: 'captives' owned by large financial services organisations such as banks, insurance companies and pension funds who use their own funds to make investments; private independent firms which raise money through private placements with institutions and some large companies; publicly listed funds; government-backed funds such as those administered by the Scottish and Welsh Development Agencies; and some local authorities. The UK has the largest venture capital industry in the EEC, accounting for 41 per cent of the Community's total pool of risk-finance at the end of 1985. On the other hand, the US venture capital industry is five times as large as the UK's. A boost was given to the American venture capital industry in the late 1970s and early 1980s by the flotation of successful venture capital-backed companies, of which Apple Computers was a prime example.

In 1985 Great London accounted for 35 per cent of venture capital investment by value in the UK and the remainder of South-East England claimed a further 25 per cent of the funds invested. These figures should be set against the fact that only 32 per cent of the total number of VAT-registered businesses in the UK in 1983 were in South-East England. Scotland, Wales and northern England contained one-third of the business stock of the UK in the same year but attracted only 17 per cent of venture capital investments in 1985. One reason for this uneven geographical pattern is that most venture capital funds operate from London, so that there is probably a lack of awareness of the opportunities available elsewhere. Geographical proximity is important in another way because most of the venture capital organisations like to monitor the performance of the companies they finance. As there is a comparative shortage of experienced venture capital executives there is an added incentive to restrict investments to companies within travelling distance of London. Scotland is the only other region to have obtained more than its 'fair share' of venture capital investments, probably because Scotland has its own indigenous financial services sector.

Just as the trends discussed here are not limited to the service sector because the available figures do not permit precise identification of the funds made over to that sector alone, so it is not possible to isolate the service sector when considering another process connected with finance that has increased in scope in recent years. There has been a merger boom in the UK which has affected the industrial and commercial sectors. In the first nine months of 1986 £11.3 billion was spent on the acquisition of companies in Britain (Scouller, 1987), which was more than in any previous year. In addition £4.5 billion was spent on buying non-British companies in the same period. Earlier merger booms occurred in 1968 and 1978, but even when prices are adjusted to allow for inflation the amounts paid in these years fell below that paid out in the first three quarters of 1986. There were fewer mergers in 1986 than in the other years, and in fact in 1986 the top five mergers accounted for 59 per cent of expenditure. Most of the finance raised was by the issue of equity (64 per cent) and debt (21 per cent), while cash accounted for only 15 per cent of total expenditure. The 1986 merger boom was dominated by manufacturing (72 per cent of expenditure), but wholesaling and retailing were also an important component; for example, the acquisition of British Home Stores by Habitat-Mothercare for £488 million. Acquisition may involve the purchase of independent companies or the sale of subsidiaries between companies. Companies engaged in mergers may have different strategies in mind. British American Tobacco (BAT) has been diversifying out of tobacco since the 1960s and in 1982 it chose insurance as its target. Hence in 1983 it bought Eagle Star for £800 million and in 1985 Hambros for £660 million. Habitat and Burton, by contrast, have engaged in industrial restructuring. Habitat acquired Mothercare for £120 million and British Home Stores with the aim of achieving much higher sales per square foot of retail space and to respond to the increasing optimal size of company. Burton grew by acquiring Peter Robinson, Collier and Debenhams (the largest, and costing £570 million). Other retailing firms involved in merger include Dixons, Argyll and the Dee Corporation.

An important consequence of mergers is their effect on market share. For example, Britain's food retailing industry, currently worth £32 billion per year, is the country's largest retail market and it has been affected by mergers and acquisitions. In 1983–4 Sainsbury, Tesco and Asda together controlled over 30 per cent of the market, and were significantly more important than Dee, with 4.2 per cent of market share, and Argyll, with 5 per cent. The dominance of the Big Three has been affected by a series of acquisitions which have increased Dee's market share to 11.1 per cent and Argyll's to 9.6 per cent in 1986–7. Thus, instead of a Big Three there is now a Big Five controlling more than 55 per cent of the market. Inevitably competition at the top end of the market has increased and analysts believe that this is more beneficial for the industry and consumers than the type of competition provided by a host of independent corner shops. As this brief example illustrates, mergers and acquisitions clearly have far-reaching effects on the nature of the market and the service offered to consumers.

## Floorspace change in England and Wales

Floorspace data (Tables 9.2 and 9.3) provide a measure of the extent of change in the service sector. Warehousing showed the greatest percentage increase, and in some regions growth has been staggering—over 200 per cent in East Anglia and the London outer metropolitan regions. In absolute terms South-East England contains the greatest area of warehousing, with 42 million square metres (452 million square feet). Without doubt warehouse provision has been one of the success stories of commercial property developments in the 1970s and 1980s. The changing practices in distribution, notably the bigger retail units, encouraged changes in warehousing. Office space has continued to expand, doubling overall between 1967 and 1984. Regionally the greatest amount of office space is in the Greater London area (Figure 9.1), although in percentage terms the Outer South-East and the outer metropolitan area grew most. Greater London, however, added nearly 8 million square metres (about 85 million square feet) over the period. Office growth was notable in all regions regardless of their economic health. The area occupied by shops also increased though not so dramatically. Unusually Greater London lagged

**Table 9.2** Commercial floorspace by region, 1967–84 (millions of square metres)

|  | Offices | | Shops | |
|  | 1967 | 1984 | 1967 | 1984 |
| --- | --- | --- | --- | --- |
| North | 1.1 | 1.89 | 3.6 | 4.5 |
| Yorkshire and Humberside | 1.9 | 3.77 | 5.3 | 6.58 |
| East Midlands | 1.1 | 2.30 | 3.4 | 5.11 |
| East Anglia | 0.6 | 1.39 | 1.6 | 2.60 |
| South-East | 13.9 | 26.5 | 18.6 | 24.84 |
| Greater London | 10.6 | 18.02 | 10.2 | 11.87 |
| Rest of South-East | 1.3 | 3.58 | 4.2 | 6.48 |
| Outer metropolitan area | 2.0 | 4.90 | 4.1 | 6.49 |
| South-West | 1.4 | 3.41 | 4.4 | 6.29 |
| West Midlands | 1.9 | 3.67 | 4.6 | 6.78 |
| North-West | 3.6 | 5.72 | 7.5 | 9.36 |
| Wales | 0.8 | 1.35 | 2.6 | 3.59 |

9.2 *continued*

| | Warehouses | | Industry | |
|---|---|---|---|---|
| | 1967 | 1984 | 1967 | 1984 |
| North | 2.9 | 7.49 | 11.8 | 14.4 |
| Yorkshire and Humberside | 6.3 | 14.4 | 30.9 | 29.2 |
| East Midlands | 4.2 | 10.9 | 17.1 | 23.4 |
| East Anglia | 2.2 | 7.49 | 5.8 | 8.20 |
| South-East | 18.7 | 42.01 | 53.2 | 53.54 |
| Greater London | 10.9 | 18.16 | 26.7 | 20.92 |
| Rest of South-East | 3.8 | 10.99 | 9.7 | 13.71 |
| Outer metropolitan area | 4.0 | 12.90 | 16.8 | 18.91 |
| South-West | 5.3 | 11.59 | 11.0 | 15.31 |
| West Midlands | 5.1 | 14.51 | 34.3 | 37.4 |
| North-West | 11.0 | 20.17 | 47.8 | 44.22 |
| Wales | 2.5 | 5.22 | 7.0 | 9.94 |

*Sources: Regional Statistics*, 1974; *Regional Trends*, 1986

**Table 9.3** Percentage change in floorspace in commercial land use by region, 1967–84

| | Offices | Shops | Warehouses | Industry |
|---|---|---|---|---|
| North | 71.8 | 25.0 | 158.2 | 22.0 |
| Yorkshire and Humberside | 77.3 | 24.1 | 126.9 | −5.6 |
| East Midlands | 109.0 | 50.0 | 159.5 | 36.8 |
| East Anglia | 131.6 | 62.5 | 240.4 | 41.3 |
| South-East | 90.6 | 33.3 | 124.5 | 0.3 |
| Greater London | 70.0 | 16.3 | 66.6 | −21.7 |
| Rest of South-East | 175.3 | 52.3 | 189.2 | 41.3 |
| Outer metropolitan area | 145.0 | 58.2 | 222.5 | 12.5 |
| South-West | 143.5 | 42.9 | 118.6 | 39.1 |
| West Midlands | 93.1 | 47.3 | 148.5 | 9.0 |
| North-West | 58.8 | 24.8 | 83.3 | −7.5 |
| Wales | 68.7 | 38.0 | 108.8 | 42.0 |

*Source: Regional Statistics*, 1976, Table 10.11; *Regional Trends*, 1986, Table 10.10.

behind in its growth rate, perhaps because of the planning authority's opposition to the development of hypermarkets. In other regions policies favouring large retail units resulted in larger increases in shop floorspace. Industrial floorspace on the other hand tells a different story. Yorkshire and Humberside, the North-West and Greater London recorded a decline in

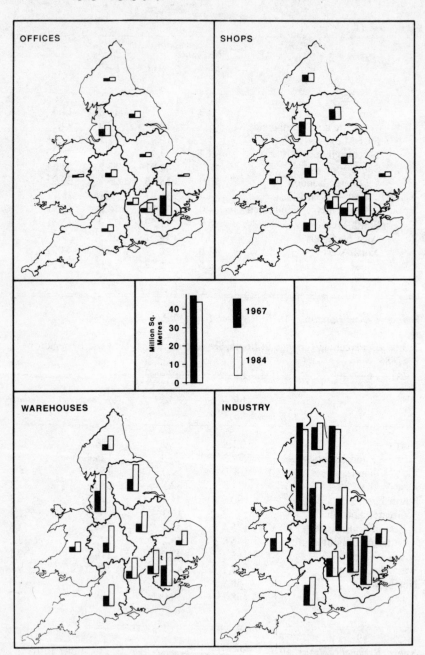

**Figure 9.1** Changes in commercial floorspace, England and Wales, 1967–84
*Source: Regional Statistics, 1974; Regional Trends, 1986*

floorspace and there was little growth in the West Midlands. The booming areas were East Anglia, Outer South-East England, South West England, Wales and the East Midlands.

## Property development

Changes in property development are intimately linked with the general fortunes of the economy and the demands for new types of structure such as retain warehouses, superstores, office complexes and conference centres. However, it ought to be remembered that property development is not a passive response to demand from other sectors but an industry in its own right. A distinction is made between the property companies which arrange the financing, marketing, leasing and renting of property and the construction companies which do the building work. Often major construction companies have their own subsidiary property companies to market their buildings, but there are also major property companies which are independent of construction. Table 9.4 shows the main property companies in the UK. Twenty out of the 25 listed are located in London: eight have prestigious W1 addresses and six have equally prestigious SW1 addresses. Only Scottish Metropolitan Property is based outside South-East England. These companies employ huge capital sums running into hundreds and, in three cases, thousands of millions of pounds. A large part of the income of many of them comes from rents, often of large office blocks for other service activities in London. Laing, Wimpey and Wates are all leading construction firms with their own property development companies, while John Lewis Properties belongs to a major retailer.

Bateman (1985) followed Ambrose and Colenutt (1975) in linking office development with the Western capitalist financial system and asserted that modern office development must be related to a 'geography of finance' to include the operation of international money markets. According to this view international variations in exchange rates, interest rates for borrowers, and interest returns for investors are now vital explanatory components in an understanding of international variatons in economic activity, including property developments. Classical rent theory, with its emphasis on utility maximisation for the occupier, is seen to be inadequate to explain a system of development where utility for the occupier may be a secondary consideration compared with profit maximisation for the financial instititutions. Office building is not necessarily a response to need, but is frequently speculative and in this sense can be compared with much nineteenth-century residential development. In short, the supply side may be more significant than the demand side in deciding where development occurs.

Demand for offices increases when the business cycle is in an upward swing. Lead times may be such that there are delays in completing large projects, and eventually supply may exceed demand, as happened in Paris in the early 1970s. Financial crises like the 1973 oil crisis which affected London might make an impact, and although national economic cycles may not be exactly in phase with international cycles the latter cannot be ignored. Whitehand (1967) showed how the cyclic nature of development affects urban

**Table 9.4** Leading British property companies, 1985 (£ millions)

|  | Capital employed | Gross rents | Net profits |
|---|---|---|---|
| Land Securities | 2282.8 | 132.1 | 114.9 |
| Hammerson | 1472.0 | 104.9 | 82.3 |
| MEPC | 1340.2 | 99.1 | 81.6 |
| Slough Estates | 727.1 | n.a. | 54.4 |
| Oldham Estates | 577.7 | 27.6 | 24.4 |
| British Land | 492.8 | 47.3 | 33.0 |
| Sterling Guarantee Trust | 399.6 | 42.6 | 24.6 |
| Laing Properties | 371.8 | 42.6 | 24.6 |
| Brixton Estates | 261.7 | 20.5 | 15.6 |
| Great Portland Estates | 300.1 | 17.3 | 16.8 |
| Haslemere Estates | 290.1 | 20.7 | 14.8 |
| Stock Conversion Investments | 282.7 | 17.8 | 19.7 |
| English Property Corporation | 273.0 | 22.3 | 21.2 |
| Capital & Counties | 242.4 | 18.9 | 13.7 |
| John Lewis Properties | 195.3 | n.a. | 21.3 |
| Country & New Town Properties | 156.4 | 13.3 | 10.5 |
| Wimpey Property Holdings | 154.5 | 8.9 | 6.6 |
| Chesterfield Properties | 152.2 | 8.7 | 7.1 |
| Property Holding & Investment Trust | 141.7 | 8.7 | 7.1 |
| Property Security Investment Trust | 141.6 | 6.0 | 9.1 |
| Percy Bilton | 129.6 | 11.9 | 10.5 |
| London Shop Properties | 123.2 | 10.5 | 9.1 |
| Wates City of London Properties | 120.1 | 3.7 | 3.6 |
| Scottish Metropolitan Property | 118.3 | 7.6 | 7.4 |
| Euston Centre Properties | 116.5 | 7.7 | 8.1 |

*Source: Times 1000,* 1986

morphology (see Chapter 5) and he has also contributed to studies of town centres and the agents responsible for their change (Whitehand and Whitehand 1983; 1984). The thrust of Bateman's argument is that office development results from deliberate investment decisions by people to secure returns on their capital. Market experience, intuition, and willingness to take risks may be more important than urban land-use theory allows for. What matters is that the inherent value of land and property should maintain the value of the assets and offer the possibility of an income as well. Above all, land is in limited supply and it cannot be lost or overexploited (at least, not as far as prime inner-city locations are concerned) in the way that other investments can.

The property market is dominated by financial institutions such as insurance companies, pension funds, and unit trusts. Property companies were active in the 1950s and 1960s, but they are a declining force, as many have sold out to financial institutions. Hamnett (1987) reently demonstrated that the Church

Commissioners (acting on behalf of the Church of England) have changed their investment strategies and have become increasingly indistinguishable from the financial institutions in respect of property development. The Commissioners have been particularly involved in office and retail development in central London so their activities are of interest in the present context. Institutional investors are very powerful, although a large part of the population has a share in their holdings. Whatever the long-term security of land and property, there may be cycles of relatively low performance or poor profitability compared with other investments. For example, rents tend to be tied to the general state of the economy, which has been weak for much of the 1980s. Consequently property investment by life assurance and investment funds has fallen and there has recently been rationalisation of property holdings. A feature of the financing of property development that will emerge in the later discussion of case studies is that local authorities often combine with property companies to secure a development they consider to be potentially beneficial to their area. The geographical implications of the temporal changes described here are that prime sites will always attract demand while those in marginal locations may become less attractive. On the other hand, trading in property seems to be an international operation, and it is an axiom that if enough institutions hold property in a centre there will be further investment there. It is an axiom that rarely fails.

Geography are naturally interested in the international character of property development. Some countries like Canada restrict overseas development, but others welcome it. British investment has often transformed the property market in other countries—for example, Belgium in the early 1970s; France; and, above all, the USA. Sometimes, as in Belgium, oversupply of offices may result in subsequent disinvestment. Exchange rates and political decisions or events are important factors which make it difficult to analyse the property market, but it is clear that an appreciation of the property market as a vehicle for profitable investment is vital to a geographical understanding of the office development process. Bateman's work reviewed here relates to office development only, but the same trends affect the development of many retail and leisure facilities.

Before examining the latter two areas in more detail it is useful to consider the contemporary situation in the ownership of property because so many ongoing developments entail a wide range of activities. Details provided by reports in *The Times* in January 1985 illustrate the position in London. Sweeping changes have taken place in the ownership of London property since the oil crisis in 1973. Traditional landlords such as the Crown Estate and the Church Commissioners continue to be important and British funding remains a significant element through pension funds and insurance companies. The British Petroleum Pension Trust, for instance, owns a large part of Berkeley Square and surrounding streets in Mayfair, including one of London's most expensive office areas. Confidence in the prospects of London's financial sector is evident in the amount of foreign investment by French, Swiss, Middle Eastern, Canadian, American and Soviet (Narodny Bank) interests. Most of these concern single buildings, but in the aftermath of the oil crisis there were some larger-scale investments, such as the acquisition of the St Martin's Property Corporation by the Kuwaiti royal family in 1974 for £107 million. The deal included 2 million square feet (190 000 square metres) of office space, but this is being increased by the projects at Hay's Wharf. Here in a half-mile stretch of the south bank of the Thames between London Bridge and Tower Bridge redevelopment is occurring which entails a further 2 million square feet of office space, a private hospital, houses and shops.

The Hay's Wharf scheme is one of many that is transforming the banks of the Thames. Formerly it was the river itself that was the thriving commercial thoroughfare associated with the Port of London, but currently it is the development of potential along the banks that offers most. Old wharves and warehouses provide ideal sites for development. The Hay's Wharf scheme involves an investment of £350 million to create London Bridge City. Local interests have opposed this and other schemes, sometimes successfully, as in the Coin Street development, and changes in market circumstances have affected other projects. For example, the King's Reach development close to Blackfriars Bridge was originally intended to include a riverside hotel before the bottom temporarily dropped out of the London hotel market. In 1985 over 250 000 square feet (23 000 square metres) of office space was being developed. More development occurred on the north bank, which is attractive because of its greater proximity to the financial district of the City. The City of London Corporation owns about a third of the City's real estate and the livery companies are also major landowners in this area, so these interests can exert a powerful influence on redevelopment. There has been a predominance of office building, although at St Katherine's Dock tourist attractions and a modern hotel have been included. Nevertheless, the World Trade Centre and International House provide office space, and the London Commodity Exchange has signed a deal to make its home at St Katherine's Dock. Among other developments under consideration are the Billingsgate, Royal Mint, City of London Boys' School and Brook Wharf sites. The dynamic process is certainly changing the urban fabric and the prospects of employment opportunities in the City.

*Retailing and recreation provision*

An obvious manifestation of retail property development is the spread of shopping centres in the USA since the first strip centre was opened in Columbus, Ohio, in 1928. Dawson (1983) noted that this centre was designed by Don M. Casto and that 20 years later the same company was involved in a development 10 km (6 miles) east of the Columbus Central Business District. Joint investors were Casto and the Pheonix Insurance Company, and it was so profitable that it led to more developments. Though successful, the Casto organisation was only in thirty-sixth place in the table of American developers. Top of the list was the Taubman Company, a post-war organisation, but it sold over half the space it developed so that the largest owner is in fact the second largest developer, the Edward J. de Bartok Corporation. Because the USA has experienced mainly private investment the centres have been located in the potentially most profitable locations—the suburban middle-

and higher-income districts. This contrasts with the situation in Europe where there has been more public sector involvement and a brake on the flight from the central areas.

Britain has witnessed much local government participation in new shopping schemes and town-centre renewal, encouraged by central government policies. The outcome is that there has been co-operation between public authorities and private developers which is central to understanding the way shopping centres have spread throughout urban Britain. The formal land-use control mechanisms operated by government and local authorities have provided the framework, spatial and structural, in which the development process and the shopping centre industry have worked. There is a parallel with the USA in that major development companies have emerged, and the ten largest accounted for over 50 per cent of the floorspace developed in 1981. Apart from Laing (Watford) and Norwich Union (Norwich) the remaining firms, which include Town and City, Ravenseft, Hammerson, EPC, Grosvenor, Capital and Counties, CIN, and Neale House, have London headquarters. Figures in Dawson (1983) show that compared with the 2.8 million square metres (30 million square feet) developed by the top ten companies, local authorities and New Town Development Corporations were responsible for a further 750 000 square metres (8 million square feet). Britain differs from the USA in that British centres have developed in response to perceived needs rather than to the pure profit motive, and as a result there is a more equitable pattern of access to centres.

Another perspective on the question of development is to consider what is happening within the constraints of a traditional shopping street. The almost instant adjustment to changed market circumstances implied in rent theory looks very unrealistic when it is recognised that city centre shops, for instance, are rarely owned by the people who occupy them. Most retailers merely own the occupational lease which hardly ever comes directly from the freeholder. A common practice is to sell properties to companies or institutions who buy them as investments. These head-leaseholders sell long subleases in their turn, and often there are further sublettings so that there is a chain of owners between the occupant and the freeholder. Retailers may be confronted by rising rents and property taxes which have in fact pushed out many established shop tenants who have been replaced by rapid-turnover and low-investment concerns trying to sell as much stock as possible before moving on when the lease expires. This helps to explain why many traditional main shopping streets have deteriorated in appearance because short-term traders have no incentive to maintain their shopfronts. Development projects have to take account of the various leasing arrangements so their implementation may well be delayed. For example, the Crown Estate, which owns almost all of Regent Street in London, is hampered by the fact that when the street was developed in the 1920s the properties were sold on very long leases at a high premium but a low fixed annual rent. Famous names like Liberty's, Dickins and Jones, and Mappin and Webb are not in fact very profitable tenants for the Crown. Since the 1960s the Crown Estate's leasing practices have taken more account of inflation, though the only way the Crown Estate can renegotiate a lease is when the head-leaseholder wants to refurbish a property because this requires the freeholder's consent. In this event leases may include a ground rent which is reviewable upwards every few years (Green, 1986). Clearly considerable expertise and patience is required in addition to capital to implement a development proposal, and this should be borne in mind when the following examples are studied.

The *Times* survey used Oxford Street in London as an example of one of the world's great shopping streets where there is little or no scope for modern shopping centres. Oxford Street contains the largest concentration of shops in Europe and is the most profitable retail street in the UK. Plans to unify the street have been put forward occasionally but they have been frustrated by the patterns of ownership and perhaps by the realisation that Oxford Street owes much of its excitement to its diversity.There are four main types of owner in Oxford Street. These include the great landed estates such as the Crown and the Church; the insurance companies and pension funds; the property companies; and in a few cases the retailers themselves. The Crown Estate owns much of Oxford Street and has been responsible for the Quadrangle West One scheme at the corner of Wardour Street, a development that includes six shops with offices above and seven apartments. Another landed estate is the Portman Family Settled Estate. Though it sold the Debenhams and John Lewis sites some time ago, Portman still owns the freehold on the north side of Oxford Street between Marks and Spencer and Marble Arch. In this area there are six shops let on a long lease to a financial institution which has given a lease to one of the UK's largest quoted property companies which

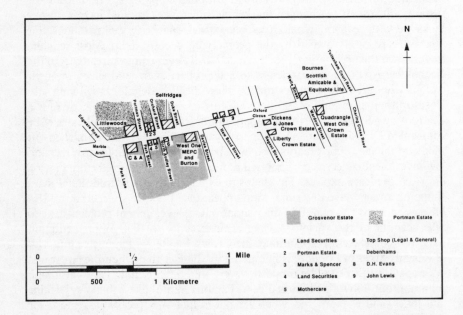

**Figure 9.2** Aspects of the pattern of property ownership in Oxford Street, London (January 1985)

in turn lets the shops to retailers. On the south side of Oxford Street the Grosvenor Estate has large land holdings and owns some of the buildings. The largest financial institutions to own property in the prime west of Oxford Street is the Prudential Assurance, but there are others, including Legal and General Assurance, and the pension funds for Mothercare and the Post Office staff. Land Securities is a large property company which has interests in shops, offices, showrooms and restaurants along the street. MEPC is another big property group which was responsible for the West One Shopping Centre above Bond Street underground station which contains 45 000 square feet (4200 square metres) of offices and the same amount of shopping space. The Burton Group took half the retail space, and the whole development was worth more than £22 million in 1985. Few retailers apart from Debenhams and John Lewis own their premises.

To date the main difference between finance and property development in respect of retailing and tourism or leisure facilities has been one of scale. Retailing has attracted much more investment than tourism and leisure, but this may change as leisure activities assume a more dominant role in our everyday lives. Just as with retailing and commercial development, some schemes have been so large that joint financial arrangements have been necessary. Prominent among these has been the well-known development in Languedoc-Roussillon in France, but there have been other examples such as Queenstown in New Zealand (Pearce, 1981) where the main public involvement was in the provision of new infrastructure. Public involvement was also a feature of the Brighton Marina project, for the Brighton Marina Act allowed the Borough of Brighton to buy the foreshore and seabed from the Crown to provide a site for development. In the foreseeable future public investment is likely to be needed for infrastructure, and there will always be pressures on governments or local authorities to provide assistance in order to maintain the prosperity of their area.

Hotel ownership has attracted much private investment connected with leisure. Unfortunately tourism is subject to fluctuations in demand, which encourages investors to keep an eye on quick returns. Large operators, however, have sought to build up suitable portfolios. Grand Metropolitan and British Transport Hotels helped to promote change in London by selling many of their holdings. Grand Metropolitan sold 19 London hotels in the early 1980s and British Transport another five. Foreign and provincial groups seeking a London flagship have helped to keep demand buoyant. Among the newcomers are comparatively small companies such as Mount Charlotte Hotels, Queens Moat Houses, Thistle Hotels, Reo Stakis and Sarova. American hotel groups such as Holiday Inns, Sheraton and Marriott are all waiting to buy, as is France's IBIS-Sphere group. The Dorchester Hotel in Park Lane was sold to Regent International, an American company, for £45 million in 1984—about £140 000 per room, which is more expensive than new building. One way of capitalising on a tourist boom is to rebuild behind an existing facade because this is relatively cheap and does not conflict with planning requirements. Between 1980 and 1984, 11 leading London hotels changed hands and were undergoing reburbishment, and there were plans affecting another 17. In its heyday Grand Metropolitan Hotels had an impressive portfolio of London properties which so far has not been matched by the newcomers despite the activities of Mount Charlotte, Taj International Hotels, Barclay Hotels, Thistle Hotels and Sarova. Mount Charlotte, for example, bought six hotels which added 2000 rooms to the group's stock. So valuable are hotels that the premium price for getting into the market is now too high for most companies, so there is a trend towards operating hotels rather than owning buildings (cf. retailing).

Increasing attention to the leisure market has resulted in sports centres and leisure centres being promoted by public authorities, often in association with private interests. The UK, Europe and North America have experienced an expansion of this type of facility, which besides offering entertainment to the general public also provides employment opportunities for many people. Drive-in cinemas have been a common feature in North America in recent years, but the concept of out-of-town or suburban cinema complexes (cf. shopping centres and superstores) is new to the UK. In July 1987 the Cinema International Corporation (CIC) Theatre Group, owned by Paramount Pictures (a subsidiary of Gulf & Western) and Universal Pictures (a subsidiary of MCA), opened a six-screen complex costing £3.5 million at High Wycombe. This is the first out-of-town multiplex in the UK and may be the forerunner of a new trend. The location was carefully chosen by CIC, one of the world's largest motion picture corporations and a transnational enterprise operating 98 screens in 14 countries. The multiplex is situated adjacent to a motorway interchange, which was a major factor in the choice of site, and it is expected that customers will travel from distances of up to 20 miles to use it. Parking for 300 cars is provided and has already proved to be inadequate, which suggests that the concept is a successful one. Catering facilities are available to entice customers from their homes and offer them something more than just a visit to a cinema, albeit one with a choice of six different shows. Not the least of this feature's benefits is the fact that it employs 40 people (see Figure 5.2). Multiplexes have been hailed as the way ahead for cinema operators, and several new multi-screen cinemas are planned or have already been opened in town centres. National Amusements, another transnational American-owned company, has initiated a programme for opening 16 multiplexes costing more than £75 million in total because they believe that there is a big future for cinema in Britain. For the time being town centre locations are favoured, but if the High Wycombe cinema's success is any guide more out-of-town multiplexes will follow. The fact that transnational companies are willing to invest heavily in this sort of venture confirms the importance of leisure facilities and ensures their continuance as service sector activities which have a geographical expression.

## Public sector development

Governments are major initiators of property development for schools, hospitals, government offices, motorways, civil engineering works and defence. Table 9.5 shows the changes in the proportion of the GDP, from which the capital expenditure listed above is derived, consumed by Western govern-

**Table 9.5** Percentage of GDP consumed by government in advanced nations, 1973 and 1984

|              | 1973 | 1984 |
|--------------|------|------|
| Belgium      | 14.7 | 17.4 |
| Denmark      | 21.7 | 25.9 |
| West Germany | 13.0 | 13.6 |
| Greece       | 12.7 | 19.0 |
| France       | 12.6 | 16.4 |
| Ireland      | 16.5 | 19.0 |
| Italy        | 14.4 | 19.4 |
| Luxembourg   | 11.4 | 15.7 |
| Netherlands  | 16.7 | 16.8 |
| Portugal     | 13.5 | 14.7 |
| Spain        | 11.3 | 12.3 |
| Sweden       | 22.5 | 27.8 |
| UK           | 18.8 | 21.9 |
| USA          | 18.5 | 18.8 |
| Japan        | 8.8  | 9.8  |

*Source: Eurostat,* 1974, Table 15; *Eurostat Review,* 1986, Table 2.1.1.

ments in recent years. In the European countries, except for West Germany and the Netherlands, the share of all governments increased, but in the USA and Japan the increase was very mediocre. The highest shares were in the welfare states of Scandinavia and the UK. Japan is notable for having less than 10 per cent of its GDP consumed by government. The reason for this is that many of the functions performed by the state in other nations are carried out by industry in Japan because company welfare replaces state welfare.

The general public is most aware of current spending —teachers' and doctors' salaries, welfare payments to pensioners or the unemployed, and armed forces pay—and in fact this does represent the greater part of public expenditure. Capital expenditure is more relevant for the purposes of this discussion, and here we are concerned with public spending on property, in particular non-residential buildings and public works (including roads). Table 9.6 shows the differences in expenditure on dwellings and other construction work between 1975 and 1982 in Western countries. A higher percentage of the gross fixed capital formation went into non-residential building in all countries. The difference in Japan is especially extreme, with twice as much going on non-residential construction as housing. In the UK, by contrast, it was less than 50 per cent more. It is impossible from these figures to say how much was government-inspired but it is possible to obtain an idea of the UK's public and private property development on a regional scale.

Table 9.7 indicates the proportion of government regional assistance to industry which was spent on land and factories. In most cases it is a relatively small proportion. Taking the total value of new construction work in one year

**Table 9.6** Construction of dwellings and non-residential buildings and civil engineering works as a percentage of national gross fixed capital formation, selected countries, 1975 and 1982

|  | Dwellings | | Non-Residential | |
|  | 1975 | 1982 | 1975 | 1982 |
|---|---|---|---|---|
| Belgium | 25.8 | 17.0 | 36.2 | 43.1 |
| Denmark | 31.7 | 21.0 | 34.8 | 34.4 |
| West Germany | 26.6 | 27.8 | 36.1 | 34.0 |
| Greece | 27.1 | n.a. | 34.5 | n.a. |
| France | 31.3 | 27.1 | 29.1 | 26.8 |
| Ireland | 24.3 | 20.7 | 29.0 | 32.2 |
| Italy | 26.9 | 27.7 | 31.3 | 31.7 |
| Luxembourg | 28.9 | 18.5 | 42.8 | 46.5 |
| Netherlands | 24.4 | 28.5 | 33.2 | 30.2 |
| Portugal | 19.3 | n.a. | 44.1 | n.a. |
| Sweden | 19.8 | 24.3 | 38.6 | 35.3 |
| Spain | 26.3 | n.a. | 35.4 | n.a. |
| UK | 22.3 | 20.3 | 33.4 | 29.4 |
| USA | 20.6 | 17.8 | 36.1 | 37.4 |
| Japan | 23.4 | 20.1 | 39.5 | 42.7 |

*Source: Eurostat Review*, 1986, Table 2.1.63/4

**Table 9.7** Government expenditure on regional assistance to industry, UK, 1984–5

|  | Total (£ millions) | Percentage on land and factories |
|---|---|---|
| North | 122 | 15 |
| Yorkshire and Humberside | 41.9 | 14.3 |
| East Midlands | 10.1 | 0 |
| South West | 13.7 | 18.2 |
| North West | 101.6 | 10.0 |
| Wales | 141.1 | 21.3 |
| Scotland | 184.5 | 12.6 |

*Source: Regional Trends*, 1986, Table 10.8.

**Table 9.8** Value of new construction work, Great Britain, 1984 (percentage of total)

| | |
|---|---|
| *New housing* | |
| Public | 4.4 |
| Private | 16.5 |
| *Other works* | |
| Public | 15.36 |
| Private industry | 10.07 |
| Private commercial | 13.40 |
| *Repairs and maintenance* | |
| Housing | 22.5 |
| Other | |
| Public | 9.1 |
| Private | 8.6 |
| Total (£ millions) | 23,238 |

*Source: Regional Trends*, 1986

**Table 9.9** New non-residential construction work, Great Britain, 1984

| | Public Works (%) | Private Works Industry (%) | Commerce (%) | Total (£ millions) |
|---|---|---|---|---|
| Great Britain | 39.5 | 25.9 | 34.3 | 9022 |
| North | 47.7 | 23.7 | 28.5 | 442 |
| Yorkshire and Humberside | 38.8 | 33.2 | 27.9 | 634 |
| East Midlands | 38.6 | 36.2 | 25.0 | 535 |
| East Anglia | 43.5 | 27.1 | 29.3 | 365 |
| South-East | 30.9 | 23.0 | 46.0 | 3636 |
| Greater London | 26.3 | 13.5 | 33.9 | 1682 |
| Rest of South-East | 34.8 | 31.3 | 33.9 | 1954 |
| South-West | 40.5 | 26.8 | 32.7 | 609 |
| West Midlands | 42.0 | 28.2 | 29.8 | 709 |
| North-West | 46.9 | 29.8 | 23.2 | 835 |
| Wales | 48.9 | 30.9 | 20.1 | 388 |
| Scotland | 57.1 | 18.6 | 24.3 | 870 |

*Source: Regional Trends*, 1986

**Table 9.10** Repair and maintenance of buildings and works, Great Britain, 1984

|  | Housing (%) | Other Works | | Total (£ millions) |
| --- | --- | --- | --- | --- |
|  |  | Public (%) | Private (%) |  |
| Great Britain | 55.8 | 22.6 | 21.5 | 9348 |
| North | 53.7 | 23.8 | 22.5 | 387 |
| Yorkshire and Humberside | 49.8 | 25.4 | 24.7 | 841 |
| East Midlands | 56.1 | 22.8 | 21.1 | 592 |
| East Anglia | 58.5 | 21.3 | 20.2 | 352 |
| South-East | 55.1 | 22.9 | 21.9 | 3379 |
| Greater London | 52.1 | 24.5 | 23.3 | 1414 |
| Rest of South-East | 57.2 | 21.8 | 20.9 | 1965 |
| South-West | 59.4 | 23.8 | 20.5 | 777 |
| West Midlands | 57.0 | 22.7 | 20.3 | 849 |
| North-West | 57.2 | 20.4 | 22.4 | 916 |
| Wales | 58.5 | 21.8 | 19.6 | 357 |
| Scotland | 58.8 | 21.2 | 20.0 | 869 |

*Source: Regional Trends, 1986*

gives an idea of the role of government (Table 9.8). The total public expenditure share of all construction work was 28 per cent of some £23.3 billion. New non-residential construction work for government amounted to just over half the total and repairs and maintenance for a further 9 per cent. Public housing accounted for 4.4 per cent. About 60 per cent of this total was spent on new construction work and the remainder on repair and maintenance. Private industrial works accounted for just over 10 per cent and commercial works 13.4 per cent.

On a regional scale there are substantial variations in public and private works. Table 9.9 presents figures which include all roads, public buildings, ports, airports, and commercial uses. Public works are particularly significant in Scotland, Wales and the North, and least important in Greater London where the biggest share goes on private commercial building. This confirms the previous reference to office floorspace in London. South-East England as a whole has a disproportionate share of the total expenditure on new buildings (40 per cent). There is very little difference in the proportions expended for either public or private works on repair and maintenance (Table 9.10), probably because the rate at which structures deteriorate is spatially random.

It has been necessary to consider government expenditure in these general terms, in which it is not possible to isolate the amount directly devoted to the service sector, because the spending described includes the cost of the infrastructure that is vital to so many services. More specifically, capital expenditure on health and education can be examined in greater detail. Public investment in health varies between countries according to their system of provision. In the USA, where private medicine is in the ascendant, there is a clear relation-

**Table 9.11** Capital expenditure of health authorities, England, 1984–5 (£ thousands)

| | | |
|---|---:|---:|
| Hospitals | | |
| New, replacement, virtual reconstruction | 191 557 | |
| Other | 418 009 | |
| Vehicles | 5 028 | |
| Acquisition of land and buildings | 3 808 | |
| Community Health Services | 39 311 | |
| Ambulance Services | 21 721 | |
| Other Services | 83 581 | |
| Staff Services | 32 389 | |
| | | |
| Total capital expenditure | | 795 404 |
| | | |
| Income on capital account | | |
| Proceeds from sales of land and buildings | 46 191 | |
| Income from other sales | 4 424 | |
| | | 50 615 |
| Net expenditure on capital account | | 744 789 |
| Net expenditure on revenue account | | 12 093 324 |

*Source: The Hospitals and Health Service Year Book, 1987*

ship between new investment and the more prosperous suburbs or outer metropolitan areas. Attempts to rectify the lack of hospitals in rural areas included the provision of the Hill–Burton Act of 1946 which allowed for the building of hospitals on a cost-sharing basis with state governments. Even with this degree of government involvement suburban and non-metropolitan areas were found to have newer private and public hospitals while the inner cities were left with the older municipal and county hospitals (Rosenberg, 1986).

In the UK most expenditure on health is undertaken by the National Health Service. Total expenditure in the financial year 1984–5 was just under £13 billion, of which £795 million was capital expenditure. Table 9.11 provides a breakdown of this expenditure, from which it will be seen that just over £191 million was spent on hospitals—for new or replacement buildings or else the virtual reconstruction of existing buildings. A further £3.8 million was spent on the acquisition of land or buildings. Thus, the greater part of capital expenditure in the Health Service is devoted to equipment and other capital items needed for the efficient running of the service. Nevertheless, an impressive amount is devoted to construction work, and many of the new hospitals are on new sites so they are an element in geographical change.

Health Service expenditure entails health-care planning in a spatial context. This process is fraught with unavoidable difficulties, and the Resource Allocation Working Party (RAWP) was initiated in 1975 to identify differences between areas. The work of RAWP has been discussed by other geographers (for example, Eyles and Woods, 1983; Joseph and Phillips, 1984) who pointed out that the distribution of capital and revenue among the Regional Health Authorities (RHAs) was reviewed in order to establish a pattern of distribution responsive, objectively, equitably and efficiently to relative needs. RHAs were ranked relative to each other in terms of revenue targets determined for each of them, which revealed that some RHAs were underfunded. An immediate consequence was the diversion of funds away from South-East England as well as a redistribution of resources within RHAs. For example, local hospitals in Tower Hamlets in East London were closed to permit concentration of facilities in the London Hospital which served outsiders in addition to residents in the North-East Thames RHA. Thus, resources were switched away from an inner-city district (Eyles *et al.*, 1982). Areas which lost resources naturally protested, for RAWP simply divided the cake and did not increase its size so that some regions were worse off than they had been previously. Other criticisms were directed at the RAWP criteria for norms. That the problem is not confined to the UK has been shown by Eyles (1985) in his study of the rationalisation of public health-care provision in New South Wales.

Haynes (1985) illustrated the problem in his review of regional anomalies in hospital bed use which tried to stress the question of equity between patients. Although not directly concerned with new building, which has been the focus of the discussion so far, his work is of interest because the intensity of bed usage may mean that a shortage of hospital accommodation in an area is being overcome by discharging patients in the minimum possible time, possibly before their recovery is complete. Haynes noted that the brunt of the cuts had been borne by the local hospital services which have the least political influence, and that there are serious within-region differences whose explanation requires more information at the subregional level. Marginal changes in a region's share of resources may make no difference to the balance of services between different diagnostic condition groups. Some differences are to be expected because each RHA is responsible for spending within its own region, but when broad diagnostic conditions are considered separately disparities between regions in hospital bed use are noticeable. Contrary to expectations the highest bed-usage rates tend to be in the northern and western parts of the country, while most minimum rates are found in the South and East. Hence a person's chances of receiving hospital treatment for a specific medical condition are by no means uniform throughout the country, though this does not mean that the chances of recovery are less where bed-usage rates are low. Nevertheless, such differences should be justified before they are perpetuated. In general Haynes supported RAWP's objectives despite the differences in provision detected. Some of these are large enough to merit a policy response, but the true problem is that it is difficult to attempt redistribution when resources are scarce.

In the case of public expenditure it is not always easy to separate capital from other costs, as the discussion of RAWP illustrates. Much the same consideration applies to expenditure on education, though here the problem is compounded by the fact that detailed educational expenditure is often the responsibility of local authorities. The British government is trying to rationalise educational spending because it disagrees with the policies followed by some local authorities, but hitherto there have been geographical variations in expenditure levels which some have related to attainment levels (for example, Kirby, 1982). Even within authorities there are variations in provision which might affect schooling standards, although the government ensures that at least minimum acceptable levels are maintained. Variations also occur in more centralised states where government plays a more decisive role in determining standards. Table 9.12 shows the capital account expenditure of local authorities in England and Wales, but it does not show how much of that expenditure was spent on buildings. Total public expenditure on education in England and Wales is of the same order as that for health, and about the same proportion (roughly 6 per cent) is accounted for by capital expenditure. Local authorities receive funding for education from the government, but they also raise finance from local taxes. The figures in Table 9.12 show that capital spending was severely restrained in the period 1977–80, and was kept in check until 1984. Public anxiety about education may have led to an increase in funding, but comparisons of Tables 9.11 and 9.12 indicates that public capital expenditure on health exceeded that on education. That does not necessarily mean that education expenditure lagged because the private sector in education is more extensive than private medicine in the UK. The position in Scotland mirrors that in England and Wales. It should also be remembered that at a time of falling school rolls there is perhaps less call for new educational building. A further point is that the figures in Table 9.12 relate to local authority education provision, which means that the universities are not included. Universities have been badly affected by financial restraints which have curtailed their building programmes. Funding is administered through the University Grants Committee (UGC), though it is proposed to change this system. There was a drop in the allocation for current expenditure in the year 1981–2 but there has been an improvement since then. The same is not true of capital expenditure, which did not vary greatly in the years between 1980 and 1984. Given the high cost of capital equipment needed by universities, the severity of the problem facing them is clear.

**Table 9.12** Capital account educational expenditure of local authorities in England and Wales and Scotland (£ thousands)

|  | *England and Wales* | *Scotland* |
|---|---|---|
| 1975–76 | 450 574 | 66 774 |
| 1976–77 | 428 156 | 88 294 |
| 1977–78 | 364 741 | 75 789 |
| 1978–79 | 332 811 | 58 241 |
| 1979–80 | 367 542 | 56 761 |
| 1980–81 | 477 762 | 58 857 |
| 1981–82 | 431 177 | 66 545 |
| 1982–83 | 474 214 | 60 827 |
| 1983–84 | 486 234 | 55 854* |
| 1984–85 | 538 909 | n.a. |

*provisional    n.a. not available
*Source:* CSO, *Annual Abstract of Statistics*, 1987

In the USA education benefits from a considerable amount of public funding, though the available figures do not distinguish between capital and current expenditure from this source. Schools are partly financed by local property-based funding; in 1984–5 that source accounted for 43.7 per cent of expenditure compared with 49.6 per cent supplied from state sources and 6.6 per cent from federal sources. Average expenditure per student was $3440, a figure which rose to about $3720 when capital and interest charges were taken into account. Education claimed 29.3 per cent of the $600 667 million spent by the states on current and capital expenditure in 1983–4. During the same financial year universities and colleges spent $84 113 million from current funds, of which $54 565 million was expended by institutions under public control. The federal government contributed 12.6 per cent of the total current fund revenue of universities and colleges, state government 28.6 per cent, student tuition and fees 22.8 per cent, and the remaining 36 per cent came from other sources. Federal government intervention in education has traditionally been limited, but since 1983 many of the Department of Education's financial programmes have been transferred to other agencies, many to the Foundation for Education Assistance, which has further reduced the scope for federal influence on education. In 1987 the overall outlay on education within the federal budget was $28 611 million, and that included expenditure on training, employment and social services. Large though this sum may seem to be, it is no more than 2.9 per cent of the budget total of $975 090 million which perhaps puts the extent of federal involvement into perspective.

## Conclusion

Developments in the service sector, particularly its private component, are inseparably linked with the operation of the real property market, and an awareness of the latter's characteristics is an essential basis for understanding the ways in which service facilities evolve within urban areas. Without the sources of finance discussed in this chapter and without the type of property development described the growth of the service sector and its changing geography would not have taken the course it has taken. What is clear is that in the UK there is a marked difference between the private and public sectors as far as the availability of finance is concerned, with the result that the private sector is in a much more buoyant state than the public sector. That is abundantly reflected in the scale of building of offices, shops and recreational facilities. On the other hand, the deprivations of the public sector, especially health and education, have been well rehearsed by many individuals. Conditions in the UK illustrate the factors and processes at work, and while the situation in other countries may be broadly similar due allowance must be made for variations arising from local circumstances in North America, Australasia and Western Europe. Some of these differences are evident from the American examples quoted in this chapter, and although the balance between private and public sector involvement is not the same as in the UK the issues raised and the debate that ensues exhibits many similarities on both sides of the Atlantic.

## Chapter 10

# Accessibility and the Usage of Facilities

Gregory (1981) defined accessibility as the relative opportunity of interaction and contact. Geometrical aspects of this relationship were explored in classical and modern location theory, whereas the structuralist and welfare schools stress the social and economic dimensions of accessibility. Although access to information, facilities and users is of great significance to the service sector, supply and demand considerations must be acknowledged. Different location principles may apply to suppliers of private and public sector activities, with the former having commercial aims and the latter perhaps being influenced by equity considerations. In order to increase efficiency and permit more local contact with decision-making some decentralisation of government administration is virtually universal. Such jurisdictional partitioning can be analysed by comparing the quality and quantity of local services allocated by differing local agencies (Pinch, 1985). 'Output' studies concentrated on what is actually provided may be concerned with issues of equality and the geographical variations in service delivery, or they may be more normative in orientation and interested in criteria that ought to govern the allocation of resources instead of explaining the patterns which actually exist. 'Territorial justice' and the just distribution of resources between political and administrative units according to normative criteria is a concept related to output studies. Investigation of accessibility and the usage of facilities is one way of analysing the distribution and utility of service facilities, and from this base it would be possible to explore the welfare issues that Pinch identified. In this chapter the geographical distribution of services representing the supply of facilities available to consumers is discussed, and in addition the demand for these facilities as demonstrated by studies of revealed accessibility is considered.

## The supply of private sector services

Private sector services exist to meet an actual or perceived potential demand and they locate where they can best serve their market. Producer services may find that a location in a capital city or financial centre is virtually a precondition for commercial success, whereas the headquarters offices of major manufacturing companies may benefit more from proximity to government decision-making centres. Perhaps retailing is the activity that has generated most research into the distribution of facilities. Initially, the hierarchical character of national patterns of provision was studied (see, for example, Carruthers 1967; R.D.P. Smith 1968) and Hillier Parker (1985) still offer a map categorising the status of retail centres which suggests that the approach retains some practical relevance despite the reservations of academic experts in the field. Comparable work, notably Berry's (1967) classic study of South-West Iowa, has been conducted on a smaller geographical scale, and there have also been investigations of intra-urban patterns (for example, Simmons 1964 on Chicago; and Potter 1982 on Stockport). Retailers are particularly sensitive to the accessibility requirements of their customers, taking full advantage of the custom created in retail agglomerations offering the benefits of cumulative attraction (Brown, 1987). They are also keenly aware of the advantages accruing from decentralisation to suburban or out-of-town centres, but they have attracted criticism as a result for not embracing the needs of the poor, old and immobile in their perceptions of the market. Developers of new enclosed or regional shopping centres attach great importance to the location of retailers within a mall, and they realise that careful management of the position of units within a scheme is necessary if they and their clients are to obtain the best returns. Concern for access to customers is matched by interest in another aspect of access to a store, that of convenience for delivery purposes. This important consideration now commands considerable attention, and it also affects the related activity of wholesaling for which the question of access to the market served is paramount.

Private education and medicine have been matters of political controversy in the UK but not necessarily so elsewhere in the world. In fact, private schools for children of nursery and primary age are virtually ubiquitous in the UK's urban areas, especially in the South. Even at the secondary level there is quite extensive provision which is increasing because of dissatisfaction with the state system. Concern about the standards of some private schools was amply justified and supervision of standards by national authorities now ensures that the most flagrant abuses are kept in check. Within the independent sector, as it prefers to be called, there is an elite layer of 'public' schools representing the cream of the private system. Membership of bodies such as the Headmasters' Conference or the Girls' School Association acts as a guide to parents in assessing school quality. Table 10.1 shows the regional distribution of teachers and pupils in the UK in 1982, and the predominance of South-East England is confirmed. At the tertiary level there are several private colleges for training (for instance, secretarial) but only one university, at Buckingham.

There is a dual public and private system in the USA. The extent of the private sector, though far outweighed by public provision, is considerable. In 1983–4 there were 28 734 private schools at grade- and high-school levels comprising 25.8 per cent of the total number of schools, according to the US National Center for Education Statistics. These schools employed 13.7 per cent of the total teaching force and catered for 12.7 per cent of the country's enrolled students. Almost 55 per cent of higher education institutions are private, including the prestigious Ivy League universities, but only 27.7 per cent of teachers and 22.7 per cent of students are in the private sector. Private

**Table 10.1** Regional distribution of teachers and pupils, UK, 1982

Teachers

| Region | Primary (thousands) | Secondary (thousands) | Comprehensive (%) | Independents (thousands) | % all schools | Regional share (%) | Special (thousands) |
|---|---|---|---|---|---|---|---|
| | | | State Sector | | | | |
| UK | 218.7 | 278.5 | 88.9 | 47.2 | 8.4 | 100 | 19.5 |
| North | 12.7 | 16.6 | 99.3 | 1.3 | 4.0 | 2.7 | 1.1 |
| Yorkshire and Humberside | 18.8 | 26.3 | 94.6 | 2.2 | 4.4 | 4.6 | 1.8 |
| East Midlands | 14.5 | 19.4 | 91.7 | 2.2 | 5.8 | 4.6 | 1.2 |
| East Anglia | 6.9 | 8.7 | 95.4 | 1.8 | 10.0 | 3.8 | 0.4 |
| South-East | 60.5 | 77.9 | 87.8 | 21.7 | 12.9 | 45.9 | 6.4 |
| South-West | 14.4 | 19.2 | 79.1 | 5.9 | 14.4 | 12.5 | 1.2 |
| West Midlands | 20.8 | 27.2 | 94.1 | 3.5 | 6.5 | 7.4 | 2.0 |
| North-West | 25.6 | 33.1 | 88.2 | 3.7 | 5.6 | 7.8 | 2.7 |
| Wales | 12.2 | 14.2 | 96.4 | 1.1 | 3.9 | 2.3 | 0.6 |
| Scotland | 24.3 | 28.1 | 100.0 | 1.2 | 2.1 | 2.5 | 1.7 |
| Northern Ireland | 8.0 | 7.8 | n.a. | 2.7 | 14.2 | 5.7 | 0.3 |

*Source: Regional Trends*, 1984, Table 6.2.

Pupils

| Region | Primary (thousands) | Secondary (thousands) | Comprehensive (%) | Independents (thousands) | % all schools | Regional share (%) | Special (thousands) |
|---|---|---|---|---|---|---|---|
| | | | State Sector | | | | |
| | 4780 | 4558.5 | 88.9 | 590.2 | 5.7 | 100 | 144 |
| | 270.8 | 271.9 | 99.6 | 16.0 | 2.8 | 2.7 | 8.8 |
| | 413.2 | 452.5 | 95.1 | 29.1 | 3.1 | 4.9 | 13.1 |
| | 337.4 | 328.7 | 91.7 | 26.7 | 3.7 | 4.5 | 9.2 |
| | 157.8 | 149.0 | 91.7 | 21.8 | 6.6 | 3.6 | 3.3 |
| | 1335.0 | 1269.2 | 87.4 | 259.5 | 8.8 | 43.9 | 46.4 |
| | 345.2 | 334.3 | 79.1 | 65.8 | 8.6 | 11.1 | 9.8 |
| | 472.4 | 451.2 | 93.9 | 42.7 | 4.3 | 7.2 | 15.1 |
| | 591.0 | 541.2 | 88.1 | 54.0 | 4.4 | 9.1 | 20.2 |
| | 267.0 | 237.2 | 96.6 | 12.3 | 2.3 | 2.0 | 4.6 |
| | 492.6 | 404.6 | 100.0 | 17.6 | 1.8 | 2.9 | 11.3 |
| | 187.6 | 118.8 | n.a. | 44.6 | 12.4 | 7.5 | 2.6 |

universities or colleges may receive limited help from the state in which they are located. Impressive though these figures are, it is clear that the majority of Americans rely on the public sector to provide the schools and colleges they need.

The American health care system is often regarded as the archetypal free market service, but since 1945 there has been increasing state involvement on behalf of the poor and the elderly (Rosenberg, 1986). Figures for 1984 issued by the American Hospital Association indicate the extent of public investment in the health-care system. Of the 6872 hospitals providing 1 339 000 beds, 341 (112 000 beds) were operated by the federal government, 1662 (203 000 beds) by state and local governments, 3366 (717 000 beds) by non-profit organisations, and 786 (100 000 beds) were run by proprietary bodies. The status of 717 hospitals (207 000 beds) was not specified, but it is clear that the federal and state involvement is such that it might be more accurate to describe the American system as mixed rather than private in character. According to McGuire *et al.* (1988), federal, state and local government agencies now account for about 40 per cent of American health-care funding, despite the opposition to so-called socialist medicine. Direct charges to patients are high and represent about one-third of total health expenditure, although the proportion varies markedly with the type of care. Physicians see themselves as individual entrepreneurs providing care on a fee-for-service basis. In theory patients can select their physician by free choice, but in fact the individual's choice is limited by ability to pay and by the nature of physical access to a practitioner. Physicians control their own supply by regulating the medical education system and by the licensing boards that certify the ability to practise. Critics argue that large corporate entities such as the pharmaceutical, hospital supply, private health insurance industries, and health maintenance organisations (HMOs) further reduce competition in what has been termed the 'medical industrial complex'.

The state entered the national health-care system as a source of finance for the construction of hospitals (Hill–Burton Act 1946) and for the insurance of the elderly (Medicare) and the poor (Medicaid). Now there is a complex interplay of the different levels of government and the private and public sectors. Each level of government has a role in financing health care for those who cannot afford the costs of private treatment, in financing the delivery of health care, and in planning the system. Consequently there has been overlapping coverage for some people and lack of cover for others. Purely private hospitals are operated by entrepreneurs whose quest for profit is constrained only by state regulations specifying minimum levels of health care. Such operators are prominent in the chronic care sector. Hospitals associated with religious orders, charities and universities resemble public hospitals because they receive public funds in various forms. Public hospitals can be subdivided into local, municipal and county hospitals, and in addition there are federal government hospitals created to meet legislative commitments to particular groups such as veterans.

In the past hospitals have been paid largely on the basis of retrospective reimbursement, but the current move towards prospective reimbursement under diagnostic related groups (DRGs) is leading to substantial changes in hospital management and financing. This system funds hospitals according to their case mix where a specific type of case (a DRG) has an agreed fee attached to it irrespective of what happens to an individual patient in a particular hospital. Provided that the extent of 'legitimate' variance across different patients can be allowed for (for example, degree of severity, home conditions on discharge) the system has some advantages, but the extent to which all the relevant variations can be taken into account is open to question. Since hospital admission is carefully controlled, the new system may have implications for the freedom of access to hospitals enjoyed by patients if their condition seems to be more complicated than the norm for their DRG.

HMOs are usually non-profit-making bodies combining the supply of health care with insurance. They are pre-paid group practices whose subscribers pay a capitation fee and in return receive fairly comprehensive health care which is either zero- or low-priced at the point of consumption. HMOs vary in the extent to which they employ physicians or own hospitals. Although HMOs are often cited as a model for the development of a health-care system there have been suggestions that they have sacrificed quality in order to reduce costs. Medicare, run by the federal government, is a contributory social insurance scheme for the elderly, whereas Medicaid, which is jointly organised by state and federal government for poor people, is non-contributory. At present about 16 per cent of total health-care spending is accounted for by Medicare and about 12 per cent by Medicaid (McGuire *et al.*, 1988). Estimates of access to health care vary, but perhaps 10 per cent of Americans have no health insurance and it is said that a total of 30 million people are inadequately catered for. It has also been claimed that there are variations in the quality of care between the insured in the private sector and the uninsured under public care.

Decentralisation of hospitals encouraged by the Hill–Burton Act of 1946 has meant that facilities have followed the market, thereby creating problems of access for the urban poor. In the 1970s and 1980s metropolitan areas have lost more hospitals by closure than non-metropolitan areas and closures have particularly affected smaller facilities in low-income districts. Levels of hospital provision also differ markedly between states, but despite this the USA has a relatively favourable persons-to-beds ratio compared with other countries.

Primary health care is also privately supplied, and besides being very competitive physicians tend to concentrate in the country's wealthier areas where the prospects are more lucrative. Shannon and Dever (1974) drew attention to the acute shortage of physicians in some parts of the country, but the reality is that the American Medical Association has been successful in resisting all but the most benign attempts to redistribute physician resources. An exception to the freedom of physicians to locate where they choose is the National Service Corps Scheme established in 1976. Under this scheme medical training is paid for on a year-to-year basis for those willing to work in communities which have a critical shortage of physicians. It is clear that, despite the range of provision available, equality of access has not been attained in the USA.

Because private medicine in the UK often uses National Health Service facilities, the two systems are not always geographically distinct. Private medicine offers patients treatment by a chosen consultant, the availability of a single hospital room, rapid arrangement of consultations, and reduced waiting times for hospital admissions. Such a service is expensive and is usually financed through an insurance scheme, but 90 per cent of insurers are also registered with a Health Service doctor. For patients needing short-term surgical care the private sector is advantageous, and currently over 4 million people are insured for private medical treatment. According to Mohan (1984) private medicine has developed unevenly, with the Thames RHAs containing 52.3 per cent of existing bed capacity in private acute hospitals (Table 10.2). There are also significant regional variations in the availability of private beds on a per capita basis. Within the capital there is a marked concentration of facilities in West London. Some dispersal of capacity is planned, but the high cost of provision means that the likely catchment area must have a good income profile and potential. Insurance cover at the county level varies greatly, being as high as 18.6 per cent of Buckinghamshire's and 13 per cent of Surrey's population, but much lower elsewhere. Since company schemes have grown some towns like Peterborough may have large numbers of employees insured.

The largest private hospitals offer about 130 beds, though a more typical size is 50–60 beds. Factors influencing the location of private hospitals include their dependence on Health Service consultant staff and the desirability of proximity to Health Service hospitals, financial support from local businesses, and the availability of redundant hospitals to circumvent planning constraints. There are signs of excess capacity in London, Birmingham and Manchester, raising the likelihood of closures (one had been reported when Mohan wrote), but in contrast to the cutbacks experienced by the state Health Service private hospitals have expanded with little constraint in recent years. It is clear that in the UK private medical provision is related to the potential market and that access to this as well as key personnel are important determinants of the pattern provided.

**Table 10.2** Number of beds in private hospitals with operating theatres, England, 1982

| RHA | No. of beds | (%) | Beds per 1000 population |
|---|---|---|---|
| North-East Thames | 1 486 | 19.4 | 39.8 |
| North-West Thames | 1 107 | 14.4 | 32.1 |
| South-East Thames | 795 | 10.4 | 22.2 |
| South-West Thames | 621 | 8.1 | 21.1 |
| Oxford | 4 654 | 5.9 | 19.2 |
| Mersey | 305 | 3.9 | 12.5 |
| Yorkshire | 447 | 5.9 | 12.4 |
| South-Western | 375 | 4.9 | 12.2 |
| Wessex | 335 | 4.4 | 12.1 |
| West Midlands | 601 | 7.8 | 11.6 |
| North-Western | 444 | 5.8 | 11.1 |
| East Anglia | 208 | 2.7 | 10.9 |
| Trent | 421 | 5.5 | 9.2 |
| Northern | 64 | 0.9 | 2.1 |
| England | 7 663 | | 16.4 |

*Source:* Medical market information; Mohan (1984).

An indication of the perceived potential of the private health-care market in the UK is provided by the recent history of the American-based American Medical International (AMI) Healthcare group in Britain. AMI Healthcare acquired a majority stake in the prestigious Harley Street Clinic in London in 1970, and since then it has built up a chain of 13 modern hospitals containing 1142 acute-care beds (about 10 per cent of private sector beds). It also runs three psychiatric hospitals and has a growing occupational health and screening business. Compared with state-run hospitals private sector institutions can often vary their staff costs according to occupancy levels, which in AMI's case average 65 per cent in acute-care hospitals. With a pool of 1800 full-time staff and 3000 part-time staff the company has scope for adopting flexible working practices. Increased out-patient work is also helping to meet overheads. A measure of the company's success is that when it sought full stock market listing in February 1988 the offer was oversubscribed between two and three times because profit growth was expected to be good at about 20 per cent. AMI Healthcare has been in the forefront of marketing private health care services, offering fixed prices for certain routine operations such as hip replacements and its own credit-care facility, the Amicard. They have not yet followed a competitor's lead in offering a fortnight's holiday at no extra cost if patients are willing to go to Spain for cosmetic surgery, but this example indicates the growing commercialisation of the private sector and the apparent potential for the effective marketing of private health care in the UK.

Leisure and recreation activities depend to a large extent on exploiting the natural and built environment. Suppliers of leisure and recreation opportunities must provide facilities giving access to the principal attractions that appeal to visitors. Grand natural features are unlikely to lose their appeal unless fashions change dramatically, but in practice the majority of tourists are interested in features of the built environment. Capital cities are usually well endowed with what Gottman (1952) termed 'national icons' which attract visitors in their thousands. Most overseas visitors to the UK spend some of the time in London and many do not venture outside it. The Tower of London and St Paul's Cathedral rank high among the country's tourist attractions, while in Paris the Eiffel Tower and Notre Dame Cathedral fulfil a similar function. Elsewhere historic houses and gardens, or magnificent cathedrals and churches also draw tourists. None of these was built for the benefit of the tourist industry, but there are purpose-built tourist facilities such as the familiar piers at British seaside resorts, the assembly rooms at inland resorts, the bandstands and the growing number of marinas. Occasionally the buildings meant to house events have become tourist attractions themselves; for example, the Wagner Festival at Bayreuth. In addition to these types of facility private companies provide hotel accommodation, places of refreshment, specialist equipment (such as ski lifts), integrated entertainment complexes such as theme parks (Disneyland attracts more paying visitors than any other facility in the world), and casinos like those in Las Vegas and Monaco.

Providers of leisure and recreation facilities are not passive. Commercial providers (for example cinemas and sports stadia) aim to make money so their actions are dictated by the need to stimulate demand, to increase profit, to invest in facilities to boost consumption, to diversify into cognate activities, and to close down what is unprofitable. Spatial consequences may result as when rationalisation by brewers deprived many rural areas of their inns because it was felt that the low population totals did not justify continued investment (Clout, 1972). Even though their aim is not primarily commercial, voluntary providers like the National Trust have to maintain their own viability in order to achieve their conservation goals (Tunbridge, 1981). Given the consumer orientation of recreation and leisure activities it is not surprising that their geographical distribution matches that of population and income.

## The supply of public sector services

Frequently public sector office space gives rise to impressive public buildings such as legislature buildings, county or town halls. The grand government quarters of Washington, London or Canberra have their less extensive counterparts in the provincial cities of Cardiff, Edinburgh, Atlanta, Boston or Adelaide. For the most part public sector provision is concerned with health, education, and parks and gardens, and it is to these that attention will be turned in this section.

### Health care

It has already been pointed out that the extent of public provision of health-care facilities in the USA is not negligible, but here emphasis is placed on the British National Health Service to illustrate the characteristics of public involvement in this field. Primary health care provides the majority of patient contacts with the health services so family doctors or general practitioners must be within reach of their patients, though this does not normally require major facilities. People rather than technology are the prime consideration. General medical practitioners are distributed roughly in proportion to population (Table 10.3), though the Thames regions are better served than the Trent RHA. List sizes also vary (Table 10.4), the largest being in Trent and the North-West, and the smallest in East Anglia, Wessex and the South-West. It is one of the great achievements of the National Health Service that GPs are well distributed throughout the country, but there are some problem areas. For example, the preponderance of elderly practitioners in inner London practices and their utilisation of answering machines because they reside elsewhere than at their surgeries is a problem. Patients in these circumstances experience difficulty in making direct contact with their GPs. There is, therefore, some evidence to confirm Hart's (1971) 'inverse care law' which states that the availability of good medical care varies inversely with the need for it. Chronic conditions have replaced acute conditions as the main workload for primary care, and attitudes towards provision have changed. Much can be achieved within the community without recourse to institutions, as the growing proportion of elderly people receiving community-based social care as opposed to surgical or medical treatment illustrates. Mental and behavioural disorders can be similarly treated, which has enabled many small hospitals to

**Table 10.3** General medical practitioners: distribution by Regional Health Authority, England, 1981 and 1985

|  | 1981 | 1985 |
|---|---|---|
| England | 24 359 | 26 190 |
| Northern | 1 537 | 1 656 |
| Yorkshire | 1 823 | 1 971 |
| Trent | 2 213 | 2 409 |
| East Anglian | 996 | 1 086 |
| North-West Thames | 2 020 | 2 117 |
| North-East Thames | 1 970 | 2 074 |
| South-East Thames | 1 897 | 2 015 |
| South-West Thames | 1 564 | 1 662 |
| Wessex | 1 462 | 1 620 |
| Oxford | 1 184 | 1 327 |
| South-Western | 1 788 | 1 983 |
| West Midlands | 2 588 | 2 796 |
| Mersey | 1 270 | 1 335 |
| North-Western | 2 047 | 2 139 |

*Source: Health and Personal Social Statistics for England*, 1982, Tables 3.27 and 3.28; 1987, Tables 3.27 and 3.28.

**Table 10.4** Average list size, England, 1981 and 1985

|  | All patients | | Elderly patients | |
|---|---|---|---|---|
|  | 1981 | 1985 | 1981 | 1985 |
| England | 2 201 | 2 068 | 334 | 317 |
| Northern | 2 237 | 2 076 | 329 | 313 |
| Yorkshire | 2 186 | 2 039 | 337 | 314 |
| Trent | 2 309 | 2 126 | 341 | 321 |
| East Anglian | 2 118 | 1 994 | 351 | 333 |
| North-West Thames | 2 194 | 2 085 | 294 | 278 |
| North-East Thames | 2 221 | 2 114 | 324 | 308 |
| South-East Thames | 2 197 | 2 092 | 375 | 354 |
| South-West Thames | 2 215 | 2 121 | 359 | 345 |
| Wessex | 2 102 | 1 998 | 350 | 336 |
| Oxford | 2 221 | 2 072 | 279 | 262 |
| South-Western | 2 053 | 1 928 | 365 | 346 |
| West Midlands | 2 233 | 2 067 | 305 | 297 |
| Mersey | 2 210 | 2 081 | 320 | 306 |
| North-Western | 2 234 | 2 104 | 348 | 326 |

*Source: Health and Personal Social Service Statistics for England,* 1982, Table 3.28; 1987, Table 3.28.

avoid closure because they can provide day care. Associated with this trend is the growth of private residential accommodation for elderly persons, which has been studied by Phillips and Vincent (1986) and by Phillips *et al.* (1987) with reference to Devon. They detected a marked spatial concentration of homes and they noted that almost 40 per cent of those in their sample had previously been used for tourist accommodation. With an ageing population this type of accommodation might become more common in the future. However, doubts about the soundness of the financial footing of many homes raise the likelihood that greater public sector involvement will become inevitable.

GPs work from surgeries, often in their own homes or else in converted premises, and they rarely cluster in agglomerations except in cases like London's Harley Street. There is a trend towards combining primary care personnel under one roof in a health centre, but as discussed on page 104 little progress in this direction had been made by 1969. Few of the health centres then existing had developed out-patient clinics or specialised diagnostic services as suggested in the original policy. Developments accelerated in the 1970s and are continuing. From a managerial perspective health centres have several advantages for improving administrative efficiency and providing specialised services, but there is a feeling that public accessibility is not necessarily improved and great care must be taken in the spatial allocation of centres. The fear that the size of health centres may introduce an impersonal feeling that creates a social-psychological barrier between patients and practitioners is unjustified in the majority of cases and should not be a bar to further development, for health centres have undoubtedly upgraded surgery provision.

Hospitals, the characteristic providers of secondary health care, include a wide range of institutions such as specialist establishments dealing with a specific form of illness (such as children's or women's diseases). Most geographical studies concern general hospitals providing acute in-patient and out-patient care. Since the hospital system inherited by the National Health Service in 1948 was the product of historical causes there were noticeable regional and intra-urban differences in provision. Partly this was because population movement had left hospitals stranded where they were no longer conveniently situated, partly because the philanthropy commonly associated with the early development of hospitals had been variable in incidence, and partly because ideas on the best locations for hospitals had changed.

Analysis of the regional pattern of allocated beds per 1000 population (Table 10.5) indicates a reduction in disparities in the period 1970–85. Overprovision of beds in the South-West Thames area has been reduced in absolute and relative terms, though the Oxford RHA's position seems to have worsened. Care must be exercised in interpreting these figures because there may be differences in the length of hospital stay or in the types of illness treated that affect the numbers of patients using the available beds. Secondary health care receives higher funding than its primary counterpart, and it seems that overall patients have access to a satisfactory range of facilities wherever they may be. Haynes (1985) indicated that notwithstanding the allocation of beds in practice there are regional anomalies in hospital bed use which mean that inequities remain in the system.

Geography plays an important part in the organisation of the Health Service,

**Table 10.5** Hospital occupancy rates per 1000 population, England, 1970-85

| | Allocated beds* | | | Occupied beds | | | Average length of stay † (days) | | |
|---|---|---|---|---|---|---|---|---|---|
| | 1970 | 1980 | 1985 | 1970 | 1980 | 1985 | 1970 | 1980 | 1985 |
| England | 9.3 | 7.8 | 6.9 | 7.6 | 6.2 | 5.6 | 11.3 | 8.6 | 7.6 |
| Northern | 9.2 | 8.3 | 7.7 | 7.4 | 6.5 | 6.1 | 11.0 | 8.3 | 7.4 |
| Yorkshire | 10.1 | 8.5 | 7.4 | 8.3 | 6.6 | 5.9 | 11.4 | 9.0 | 7.6 |
| Trent | 7.4 | 7.0 | 6.4 | 6.1 | 5.5 | 5.0 | 10.6 | 8.0 | 6.9 |
| East Anglian | 8.1 | 7.1 | 6.4 | 6.6 | 5.5 | 5.0 | 10.2 | 8.1 | 7.3 |
| North-West Thames | 9.8 | 7.9 | 6.8 | 8.0 | 6.6 | 5.7 | 11.9 | 9.0 | 8.0 |
| North-East Thames | 9.1 | 7.8 | 7.2 | 7.4 | 6.5 | 6.1 | 12.3 | 9.7 | 8.3 |
| South-East Thames | 9.3 | 7.8 | 6.7 | 7.5 | 6.4 | 5.5 | 12.0 | 8.9 | 7.7 |
| South-West Thames | 13.0 | 8.4 | 7.5 | 11.0 | 7.2 | 6.4 | 11.6 | 8.4 | 7.7 |
| Wessex | 8.7 | 7.0 | 6.2 | 7.1 | 5.6 | 4.9 | 10.0 | 7.6 | 7.4 |
| Oxford | 7.9 | 5.9 | 5.2 | 6.2 | 4.6 | 4.1 | 8.9 | 7.5 | 7.0 |
| South-Western | 10.4 | 8.1 | 7.0 | 8.7 | 6.5 | 5.6 | 10.7 | 7.9 | 7.6 |
| West Midlands | 8.2 | 7.0 | 6.4 | 6.8 | 5.6 | 5.1 | 11.1 | 8.6 | 7.5 |
| Mersey | 10.3 | 8.8 | 7.6 | 8.2 | 7.2 | 6.4 | 13.2 | 9.8 | 7.9 |
| North-Western | 8.9 | 7.8 | 7.3 | 7.4 | 6.2 | 5.9 | 11.3 | 8.5 | 7.3 |

*Source: Health and Personal Social Statistics for England*, 1982, Tables 4.7 and 4.8; 1987, Tables 4.7 and 4.8.
*Staffed beds at 31 December, including unavailable beds
† All medical and surgical specialities, including gynaecology and pre-convalescent departments, and for 1980 also including nuclear medicine, pathology and radiology.

which operates on a territorial basis in that England is divided up among Regional Health Authorities (RHAs). RHA boundaries do not correspond with those of the Economic Planning Regions, and neither are they defined according to medical criteria such as the distribution and relative prevalence of disease. Some compromises have been effected, but boundaries are co-terminous with those of local authority areas. Since 1982 the District Health Authorities (DHAs), serving about 250 000 people, have become the most significant functional unit. They provide a comprehensive health service including hospitals, community and domiciliary care. They are required to study an area's health needs to discover where provision falls below the accepted standards. Grime and Whitelegg (1982) provide a detailed case study of the Blackburn Health District which illustrates the problems encountered in health-care provision and the kinds of solution adopted. Table 10.6 shows the scope of one RHA's responsibility and the scale of provision among its constituent DHAs. It is fair to say that the public health care system in the UK is impressive despite the strength of criticisms that the emphasis on managerial efficiency desired by government is impeding clinical work. The traditional approach implicit in the foregoing paragraphs has been challenged by

**Table 10.6** Resources allocated by North-East Thames Regional Health Authority, by district, 1983-4.

| DHA | Population | Expenditure (total) £ | Per capita expenditure £ | Total beds | Beds per 1000 |
|---|---|---|---|---|---|
| Barking, Havering and Brentwood | 465 000 | 64 455 300 | 138.61 | 3 161 | 6.80 |
| Basildon and Thurrock | 280 900 | 43 000 000 | 153.08 | 1 571 | 5.59 |
| Bloomsbury | 130 300 | 107 000 000 | 821.18 | 2 765 | 21.22 |
| City and Hackney | 188 500 | 72 500 000 | 384.62 | 1 926 | 10.22 |
| Enfield | 262 100 | 28 771 200 | 109.77 | 1 476 | 5.63 |
| Hampstead | 106 100 | 59 100 000 | 557.02 | 1 166 | 10.99 |
| Haringey | 204 600 | 33 000 000 | 161.29 | 1 160 | 5.67 |
| Islington | 162 900 | 43 003 000 | 263.98 | 1 154 | 7.08 |
| Mid Essex | 272 200 | n.a. | n.a. | 1 394 | 5.12 |
| Newham | 212 300 | 32 330 000 | 152.28 | 986 | 4.64 |
| North-East Essex | 283 900 | 50 000 000 | 176.12 | 3 078 | 10.84 |
| Redbridge | 227 800 | 32 000 000 | 140.47 | 1 660 | 7.29 |
| Southend | 317 900 | 35 300 000 | 111.04 | 2 088 | 6.57 |
| Tower Hamlets | 144 500 | 60 000 000 | 415.22 | 740 | 5.12 |
| Waltham Forest | 215 700 | 55 000 000 | 254.98 | 2 151 | 9.97 |
| West Essex | 256 900 | 29 000 000 | 112.88 | 820 | 3.19 |

*Source: Hospital Administrators' Year Book.*
n.a. not available

Humphreys (1985) who, drawing his examples from remote areas in Queensland, argued that inasmuch as health-care facilities are public goods their provision is a matter lying within the political arena. He favoured a political economy approach as a more productive method of addressing the problem of allocating health-care resources.

*Education*

State education in most countries dates from the recognition that after the Industrial Revolution a literate work-force capable of understanding written instructions was needed. Guidance and control, advice and assistance must be provided by the state so government lays down policy and sets standards on teacher training, examinations and inspection. Funds are allocated, performance statistics are collected, and ultimately a government minister is responsible for the education system's well-being. Because everyone has some stake in education it is a highly political issue, and one with geographical implications. For example, falling school rolls lead to amalgamations and closures resulting in new patterns of movement for pupils. A UNESCO (1981) comparison of educational organisations around the world confirmed the existence of broad similarities. Normally there is a threefold division, but sometimes there is a non-compulsory nursery or kindergarten sector for 3–5-year-olds. Differences emerge in the number of years devoted to each stage, the age of commencement, and the age of finishing. There is general uniformity in primary, or elementary, education which typically extends from 6 or 7 to 11 or 12 years. Secondary education may extend for a further 4 or 6 years, and may be followed by tertiary (university or college) education, whose length varies considerably.

Within individual countries there may be deviations from the above norms because the delivery of education systems may be in the hands of different authorities. In federal countries like the USA or Australia differences between individual states may be considerable, whereas in a unitary state like France national uniformity is more prominently emphasised. In the UK education is primarily administered by local authorities under central government guidance, which gives the local authorities some degree of discretion to adopt systems which suit them. This may change because currently the government is trying to increase its power which may lead to more uniformity.

Variety within the educational system of the USA stems from the fact that the Constitution makes no reference to education. Instead, Article 10 confers upon the states powers in those areas which are not specifically denied to them or reserved to the Federal government. Hence power over education and legal responsibility for the maintenance of education systems resides in the states, though the Federal government has enacted legislation affecting education on a nation-wide basis (for example, the Morrill Act of 1862 which appropriated land for the setting up of agricultural and mechanical colleges, the Smith–Hughes Act of 1957 which subsidised vocational-technical training, and more recently, during the Johnson administration of the 1960s, Operation Headstart, designed to reduce inequalities in educational opportunity). There is a strong belief that education is best provided for by the local community, and thus the school district with its elected board of between three and nine members is the basic educational administrative unit throughout the USA except in the South, where the county is the unit, and in New England, where it is the township. In 1950 there were about 90 000 school districts in the USA, but in the interests of greater efficiency this total was reduced to 15 747 by 1983. In most states there is a State Board of Education which is in effect a legislative body empowered to formulate policies, fix the school leaving age, lay down codes, and approve courses of study. Board members may be elected, appointed or *ex officio* and it is the duty of the State Department of Education under the State Superintendent of Schools (or the Commissioner for Education) to implement these policies. By contrast the US Office of Education, which is part of the Federal Department of Health, Education and Welfare, has limited functions confined largely to research, the administration of federal education grants, and providing services to local, state, national and international agencies. Public education is the most significant component of US provision accounting for about 75 per cent of the total number of schools, employing 86 per cent of the country's teachers, and catering for 87 per cent of the student population. The system is not without its faults and critics, especially where there have been disputes concerning ethnic groups, but most American children benefit from access to good educational facilities.

Enrolment rates (primary and secondary levels combined), expressed as a percentage of the age group eligible, provide a measure of accesss to education. Table 10.7 gives details of enrolment rates, and on this criterion the USA performs very well with a figure of 102 per cent, which arises because actual attendance goes beyond the specified age limits. Generally the percentage for both sexes is over 90, but Portugal, Italy, Austria and Germany have lower figures. This may reflect the true state of enrolment in Portugal and Italy because their illiteracy rates are quite high, though in the Germanic states the statistics are anomalous due to differences in the ages to which the figures refer compared with the UN standard. These figures, which are not easy to interpret, are of value for comparisons with less developed countries. Illiteracy is a more useful measure. Very few Westerners are illiterate, despite the existence of a small proportion of adults who find themselves illiterate due to childhood illness or migration from another language area. Most national governments evidently do not believe that they have an illiteracy problem worth recording.

School provision is naturally related to the distribution of potential pupils.

**Table 10.7** Education in advanced nations, 1982

|  | Percentage of GNP spent on education | | | Illiteracy rate (%) | | Enrolment rate (%) | |
|---|---|---|---|---|---|---|---|
|  | 1970 | 1977 | 1982 | males | females | males | females |
| Australia | 4.2 | 6.5 | 6.0 | – | – | 99 | 100 |
| Austria | 4.6 | 5.5 | 5.6 | – | – | 81 | 80 |
| Belgium | – | 6.5 | 6.1 | – | – | 94 | 95 |
| Canada | 8.9 | 8.3 | 7.7 | – | – | 94 | 94 |
| Denmark | 6.8 | 6.7 | 6.3 | – | – | 92 | 92 |
| Finland | 6.1 | 6.2 | 5.7 | – | – | 84 | 89 |
| France | 4.9 | 5.5 | 3.5 | – | – | 94 | 98 |
| West Germany | 3.7 | 4.7 | 4.7 | – | – | 78 | 80 |
| Greece | 2.0 | 2.0 | 2.3 | 6 | 17 | 95 | 89 |
| Ireland | 5.0 | 6.3 | 6.8 | – | – | 95 | 100 |
| Italy | 4.0 | 4.5 | 4.6 | 4 | 5 | 85 | 82 |
| Japan | 3.9 | 5.5 | 5.8 | – | – | 96 | 97 |
| Netherlands | 7.7 | 8.4 | 8.1 | – | – | 98 | 96 |
| New Zealand | 4.8 | 5.4 | 5.6 | – | – | 91 | 92 |
| Norway | 6.0 | 7.6 | 8.1 | – | – | 96 | 98 |
| Spain | 2.1 | 2.1 | – | 4 | 9 | 96 | 96 |
| Sweden | 7.7 | 8.4 | 9.1 | – | – | 90 | 94 |
| Switzerland | 4.0 | 5.2 | 5.0 | – | – | – | – |
| USA | 6.6 | 6.3 | 6.4 | – | – | 98 | 102 |
| UK | 5.3 | 5.9 | 5.7 | – | – | 91 | 93 |

*Source:* Unesco (1982)

Particular problems arise in thinly populated areas which may be solved by subsidising small uneconomic schools (some Scottish islands have one teacher to a dozen or fewer pupils), closing schools and transferring pupils to a larger school daily by bus or by boarding (children from Mull board in Oban during the week), providing distance learning by radio and correspondence (as in Northern Territory, Australia), or by employing peripatetic teachers (as on the Falkland Islands). Small schools are comparatively expensive because of the indivisibility of fixed costs (heat and light) and variable costs (teachers' salaries). Phillips and Williams (1984) documented the problems of cost per pupil in Cumbrian primary schools (Figure 10.1) and they also showed how long daily bus journeys are imposed on Gloucestershire schoolchildren (Figure 10.2). Cloke (1979) demonstrated how school closures were a common feature of rural areas in Warwickshire and Devon (Figure 10.3). Most parishes affected by closure were experiencing withdrawal of other public and private services such as post offices and stores, so the loss of a school is critical to local community life for it is often the venue for village activities. Where population growth justifies new schools, as in the New Towns, a hierarchical arrangement of primary feeders to secondary schools has been favoured (the case of Harlow New town is illustrated in Figure 10.4).

However important education may be, Table 10.8 shows that teachers do not comprise a large proportion of the work-force or of service workers in advanced nations. Within countries the distribution of teachers usually matches that of pupils, but differences between areas can be indicated by the pupil–teacher ratio. Differences are large in the USA (Figure 10.5) where the pattern is less coherent than that for spending per pupil (Figure 10.6). A low pupil–teacher ratio is considered desirable and is claimed to be an advantage of private education. Table 10.1 suggests that British independent schools have lower ratios than state schools, but even in this sector South-East and South-West England are more favoured than other regions. Interestingly, the state sector in Scotland has lower ratios than its private sector counterpart so it is not invariably true that the state sector fares worse.

The quality of access may also be affected by the extent of overcrowding in classrooms. Government figures imply a high degree of overcrowding in England and Wales, but a breakdown of county and district authorities published in the *Guardian* (22 May 1984) revealed that the regional average masked notable variations between authorities. Gateshead, for example, had only 7.5 per cent of primary pupils in classes of over 30 compared with 47.9 per cent in Birmingham. Figure 10.7 shows the proportion of overcrowded classes among districts in the former metropolitan counties. The explanation for the differences most probably lies in the differing policies of authorities towards education spending. Labour authorities such as Liverpool and Sheffield have been more reluctant to impose economy cuts on education than Conservative administrations such as Birmingham.

*Leisure and recreation*

Public authorities play an important role in providing facilities for leisure and recreation, ranging from playing fields, through swimming pools, sports

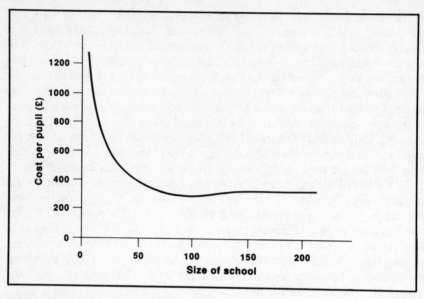

**Figure 10.1** Primary school costs per pupil by size of school
*Source:* after Phillips and Williams (1984)

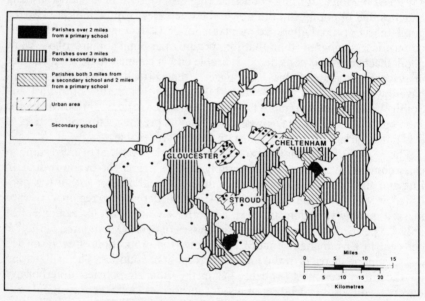

**Figure 10.2** Access to schools in Gloucestershire, 1977
*Source*: after Phillips and Williams (1984)

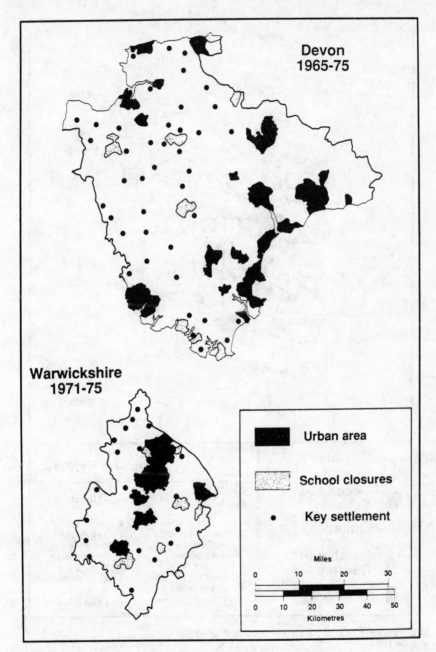

**Figure 10.3** School closures in Warwickshire and Devon
*Source*: after Cloke (1979)

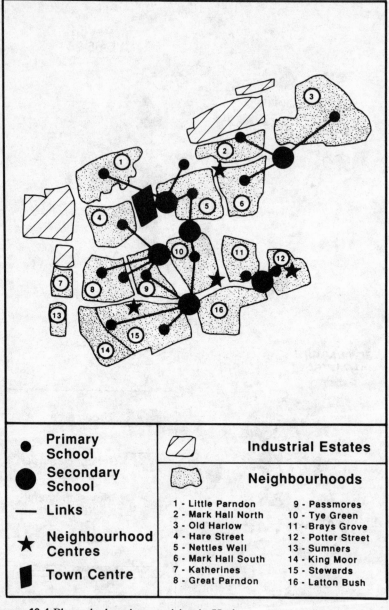

**Figure 10.4** Planned education provision in Harlow
*Source*: Harlow New Town Corporation, 1977

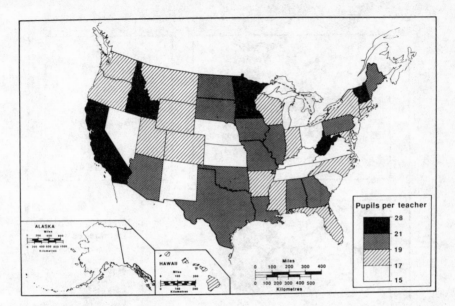

**Figure 10.5** Pupils per teacher, USA, 1981
*Source: World Almanac*, 1985

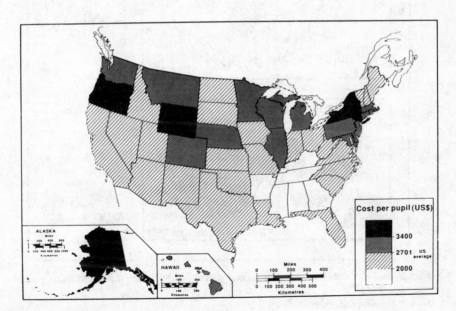

**Figure 10.6** Cost per pupil per state, USA, 1980–1
*Source: World Almanac*, 1985

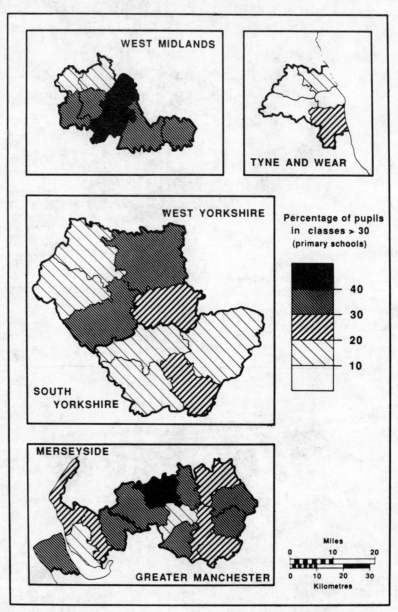

**Figure 10.7** Proportion of pupils in classes of over 30 in primary schools in metropolitan counties, 1983
*Source: Guardian* 22 May 1984, p. 13

centres, tennis courts, and bowling greens to halls and meeting places. Access to open space for recreation was recognised as an important need in the aftermath of urban growth that accompanied the Industrial Revolution and Britain pioneered the concept of urban public space. The Victorians and Edwardians viewed parks as being primarily for healthy outdoor exercise, an assumption

**Table 10.8** Teachers in advanced nations

|  | Teacher numbers | Teachers as % of work-force | Teachers as % of service workers |
|---|---|---|---|
| Belgium | 46 484 | 0.7 | 1.2 |
| Canada | 286 200 | 1.76 | 2.66 |
| Denmark | 58 957 | 1.78 | 3.0 |
| Finland | 59 701 | 1.83 | 3.3 |
| France | 582 494 | 1.68 | 3.1 |
| West Germany | 678 296 | 1.64 | 3.2 |
| Greece | 49 672 | 0.80 | 2.2 |
| Ireland | 36 030 | 1.80 | 4.0 |
| Italy | 796 565 | 2.18 | 4.9 |
| Japan | 1 191 874 | 1.49 | 3.0 |
| Netherlands | 100 895 | 1.06 | 2.1 |
| New Zealand | 26 210 | 1.24 | 2.2 |
| Norway | 50 650 | 1.96 | 3.4 |
| Portugal | 93 959 | 1.52 | 4.1 |
| Spain | 235 267 | 0.98 | 2.1 |
| Sweden | 100 448 | 1.89 | 3.09 |
| UK | 576 047 | 1.60 | 2.8 |
| USA | 3 133 000 | 2.06 | 3.1 |

*Source: Unesco, 1984*

that became institutionalised in official thinking. The standard measure of open space provision was laid down in 1925 as 6 acres (2.4 hectares) per 1000 population and this persists to the present day. This arbitrary assumption is based on presumed numbers of people likely to be engaged in particular sports, but there is growing evidence that this standard does not correspond to contemporary needs or wishes. Various surveys of parks in the 1970s such as those by the Greater London Council and Edinburgh Corporation (Table 10.9) showed that the predominant use of parks was for such informal passive activities as sitting, walking and running because only a minority played organised sport. The general ratio of park to playing fields space is 1:4, but 75 per cent of local authorities feel dissatisfied with the distribution of parks in their area. Only half the authorities consulted had a location policy, and most of these adopted the GLC's hierarchical scheme for provision. Though not a major element in service sector provision, parks and gardens make a notable contribution to the urban landscape as well as accounting for some service sector employment.

## The usage of facilities: studies of revealed accessibility

Studies of the actual use of facilities, or the revealed accessibility, must complement consideration of the supply of services which indicate the potential

**Table 10.9** Activities in urban parks (percentage of all visits)

| | |
|---|---|
| *GLC* | |
| General (walking, sitting) | 86 |
| Observing events and people | 19 |
| Playing with children | 12 |
| Social activities | 10 |
| Organised sport | 6 |
| Entertainments | 3 |
| Activities with animals | 2 |
| *Edinburgh* | |
| Informal, passive pursuits | 67 |
| Children's play | 14 |
| Casual ball games | 15 |
| Organised sport | 3 |

*Sources:* GLC, 1968; Edinburgh Planning Dept., 1969

accessbility to users. Micro-scale studies make use of gravity interaction models and related concepts for their methodology, as was briefly described in Chapter 4. Macro-scale studies tend to base their findings on standard carto-graphic analysis. Whichever approach is being discussed here, there is little point in distinguishing between the public and private sectors for the principles at issue are the same for both.

*Micro-scale studies*

Travel minimisation and the role of distance are important concepts in micro-scale studies, and early developments concerned shopping behaviour. Berry's (1967) renowned study of South-west Iowa set the tone with its emphasis on aggregate behaviour, distances, and directions of alternative kinds of shopping trips (for example, convenience, comparison and speciality). Countless studies have replicated Berry's work, which still has validity, although modern trends in consumer behaviour have reduced its predictive capacity. Earlier Applebaum (1940) had focused interest on the delimitation of trade areas, and earlier still Reilly (1929) attempted to predict the attractive power of centres and hence their use by consumers. Reilly's gravity formulations were subse-quently developed by Huff (1963) and Lakshmanan and Hansen (1965) (see Chapter 4), but for some these methods were too deterministic. Rushton (1981) developed the idea of *revealed space preference*, suggesting that consumers rank all alternative shopping centres on a scale of preference. Potter (1979) amplified this behaviouralist interpretation by distinguishing between *consumer information fields* and *consumer usage fields*. He found that these fields were wedge-shaped and that the angles of the information and usage fields increased as social status improved. Age and family size were other important factors, and it was noted that directional bias tended to favour downtown as opposed to uptown centres.

Investigations have been conducted into the images of the retail environment, consumer learning and decision-making, and variability in overt behaviour. All these studies suffered from the defect of presenting a static picture of the consumer's activity which may not have general applicability. Recent work utilising panel (or longitudinal) surveys is more relevant for the description and analysis of spatial behaviour involving recurrent choice and movement, and for assessing change in behaviour over time. Wrigley *et al.* (1985) used this approach to study grocery shopping in Cardiff. Current computing power and storage capabilities mean that the large volume of data generated by a panel survey can be handled, so new methods of retail analysis and forecasting which cannot be matched by conventional cross-sectional data are being evolved.

One justification for the new approach is that during the past 20 years the face of British retailing has been transformed, not least because of the intensification of competition among a few major multiples, to such an extent that adjustments in shopping behaviour were only to be expected. Previously, most of the conventional wisdom about routine shopping behaviour in the UK was derived from sample surveys carried out in towns such as Watford, Coventry, Oxford and part of north London during the period 1969–76 (Guy, 1985). Among the topics that can be analysed and used in forecasting with the aid of the new data are patterns of repeat buying at stores, the interaction of store choice and brand choice, the relationship between household income and shopping behaviour, the degree of loyalty to grocery stores, the nature of multi-stage and multi-purpose shopping journeys and the identification of shopping bundles, the market performance of particular stores or store groups, the usage of edge-of-city and within-city superstores, and a comparison of the shopping behaviour of women in full-time, part-time or no paid employment. Above all the Cardiff survey contained detailed locational information on consumer travel and purchasing habits that greatly enhances our understanding of consumer behaviour. Already a modified version of the Cardiff survey design is being applied in California, and in fact there is great potential for cross-cultural comparisons.

A strong concern with the link between residential location and consumer behaviour is the basis of ACORN (A Classification of Residential Neighbourhoods) which is a method of defining and reaching target audiences on a geographical level (Clark, 1982). Although it was designed with the British market in mind, ACORN is actually operated by Consolidated Analysis Centres Inc. (CACI), an American market analysis group. Central to ACORN is the idea that areas possessing similar demographic and social characteristics will share common lifestyle features irrespective of their location in the country. Burglars have long known that where people live is related to what products they buy and own, and now marketing men are exploiting the same notion. Types of housing and the kinds of people living in an area are precisely defined using 40 variables extracted from the population census. Census enumeration districts (of about 150 households) provide the geographical base, and 11 types of neighbourhood are recognised which can be further subdivided. Since postcodes are known for each enumeration district lists of all areas and residences of a specified type can be produced. Like other marketing classifications, ACORN depends on probabilities and relies on stereo-types, but in contrast to the one-dimensional classifications based on class, age or income it uses 15 social and economic variables, 12 relating age and household, and 13 related to housing. The old socio-economic groups deter-mined by how a person earns a living rather than on what is actually earned could be misleading; for example, clergymen are AB in social status but are more likely to be E in spending power. ACORN's real advantage is that besides identifying what the market is it reveals where it can be contacted.

ACORN has proved its worth as a media tool in helping to select which products to promote in particular markets, in deciding how to define market and sales territories, in choosing the appropriate media for the task in hand, and in locating sites for poster displays. Building societies, TV rental companies and brewers are now keen users, but a striking example of ACORN's value is provided by the experience of the freezer food company Bejam. Traditionally Bejam regarded its market in socio-economic terms as ABC1, but it was shown that actually the highest degree of penetration was achieved in ACORN group B (modern family houses, higher incomes). In-store interviews confirmed this finding, so Bejam now rank all major shop-ping districts in the country according to an index of freezer potential. Site selection staff have a guide to where they should seek new outlets using a Local Expenditure Zone system which divides the country into 1101 retail catchment areas. The population characteristics in each zone are matched with the national index of freezer potential to derive a grade for each shopping district according to quality dependent on the type of customer available. Bejam's marketing manager is enthusiastic about what he calls the 'most sig-nificant marketing tool since the first census'. As with the Cardiff consumer survey, ACORN can only function because of the availability of modern com-puting power, but it is relatively cheap and it has demonstrated its value to firms seeking the most profitable markets for their products. Compared with older methods using central place and gravity model principles the modern emphasis on longitudinal surveys of consumer behaviour and methods of market segmentation like ACORN are better adapted to the contemporary retail environment. Companies find it easier to plan how to reach their potential customers, and more information can be made available about consumers' access to and usage of facilities.

From the geographical viewpoint medical visits have much in common with shopping trips in that distance greatly influences them. Because it is hard to find reasons for the non-availability or non-utilisation of facilities and because available data relate to attendance, existing studies of patient behaviour rely on interpretation of revealed behaviour. Phillips (1981) examined acces-sibility to medical practitioners in West Glamorgan using three socially dis-tinct pairs of sub-areas with similar medical practitioner provision and a fourth pair of low-status areas, only one of which possessed medical prac-titioner services. Distance and socio-economic variables were found to inter-act so that distance did not determine the observed pattern. Place of previous residence seemed to be highly significant in explaining utilisation patterns, suggesting that inertia is an important element if patients are satisfied with a GP. As expected, low-status patients had less favourable attitudes to travel to a surgery unless they lived close to a health centre, and they were apparently inhibited by administrative procedures and bureaucratic attitudes at the surgery. Administrative features of the service rather than treatment gave most cause for dissatisfaction. On the whole the low-status people used the service more than high-status people, though the difference was not statistically significant. Differences in usage are also related to age and sex, for older people generally use the services more than younger groups and females attend more than males. Young mothers make considerable use of medical services, and there are obvious differences between male and female usage of facilities which depend on gender. Nevertheless there is evidence that women make more routine use of preventive medicine and follow-ups than men. Phillips reported a Wisconsin study which, having removed from the analysis those women who had given birth in the preceding 12 months, found that women paid an average 2.9 visits per year compared with 1.9 for men.

Studies of hospital utilisation have concentrated on the distance decay function, but it is important to realise, as Morrill and Earickson (1968a, 1968b) did, that hospitals do not offer homogeneous services and that patients do not have common needs. The 'hospital problem' is something more than a simple ratio of capacity to demand. The Chicago Regional Hospital Study concluded that significant variations among hospitals must be understood and also the variations among patients which affect the location and use of hospitals. At the time of the study there were over 100 hospitals in Chicago varying greatly in size and specialisation, control, religious affiliation, and location. A five-tier hierarchy was recognised, the fifth-level consisting of long-term institutions, and not surprisingly there was a strong correlation between size and the range of services offered. The largest hospitals tend to provide specialised diagnostic and treatment facilities and personnel enabling them to handle unusual or difficult cases. Such hospitals attract patients from further afield than smaller hospitals, and they can be regarded as having a different output. However, the greater complexity of their output helps to explain the diseconomies of scale that accompany increased size. In reality there are marked differences in the level of service, the kinds of residence and intern programmes, and the number of medical staff as well as in the overall size of hospitals. It was also found that patients vary in their preference for hospitals of different kinds, their ability to pay, and their location with respect to hospitals. Hospitals of unusual quality or renown would attract patients from a greater distance, while isolated hospitals were more dependent on their immediate vicinity than those in competitive clusters. However, there were deviations from the expected pattern attributable to the reputation of the hospital, possible discrimination in the case of black citizens, and religious affiliation. Later Morrill *et al.* (1970) found that referral practice related to physician affiliation explained why certain patients travelled beyond the nearest hospital. The significance of social and economic distinctions and religious preferences was also confirmed, all of which suggests that there is a sufficient lack of a common distance decay function to raise problems in applying this concept in health-care planning, at least in situations where private medicine is the rule. On the other hand, Haynes and Bentham (1979) did find that distance affected out-patient attendance at a new hospital in Kings Lynn in the UK, and Magnusson (1980) also confirmed the importance of distance in his study of visits to an emergency department in Stockholm. Other studies have also established the importance of distance decay in the use of emergency departments.

Usage of leisure facilities can be analysed in the same way as shopping or medical visits, but school attendance is compulsory so there is no call for comparable work on education. In the case of education there are problems of school provision and the delimitation of catchment areas to be solved. Spatial analysis has proved useful in this respect (Hodgart, 1978). Yeates's (1968) work in Grant County, Wisconsin, is a good example in which linear programming was used to modify school district boundaries in the interests of greater efficiency. For example, the existing system exhibited much inefficiency, 18 per cent of high school students being in the wrong districts, and Yeates was able to propose a possible remedy for this.

*Macro-scale studies*

Macro-scale studies of the use of retail facilities depends on the availability of figures such as sales or turnover data. National-level sales in the UK could be analysed (Thorpe 1968; Price 1970) when the Census of Distribution was published, but since its demise the substitutes in the form of Business Monitors and Retail Inquiries have not proved satisfactory replacements because they do not provide disaggregated figures of use to geographers (Jones P.M., 1984). The USA is better served in this respect by its Census of Retail Trade, even if the interval between censuses is regarded as too long (Richards, 1984). Despite the limitations of official statistics there are sufficient indications in the business sections of daily newspapers to endorse the view that a very healthy level of usage is achieved by retail outlets in a variety of countries.

International tourist movements are better recorded. First-rank countries with over 10 million arrivals per annum are exclusively European or North American (Table 10.10). Trends in these countries are shown separately in Table 10.11, from which it will be seen that all except Canada and Italy exhibited considerable growth in the 1970s. Italy maintained a steady level of involvement, but Canada's figures actually declined. Spain remained the most popular tourist destination, with France and the UK achieving a marked increase, but the most spectacular growth was in Czechoslovakia, where arrivals increased by over 400 per cent. Nearly half the countries recording over 1 million arrivals are also European, the remainder being in Latin America, the Far East and the Middle East. Third World countries are strongly represented in the 500 000–999 999 category, and they had the highest growth rates apart from Czechoslovakia. Very few countries registered a decline in tourist arrivals though the inclusion of Switzerland in this group will puzzle some. Less surprising is the decline in Afghanistan, Ethiopia, Madagascar and the Sudan. Impressive though the figures are, it must be remembered that they represent a very small proportion (under 10 per cent) of the world's population, so that the potential for the expansion of tourism as living standards rise is great.

The emphasis on the Western nations in the overall figures underlines the importance of providing facilities if visitors are to be attracted. It is also clear

**Table 10.10** Tourist arrivals, 1980

|  | No. of countries |
|---|---|
| 10 000 000+ | 8* |
| 1 000 000–9 999 999 | 32† |
| 500 000–999 999 | 9‡ |
| 100 000–499 999 | 30 |
| Under 100 000 | 25 |

*Source: World Statistics in Brief,* Department of International Economic and Social Affairs, Statistical Office, Statistical Papers, Series 5, no. 6, United Nations, New York, 1981.

*Austria, Canada, Czechoslovakia, France, Italy, Spain, UK, USA.
†Argentina, Bahamas, Belgium, Brazil, Bulgaria, Colombia, Egypt, East Germany, West Germany, Greece, Hungary, Ireland, Israel, Japan, Jordan, Malaysia, Mexico, Morocco, Netherlands, Norway, Poland, Portugal, Romania, Singapore, Switzerland, Syria, Thailand, Tunisia, Turkey, USSR, Uruguay, Yugoslavia.
‡Australia, Guatemala, India, Indonesia, Iran, Iraq, Malta, Philippines, Venezuela.

**Table 10.11** Trends in tourist arrivals: major destinations, 1970–80 (thousands)

|  | 1970 | 1975 | 1979/80 | CHANGE 1970–79/80 (%) |
|---|---|---|---|---|
| Austria | 9 753 | 11 540 | 12 875* | +32 |
| Canada | 14 184 | 13 662 | 12 267 | −14 |
| Czechoslovakia | 3 545 | 13 863 | 18 350 | +418 |
| France | 13 700 | 13 064 | 28 000* | +104 |
| Italy | 14 189 | 15 500 | 14 699* | +4 |
| Spain | 24 105 | 30 122 | 38 902* | +61 |
| UK | 6 692 | 8 844 | 12 498* | +87 |
| USA | 13 167 | 15 698 | 20 016* | +52 |

*Source:* As Table 10.10.
*1979.

that, whatever British tourists' prejudices may be, a favourable climate is not the only attraction for visitors. Within individual countries capital cities remain important destinations, especially for foreigners, but tourism embraces a wider definition than international travel and there are regions which attract indigenous holidaymakers in most countries. In the UK, for example, domestic holidays are generally taken in the South-West, South and South-East, though the Lake District of northern England is a popular exception. As with retailing, all the evidence points to the flourishing nature of the tourist industry with the concomitant of a good rate of usage for its facilities. Pearce (1987) argued that studies of international travel flows deal with a single scale of analysis, whereas in reality movements also occur on an intra-national scale as well as within the cities and resorts visited. Pearce advocated an integrated approach embracing all three levels to provide a better under-standing.

In the case of health care, Cullis and West (1979) distinguished between *horizontal equity*, implying equal access to care and equal resource provision for patients suffering from a particular complaint regardless of where they live, and *vertical equity*. This latter refers to the extent to which individuals suffering from different disorders receive appropriately different medical attention. These two aspects of equity are structured and internal to any health system and must not be confused with forms of inequality in the use of services. Conventionally health service utilisation is investigated in the aggre-gate with the suggestion that variations are caused by consumer characteris-tics (age, sex, income, personal mobility) and by the influence of such facility attributes as size, cost, quality and location. The individual's perception of a service, of facilities and their accessibility is relevant (Joseph and Phillips, 1984). Uneven population distribution and the fixed locations of medical facilities means that uniform availability is impossible to achieve because geo-graphical constraints prevent the supply of facilities adjacent to all prospec-tive users, and for this reason health care is not a 'pure' public good.

The supply of a service is a prerequisite for accessibility (Joseph and Phillips, 1984), and this availability depends on the state of medical technology and the allocation of resources to health care. Socio-organisational factors including cost, intake policy, and specialisation of the provider could give rise to differ-ential access to care. There is a distinction between *locational accessibility*, crudely measured in mileage terms, and *effective accessibility*, concerned with whether a facility is always open or available to people. Economic barriers are an important influence on health care accessibility, but their significance varies according to the type of health-care system. In the UK waiting times for treatment vary for private and Health Service patients, and there are marked variations within the state system according to location. Figure 10.8 identifies the North Midlands and the North as the worst areas for waiting, although delays are highly likely in a belt stretching from East Anglia to cen-tral southern England and the South-West. There are further differences in the metropolitan regions. Selected examples, quoted in Table 10.12, provide extra evidence of the nature of this problem. If health care were a simple good (a uniform service available at identical facilities) many of the difficulties could be overcome, but this is not the case and its complexity is increasing steadily. What consumers may want is not an amorphous and generalised service called 'health care' but access to specific types of treatment or com-binations of treatment, the availability of which depends largely on the organisational attributes of the delivery system.

Empirical studies have focused on actual utilisation or barriers to utilisation. Bradshaw (1972) identified normative, felt, expressed, and com-parative needs. Normative need is professionally determined by a doctor; felt

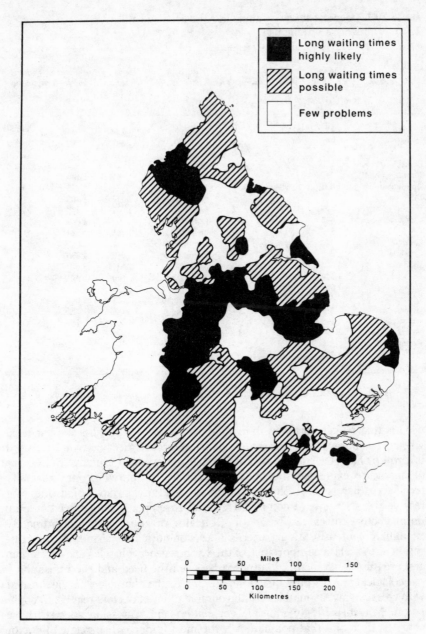

**Figure 10.8** NHS waiting lists
*Source: Guide to Hospital Waiting Lists*, 1985, College of Health

**Table 10.12** General surgery waiting lists, England and Wales, 1985 (HAAs with longest waiting lists)

| Health Authority Area | Patients on waiting list | Non-urgent cases | Patients waiting over 1 year (%) | Health Authority Area | Patients on waiting list | Non-urgent cases | Patients waiting over 1 year (%) |
|---|---|---|---|---|---|---|---|
| Barking | 1 457 | 1 419 | 9 | Lewisham | 1 729 | 1 594 | 27 |
| Barnet | 1 901 | 1 735 | 28 | Lincs N | 1 842 | 1 590 | 34 |
| Bath | 1 241 | 1 056 | 29 | Lincs S | 1 813 | 1 757 | 42 |
| Berkshire E | 1 728 | 1 809 | 32 | Liverpool | 1 822 | 1 821 | 23 |
| Birmingham C | 1 912 | 1 848 | 27 | Medway | 1 145 | 1 140 | 7 |
| Birmingham N | 1 001 | 984 | 17 | Newcastle | 1 374 | 1 320 | 4 |
| Brighton | 1 172 | 1 166 | 26 | Northampton | 1 577 | 1 385 | 48 |
| Bristol & Weston | 1 779 | 1 715 | 22 | Norwich | 1 002 | 897 | 23 |
| City & Hackney | 1 643 | 1 367 | 32 | Oldham | 1 099 | 1 063 | 51 |
| Clwyd | 1 177 | 1 130 | 9 | Oxfordshire | 1 161 | 1 084 | 11 |
| Crewe | 2 343 | 2 190 | 72 | Pembrokeshire | 1 249 | 1 023 | 67 |
| Cumbria E | 1 251 | 1 251 | 43 | Scunthorpe | 1 842 | 1 830 | 37 |
| Doncaster | 1 050 | 905 | 40 | Sheffield | 2 627 | 2 420 | 55 |
| Dorset E | 1 328 | 1 245 | 28 | Shropshire | 2 610 | 2 327 | 44 |
| Exeter | 1 068 | 1 029 | 0 | Somerset | 1 231 | 1 121 | 27 |
| Glamorgan Mid | 2 457 | 2 436 | 40 | Southampton | 2 121 | 2 011 | 34 |
| Glamorgan S | 1 539 | 1 336 | 34 | Staffs N | 2 189 | 1 755 | 41 |
| Gloucester | 1 109 | 984 | 32 | Tees S | 1 789 | 1 780 | 53 |
| Gwent | 1 430 | 1 335 | 16 | Warrington | 1 772 | 1 772 | 63 |
| Hounslow | 1 291 | 1 258 | 44 | West Lambeth | 1 146 | 1 101 | 52 |
| Hull | 1 231 | 1 231 | 41 | Wolverhampton | 1 606 | 1 601 | 21 |

*Source: Guide to Hospital Waiting Lists*, 1985, College of Health, quoted in *The Times*, 25 November 1985

need is that perceived by an individual; and expressed need is the felt need when it has been transformed into a demand for a service. Comparative need is a group characteristic and is professionally determined, usually on the basis of aggregate expressed demand; for example, if retired people normally receive regular general physical examinations, any group which does not receive the service is in comparative need. Attempts to gauge need employ unsatisfactory measures based on ill-health or morbidity. Unfortunately examination of utilisation patterns does not normally permit the identification of the relative importance of the various geographical, socio-economic, and organisational factors interposed between the need and the utilisation.

Ecological studies pose questions relating to the characteristics associated with areas having favourable or unfavourable ratios of doctors relative to population. Not surprisingly multiple correlation and regression analyses have consistently found that population is the most important correlate of doctor supply at a variety of geographical scales. Problems of multicollinearity make it difficult to explore the importance of other variables even when the population effect is controlled. Joseph and Phillips (1984) discuss other difficulties of this type of analysis, including the problem of evaluating non-pecuniary influences on the location of doctors. Cross-cultural comparisons clearly present further problems. As always the reality of the 'ecological fallacy' might lead the investigator to make false inferences about individual behaviour.

Accessibility to GPs can be measured by using the ratio of population to GPs, but there are problems relating to the uniqueness of place when the scale of enquiry is reduced to the urban level. Moreover, the implication that boundaries are impermeable is not justified for medical services. Regional accessibility measures suffer from the defect that accessibility is equated with that of a region's centroid, an assumption that becomes increasingly unreasonable as the size of region grows. British practice uses service norms as a measure of availability, so that areas with a list size of 2500 or more are regarded as underserviced. Index measures summarising regional distributions (for example, location quotients) could be used as an alternative. Distance decay functions of varying gradient according to the specialised nature of the facility can be examined, but relationships are not simple and straightforward. Knox (1978; 1979a; 1979b) devised a comparatively sophisticated measure of intra-urban variability in access to GPs which discriminated between areas of over- and underprovision of doctors. Like all measures of potential physical accessibility, Knox's model is affected by problems relating to the distance exponent and by questions of the elasticity of supply of doctors' services. It should always be remembered that availability of access does not mean that patients will take advantage of the opportunities afforded them.

Educational performance provides an indication of the value of access to education. Despite the state's legitimate interest in performance it is a controversial issue because of its bearing on teacher competence, student ability, the fair distribution of resources and political matters. Nevertheless, examination success or failure is the only effective quantitative measure. Universities in South-East England award the highest proportion of first-class degrees (Lynn, 1979); this area, of course, contains the universities of Oxford, Cambridge and London, internationally renowned centres of learning that may attract higher-calibre students or benefit from superior teaching. Alternatively they may treat their students more leniently than their counterparts elsewhere. In short, it is not easy to interpret spatial variations in academic performance.

Performance in school examinations is depicted in Figures 2.1 and 10.9. In showing school leavers who left with no graded results, Figure 10.9 effectively presents a geography of failure. Wales, Scotland and Northern Ireland have a higher than average proportion who fail to achieve (compare Strathclyde's 31.1 per cent failure rate with the 4.9 per cent of Buckinghamshire and West Sussex). Again, South-East England (except for London) has the lowest overall failure rates. Conversely, school leavers with formal qualifications are numerous in Buckinghamshire, Hertfordshire and Surrey. Wales is generally better than England, where the West Country and the Midlands have comparatively low levels of achievement. Coates and Rawstron (1971) observed similar patterns in the 1960s, but the 1974 boundary changes inhibit direct comparison. Scotland cannot easily be compared with England and Wales because the Scottish education system is different and its H grades are not wholly comparable with A levels. In Scotland the more remote areas have a higher proportion of successful candidates; thus the 34 per cent success rate in the Western and Northern Isles exceeds that of Strathclyde and the Lothians, containing Glasgow and Edinburgh respectively, which have the

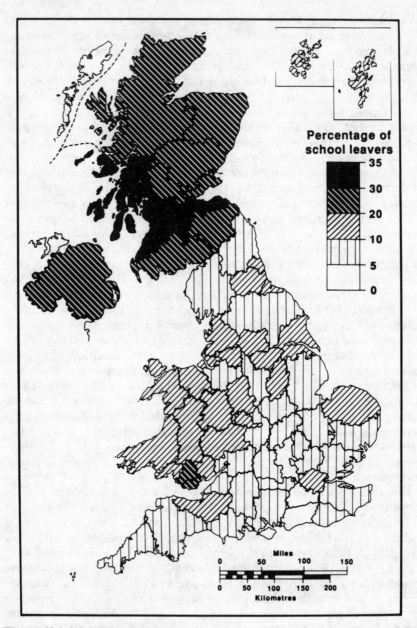

**Figure 10.9** School leavers with no grade results, 1982
*Source: Regional Trends*, 1985

lowest rates. The patterns are quite complex, but rural counties and conurbations seem to enjoy less success than outer suburban areas or very remote rural places. It is difficult to better the explanations offered by Coates and Rawstron (1971), though no one has followed up their pioneering work to unravel the reasons for these quite marked anomalies. Perhaps what D.M.

**Table 10.13** Female participation in education, 1977–8

| | Female students (%) | | | Female teachers (%) | | |
|---|---|---|---|---|---|---|
| Level: | Primary | Secondary | Tertiary | Primary | Secondary | Tertiary |
| Australia | 49 | 49 | 44 | 71 | 46 | – |
| Austria | 48 | 50 | 41 | 74 | 51 | 13 |
| Belgium | 49 | 49 | 43 | – | 58 | – |
| Canada | 49 | 49 | 48 | – | – | 14 |
| Denmark | 49 | – | 46 | 52 | – | – |
| Finland | 49 | 52 | 50 | – | – | 22 |
| France | 49 | 51 | 50 | 67 | – | – |
| West Germany | 48 | 52 | 40 | 62 | 40 | – |
| Greece | 48 | 43 | 38 | 48 | 54 | – |
| Iceland | 49 | 46 | – | 54 | 29 | 12 |
| Ireland | 49 | 52 | 38 | 73 | – | – |
| Italy | 49 | 47 | 41 | 85 | 56 | – |
| Japan | 49 | 49 | 33 | 56 | 26 | 13 |
| Netherlands | 49 | 47 | 36 | 45 | – | – |
| New Zealand | 49 | 47 | 36 | 45 | – | – |
| Norway | 49 | 49 | 44 | 55 | – | 18 |
| Portugal | 48 | 50 | 42 | 81 | 56 | 29 |
| Spain | 49 | 49 | 40 | 58 | – | 20 |
| Sweden | 49 | 51 | 44 | 81 | 47 | – |
| Switzerland | 48 | 50 | 28 | – | – | 7 |
| UK | 49 | 49 | – | 78 | 48 | – |

*Source:* UNESCO

Smith (1977) called one's 'life chances' are spatially unequal, or perhaps there are differences in the ability to make use of the available opportunities.

Without equality in education girls are likely to be disadvantaged in the employment market. Table 10.13 shows that at primary and secondary levels female participation compares with the proportion of females in the population, but at the tertiary level only Finland and France and the USA have equality of numbers. In some countries there is a substantial inequality which is matched by the low percentage of female staff, for example, only 28 per cent in Switzerland, 33 per cent in Japan and 36 per cent in the Netherlands. Such imbalance is self-perpetuating, for fewer female graduates means that there are fewer potential female academics to be recruited. Coates and Rawstron (1971) found regional variation in the proportions of the sexes staying on for advanced courses at British schools and proceeding to higher education. Areas with a tradition of working women (such as South-East England) had higher female participation rates than areas like East Anglia where fewer women worked. They suggested that a lower value was placed on girls' education in some areas.

The greater discrepancies in access to tertiary education arise because after a specified age (16 in the UK, 15 in Australia) education is no longer compulsory. Successful school leavers can progress to higher education in pursuit of degrees or diplomas which are frequently prerequisites for many careers. For this reason about 40 per cent of American high school students proceed to some form of higher education. In 1985 nearly 28 per cent of the population aged 18–24 were enrolled in colleges or universities, and 52.5 per cent of these were women. Although a university degree does not guarantee a job, it qualifies people for applying for specified posts. It enables people to pursue further study in the professions such as law and accountancy, and since these professions are among the better paid in Western society higher education is also viewed as a passport to higher monetary reward and social status. Alternatively higher education can be regarded as a means of personal fulfilment through meeting intellectual challenges. Participation in education beyond the compulsory age is thus dependent on a mixture of motivations and ability, but is essentially voluntary.

Figure 10.10 illustrates variations in the percentage of pupils in the UK staying on at school after age 16. The prosperous South of England and the Celtic fringe of Scotland, Wales and Northern Ireland stand out as above average. Percentages range from as high as 51 per cent in the Highlands to as low as 17 per cent in Somerset. Coates and Rawstron (1971) attributed the high figures in South-East England for the 1960s to the greater number of affluent middle-class parents seeking better employment prospects for their children. Consequently, Surrey, one of the country's highest income areas, had 46 per cent staying on, doubtless influenced by the greater opportunity in the London region with its demand for trained personnel. Economic opportunities are so low in the Celtic fringe that the only way to progress is to obtain qualifications, even if eventually that means migrating. Where youth unemployment is as high as it is in these areas additional years in school might seem preferable to idleness. Coates and Rawstron noted that in Wales education is a highly valued aspect of the culture, which in some cases may be a by-product of the difficulties inherent in mastering two languages.

## Conclusion

The concept of accessibility adopted in this chapter is a broad one, but it is very suitable for an analysis of the service sector. It has been argued that the supply of facilities must be taken into account in any assessment of accessibility, and it has been shown that the criteria employed to determine the extent of provision differed greatly between the private and public sectors, especially in respect of location. That there are inequalities in service provision cannot be doubted, for, as Freestone (1977) observed, geographical location is itself a potent cause of inequality. The implication of this should not be ignored and several workers have addressed this problem. Badcock (1977), for instance, viewed the city as essentially a system of resource allocation and referred to

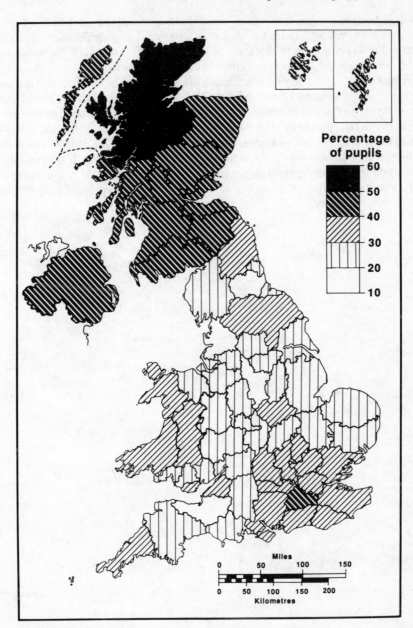

**Figure 10.10** Pupils aged over 16 staying on at school, 1982
*Source: Regional Trends*, 1985

social polarisation in Australian cities. Awareness of the existence of disadvantaged groups in cities has given rise to policies of positive discrimination intended to bring help to the areas of greatest need. Bondi (1987) considered the allocation of education resources within Manchester and urged the need for more studies of a similar type. Her work illustrates the continuing need for exploring the meaning of accessibility. The distinction between the public and private sectors is less important to the evaluation of the demand for services. For predictive purposes accessibility and the usage of facilities are usually measured with the aid of interaction models which may be used to calculate the extent of attraction of a single facility or a group of facilities. It is impossible to study the changing geography of the service sector without being aware of the variations in the patterns of usage and the different degrees of accessibility that influence them.

*Chapter 11*

# Conclusion

If economic geography is 'fundamentally concerned with the ways in which economic activities are arranged on the surface of the earth and with the processes which lead to such spatial patterns' (Lloyd and Dicken, 1977), then agricultural and industrial activities have been better served in the literature than the service sector. Taken as a whole, as has been attempted in this book, the latter has suffered from what Daniels (1985) called 'long-standing neglect'. On the other hand, certain branches of service activity such as retailing, health care, and leisure and recreation have been investigated in depth, resulting in the production of an impressive body of knowledge. The very range of activities covered highlights a problem: some are straightforwardly commercial, but others cannot be regarded simply as commercial undertakings. This difficulty can be overcome if one thinks 'in terms of a spectrum which stretches from commodities whose expected utility theory fits very well to those where it fits badly, [and] health care is at the latter end' (McGuire *et al*. 1988). In this way it is possible to include all the activities covered in this book within the market approach adopted, but the questions of equity raised by health care and education mean that alternative viewpoints must be acknowledged. Allowing for the different interpretations that necessarily arise, an attempt has been made to present an integrated view of the service sector by drawing on existing specialised work in the belief that there is a combined tertiary and quaternary economic system that merits study in its own right. There seems to be ample justification for this because of the importance of services as a source of wealth and employment in the advanced economies. Without a doubt the post-industrial society has arrived in many parts of the world and should be given the prominence it deserves.

Lloyd and Dicken (1977) championed the advantages of viewing the world in systems terms to emphasise the wholeness and interdependence among the system's components. They argued that from the geographical viewpoint the elements of the system clearly have a physical expression in space in the shape of what they call the 'economic furniture' of the landscape. Geographers are interested in the ways in which this furniture is arranged, but, as Lloyd and Dicken caution, the elements are not in themselves the system. They identified management structures providing the necessary organisation and control for the system's function; maintenance structures seeking to preserve the stability of the system; and adaptive structures that look to the future to prepare for new demands. Though this classification has not been consciously followed in the text it is not inappropriate. Attention has been devoted to the management structures of government bureaux, firms and companies, and the geographical patterns they have generated. Less prominence has been given to maintenance structures, although they have not been ignored. In the chapter on the impact of technology, adaptive structures were considered. Lloyd and Dicken had a fourth category, the actual work done by the service sector, and this, too, has been incorporated at many points in the book.

No study of the service sector can ignore its dynamic nature: working practices are being changed by innovations; the sector's occupational structure is changing as new types of work emerge and old ones disappear. Economic change is affecting the opportunities available, and social and political change is altering the character of the demand for and the supply of facilities. Since service growth and urbanisation appear to be linked, service sector change is likely to be evident in the urban structure. Some changes affecting the urban structure have been mentioned in various chapters, but there have been few empirical studies devoted to the changing geography of a nation's service sector. An exception is Kirn's (1987) examination of growth and change in the service sector of the USA from a spatial perspective. He commented that the size and diversity of the service sector makes our understanding of its many characteristics quite limited. His study covered the period 1958–77, and he proposed a number of hypotheses relating to changes in the geography of the service sector. Most change in the spatial pattern of service location was expected in producer services which were thought to be more significant in regional development processes. Movement down the urban hierarchy in line with population movement was anticipated, and it was believed that growth would be particularly strong in the nation's fastest-growing region. The role of producer services in regional development should be reflected in relationships between population and economic growth and the location and growth of producer services. Places specialising in producer services should grow more rapidly than those specialising in consumer services or manufacturing. Consumer services would adapt themselves to population and income change, and would be instrumental in the growth of many metropolitan centres.

Kirn found that the spatial distribution of American service activities changed significantly in his study period and that the major focus of change was in business and professional services, and finance, insurance and real estate. Besides becoming more evenly distributed spatially, the service structures of different levels of the urban hierarchy became more alike due to downfiltering of a number of service industries, though not all producer services downfiltered to the same extent. Decentralisation of manufacturing must have had some effect on producer services, and it was noted that most of the services that decentralised also experienced strong overall growth. This suggests that demand for them grew at all levels of the hierarchy. Consumer services were affected by the shift of population growth to non-metropolitan places in the 1970s. On this evidence Kirn's hypotheses successfully identified trends that are worthy of special consideration in studies of service sector geography.

Comparable investigations of countries other than the USA are awaited. Kirn's work in distinguishing between regions within the USA drew attention to the progress made by the South. Even so, the North-East, with the dominant service centre in New York, retained its supremacy. Keinath also examined the spatial component of the USA's post-industrial soc the period 1971-8. He found that the American manufacturing be ...as becoming more specialised in manufacturing while the SunBelt was becoming more diversified and experiencing relative post-industrial growth. In his opinion the economic power base of the nation is beginning to tilt towards the periphery, and this tilt is not the result of a mere diffusion of the characteristics of the core but represents the beginning of a new kind of economy that is fundamentally different from the older one both nationally and peripherally. Applied to the UK this core–periphery dichotomy seems less convincing, but service sector growth has largely occurred outside the old-established manufacturing areas comparable to the American manufacturing belt. In the UK it is the South-East England core which is benefiting most from service sector expansion to achieve a level of prosperity that is noticeably lacking in the periphery.

Borchert (1978) adopted a different perspective, arguing that the larger organisations dominate the allocation process and have become the major control points in the nation's economy. The organisations' administrative buildings command the skylines and extensive land areas at their control points, and they are among the leading shapers of the images of downtown districts, cities and regions. His study covered changes that took place in the USA between 1927 and 1971, and he found that the distribution of main control points resembles the pattern of metropolitan population or employment. The concentration of control in New York was over ten times as large as the mean for the next seven cities. Private corporations that exceeded the national growth rate did so by specialising in fast-growth parts of the economy, acquiring other firms, diversifying, or conglomerating. Very large government-controlled business organisation firms grew from a small base to become some of the nation's largest conglomerates and diversified financials. Overall the North-East's share declined, but within that region the New York–Hartford area experienced greater concentration. A regional income and savings base was a prerequisite for development, which explains the degree of inertia in the location of control points. As a generalisation, which seems to apply to other countries as well, there was great instability in the relative strength of different classes of industry and in the relative fortunes of individual firms. By contrast, there was also much stability, as the large organisations grew even larger and more diverse. This conclusion can certainly be related to much of what has been discussed in this book.

Without a doubt service sector growth is an engine of change in the geography of advanced industrial nations. Whether the developing world will seek to emulate the more prosperous countries by entering the post-industrial stage themselves remains to be seen. Until they do differences will persist at the global level, but even at smaller geographial scales all the evidence suggests that development associated with this major economic activity will be spatially uneven. Clearly there is a need for greater understanding of the background to, and the processes which are influencing, change in the geography of the service sector, and it is hoped that this work has made a contribution towards this end.

# Bibliography

Abler, R. and Falk, T. (1981), 'Public information services and the changing role of distance in human affairs', *Economic Geography*, 57, 10–22.

Adrian, C. (1984), 'Institutional constraints on the post-war provision of fire services in Sydney', *Australian Geographer*, 16, 38–54.

Airey, D. (1978), 'Tourism and the balance of payments', *Tourism International Research–Europe*, 3rd quarter, 2–16.

Alexander, I. (1979), *Office Location and Public Policy*, London, Longman.

Ambrose, P. and Colenutt, B. (1975), *The Property Machine*, Harmondsworth, Penguin.

Antonelli, C. (1987), 'The determinants of the distribution of innovative activity in a metropolitan area: the case of Turin', *Regional Studies*, 21, April, 85–94.

Applebaum, W. (1940), 'How to measure the value of a trading area', *Chain Store Age*, November, 92–94, 111–14.

Armstrong, R.B. (1979), 'National trends in office construction, employment and headquarters location in US metropolitan areas' in Daniels (1979, 61–94).

Askew, I. (1983), 'The location of service facilities in rural areas: a model for generating and evaluating alternative solutions', *Regional Studies*, 17 (5), 305–13.

Badcock, B.A. (1977), 'Educational achievement and participation rates in Sydney', *Australian Geographer*, 13, 325–31.

Bannock, G. (1981), 'The clearing banks and small firms', *Lloyds Bank Review*, 142, October, 15–25.

Bateman, M. (1985), *Office Development: A geographical Analysis*, London, Croom Helm.

Beavon, K.S.O. (1977), *Central Place Theory: A Reinterpretation*, New York, Longman.

Bell, D. (1974), *The Coming of the Post-industrial Society*, London, Heinemann.

Bennett, R.J. (1980), *The Geography of Public Finance*, London, Methuen.

Bennison, D.J. and Davies, R.L. (1980), 'The impact of town centre shopping schemes in Britain: their impact on traditional retail environments', *Progress in Planning*, 14, 1–104.

Berry, B.J.L. (1967), *Geography of Market Centres and Retail Distribution*, Englewood Cliffs, NJ, Prentice Hall.

Beyers, W.B. and Alvin, M.J. (1985), 'Export services and post industrial society', *Papers of the Regional Science Association*, 57, 33–45.

Bird, J.H. and Witherwick, M.E. (1986), 'Marks and Spencer: the geography of an image', *Geography*, 71 (4), 305–19.

Blomley, N.K. (1985), 'The Shops Act (1950): the policies and the policing', *Area*, 17 (1), 25–33.

Body, R. (1984), *Farming in the Clouds*, London, Temple Smith.

Bondi, L. (1987), 'Education, social needs and resource allocation: a study of primary schools in Manchester', *Area*, 19(4), 333–43.

Borchert, J.R. (1978), 'Major control points in American economic geography', *Annals of the Association of American Geographers*, 68 (2), 214–32.

Bradshaw, J. (1972), 'The concept of social need', *New Society*, 30 March, 640–3.

Bramley, G. (1986), 'Defining equal standards in local public services', *Urban Studies*, 23, 391–412.

Breheny, M.J., Green, J. and Roberts, A.J. (1981), 'A practical approach to the assessment of hypermarket impact', *Regional Studies*, 15, 459–74.

Brown, S. (1987a), 'A perceptual approach to retail agglomeration', *Area*, 19(2), 131–40.

Brown, S. (1987b), 'Institutional change in retailing', *Progress in Human Geography*, 11 (2), 181–182.

Brown, S. (1987c), 'The complex model of city centre retailing: an historial application', *Transactions, Institute of British Geographers*, new series, 12 (1), 4–18.

Bunce, V.J. (1983), 'Revolution in the high street? The emergence of the enclosed shopping centre', *Geography*, 68 (4), 307–18.

Burgess, E.W. (1923), 'The growth of the city', *Proceedings of the American Sociological Society*, 18, 85–9.

Burkart, A.J. and Medlik, S. (1981), *Tourism: Past, Present and Future*, London, Heinemann.

Burns, W. (1959), *British Shopping Centres: New Trends in Layout and Distribution*, London, Leonard Hill.

Burtenshaw, D. (1985), 'The future of the European city: a research agenda', *The Geographical Journal*, 151(3), 365–370.

Carruthers, I. (1967), 'Major shopping centres in England and Wales', *Regional Studies*, 1, 65–81.

Carter, H. (1972), *The Study of Urban Geography*, London, Edward Arnold.

Central Office of Information (COI) (1984), *Britain: An Official Handbook*, London, HMSO.

Central Statistical Office (1986), *UK Balance of Payments 1986*, London, HMSO.

Chester, T.E. (1979), 'A better way to pay for health care? An essay in comparative analysis', *National Westminster Bank Quarterly Review*, November, 12–25.

Chester, T.E. (1981), 'Market forces and health economics—a case study of Switzerland', *National Westminster Bank Quarterly Review*, November.

Chester, T.E. and van Oss, M.G.M. (1984), 'Economic priorities and social expenditure: a comparison of Dutch and British Health Service policies', *National Westminster Bank Quarterly Review*, February, 31–40.

Christaller, W. (1933), *Die zentralen Orte in Süddeutschland*, Jena, Fischer; translated by C.W. Baskin as *Central Places in Southern Germany*, Englewood Cliffs, NJ, Prentice Hall, 1966.

Clark, E. (1982), 'ACORN finds new friends', *Marketing*, 16 December, 29–35.

Cloke, P.J. (1979), *Key Settlements in Rural Areas*, London, Methuen.

Cloke, P.J. (1985), 'Counter-urbanisation: a rural perspective', *Geography*, 70 (1), 13–23.

Clout, H.D. (1972), *Rural Geography: An Introductory Survey*, Oxford, Pergamon.

Coates, B.E. and Rawstron, E.M. (1971), *Regional Variations in Britain*, London, Batsford.

Cocheba, D.J., Gilmer, R.W. and Mack, R.S. (1985), 'Measuring changes in service sector activity: data refinement recommendations and their impact on a study of the Tennessee Valley', *Growth and Change*, 16 (4), 20–42.

Cocheba, D.J., Gilmer, R.W. and Mack, R.S. (1986), 'Causes and consequences of slow growth in the Tennessee Valley's service sector', *Growth and Change*, 17 (1), 51–65.

Collins, L. and Walker, D.F. (eds) (1975), *Locational Dynamics of Manufacturing Industry*, Chichester, Wiley.

Cooper, C. (1987), 'The changing administration of tourism in Britain', *Area*, 19 (3), 249–53.

Crawford, R.J. (1973), 'A comparison of the internal urban spatial pattern of unit and branch bank offices', *The Professional Geographer*, 25 (4), 353–6.

Cullis, J.G. and West, P.A. (1979), *The Economics of Health. An Introduction*, Oxford, Martin Robertson.

Damesick, P. (1979), 'Offices and inner-urban regeneration', *Area*, 41–7.

Daniels, P.W. (1979), *Spatial Patterns of Office Growth and Location*, London, Bell.

Daniels, P.W. (1982), *Service Industries: Growth and Location*, Cambridge, Cambridge University Press.

Daniels, P.W. (1983a), 'Service industries: supporting role or centre stage', *Area*, 15 (4), 301–9.

Daniels, P.W. (1983b), 'Modern technology in provincial offices: some empirical evidence', *Service Industries Journal*, 3, 21–41.

Daniels, P.W. (1985), *Service Industries: A Geographical Appraisal*, London, Methuen.

Daniels, P.W. (1986a), 'Office location in Australian metropolitan areas: centralisation or dispersal?' *Australian Geographical Studies*, 24 (1), 27–40.

Daniels, P.W. (1986b), 'Foreign banks and metropolitan development: a comparison of London and New York', *Tijdschrift voor Economische en Sociale Geografie*, 77, 269–87.

Daniels, P.W. (1986c), 'Producer services in the Post-Industrial Space Economy' in Martin, R. and Rowthorn, B. (eds), *The Geography of Deindustrialisation*, London, Macmillan.

Darin-Drabkin, H. (1977), *Land Policy and Urban Growth*, Oxford, Pergamon.

Davies, R.L. (1976), *Marketing Geography: With Special Reference to Retailing*, London, Methuen.

Davies, R.L. (1978), 'Retailing in the city centre: the character of shopping streets', *Tijdschrift voor Economische en Sociale Geografie*, 69, 270–5.

Davies, R.L. (1984), *Retail and Commercial Planning*, London, Croom Helm.

Davies, R.L. and Howard, E.B. (1986), 'The changing retail environment and the Shops Act 1950', *Area*, 16 (3), 236–40.

Davies, R.L. and Rogers, D.S. (eds) (1984) *Store Location and Store Assessment Research*, Chichester, John Wiley.

Dawson, J.A. (1979), *The Marketing Environment*, London, Croom Helm.

Dawson, J.A. (1982a), *Commercial Distribution in Europe*, London, Croom Helm.

Dawson, J.A. (1982b) 'The growth of service industries', in Johnston and Doornkamp (1982).

Dawson, J.A. (1983), *Shopping Centre Development*, London, Longman.

Dawson, J.A. (1985), 'Shopping centre development in Canberra' in Dawson and Lord (1985, 185–205).

Dawson, J.A. and Lord, D.J., (1985), *Shopping Centre Development: Policies and Prospects*, London, Croom Helm.

Delobez, A. (1985), 'The development of shopping centres in the Paris region', in Dawson and Lord (1985, 126–60).

Dicken, P. (1986), *Global Shift. Industrial Change in a Turbulent World*, London, Harper and Row.

Dicken, P. and Lloyd, P.E. (1981), *Modern Western Society. A geographical Perspective on Work, Home and Well-being*, London, Harper and Row.

Dunn, R. and Wrigley, N. (1984), 'Store loyalty for grocery products: an empirical study', *Area*, 16 (4), 307–14.

Dunning, J.H. (1983), 'Changes in the level and structure of international production: the last one hundred years' in Casson, M. (ed.), *The Growth of International Business*, London, George Allen and Unwin.

Eckstein, A.J. and Heien, D.M. (1985), 'Causes and consequences of service sector growth: the US experience', *Growth and Change*, 16 (2), 12–17.

Edgington, D.W. (1982), 'Changing patterns of Central Business District office activity in Melbourne', *Australian Geographer*, 15, 231–42.

Edwards, L.E. (1983), 'Towards a process model of office-location decision making', *Environment and Planning A*, 15, 1327–42.

Enderwick, P. (1987), 'The strategy and structure of service sector multinationals: implications for potential host regions', *Regional Studies*, 21(3), 215–24.

Erickson, R.A. (1986), 'Multinucleation in Metropolitan Economies', *Annals of the Association of American Geographers*, 76(3), 331–46.

Erickson, R., Gavin, N. and Cordes, S. (1986), 'Service industries in interregional trade: the economic impacts of the hospital sector', *Growth and Change*, 17(1), 17–27.

Eyles, J., (1985), 'From equalisation to rationalisation: public health care provision in New South Wales', *Australian Geographical Studies*, 23(2), 243–68.

Eyles, J. (1986), *A Geography of the National Health. An Essay in Welfare Geography*, London, Croom Helm.

Eyles, J., Smith, D.M. and Woods, K.J. (1982), 'Spatial resource allocation and state practice: the case of health service planning in London', *Regional Studies*, 16(4), 239–53.

Eyles, J. and Woods, K.J. (1983), *The Social Geography of Medicine and Health*, London, Croom Helm.

Florida, R.L. and Kenney, M. (1988), 'Venture capital, high technology and regional development', *Regional Studies*, 22(1), 33–48.

*Fortune International* (1987), 'The Service 500', 115, 12 June.

Freeman, M. (1987), 'Property development in the CBD: concentration or dispersal?'. *Area*, 19(2), 123–9.

Freestone, R. (1977), 'Provision of child care facilities in Sydney', *Australian Geographer*, 13, 315–25.

Fryer, D.D. (1987), 'The political geography of international lending by private banks', *Transactions, Institute of British Geographers*, new series, 12(4), 413–32.

Garner, B.J. (1966), *The Internal Structure of Retail Nucleations*, Research series 12, Northwestern University, Department of Geography.

Gassman, H.P. (1981), 'Is there a fourth economic sector?', *OECD Observer*, 113, November, 18–25.

Gershuny, J. and Miles, I. (1983), *The New Service Economy*, London, Frances Pinter.

Gertler, M.S. (1986), 'Regional dynamics of manufacturing and non-manufacturing investment in Canada', *Regional Studies*, 20 (6), 523–34.

Giggs, J.A. (1973), 'The distribution of schizophrenia in Nottingham', *Transactions, Institute of British Geographers*, 59, 5–76.

Gillespie, A.E. and Goddard, J.B. (1986), 'Advanced telecommunications and regional economic development', *The Geographical Journal*, 152(3), 383–97.

Gillespie, A.E. and Green, A.E. (1987), 'The changing geography of producer services employment in Britain', *Regional Studies*, 21(5), 397–412.

Goddard, J.B. (1967), 'Changing office location patterns within Central London', *Urban Studies*, 4, 276–84.

Golledge, R.G., Brown, L.A. and Williamson, F. (1972), 'Behavioural approaches in geography: an overview', *Australian Geographer*, 12, 59–79.

Goodall, B. (1972), *The Economics of Urban Areas*, Oxford, Pergamon, 47–9.

Gottman, J. (1952), 'The political partitioning of our world: an attempt at analysis', *World Politics*, 4, 512–19.

Greater London Council (1969), *Greater London Development Plan: Statement*, London, GLC.

Greater London Council (1985), *Planning for Shopping*, GLC Conference, 26 April, London, GLC.

Greater London Council (1986), *Survey of Offices in London*, Report 1: *Background to the Design and Implementation of the Survey*; Report 2: *Preliminary Findings on Employment Use of Floorspace and Location*; Report 3: *New Technology Analysis: Preliminary Findings*, GLC March.

Green, A.E. and Howells, J. (1987), 'Spatial prospects for service growth in Britain', *Area*, 19(2), 111–22.

Green, S. (1986), *Who owns London?*, London, Weidenfeld and Nicolson.

Gregory, D. (1981), 'Accessibility' in Johnston (1981).

Grime, L.P. and Whitelegg, J. (1982), 'The geography of health care planning: some problems of correspondence between local and national policies', *Community Medicine*, 4, 201–8.

Guy, C.M. (1980), 'Policies for the location of large new stores—a case study', *Area*, 12(4), 279–284.

Guy, C.M. (1985), 'The food and grocery shopping behaviour of disadvantaged consumers: some results from the Cardiff consumer panel', *Transactions, Institute of British Geographers*, new series, 10, 181–90.

Hagerstrand, T. (1967), *Innovation Diffusion as a Spatial Process*, Chicago, University of Chicago Press.

Hall, P. (1987), 'The anatomy of job creation: nations, regions and cities in the 1960s and 1970s', *Regional Studies*, 21(2), 95–106.

Hamnett, C. (1987), 'The church's many mansions: the changing structure of the Church Commissioners' land and property holdings, 1948–1977', *Transactions, Institute of British Geographers*, new series, 12(4), 465–81.

Harrington, J.W., Jnr, Burns, K. and Man Cheung (1986), 'Market-oriented foreign investment and regional development: Canadian companies in Western New York', *Economic Geography*, 62(2), 155–66.

Harris, C.D. and Ullman, E.L. (1945), 'The nature of cities', *Annals of the American Academy of Political Science*, 242, 7–17.

Harrison, A. and Gretton, J. (1986), 'Health care UK', *Policy Journal*, 362–709.

Hart, J.T. (1971), 'The inverse care law', *Lancet*, 405–12.

Harvey, D. (1981), 'Marxist geography' in Johnston (1981: 209–12).

Hayes, M. (1986), 'Your good health: access to health and health-care in Northern Ireland', *Regional Studies*, 20(6), 493–504.

Haynes, R.M. (1985), 'Regional anomalies in hospital bed use in England and Wales', *Regional Studies*, 19(1), 19–28.

Haynes, R.M. (1987), *The Geography of the Health Services in Britain*, London, Croom Helm.

Haynes, R.M. and Bentham, C.G. (1979), 'Accessibility and the use of hospitals in rural areas', *Area*, 11(3), 186–91.

Hepworth, M. (1986), 'The geography of technological change in the information economy', *Regional Studies*, 20(5), 407–24.

Hepworth, M. (1987), 'Information technology as spatial systems', *Progress in Human Geography*, 11(2), 157–80.

Herbert, D.T. and Thomas, C.J. (1982), *Urban Geography. A First Approach*, Chichester, John Wiley.

Highlands and Islands Development Board (HIDB) (1985), *The Highland Region*, Inverness, HIDB.

Hillier Parker (1985), *Shopping Centres of Great Britain*, Hillier Parker May and Rowden.

Hirst, J. and Taylor, M.J. (1985), 'The internationalisation of Australian banking: further moves by the ANZ', *Australian Geographer*, 16(1), 291–5.

Hirst, J., Taylor, M.J. and Thrift, N.J. (1982), 'The geographical pattern of Australian Trading Banks' overseas representation' in Taylor and Thrift (1982).

Hodgart, R.L. (1978), 'Optimizing access to public services: a review of problems, models and methods of locating central facilities', *Progress in Human Geography*, 2(1), 17–48.

Holmes, J.H. (1985), 'Policy issues concerning rural settlement in Australia's pastoral zone', *Australian Geographical Studies*, 23(1), 3–27.

Holmstrom, B. (1985), 'The provision of services in a market economy' in Inman (1985, 183–213).

Horwood, E.M. and Boyce, R.R. (1959), *Studies of the Central Business District and Urban Freeway Development*, Seattle, University of Washington Press.

Howells, J. and Green, A.E. (1986), 'Location, technology and industrial organisation in the UK services', *Progress in Planning*, 26, 83–184.

Howells, J. (1984), 'The location of research and development: some observations and evidence from Britain', *Regional Studies*, 18(1), 13–29.

Howells, J. (1987), 'Development in the location, technology and industrial organisation of computer services: some trends and research issues', *Regional Studies*, 21(6), 493–504.

Hoyt, H. (1939), *The Structure and Growth of Residential Neighborhoods in American Cities*, Washington, DC, Federal Housing Administration.

Huff, D.L. (1963), 'A probability analysis of shopping centre trade areas', *Land Economics*, 53, 81–9.

Hulten, C.R. (1985), 'Measurement of output and productivity in the service sector' in Inman (1985, 127–30).

Humphreys, J.S. (1985), 'A political economy approach to the allocation of health care resources: the case of remote areas in Queensland', *Australian Geographical Studies*, 23(2), 222–42.

Inman, R.P. (ed) (1985), *Managing the Service Economy. Prospects and Problems*, Cambridge, Cambridge University Press.

Jackson, J. (1985), Community health care in Victoria, *Australian Geographical Studies*, 23(2), 312–4.

James, F.J. (1985), 'Economic impacts of private reinvestment in older regional shopping centres', *Growth and Change*, 16(3), 11–24.

Jarrett, M.J. and Wright, M. (1982), 'New initiatives in the financing of smaller firms', *National Westminster Bank Quarterly Review*, August 40–52.

Johnston, R.J. (1979), *Geography and Geographers. Anglo-American Human Geography since 1945*, London, Edward Arnold.

Johnston, R.J. (ed) (1981), *The Dictionary of Human Geography*, Oxford, Basil Blackwell.

Johnston, R.J. and Doornkamp, J.C. (1982), *The Changing Geography of the United Kingdom*, London, Methuen.

Jones, P. (1981), 'Retail innovation and diffusion—the spread of ASDA stores' *Area*, 13(3), 197–201.

Jones, P. (1984), 'Retail warehouse development in Britain', *Area*, 16(1), 41–7.

Jones, P. (1988), 'The geographical development of convenience stores in Britain', *Geography*, 73(2), 146–9.

Jones, P.M. (1984), 'General sources of information. B: Within the UK' in Davies and Rogers (1984, 139–62).

Joseph, A. and Phillips, D. (1984), *Accessibility and Utilization: A Geographical Perspec-*

*tive on Health Care Delivery*, London, Harper and Row.

Keil, S. and Mack, R. (1986), 'Identifying export potential in the service sector', *Growth and Change*, 17(2), 1–10.

Keinath, W.F., Jnr (1985), 'The spatial component of the post-industrial society', *Economic Geography*, 61(3), 223–40.

Kellerman, A. (1981), 'The use of standard distance as an equity criterion for public facility location', *Area*, 13(3), 245–9.

Kellerman, A. (1983), 'The suburbanisation of retail trade: the Israeli case', *Area*, 15(3), 219–22.

Kellerman, A. (1985a), 'The evolution of service economies: a geographical perspective', *The Professional Geographer*, 37(2), 133–42.

Kellerman, A. (1985b), 'The suburbanisation of retail trade: a US nationwide view', *Geoforum*, 16(1), 15–23.

Kellerman, A. and Krakover, S. (1986), 'Multi-sectoral urban growth in space and time: an empirical approach', *Regional Studies*, 117–29.

Kendrick, J.W. (1985), 'Measurement of output and productivity in the service sector' in Inman (1985, 113–23).

King, L.J. (1984), *Central Place Theory*, Beverly Hills, CA, Sage.

Kirby, A. (1982), *The Politics of Location: An Introduction*, London, Methuen.

Kirby, A. (1985), 'Leisure as a commodity: the role of the state in leisure provision', *Progress in Human Geography*, 9(1), 64–84.

Kirby, D.A. (1984), 'Shops Act 1950: Restrictions on Trading', *Area*, 16(3), 233–5.

Kirkland, R.I. (1987), 'The bright future of service exports', *Fortune International*, 115(3), June, 26–30.

Kirn, T.J. (1987), 'Growth and change in the service sector of the US: a spatial perspective', *Annals of the Association of American Geographers*, 77(3), 353–72.

Knippenberg, H. and van der Wusten, H. (1984), 'The primary school system in the Netherlands, 1900–1980', *Tijdschrift voor Economische en Sociale Geografie*, 75, 177–85.

Knox, P.L. (1978), 'The intraurban ecology of primary medical care: patterns of accessibility and their policy implications', *Environment and Planning A*, 10, 415–35.

Knox, P.L. (1979a), 'The accessibility of primary care to urban patients: a geographical analysis', *Journal of the Royal College of General Practitioners*, 29, 160–8.

Knox, P.L. (1979b), 'Medical deprivation, area deprivation and public policy', *Social Science and Medicine*, 13D, 111–21.

Kravis, I.B. (1985), 'Services in world transactions' in Inman (1985, 135–60).

Kutay, A. (1986), 'Optimum office location and the comparative statistics of information economics', *Regional Studies*, 20(6), 551–64.

Langdale, J. (1983), 'Competition in the United States long distance telecommunications industry', *Regional Studies*, 17(6), 393–409.

Langdale, J. (1985), 'Electronic funds transfer and the internationalisation of the banking and finance industry', *Geoforum*, 16, 1–13.

Lakshmanan, T.R. and Hansen, W.G. (1965), 'A retail market potential model', *Journal of the American Institute of Planners*, 31, 134–43.

Lawson, F. and Baud-Bovy, M. (1977), *Tourism and Recreational Development*, London, Architectural Press.

Laulajainen, R. and Gadde, L.-E. (1986), 'Locational avoidance: a case study of three Swedish retail chains', *Regional Studies*, 20(2), 131–40.

Leahy, E.P. and Hill, J.A. (1981), 'The spatial distribution of international monetary reserves', *The Geographical Review*, 71(1), 64–82.

Le Grand, J. and Robinson, P. (1976), *The Economics of Social Problems*, London, Macmillan.

Levitt, R. (1977), *The Reorganised National Health Service* (2nd ed), London, Croom Helm.

Levitt, R. and Wall, A. (1984), *The Reorganised National Health Service* (3rd ed), London, Croom Helm.

Ley, D. (1980), 'Liberal ideology and the postindustrial city', *Annals of the Association of American Geographers*, 70(2), 238-58.

Ley, D. (1985), 'Downtown or the suburbs? A comparison of two Vancouver head offices', *The Canadian Geographer*, 29(1), 30-43.

Ley, D. and Hutton, T. (1987), 'Vancouver's corporate complex and producer services sector: linkages and divergence within a provincial staple economy', *Regional Studies*, 21(5), 413-22.

Lloyd, P.E. and Dicken, P. (1977), *Location in Space: A Theoretical Approach to Economic Geography* (2nd ed), London, Harper and Row.

London Health Planning Consortium (1981), *Primary Health Care in Inner London*, May.

Lord, J.D. (1985), 'The malling of the American landscape' in Dawson and Lord (1985, 209-25).

Losch, A. (1954), *The Economics of Location*, New Haven, CT, Yale University Press.

Love, J.H. and McNicoll, I.H. (1988), 'The regional economic impact of overseas students in the UK: a case study of three Scottish Universities', *Regional Studies*, 22(1), 11-18.

Lynn, R. (1979), 'The social ecology of intelligence in the British Isles', *British Journal of Social and Clinical Psychology*, 18, 1-12.

Magnusson, G. (1980), 'The role of proximity in the use of hospital emergency departments', *Sociology of Health and Illness*, 2, 202-14.

Malecki, E.J. (1980), 'Techological change: British and American research themes', *Area*, 12(4), 253-9.

Malecki, E.J. (1982), 'Federal spending in the USA. Some impacts on metropolitan economies', *Regional Studies*, 16(1), 19-35.

Martin, W.H. and Mason, S. (1980), *The UK Sports Market*, Sudbury, Suffolk, Leisure Consultants.

Marshall, J.N. (1985), 'Services and regional policy in Great Britain', *Area*, 17(4), 303-8.

Marshall, J.N. and Bachtler, J. (1987), 'Services and regional policy', *Regional Studies*, 21(5), 471-5.

Mason, C. (1987), 'Venture capital in the United Kingdom: a geographical perspective', *National Westminster Bank Quarterly Review*, May, 47-59.

Massey, D. (1984), *Spatial Divisions of Labour. Social Structures and the Geography of Production*, London, Macmillan.

Mathieson, A. and Wall, G. (1982), *Tourism: Economic, Physical and Social Impacts*, London, Longman.

McGuire, A., Henderson, J. and Mooney, G. (1988), *The Economics of Health Care. An Introductory Text*, London, Routledge and Kegan Paul.

McKinnon, A.C. (1981), 'The historical development of food manufacturers' distribution system', University of Leicester.

McKinnon, A.C. (1983), 'The development of warehousing in England', *Geoforum*, 14, 389-99.

Mohan, J. (1984), 'Geographical aspects of private hospital developments in Britain', *Area*, 16(3), 191-9.

Morrill, R.L. and Earickson, R.J. (1968a), 'Hospital variation and patient travel distance', *Inquiry*, 5, 26-34.

Morrill, R.L. and Earickson, R.J. (1968b), 'Variation in the character and use of hospital services', *Health Services Research*, 3, 224-38.

Morrill, R.L., Earickson, R.J. and Rees, P. (1970), 'Factors influencing distances travelled to hospitals', *Economic Geography*, 46, 161-171.

Murdie, R.A. (1965), 'Cultural differences in consumer travel', *Economic Geography*, 41, 211–33.

Murphy, P.E. (1986), *Tourism. A Community Approach*, Methuen, London.

Murphy, R.E. (1966), *The American City and Urban Geography*, New York, McGraw-Hill.

Norton, R.E. (1987), 'Citibank wows the consumer', *Fortune International*, 115(12), 38–43.

Organisation for Economic Co-operation and Development (OECD), Tourism Committee, (1985), *Tourism Policy and International Tourism in OECD Member Countries*, OECD, Paris.

Organisation for Economic Co-operation and Development (1985), 'Tourism', *OECD Observer*, September.

Organisation for Economic Co-operation and Development (1986), 'Liberalisation of trade and investment in the services sector. The role of the OECD CODES', *OECD Observer*, March, 25–7.

Organisation for Economic Co-operation and Development (1987), 'The cost of education: doing better with less', *OECD Observer*, January, 25–7.

O'hUallachain, B. (1985), 'Spatial patterns of foreign direct investment in the United States', *The Professional Geographer*, 37(2), 154–62.

Pacione, M. (1986), *Medical Geography: Progress and Prospect*, London, Croom Helm.

Parker, A.J. (1975), 'Hypermarkets: the changing pattern of retailing', *Geography*, 60, 120–4.

Patton, S.G. (1985), 'Tourism and local economic development; factory outlets and the Reading SMSA', *Growth and Change*, 16(3), 64–73.

Pearce, D. (1981), *Tourist Development*, London, Longman.

Pearce, D. (1987), *Tourism Today: A Geographical Analysis*, London, Longmans.

Peck, F. and Townsend, A. (1987), 'The impact of technological change upon the spatial pattern of UK employment within major corporations', *Regional Studies*, 21(3), 225–40.

Phillips, D.R. (1981) *Contemporary Issues in the Geography of Health Care*, Norwich, Geo Books.

Phillips, D. and Williams, A. (1984), *Rural Britain: A Social Geography*, Oxford, Blackwell.

Phillips, D.R. and Vincent, J.A. (1986), 'Private residential care for the elderly: geographical aspects of developments in Devon', *Transactions, Institute of British Geographers*, new series, 11(2), 155–73.

Phillips, D.R., Vincent, J.A. and Blacksell, S. (1987), 'Spatial concentration of residential homes for the elderly: planning responses and dilemmas', *Transactions, Institute of British Geographers*, new series, 12(1), 73–83.

Pinch, S. (1985), *Cities and Services. The Geography of Collective Consumption*, London, Routledge and Kegan Paul.

Porat, M. (1977), *The Information Economy: Definition and Measurement*, Washington, DC, US Department of Commerce, Office of Telecommunications, Special Publication 77–12(1).

Potter, R.B. (1979), 'Perception of urban retailing facilities: an analysis of consumer information fields', *Geografiska Annaler*, 61B, 19–27.

Potter, R.B. (1982), *The Urban Retailing System: Location, Cognition and Behaviour*, Aldershot, Gower.

Pred, A (1977), *City Systems in Advanced Economies*, London, Hutchinson.

Price, D.G. (1970), 'An analysis of retail turnover in England and Wales', *Regional Studies*, 4, 459–72.

Price, D.G. (1985), 'Data bases and superstore development: a comment', *Transactions, Institute of British Geographers*, new series, 10, 377–9.

Price, D.G. and Cummings, A.J. (1977), *Family Planning clinics in London. A geographical view*, Polytechnic of Central London, School of the Social Sciences and Business Studies, Research Working Paper 2.

Proudfoot, M.J. (1937), 'City retail structure', *Economic Geography*, 13, 425–8.

Rajan, A. and Cooke, G. (1986), 'The impact of information technology on employment in the financial services industry', *National Westminster Bank Quarterly Review*, August, 21–35.

Rees, J. (1978), 'Manufacturing headquarters in a post-industrial urban context', *Economic Geography*, 54, 337–54.

Reilly, W.J. (1929), *Methods for the Study of Retail Relationships*, Research monograph no. 4 of the Bureau of Business Research, University of Texas.

Reilly, W.J. (1931), *The Law of Retail Gravitation*, New York, Knickerbocker Press.

Reiner, T.A. and Wolpert, J. (1981), 'The non-profit sector in the metropolitan economy', *Economic Geography*, 57(1), 23–33.

Richards, D. (1984), 'General sources of information. A: Within North America' in Davies and Rogers (1984).

Robinson, H. (1976), *A Geography of Tourism*, London, Macdonald and Evans.

Rogers, D.S. (1984), 'Trends in retailing and consumer behaviour. A: Within North America' in Davies and Rogers (1984, 11–28).

Rosenberg, M.W. (1986), 'National systems of health care delivery' in Pacione (1986).

Rothwell, R. (1982), 'The role of technology in industrial change: implications for regional policy', *Regional Studies*, 16(5), 361–9.

Royle, S.A. (1984), 'Constraints upon the location of a retail noxious facility: the case of the sex shop', *Area*, 16(1), 49–53.

Rushton, G. (1969), 'An analysis of behaviour by revealed space preference', *Annals of the Association of American Geographers*, 59, 391–400.

Rushton, G. (1981), 'The scaling of locational preferences' in K.R. Cox and R.G. Golledge (eds), *Behavioural Problems in Geography Revisited*, London, Methuen, 67–92.

Salt, J. (1985), 'Europe's foreign labour migrants in transition', *Geography*, 70(2), 151–8.

Scheiber, G.J. (1985), 'Health spending: its growth and control', *OECD Observer*, November, 13–17.

Schoenberger, E. (1985), 'Foreign manufacturing investment in the US: competitive strategies and international location', *Economic Geography*, 61, 241–59.

Scouller, J. (1987), 'The United Kingdom merger boom in perspective', *National Westminster Quarterly Review*, May, 14–30.

Seeley, J.E. (1981), 'Introduction: new directions in public services', *Economic Geography*, 57(1), 1–9.

Semple, R.K. (1985), 'Quarternary place theory: an introduction', *Urban Geography*, 6, 285–96.

Semple, R.K. and Phipps, A.G. (1982), 'The spatial evaluation of corporate headquarters within an urban system', *Urban Geography*, 3, 258–279.

Shannon, G.W. and Dever, G.E.A. (1974), *Health Care Delivery: Spatial Perspectives*, New York, McGraw-Hill.

Shannon, G.W., Spurlock, C.W., Gladin, S.T. and Skinner, J.L. (1975), 'A method for evaluating the geographic accessibility of health services', *The Professional Geographer*, 27(1), 30–6.

Simmons, J. (1964), *The Changing Pattern of Retail Location*, Department of Geography, Research Paper, no. 92, University of Chicago.

Simon, H.A. (1959), 'Theories of decision making in economics and behavioural science', *American Economic Review*, 49, 253–83.

Smailes, A.E. (1953), *The Geography of Towns*, London, Hutchinson.

Smith, C.J. (1981), 'Urban structure and the development of national support systems for service dependent populations', *The Professional Geographer*, 33(4), 457-65.

Smith, D.M. (1977), *Human Geography: A Welfare Approach*, London, Edward Arnold.

Smith, D.M. (1979), *Where the Grass is Greener. Living in an Unequal World*, Harmondsworth, Penguin.

Smith, D.M. (1981), 'Marxian economics' in Johnston (1981: 203-9).

Smith, R.D.P. (1968), 'The changing urban hierarchy', *Regional Studies*, 2, 1-19.

Sparks, L. (1986), 'The changing structure of distribution in retail companies: an example from the grocery trade', *Transactions, Institute of British Geographers*, new series, 6(1), 104-25.

Stalson, H. (1985), 'US trade policy and international service transactions' in Inman (1985, 161-78).

Stanback, T.M. (1979), *Understanding the Service Economy: Employment, Productivity, Location*, Baltimore, MD, Johns Hopkins University Press.

Stanback, T.M., Bearse, P.J., Noyelle, T.J. and Karasek, R.A. (1981), *Services: The New Economy*, Totowa, NJ, Allanhead, Osmun.

Stanback, T.M. and Noyelle, T.J. (1982), *Cities in Transition*, Totowa, NJ, Allanhead, Osmun.

Stimson, R.J. and Adrian, C. (1987), 'Australian capital city property development, foreign investment and investor attitudes', *Australian Geographical Studies*, 25(1), 41-60.

Storper, M. (1985), 'Oligopoly and the product cycle: essentialism in economic geography', *Economic Geography*, 61(3), 260-82.

Summers, R. (1985), 'Services in the international economy' in Inman (1985, 27-48).

Swaney, J.A. and Ward, F.A. (1985), 'Optimally locating a national public facility: an empirical application of consumer surplus theory', *Economic Geography*, 61(2), 172-80.

Taylor, M.J. and Thrift, N.J. (eds) (1982), *The Geography of Multinationals*, London, Croom Helm.

Taylor, M.J. and Thrift, N.J. (1983), 'Business organisation, segmentation and location', *Regional Studies*, 17(6), 445-65.

Taylor, M. and Thrift, N. (eds) (1986), *Multinationals and Restructuring the World Economy*, London, Croom Helm.

Thorpe, D. (1968), 'The main shopping centres of Great Britain, 1961: their location and structural characteristics', *Urban studies*, 5, 165-206.

Tiebout, C.M. (1957), 'Location theory, empirical evidence and economic evolution', *Papers of the Regional Science Association*, 3, 74-86.

Todd, D. (1980), 'The defence sector in regional development', *Area*, 12(2), 115-21.

Torkildsen, G. (1983), *Leisure and Recreation Management*, London, Spon.

Toyne, P. (1974), *Organisation Location and Behaviour. Decision-making in Economic Geography*, London, Macmillan.

Tunbridge, J.E. (1981), 'Conservation Trusts as geographic agents: their impact upon landscape, townscape and land use', *Transactions, Institute of British Geographers*, new series, 6(1), 104-25.

Tunbridge, J.E. (1986), 'Warehouse functions, insurance plans and inner city revitalisation: a Canadian research note', *The Canadian Geographer*, 30(2), 146-54.

Unesco (1981), *International Yearbook of Education*, Vol. 33, Paris, International Bureau of Education, Unesco.

Unesco (1982), *International Yearbook of Education*, Vol. 34, Paris, International Bureau of Education, Unesco.

Vance, J.E. (1970), *The Merchant's World: The Geography of Wholesaling*, Englewood Cliffs, NJ, Prentice Hall.

Veljanovski, C. (1987), 'British cable and satellite television policies', *National Westminster Bank Quarterly Review*, November, 28–40.

Vincent, P., Chell, E. and Haworth, J. (1987), 'Regional distribution of consultancy firms servicing the MAPCON scheme: a preliminary analysis', *Regional Studies*, 21(6), 505–18.

Walmsley, D.J. and Sorensen, A.D. (1980), 'What Marx for the radicals? An antipodean viewpoint', *Area*, 12(2), 137–41.

Watts, H.D. (1975), 'The market area of a firm' in Collins and Walker (1975).

Watts, H.D. (1977), 'The impact of warehouse growth', *The Planner*, 63, 105–7.

Watts, H.D. (1987), 'Producer services, industrial location and uneven development', *Area*, 19(4), 353–5.

Wheeler, J.O. (1986), 'Corporate spatial links with financial institutions: the role of the metropolitan hierarchy', *Annals of the Association of American Geographers*, 76(2), 262–74.

Wheeler, J.O. and Brown, C.L. (1985), 'The metropolitan corporate hierarchy in the US South, 1960–80', *Economic Geography*, 61, 66–78.

White, R. (1984), 'Multi-national retailing: a slow advance?', *Retail and Distribution Management*, March–April, 8–13.

Whitehand, J.W.R. (1967), 'Fringe belts: a neglected aspect of urban geography', *Transactions, Institute of British Geographers*, 41, 223–33.

Whitehand, J.W.R. (1983), 'Renewing the local CBD: more hands at work than you thought?', *Area*, 15(4), 323–6.

Whitehand, J.W.R. and Whitehand, S.M. (1983), 'The study of physical change in town centres: research procedures and types of change', *Transactions, Institute of British Geographers*, new series, 8(4), 483–507.

Whitehand, J.W.R. and Whitehand, S.M. (1984), 'The physical fabric of town centres: the agents of change', *Transactions, Institute of British Geographers*, new series, 9(2), 231–47.

Williams, G.A. (1985), *When was Wales?*, Harmondsworth, Penguin.

Williams, M. (1966), 'The Parkland towns of Australia and New Zealand', *Geographical Review*, 56, 234–45.

Wolch, J.R. (1980), 'Residential location of the service-dependent poor', *Annals of the Association of American Geographers*, 70(3), 330–41.

Wolch, J.R. and Geiger, R.K. (1986), 'Urban restructuring and the not-for-profit sector', *Economic Geography*, 62(1), 3–18.

Wolpert, J.T. and Reiner, T.A. (1984), 'Service provision by the not-for-profit sector: a comparative study', *Economic Geography*, 60(1), 28–37.

Wood, P.A. (1986), 'The anatomy of job loss and job creation: some speculations on the role of the 'producer service' sector', *Regional Studies*, 20(1), 37–46.

World Bank (1983), *World Development Report*, Oxford, Oxford University Press.

Wrigley, N. (1984), 'Geographical evidence to the Committee of Inquiry on the Shops Act', *Area*, 16(3), 233.

Wrigley, N., Guy, C. and Dunn, R. (1984), 'Sunday and late-night shopping in a British city: evidence from the Cardiff consumer panel', *Area*, 16(3), 236–40.

Wrigley, N., Guy, C., Dunn, R. and O'Brien, L. (1985), 'The Cardiff consumer panel: methodological aspects of the conduct of a long term survey', *Transactions, Institute of British Geographers*, new series, 10(1), 63–76.

Yeates, M. (1968), *An Introduction to Quantitative Analysis in Economic Geography*, New York, McGraw-Hill.

# Index